The 21st Century Webster's
Family Encyclopedia

The 21st Century Webster's Family Encyclopedia

Volume 5
Hill - Lanz

1999 Edition

IMPORTED BY/IMPORTE PAR
DS-MAX CANADA
RICHMOND HILL, ONTARIO
L4B 1H7

ENGLAND
WENTWALK LTD.
278A ABBEYDALE ROAD, WEMBLEY
MIDDLESEX, HA0 1NT

MALAYSIA
PRO ENTERPRISE SDN BHD
LOT 605, SS13/1K, OFF JLN.
KEWAJIPAN, 47500 SUBANG JAYA
SELANGOR D.E., MALAYSIA

DS-MAX
IRVINE, CA 92618
IMPORTER: #16-1241510
949-587-9207

TRIDENT PRESS INTERNATIONAL
Copyright © 1999, Uitgeverij Het Spectrum BV, Utrecht

ISBN 1-55280-460-7

All rights reserved

Copyright under the Universal Copyright Convention; the International Copyright Union; Pan-American Conventions of Montevideo, Mexico, Rio de Janeiro, Buenos Aires and Havanna

Printed in Peru

The 21st Century Webster's Family Encyclopedia
is based on the Spectrum Database

editors:
Bart Drubbel
Tjeerd van der Velde
Saskia van Iperen

Hill, James Jerome (1838-1916), U.S. railroad magnate. After purchasing the St. Paul and Pacific Railroad, he extended it to the Pacific at Seattle (1893). Later, working with J.P. Morgan, he consolidated his holdings in the Great Northern Railway Company.
See also: Railroad.

Hill, Joe (Joseph Hillstrom; 1879-1915), legendary Swedish-born U.S. labor organizer for the Industrial Workers of the World. He immigrated to the United States in 1902 and was the author of many songs of the early socialist labor movement. He was convicted of murdering a man in Utah in 1915 and sentenced to death, though many people believed that he was innocent. His funeral was attended by about 30,000 people.
See also: Labor movement.

Hill, Octavia (1838-1912), English social reformer. She was instrumental in improving housing conditions for London's poor and in establishing and preserving the city's parks and playgrounds. Hill also served on the board of several charitable organizations, and her concern for the preservation of natural beauty and historic structures led to the formation of the National Trust.

Hillary, Sir Edmund Percival (1919-), New Zealand explorer and mountaineer. In 1953 he and Tenzing Norkay, a Sherpa from Nepal, were the first to reach the summit of Mt. Everest, the world's highest mountain.
See also: Mount Everest.

Hillel (c.70 B.C.-10 A.D.), Jewish scholar born in Babylonia, one of the founders of rabbinic Judaism, and ethical leader of his generation. He was opposed by Shammai, another teacher. His "Seven Rules" of exegesis laid the groundwork for a liberal interpretation of scriptural law.
See also: Judaism.

Hilliard, Nicholas (1537-1619), English miniature painter. As court artist to Elizabeth I, his style was characterized by exquisite jewellike detailing and fine drawing.

Hillman, Sidney (1887-1946), U.S. labor leader. A Lithuanian immigrant, who came to the United States in 1907, Hillman became the first president of the Amalgamated Clothing Workers (1914), a post he held until his death. He supported industrial unions, helped to found the Congress of Industrial Organizations (CIO), and advised government on labor relations.
See also: Labor movement.

Hills, Carla Anderson (1934-), U.S. government official. As Secretary of Housing and Urban Development (1975-77) under President Gerald R. Ford, she was the third woman Cabinet member in U.S. history. In 1989 President George Bush appointed her as a special trade representative.

Hilo (pop. 35,400), city on the eastern shore of Hawaii Island. The state's second-largest city and Hawaii County's seat of government, it is also the southernmost large city in the United States. Ancient Polynesian sailors settled Hilo, and a U.S. mission was opened c.1820. It is a leading exporter

of sugar cane and coffee and a hub for tourists visiting the nearby volcanic region.
See also: Hawaii.

Hilton, Conrad Nicholson (1887-1979), U.S. hotel chain founder. Beginning with his first hotels in New Mexico and Texas, Hilton expanded his holdings to most major U.S. and foreign cities and resort areas. By 1967 Hilton hotels were in 37 nations, and the international operation of the company became a subsidiary of Trans World Airlines (TWA).

Hilton, James (1900-54), English novelist. His books include *Lost Horizon* (1933), *Good-bye, Mr. Chips* (1934), and *Random Harvest* (1941), which were made into films.

Himalayas, highest mountain system in the world, over 1,500 mi (2,410 km) long, extending from Pakistan through India, Tibet, Nepal, Sikkim, and Bhutan. The northern range is called the Trans-Himalayas. The southern range has three parallel zones: the Great Himalayas, including the 29,028-ft (8,848-m) Mt. Everest, the Lesser Himalayas, and the southernmost Outer Himalayas.

Himmler, Heinrich (1900-45), German Nazi leader. A founder of the Nazi party, head of the SS from 1929 and of the Gestapo from 1936, he was responsible for the murder of millions in concentration camps. Named interior minister in 1943, he became the main leader of Germany's internal affairs. He was captured by the British army in 1945 and committed suicide.
See also: Holocaust; Nazism.

Hindemith, Paul (1895-1963), German-born U.S. composer and teacher. Denounced as a modernist because of his dissonant harmonies and counterpoint, he was banned by the Nazis in Germany and immigrated to the United States in 1937. He later returned to more tonal, neoclassical forms. Among his major works are the symphony (1934) and opera (1938) *Mathis the Painter*, *Symphonic Metamorphoses on Themes of Carl Maria von Weber* (1943), and *The Four Temperaments* (1944).

Hindenburg *See:* Airship.

Hindenburg, Paul von (1847-1934), German general, president of Germany (1925-34). Together with Ludendorff he directed German military strategies in World War I. As president he was chiefly a figurehead. In 1933 he appointed Hitler chancellor.
See also: World War I.

Hindenburg Line *See:* Siegfried Line.

Hindi, official language of India, a written form of Hindustani. It is written in Devanagari script, reading from left to right. Hindi belongs to the Indic group of the Indo-European family of languages.

Hinduism, chief religion of India, embracing many different sects and trends. In terms of numbers of adherents, it is the third largest of the world's

religions, after Christianity and Islam. Hinduism is based on the Veda, sacred writings dating back some 3,000 years. The Veda comprised four types of writing: the Samhita, which in turn consists of 4 books of hymns, chants, and prayers—the Rig-Veda, the Sama-Veda, the Yajur-Veda, and the Atharva-Veda; the Brahmanas, which are prose; the Aranyakas, containing instructions for meditation; and the Upanishads, mystical works stating the Veda's doctrine of the soul.
Between 800 B.C. and 500 B.C. Hinduism began to change under the impact of two new, rival religions: Buddhism and Jainism. It absorbed many village and tribal gods into a pantheon dominated by Brahma (the creator), Vishnu (the preserver), and Shiva (the destroyer). In this period important social and philosophical changes occured: the caste system was established, and the learned Brahman, often a priest, became the supreme figure in society. The doctrine of reincarnation and the transmigration of the soul also became part of the creed. A further addition was the concept of *karma*, the idea that every individual is punished for wrongdoing and rewarded for righteousness, if not in the present life, then in a reincarnation. The aim of every Hindu should be to rise, through just living, higher and higher in the scale of existence with each reincarnation, finally attaining absorption into the personality of Brahma. Hinduism has various subcults, of which those of Shiva, Vishnu, Krishna, Shakti, and the Matris are the most important.

Hindu Kush, mountain range in Asia, stretching about 500 m (800 km) from northeast Afghanistan to north Pakistan. High-altitude passes cross the range. The highest peak is Tirich Mir (25,260 ft/ 7,699 m).

Hines, Earl 'Fatha' (1905-83), U.S. jazz musician, pianist and composer. A member of Louis Armstrong's group, the Hot Five (late 1920s), he later formed a band of his own, featuring Charlie Parker and Dizzy Gillespie, which introduced bebop. Hines's powerful percussive style greatly influenced modern piano techniques.
See also: Jazz.

Hinton, S(usan) E(loise) (1948-), U.S. author of books for teenagers. Her novels are set in Tulsa, Okla., where Hinton was born and raised. Her characters, often teenagers themselves, reject authority and must cope with the problems of poverty, drug abuse, and violence on their own. Hinton's first and most widely recognized novel, *The Outsiders* (1967), written when she was 16, is noted for its action and harshly realistic characters. Her other works include *That Was Then, This Is Now* (1971), *Rumble Fish* (1975), and *Tex* (1979).

Hip, freely movable ball-and-socket joint formed by the cup-shaped hollow of the pelvic bone and the smooth, rounded head of the thighbone. The adult hipbone combines three bones that are separate in youth: the ilium, ischium, and pubis.

Hipparchus (c.180 B.C.-125 B.C.), Greek scientist, pioneer of systematic astronomy. He compiled the first star catalog and ascribed magnitudes to stars. He also estimated the size of the moon and its distance from the earth, and was probably the first to discover the precession of the equinox.
See also: Equinox.

Hipparchus (6th century B.C.), Greek political figure. Son of Pisistratus, ruler of Athens in the mid-500s, Hipparchus shared power with his brother, Hippias, when their father died in 527. A patron of the arts, Hipparchus brought the poets Anacreon and Simonides to Athens. He got involved in a plot to overthrow his brother and was killed when the revolt was suppressed.
See also: Greece, Ancient.

Hippies, anti-establishment subculture in the U.S. in the 1960s, principally people under 25 who rejected conservative values and traditional authority. Opposed to the Vietnam War and known for loose sexual conventions, use of drugs, and long hair, hippies gravitated to the East Village in New York City and the Haight-Ashbury district in San Francisco.

Hippocampus *See:* Seahorse.

Hippocrates (c.460-c.377 B.C.), Greek physician often called the father of medicine. He was probably the author of the *Hippocratic Collection*, some 70 books on all aspects of ancient medicine. The Hippocratic Oath, a statement of medical ethics and good practice, is still sworn to by graduates of many medical schools.
See also: Medicine.

Hippodrome, any open or closed structure for circuses or similar spectacles. Originally a Greek outdoor course for horse and chariot races, it was adopted by the Romans, who built numerous hippodromes. Shaped like the letter U, with tiers of open seats on 3 sides and closed across the fourth by an area for distinguished guests, such a stadium was frequently up to 400 ft (120 m) wide and 700 ft (210 m) long. The most famous hippodrome was the Circus Maximus at Rome, which could hold over 300,000 spectators.

Hippopotamus, one of the largest living terrestrial mammals (*Hippopotamus amphibius*), distantly related to the pig, widespread in Africa. Hippopotamuses generally are about 5 ft (1.6 m) tall and weigh about 5 tons (4,500 kg). They have massive bodies set on short legs, each with four toes with hoof-like nails. Their noses, eyes, and ears are on top of their heads, which allows them to spend most of the day submerged in rivers. At night they come on land to graze.

Hirohito (1901-89), emperor of Japan from 1926 until his death. After World War II the recognition of the emperor as a god was rescinded, and Hirohito became a "symbol of the state and unity of the people," without political or sovereign power. He was instrumental in persuading the government to accept unconditional surrender in World War II.
See also: Japan.

Hiroshige, Ando (1797-1858), Japanese painter and printmaker of the *ukiyo-e* (popular) school led by Hokusai. He is famous for his sets of woodblock color prints depicting atmospheric landscapes of snow, rain, mist, and moonlight. These inspired a number of his contemporaries in the West, including Edouard Manet and James Whistler. Among his works is *53 Stages of the Tokaido Highway* (1833), a series of landscapes.

Hiroshima (pop. 1,071,900), industrial city on Honshu Island, Japan, located on a bay in the Inland Sea, capital of Hiroshima Prefecture. A thriving industrial and commercial center, it was chosen as the target for the U.S. atomic bomb attack of Aug. 6, 1945. There were at least 80,000 people killed, many more injured or made ill by radiation, and nine-tenths of the city was destroyed. It has been largely rebuilt since 1950 and is again an important industrial marketing center.
See also: Japan; Nuclear bomb; World War II.

Hispanic Americans, in the United States, those who have come from Spanish countries or their descendants. There are approximately 20 million Hispanic Americans, making up some 8% of the U.S. population, the second-largest minority in the country after African Americans. Thanks to both a high birth rate and continued immigration, Hispanic Americans are expected to become the largest minority in the United States in the 21st century.
Hispanic Americans are unified in certain important respects, principally the Spanish language and the Roman Catholic religion. Their diversity stems from differences of history and culture among their various countries of origin as well as the causes and circumstances leading to immigration to the United States.
The majority of Hispanic Americans, some 63%, are of Mexican descent. Puerto Ricans comprise 12% and Cubans 5% of the total. The remaining 20% come from Spain and countries of South and Central America, including Colombia, the Dominican Republic, Ecuador, Guatemala, El Salvador, and Nicaragua. Consequently, Hispanic Americans are referred to broadly as Latinos. More specifically, Mexican Americans are known as Chicanos and, more recently, Puerto Ricans living in New York City are sometimes known as Nuyoricans. Broadly speaking, Mexicans are ethnically a mixture of Spanish and Indians; Puerto Ricans are a mixture of Spanish and black Africans; and Cubans are chiefly of Spanish descent. These distinct ethnic characteristics correspond to the history of the Spanish conquest, colonization, and settlement of the Caribbean and the Americas. In addition to these ethnic differences, Hispanic Americans come from different periods of immigration at different points in the history of the United States as well as in the histories of their respective countries of origin.
Though the Spanish were a significant presence in Florida as early as the 16th century, Spanish influence in North America proved to be strongest in California and the Southwest. In the aftermath of the Mexican American War (1846-48), there were some 80,000 Mexican Americans living in Colorado, Nevada, Utah, New Mexico, Arizona, Wyoming, and California. From the early 20th century, immigration from Mexico grew. By 1930 about 680,000 Mexicans had come to the United States, and, since World War II, from the 1950s to the 1980s, immigration has continued. Puerto Rico has been a U.S. possession since 1898 and its people U.S. citizens since 1917, but the major wave of immigration took place between 1940 and 1960, when some 545,000 Puerto Ricans came to the United States, principally to New York City. Cubans emigrated to the United States in large numbers as the result of Fidel Castro's successful revolution. From 1959 to 1980, about 625,000 Cubans emigrated to the United States. In addition, the 1970s saw large numbers of Central Americans, especially from El Salvador and Nicaragua, fleeing civil war, political persecution, or economic hardship.

Throughout the 20th century, the U.S. government has adopted various policies aimed at limiting or reversing Hispanic immigration, including, at one time, a program of repatriation. More recently, the U.S. government has adjusted its immigration policy to correspond to its foreign policy. As a result, Central Americans fleeing war and political unrest in their countries throughout the 1980s were refused political asylum in most cases. More recently, the U.S. government, in an attempt to deal with large numbers of illegal aliens, extended a limited amnesty to those who registered with the immigration authorities by a certain date.

The history of official U.S. resistance to Hispanic immigration has gone hand in hand with discrimination. Ironically, it has been in response to discrimination and to problems of education and economic opportunity that Hispanic Americans, in all of their diversity, have forged a common ground and have come to participate more directly and effectively in U.S. life. Through their own efforts, Hispanic Americans have improved working conditions for many immigrants, won widespread acceptance of bilingual education, and have broken down many of the barriers of discrimination. As a result, many Hispanic Americans have become prominent in U.S. life. Celia Cruz, Cesar Chavez, and Roberto Clemente are readily recognized. Joseph Montoya served as senator from New Mexico, Bob Martinez was governor of Florida, and, under President George Bush, Lauro Cavazos was secretary of education and Manuel Lujan is secretary of the interior.

Hispaniola, second largest island in the West Indies, located west of Puerto Rico and east of Cuba. The island is shared between the Republic of Haiti (west) and the Dominican Republic (east).

Hiss, Alger (1904-), U.S. public official accused of spying for the USSR. Hiss was an adviser to the U.S. State Department on economic and political affairs. In 1948 he was brought before the House Committee on Un-American Activities (HUAC), and in 1950 he was convicted of perjury. He served 4 years in prison. Maintaining his innocence, Hiss has devoted the rest of his life to clearing his name. Legal scholars are sharply divided on his guilt.

Histamine *See:* Allergy; Antihistamine.

Histology, scientific study of the structure of the tissues that make up organisms.

Histoplasmosis, infectious disease that is endemic in parts of Africa, South America, and the United States, caused by the fungus *Histoplasma capsulatum*. It is characterized by damage to the lungs and occasional anemia, with ulcerations of the mouth and the gastrointestinal tract, enlargement of the liver and spleen, disorder of the lymph glands, and necrosis (tissue death) of the adrenal glands. If not treated early with an antifungal agent, a severe attack can be fatal. It is particularly common in infants and older men.

History, study of the past through documents, reports, and other artifacts. The past can be inferred through many sources—chronicles, myths, buildings, monuments, business documents, newspapers, works of art, archeological objects. Earlier times for which no such sources exist are known as *prehistory*. History as a branch of knowledge is generally confined to the

written records of human activities, which limits its scope to the invention of writing, about 5,000 years ago.
The oldest historical writings stem from China, where archeologists found historical records written before 1,000 B.C. In the older civilizations of Egypt and Mesopotamia historical records also appear soon after the introduction of writing. The conscious writing of history is generally considered to have begun in Greece about the 5th century B.C. with Herodotus's description of the wars between Greece and Persia. What made his work history was his conscious attempt to record events of importance and to set forth the motivations of the people involved. This causal approach to events of the past earned Herodotus the title "Father of History," although, unlike modern historians, he did not try to verify all his facts and mixed tradition, oral remembrances, and fable along with actual occurrences and customs. A more analytical method of writing about the past was developed by his successor, Thucydides, whose *History of the Peloponnesian War* is a grave, authentic account of the 27-year war between Athens and Sparta. A third great Greek historian, Xenophon, concentrated more on the purely narrative aspects of history. These types of historical writing, the compendious, the analytical, and the narrative, are still in evidence today. Roman historians include Livy (*History from the Founding of the City*), Tacitus (*Annals* and *Histories*), and Julius Caesar (*Commentaries*), although Caesar's work tends more towards reportage than pure history. During medieval times, Christian monks developed the idea of a *universal history*, which attempted to unite Christian history with the Greek and Roman records. Eusebius's *Ecclesiastical History* is an example, as is Saint Augustine's *City of God*, which presented, in addition, a philosophy of history. At the same time, annals of events called *chronicles* were compiled, mainly by members of the clergy. Bede's *Ecclesiastical History of the English Nation* was the great historical work of the Middle Ages. In more modern times, history developed into a serious discipline pursued by scholars. Edward Gibbon's *History of the Decline and Fall of the Roman Empire* (1776-88) is an early example of dedicated and thorough scholarship. In the 1800s critical, objective history developed into an academic discipline, as exemplified by the works of the German historian Leopold von Ranke and his followers. This German school established canons of criticism and methods of historical analysis that are still in evidence today. The 20th century saw a broadening of the scope of history to include more than the concentration on political events that characterized history up until the 19th century. Today, events of the past are analyzed using tools from many disciplines, including economics, psychology, sociology, and anthropology. Our technological society also fostered an interest in the history of science and in the effect technology has on society. Today, all aspects of the life of peoples and societies form the proper concern of historians.

Hitchcock, Lambert (1795-1852), U.S. cabinetmaker who, in 1818, established a furniture factory at Barkhamsted, Conn. Hitchcock chairs, black with stenciled designs, combined simplicity with elegance. They are now collector's pieces.

Hitchcock, Sir Alfred Joseph (1899-1980), British film director known for his skillful suspense and macabre humor. He made over 50 films, among the best of which were *The Thirty-Nine Steps* (1935), *The Lady Vanishes* (1938), and, in Hollywood, *Rebecca* (1940), *Spellbound* (1945), *Notorious* (1946), *Rear Window* (1954), and *Psycho* (1960).

Hitler, Adolf (1889-1945), Austrian-born dictator of Germany, founder of the Nazi party. Drafted in World War I, he was wounded and awarded the Iron Cross. He blamed the German defeat in the war on Jews and Communists, and in 1920 helped to found the National Socialist (Nazi) Workers Party. In 1923, after an abortive coup against the Bavarian government (the "beer hall putsch"), he served 9 months in prison. There he wrote *Mein Kampf* (My Struggle), an anti-Semitic, anti-Communist diatribe outlining his strategy for remaking Germany and becoming a conquering power throughout Europe. The Nazi party grew rapidly after the outbreak of economic depression in 1929, becoming the largest single party in the country. Although the Nazis never won a national election, their paramilitary street violence made them a powerful force. In 1933 Hitler was named chancellor, and in 1934 he secured his position by liquidating potential opponents within the party. The opposition was crushed, all other parties were outlawed, concentration camps were established, trade unions were eliminated or placed under state control, and anti-Semitism became state policy, enacted into law. In the meantime, a war economy was established. Hitler had the main responsibility for German war strategy, and despite a failed military coup against him in 1944, he remained in complete control of the German armed forces and insisted on fighting on in the face of defeat. He committed suicide in Apr. 1945 in his bunker in Berlin, as Soviet troops entered the city.
See also: Holocaust; Nazism; World War II.

Hittites, Indo-European people of the Middle East in the 2nd millennium B.C. Of unknown origin, they appear to have first settled in southern Turkey (c.1900 B.C.); they conquered central Turkey and became a dominant power. The downfall of the Hittite empire came about 1200 B.C. when it was overrun and fragmented by a vast migration of uncertain origin, called by the Egyptians "peoples of the sea."

Hives, or urticaria, itchy skin condition characterized by the formation of welts with surrounding erythema (reddening) due to histamine release in the body's tissues. It is usually provoked by allergy to food, pollens, fungi, drugs, or parasites, but it may be symptomatic of infection, systemic disease, or emotional disorder. *Dermographism* is a condition in which slight skin pressure produces marked hives, like linear marks that appear after writing on the skin.

Hoatzin (*Opisthocomos hoatzin*), bird that lives in the flooded forests bordering the rivers of northern South America. The adult, which is slightly larger than a pigeon, has a long crest and blue cheeks. It can barely fly, its flight muscles being small to make way for a large crop in which it stores its meals of leaves and fruit. The chicks have 2 movable claws on each wing that help them clamber through foliage. When alarmed, they jump into the water, swimming and even diving easily, then clamber back up the tree when danger has passed.

Hoban, James (1762-1831), Irish-born U.S. architect. He designed and built the White House (1792-1801) and supervised construction of the Capitol and other buildings in Washington, D.C.

Hobart (pop. 183,500), capital of the island of Tasmania, south of the eastern tip of the Australian mainland. This port city, founded in 1804, was originally involved in Antarctic whaling. It took on its present name in 1881. Its industries include textiles, metal products, chemicals, and glass.
See also: Tasmania.

Hobart, Garret Augustus (1844-99), U.S. vice president (1897-79) in the McKinley administration. He was speaker of the New Jersey State Assembly (1873-74) and president of the state senate (1880-82). Upon his death, Theodore Roosevelt was appointed to complete his term.

Hobbema, Meindert (1638-1709), Dutch landscape painter, taught by Jacob van Ruisdael. His atmospheric river scenes and his later forest and road landscapes, such as *The Avenue at Middelharnis* (1689), foreshadowed John Constable and others.

Hobbes, Thomas (1588-1679), English political philosopher who sought to apply rational principles to the study of human nature. In Hobbes's view, humans are materialistic and pessimistic, their actions motivated solely by self-interest, thus a state's stability can only be guaranteed by a sovereign authority, to which citizens relinquish their rights. *Leviathan* (1651), his most celebrated work, expresses these views. Hobbes saw matter in motion as the only reality; even consciousness and thought were but the outworkings of the motion of atoms in the brain. During and after his lifetime, Hobbes was known as a materialist and suspected of atheism, but in the 20th century his reputation as an able thinker has overshadowed his former notoriety.
See also: Philosophy.

Hobby, Oveta Culp (1905-), U.S. publisher and public servant. Director of the Women's Army Corps (1942-45), she became the first secretary of the Department of Health, Education, and Welfare under President Dwight D. Eisenhower (1953-55). She became chairperson of the board of the Houston *Post* in 1965.

Hobson, Laura Zametkin (1900-86), U.S. author born in New York City, the setting for most of her novels. Her most famous work, *Gentleman's Agreement* (1947), deals with prejudice and religious intolerance. In *The Tenth Month* (1971) and *Consenting Adults* (1975), Hobson addressed the controversial issues of unwed motherhood and homosexuality, respectively. Her other works include *The Celebrity* (1951), *First Papers* (1964), and *Over and Above* (1979).

Hochhuth, Rolf (1931-), German playwright whose first controversial play, The Deputy (1963), attacked Pope Pius XII for his stand on the Jews in World War II, and whose second, Soldiers (1967), portrayed Winston Churchill as a murderer.

Ho Chi Minh (Nguyen Van Thanh; 1890-1969), president of North Vietnam (1954-69). From 1911 to 1941 he lived in England, France, the USSR, and China. He helped found the French Communist Party and, later, founded the Vietnamese Communist Party. In 1941 he returned to Vietnam and organized an independence movement, the Viet Minh, that fought against

the Japanese in World War II and then against the restored French colonial government. After the decisive Viet Minh victory over the French at Dien Bien Phu in 1954, Vietnam was temporarily divided at the 17th parallel, and Ho became president of North Vietnam. South Vietnam's refusal to hold national elections led to the Vietnam War, during which Ho and his military commander, Gen. Vo Nguyen Giap, proved resolute and tenacious war leaders. In failing health, Ho lived to see the Tet offensive of 1968 and the start of peace negotiations that led ultimately to North Vietnamese victory.
See also: Vietnam War.

Ho Chi Minh City (pop. 3,924,400), formerly Saigon, city in Vietnam, 60 mi (97 km) from the South China Sea, on Saigon River. An industrial center and river port with a trade in rice and textiles, the city was established as an Annamese settlement in the 17th century and was taken by the French in 1859. The city was capital of South Vietnam (1954-75) and suffered considerable damage during the Vietnam War.
See also: Vietnam.

Höchstädt, Battle of *See:* Blenheim, Battle of.

Hockey, game played on ice in which 2 opposing teams of skaters, using curved sticks, try to shoot a flat, rubber disk called a puck, into the opposing goal, which is 4 ft (1.2 m) high and 6 ft (1.8 m) wide. Each goal scored is 1 point and the team with the most goals at the end of the game is the winner. The ice surface, or rink, is usually 200 ft (61 m) long and 98 ft (30 m) wide and is divided into three zones: offensive, defensive, and neutral. Each team has 6 players on the ice at once: 1 center, 2 wings, 2 defensemen, and 1 goaltender. Together, the center and wings are called forwards and they try to score goals for their team, while the defensemen work to prevent the opposing team from getting chances to score. The goaltender, or goalie, is the last line of defense and always plays directly in front of his team's goal, in an area called the crease. The goalie's only job is to prevent shots by the opposing team from entering the goal. Penalties of varying length are handed out by the referee to a player who breaks the rules, and the team must play with one less skater for the duration of their player's penalty. The most popular league is the National Hockey League (NHL) which consists of 21 teams from the United States and Canada. Hockey is played worldwide, with the Soviet Union historically dominating most Olympic and international competition.
Field hockey, a variation of ice hockey, is played outdoors and on foot. The 2 teams try to shoot a small ball into a slightly larger goal: 7 ft (2.13 m) high and 12 ft (3.66 m) wide. The field is 100 yards (91 m) long and 60 yards (55 m) wide and each team plays 11 players at once: 5 forwards, 3 halfbacks, 2 fullbacks, and a goaltender. Field hockey is an international sport and women's field hockey became an Olympic sport at the 1980 Summer Games.

Hockney, David (1937-), English artist whose emphases are on figurative work and brilliant color. His characteristic painting *A Bigger Splash* (1967) was also the title of a semi-autobiographical documentary film (1974).

Hodgkin, Alan Lloyd (1914-94), English physiologist awarded (with A. F. Huxley and J. Eccles) the 1963 Nobel Prize for physiology or medicine

for his work on the chemical basis of nerve impulse transmission.
See also: Physiology.

Hodgkin, Dorothy Mary Crowfoot (1910-94), British chemist awarded the 1964 Nobel Prize for chemistry for determining the structure of vitamin B_{12}.
See also: Chemistry.

Hodgkin's disease, or lymphadenoma, form of cancer affecting the lymphatic system. It was named for Thomas Hodgkin, the English physician who first described the disease in 1832. It usually causes swelling of lymph glands in the neck, armpits, or the groin. The lymph glands manufacture lymphocytes, a type of white blood cell that fights the spread of infection. In Hodgkin's disease, these cells proliferate in a variety of abnormal forms, leaving the body with fewer normal lymphocytes to fight infection. As the disease progresses, the body becomes less able to combat infections, and damage to vital organs occurs.
See also: Lymphatic system.

Hoffa, James Riddle (1913-75?), U.S. labor leader, president of the International Brotherhood of Teamsters from 1957. After an investigation (led by U.S. attorney general Robert F. Kennedy) into his underworld links, Hoffa was convicted in 1964 of tampering with a jury over a bribery charge and jailed from 1968 to 1971, when Richard M. Nixon commuted his sentence. In 1975 he disappeared mysteriously and is thought to have been murdered.
See also: Labor movement.

Hoffer, Eric (1902-1983), self-educated U.S. author and philosopher. A migratory worker and longshoreman until 1967, he won immediate acclaim with his first book, *The True Believer* (1951), a study of mass movements. *The Passionate State of Mind* (1955), a volume of maxims, followed.

Hoffman, Dustin (1937-), U.S. actor, known for his versatility in portraying different character types. Hoffman made his film debut in *The Tiger Makes Out* (1967) and became famous with his performance in *The Graduate* (1967). He was awarded the Academy Award for best actor for *Kramer vs. Kramer* (1979) and *Rain Man* (1988). His other films include *Midnight Cowboy* (1969), *All the President's Men* (1976), *Tootsie* (1982), *Rain Man* (1988), *Outbreak* (1995), and *Sleepers* (1996). At the 1996 Venice Film Festival he was awarded a Golden Lion for his works.

Hoffmann, E(rnst) T(heodor) A(madeus) (1776-1822), German romantic author, composer, and critic. He is best remembered today for his fantastic short stories,which inspired E.A. Poe and others, and the opera *Tales of Hoffmann*, composed by J.L. Offenbach and based on 3 of his stories.

Hofman, Josef (1876-1957), Polish-born U.S. pianist who made a spectacular debut in New York City at the age of 11. He was noted for his authoritative interpretations of the works of Chopin and Liszt.

Hofmann, Hans (1880-1966), German-born U.S. artist and teacher, prominent in the abstract expressionism movement. His vigorous and colorful style, inspired by Wassily Kandinsky, is exemplified by *The Gate* (1959). In 1934 he opened the influential Hans Hofmann School of Fine Arts in New York City.

Hofmannsthal, Hugo von (1874-1929), Austrian neoromantic poet and dramatist. His early style was influenced by the German poet Stefan George (1868-1933) and the Pre-Raphaelites. His adaptation of Sophocles' *Elektra* (1903) was made into an opera by Richard Strauss in 1909, beginning a long collaboration, including *Der Rosenkavalier* (1911), *Ariadne auf Naxos* (1912), and *Die Frau ohne Schatten* (1919). His poems, plays such as *Jedermann* (Everyman, 1911), and opera librettos make him a major figure of Austrian literature.

Hog, pig, or swine, domestic animal (family Suidae) bred for its flesh and fat. Hogs are descended from the wild boars (*Sus scrofa*)of Europe and Asia, which live in small herds in woodland. The weight of the male, or *boar*, can be up to 400 lb (181 kg), while the female, or *sow*, only weighs 300 lb (136 kg). The boar has tusks up to 1 ft (30 cm) long and can be dangerous. Hogs were probably among the earliest domesticated animals. They were allowed to run free in the woods, feeding on seeds such as acorns. Domestic hogs have retained the varied diet of their ancestors and will eat roots, fallen fruit, and even meat. A sow produces litters of up to 12 piglets.

Hogan, Ben (1912-), U.S. professional golfer. His achievements include winning the PGA Championship (1946, 48), U.S. Open (1948, 50, 51, 53), Masters (1951, 53) and British Open (1953).

Hogarth, William (1697-1764), British painter and engraver. He is best known for his 3 series of moralistic and satirical engravings, *The Harlot's Progress* (1732), *The Rake's Progress* (1735), and *Marriage à la Mode* (1745). His first success was as a portraitist, and some of his finest works, such as *Captain Thomas Coram* (1740) and *The Shrimp Girl* (1760), are in this field.

Hogg, Helen Sawyer (1905-), U.S.-born Canadian astronomer noted for her *Catalogue of Variable Stars in Globular Clusters* (1939). Her work involved measurement of the period of variable stars, which helps to determine their distance from earth.

Hognose *See:* Adder.

Hogweed *See:* Ragweed.

Hohenstaufen, medieval German dynasty of Swabian origin whose members ruled Germany and the Holy Roman Empire. The great Hohenstaufen emperors were Conrad III, Frederick I Barbarossa, Henry VI, Frederick II, and Conrad IV. Their concept of a strongly centralized empire brought them into continual conflict with the papacy and with the 2 powerful opposing groups, Guelphs and Ghibellines.

Hohenzollern, German ruling dynasty that first rose to prominence in the 12th century. In 1192 Frederick III of Zollern became the ruler of Nurem-

burg, and his descendants founded the Swabian and Franconian lines. From the latter were descended the electors of Brandenburg and the dukes and kings of Prussia, who ruled as emperors of Germany, 1871-1918.
See also: Germany.

Hohokam *See:* Pima.

Hokusai, Katsushika (1760-1849), Japanese painter, printmaker, and book illustrator, greatest master of the Japanese *ukiyo-e* (popular) school. Interested in every aspect of life, Hokusai worked under a number of different names in a variety of styles, producing over 30,000 drawings of great imagination, compositional mastery, and technical excellence. The most famous collections are *36 Views of Fuji* (1823-29) and *Mangwa, or Ten Thousand Sketches* (1814-18), many of which were admired in Paris and London as well as in the Far East.

Holbein, name of 2 German painters, **Hans Holbein the Elder** (c.1465-1524) was a German Gothic painter of great distinction, best known for his many altarpieces and other church decorations, such as the Kaisheim altar (1502). His middle and later work may have been influenced by Grünewald. His son, **Hans Holbein the Younger** (1497?-1543), a religious painter and portraitist, lived in many European countries and later entered the service of Henry VIII of England, whose most famous portraits are by him.

Holberg, Ludvig (1864-1754), Norwegian-born Danish playwright and educator. A professor at the University of Copenhagen, he was a philosopher and historian as well as an author. His plays were mainly comedies influenced by earlier Roman works. The comedy *Erasmus Montaus* (1731), the satirical poem *Pedar Paars* (1719-20), and *History of the Danish Kingdoms* (1732-35) are among his best known works.

Hölderlin, Johann Christian Friedrich (1770-1843), German lyric poet, noted for the grandeur of his images, derived from classical Greek themes. Among his best-known poems are *Bread and Wine*, *The Rhine*, and *The Death of Empedocles*. *Hyperion* is a semi-autobiographical prose novel.

Holding company, in finance, company that holds a majority or substantial minority of the stock in another company or companies in order to control policies. The constituent corporations of a holding company are called *subsidiaries*. By *pyramiding* such companies, that is, by creating additional companies to control the stock of holding companies lower in the pyramid, the firm at the apex can control assets many times greater than its own.
See also: Corporation.

Holiday, originally *holyday*, day commemorating an event, person, or religious occasion on which people set aside their normal work to rest, celebrate, or pray. Seasonal days of pagan origin are still celebrated at the summer solstice, the harvest, and the end of winter.

Holiday, Billie (Eleanora Fagan; 1915-59), U.S. jazz singer. She started her career at 16, singing in Harlem cafés and night spots. Her highly individual style was soon recognized, and she sang with many famous bands and small

groups in the 1930s and 1940s. In later years she suffered from heroin addiction.
See also: Jazz.

Holinshed's Chronicles, or *Chronicles of England, Scotland, and Ireland*, purported histories of the 3 countries, largely edited by Raphael Holinshed (d. c.1580). Colorful, imaginative, and inaccurate, they provided plots for many Elizabethan dramatists, including William Shakespeare.

Holistic medicine, approach to health and medical care based on the principle that the "whole" person must be treated comprehensively, taking physical, psychological, and environmental factors into account. Treatments include herbs, acupuncture, relaxation therapy, yoga, meditation, vitamin therapy, and biofeedback (body self-monitoring technique). Traditional medicines and surgery are generally avoided.

Holland *See:* Netherlands.

Holland, John Philip (1840-1914), Irish-born U.S. inventor who built the first fully successful submarine, the *Holland*, launched in 1898 and bought by the U.S. Navy in 1900.
See also: Submarine.

Holland Tunnel *See:* Hudson River tunnels.

Holly, any of various species of evergreen trees and shrubs (genus *Ilex*) with glossy, spiny leaves and red or black fruits, usually called berries. The European holly (*I. acquifolium*), used at Christmas and in early pagan ritual, is very similar to the common American holly (*I. opaca*), but there are some species in the Americas that are not evergreen and not spiny. Yaupon (*I. vomitoria*), a holly of the southeastern states, has leaves containing large amounts of caffeine and was used by Native Americans to induce vomiting. The leaves of South American maté (*I. paraguayensis*) are dried and used to make maté tea.

Holly, Buddy (Charles Hardin Holly; 1936-59), U.S. singer, guitarist, and composer, one of rock music's first major performers. Holly's style combined several components of country music with a powerful background rhythm. In 1957 his band, the Crickets, recorded the hit song, "That'll Be the Day." In the same year, Holly released a solo hit, "Peggy Sue." His career was cut short when he was killed in a plane crash outside of Mason City, Iowa.

Hollyhock (*Althaea rosea*), one of the tallest garden flowers. Its flowers grow on short stems along the tall, upright main stalk and open in succession from the bottom of the stem upwards. Cultivated from earliest times because it was thought to have healing properties, it has spread from its native China to the United States via Europe.

Hollywood (pop. 210,000), district of Los Angeles, Calif. Its name became synonymous with the U.S. film industry in the 1920s. Few films are made there, but it now produces a large percentage of U.S. television material.
See also: California.

Holmes, Oliver Wendell (1809-94), U.S. author and physician. The father of jurist Oliver Wendell Holmes, Jr., he is best known for his light essays and poems, which appeared in the *Atlantic Monthly* from 1857, and in book form as *The Autocrat of the Breakfast-Table* (1858) and 3 sequels. He taught at Harvard, 1847-82; his paper *The Contagiousness of Puerperal Fever* (1843) is considered the first major contribution to medicine by an American.

Holmes, Oliver Wendell, Jr. (1841-1935), U.S. jurist, Supreme Court justice (1902-32). He is often called the Great Dissenter, but this reflects the significance rather than the number of his dissenting judgments. In *Lochner* v. *New York* (1905) and *Hammer* v. *Dagenhart* (1918) he reinforced arguments for legislative checks on the economy. His dissent in *Abrams* v. *United States* (1919) was a powerful defense of free speech.

Holmes, Sherlock, fictional detective created by the English author Sir Arthur Conan Doyle. Holmes solves difficult crimes through observation and deduction. A complex character, he has knowledge of chemistry, literature, and the arts, and is an accomplished violinist. He is assisted by his close friend and partner, Dr. John Watson. Holmes first appeared in the novel *A Study in Scarlet* (1887).
See also: Doyle, Sir Arthur Conan.

Holmium, chemical element, symbol Ho; for physical constants see Periodic Table. Holmium was discovered spectroscopically in 1878 by M. Delafontaine and J.L. Soret. It occurs in gadolinite and other rare-earth minerals and is commercially obtained from monazite. Elemental holmium is prepared by reducing its anhydrous chloride with calcium metal. Holmium is a silvery, soft, reactive metal. It has interesting magnetic properties. Holmium belongs to the series of elements known as the rare-earth metals. Ion-exchange and solvent extraction techniques have led to much easier isolation of these elements. Holmium and its compounds are used in carbon-arc lighting applications, special types of glass, enamels, and refractory materials.

Holocaust, term applied to the systematic execution of 6 million European Jews by the German Nazi regime, 1933-45. Adolf Hitler had exploited anti-Semitic feelings in his rise to power and later called for a "final solution to the Jewish question." Most Jews in countries overrun by the Nazis who did not emigrate in time were victims of the Holocaust, which effectively obliterated the Jewish secular and religious life that had flourished in Europe for centuries.
See also: Nazism; World War II.

Holography, technique for recording and reproducing 3-dimensional images by means of laser beams. The picture taken by the technique, the *hologram*, is a piece of photographic film that records not the scene itself but the unfocused pattern of light waves coming from the scene. A hologram is made by illuminating both the scene and the film with laser light, which has the important property of containing light of only 1 color (or wavelength). Light reflected from objects in the scene interferes with light from the direct, or *reference*, beam, producing a light-and-dark pattern of interference fringes. When light from a laser is passed through the developed hologram, the original pattern of light from the scene viewed is recreated in every respect. Thus the original scene will be visible in 3 dimensions, and the person viewing can look "behind" it by moving his or her head sideways. The method was invented in the 1940s by D. Gabor, who received the Nobel Prize in physics in 1971 for his work.

Holst, Gustav Theodore (1874-1934), English composer. He is best known for *The Planets* (1914-16), a massive symphonic suite, each piece representing a planet characterized in myth and astrology. Its popularity has overshadowed his other works, such as the opera *Savitri* (1908).

Holy Alliance, collective security agreement created at the Congress of Vienna in 1815 by Russia, Austria, and Prussia and later joined by most other European powers (excluding Britain, Turkey, and the Vatican). Its avowed aim was to promote mutual relations according to Christian principles. It had little importance in itself, except as a symbol of reaction; revolts in Spain and Naples in the 1820s were suppressed in its name.
See also: Vienna, Congress of.

Holy Bible *See:* Bible.

Holy Grail, legendary talisman, given various forms in various legends. In his *Conte del Graal* (c.1180) Chrétien de Troyes made it the chalice from which Christ drank at the Last Supper and that was used to catch his blood on the Cross. The knight Perceval, as in the poem by Wolfram von Eschenbach *Parzival* (1210), seeks the Grail to redeem himself and others. *Queste del Saint Graal* (1200) linked the Grail with the Arthurian legends and was the source of Thomas Malory's *Morte d'Arthur* (1470). The Grail legends have inspired such modern writers as T.H. White, T.S. Eliot, and Alfred Lord Tennyson, and also Richard Wagner's operas *Lohengrin* (1848) and *Parsifal* (1882).

Holy Land *See:* Palestine.

Holy Roman Empire, European empire centered in Germany that endured from medieval times until 1806. It was effectively established in A.D. 962 when the pope crowned Otto I, king of Germany, emperor of Rome. It derived its political claim to the Roman Empire based on Charlemagne's belief that his empire was the legitimate successor to ancient Rome. In theory, the Holy Roman emperor was God's temporal ruler of all christians. In reality, the political control was somewhat different. At its height, it included all the German principalities, Austria, Bohemia, Moravia, Switzerland, the Low Countries, eastern France, and northern and central Italy. Up until 1562 the emperor was crowned by the pope, thereafter the coronation was performed in Frankfurt. The Holy Roman Empire was in constant conflict with the pope and the Italian states over temporal and religious issues. It was seriously weakened by the Reformation which challenged the allegiance of German Protestant princes to the emperor. The Thirty Years War (1618-1648) almost totally destroyed the German people and the Holy Roman Empire. In fact, it never recovered from this conflict. France emerged as a central power from the war and its continued military successes, from the time of Louis XIV to Napoleon I, eradicated the political reality of the Holy Roman emperor. The official end came in 1806 when Francis II renounced the title, proclaiming himself Francis I, emperor of Austria.

Holy wars *See:* Crusades.

Holy Week, in the Christian church year, week preceding Easter, observed in most churches as a time of solemn devotion to the passion of Christ. From the 4th century the events of the week of the crucifixion have been liturgically reenacted, now especially on Palm Sunday, Maundy Thursday, Good Friday, Holy Saturday, and Easter Sunday.
See also: Christianity.

Home, Lord (1903-95), British politician, prime minister (1963-64). Early in his career he served as a Conservative party member in the House of Commons (1931-45). He was also foreign secretary (1960-63, 1970-74).
See also: United Kingdom.

Home economics, in education, all the disciplines necessary to home maintenance: cooking, nutrition, sewing, the nature and use of textiles, household equipment, and budgeting. Originally it was not considered a scholastic subject, but today it is a common high school elective, and colleges offer degree courses in it. In the United Kingdom it is called domestic science.

Homelessness, term coined in the 1980s to describe the growing condition of mostly city-dwelling people who have no permanent place to live. In the United States, causes of homelessness range from untreated mental illness to joblessness among the poor and lack of low-income housing. The total number of homeless people in the U.S. is thought to be in the millions.

Homeopathy, system of treating disease by administering small doses of a drug that would cause a healthy person to have the symptoms of the disease under treatment. Homeopathy takes a holistic approach, claiming to treat the physical, emotional, and mental states of the patient at once. Homeopathy was introduced in the West by the German doctor Samuel Hahnemann (1755-1843), author of the controversial *Organon of the Art of Healing*.
See also: Hahnemann, (Christian Friedrich) Samuel.

Homeostasis, self-regulating mechanisms through which biological systems maintain a stable internal condition in the face of changes in the external environment. The French physiologist Claude Bernard (1813-78) was the first to show that the internal environment of any living organism is maintained within certain limits. Homeostasis is generally achieved through on-off control and feedback control. Hormones often play a vital role in it.
See also: Bernard, Claude.

Homer (8th century B.C.?), Greek epic poet to whom are ascribed the *Iliad* and *Odyssey*, universally regarded as among the greatest works of western literature. Both poems deal with events related to the Trojan War. The *Iliad* is about a single episode of the war—the anger of the Greek warrior, Achilles, and its tragic results. The *Odyssey* tells of the adventures and quests of another Greek warrior, Odysseus, after the war. Historically, there has been much debate about whether the poems were really written by one author, but most scholars now believe that they were.
See also: Iliad; Odyssey.

Homer, Winslow (1836-1910), U.S. painter who often worked in watercolor, best known for his landscapes and sea studies of New England and Florida, such as *Gulf Stream* (1899). Originally an illustrator, he recorded the Civil War for *Harper's Weekly*. His quasi-impressionist paintings revolutionized the style of U.S. painting in the 1880s and 1890s.

Home Rule, U.S. system of self-government under which some states grant cities and counties the right to adapt their own charters and laws, provided these do not conflict with the state and federal constitutions. The system, which arose in the 19th century, led to the rise of autonomous city and county government.

Homestead Act, act of the U.S. Congress (1862) granting 165 acres (65 hectares) of unoccupied land for small sums of money, to any citizen who lived on the land for 5 years. The act helped to encourage westward movement.
See also: Westward movement.

Homestead Strike, bitter labor dispute (1892) between steel workers and the Carnegie Steel Company, in Homestead, Pa., a landmark in the history of the U.S. labor movement. A clash between strikers and the company's 300 Pinkerton private guards left 10 dead. The national guard was sent in, and the strike was broken, but at a high cost to the reputations of Carnegie and President Benjamin Harrison.
See also: Labor movement.

Homicide, killing of a human being by another. Criminal homicide is classified as either murder or manslaughter. Some homicides are determined to be excusable or justifiable, based on such circumstances as self-defense. Sentencing for homocide varies between U.S. states, some of which consider it a capital offense.
See also: Crime.

Homing pigeon, bird of the family Columbidae able to return to its loft from vast distances, selectively crossbred to combine speed and stamina. The racing of homing pigeons has been a popular sport since the 19th century. A well-trained bird may travel over 1,000 mi (1,600 km).

Homo erectus, early species of human being, having larger teeth and smaller brains than modern humans (*Homo sapiens*). They lived from about a million and a half years ago to 300,000 years ago. *Homo erectus* probably originated in Africa and later moved into Asia and Europe. Fossils of *Homo erectus* have been found in Indonesia (Java), China, and Kenya. *Homo erectus* made stone tools and used fire.
See also: Heidelberg man; Java man; Peking man.

Homogenization, process to delay the separation of fat in milk, an unstable emulsion containing fat globules that tend to coalesce. In homogenization the milk is heated to about 140°F (60°C) and passed at pressure through small openings. The fatty clusters are broken up by shearing as they pass through the holes, by the action of pressure, and by impact with components of the homogenizer.

Homo habilis, oldest species of human being yet discovered, believed to have lived in Africa about 2 million years ago, probably the first known human to make stone tools. The brain of *Homo habilus* seems to have been about half the size of the modern human brain. Fossil discoveries in Kenya suggest that *Homo habilis*, like apes, spent a great deal of time in trees.
See also: Australopithecus; Homo erectus.

Homologue, in biology, structure or organ with the same evolutionary origin as an apparently different structure in another species. For example, there is little apparent similarity between a horse's leg and the flipper of a whale, but they have similar embryonic histories and are therefore homologues.
See also: Biology.

Homo sapiens, species of humans approximately 450,000 years old, with the oldest known fossil remains dating back about 375,000 years. Neanderthal man is the most well known example of *Homo sapiens* and lived in Africa, Asia, and Europe from 100,000 to 35,000 years ago. Modern human beings are classified as a subspecies of *Homo sapiens*, *Homo sapiens sapiens*.

Homosexuality, sexual attraction to persons of one's own sex. Female homosexuality is called lesbianism. Although many theories have tried to account for homosexuality as a deviation from the norm, in 1975 the American Psychiatric Association removed homosexuality from its list of mental disorders. Homosexuality was widely accepted in ancient Greece, and there have been prominent homosexuals throughout history. However, legal persecution and public censure have forced homosexuals to live restricted and secret lives. In the United States hostility towards and discrimination against homosexuals remains widespread. Since the 1960s the gay rights movement has fought vocally for housing, employment, and other rights. In the 1980s the AIDS epidemic provided an excuse for a new rise in anti-homosexual attitudes. Homosexual acts between consenting adult and conducted in private remain illegal in many states, although they are rarely prosecuted.

Honduras (Republic of), country in Central America bordered by the Caribbean Sea, Nicaragua, El Salvador and the Pacific Ocean, and Guatemala. The capital is Tegucigalpa.
Land and people. Most of Honduras is mountainous, but there are swamps and forests in the east, along the Mosquito Coast. Enclosed within the mountain ranges are several basins that have become the major population centers. The official language is Spanish, and Roman Catholicism is the dominant religion.
Economy. U.S.-owned banana and coffee plantations dominate the economy, and the bulk of the population works on the land. Coffee replaced bananas as the main export in 1975; other exports are timber, meat, cotton, and tobacco. There is little industry, and transport facilities are poor.
History. From the 4th to the 7th centuries the ancient city of Copán was a center of the civilization of the Mayas, but when Columbus reached the Honduran coast on his 1502 voyage, the country was inhabited only by seminomadic tribes. A Spanish colony for almost 300 years, Honduras was generally governed from Guatemala. In 1821 it won independence from Spain and became part of the Mexican empire, along with 4 other Central

Honduras

Capital:	Tegucigalpa
Area:	43,277 sq mi (112,088 sq km)
Population:	5,862,000
Language:	Spanish
Government:	Presidential republic
Independent:	1838
Head of gov.:	President
Per capita:	U.S. $600
Mon. unit:	1 Lempira = 100 centavos

American States. Subsequently the 5 states formed the United Provinces of Central America, of which the Honduran patriot Francisco Morazán was president until its dissolution in 1838. Since that time, Honduras has been an independent republic. Its history has been marked by conflicts, revolutions, and military rule. The 1980s saw occasional border clashes with neighboring Nicaragua, and although more democratic structures have been imposed, rightist military officers generally dominated politics. The 1990s were characterized by violations of human rights by the military.

Honecker, Erich (1912-94), leader of East Germany (1971-89). He joined the Communist Party (1929) as a youth and was imprisoned by the Nazis (1935-45). After World War II, he rose to the top of the political ranks in East German and Communist Party politics. He resigned in 1989, not long before the beginning of the process of German reunification. In 1992 he was tried for his involvement in the killings of people who had tried to escape from East Germany. Due to his poor health, the trial was discontinued.

Honegger, Arthur (1892-1955), Swiss-French composer, member of the French Les Six group, best known for his popular *Pacific 231* (1923) and his oratorio *King David* (1921-23).

Honey, sweet substance made through enzyme action by bees from the nectar of flowers. As a sweetener, there is very little difference between honey and sucrose (table sugar), although the former does contain minimal quantities of vitamins, minerals, and amino acids. Honey is available in comb or syrup form. There are different types depending on what flowers the bees have fed on; some popular varieties are sage, clover, and wildflower.

Honey badger *See:* Ratel.

Honey bear *See:* Sloth bear.

Honey bee *See:* Bee.

Honeyeater, any of several birds of the family Maliphagidea, native to Australia, New Zealand, and the Pacific Islands. They feed on nectar and insects and some are pests in orchards because they eat flowers and fruit. Some species are very rare or extinct because they have been hunted and their forest homes cut down. The moho, which ranged as far as Hawaii, was prized for its yellow and black feathers, used by the Hawaiians for ceremonial cloaks. It is now extinct.

Honey locust, any of several trees (genus *Gleditsia*) of the pea family. Often used for its shade and ornamentation, the honey locust is commonly found in the eastern United States. It has large flat pods whose pulp cattle eat. Its wood is often used for railroad ties, fence posts, or fuel.

Honeysuckle, common name for shrubs and vines of the family Caprifoliaceae, found in the Northern Hemisphere. Their flowers contain a large amount of nectar, which makes them a favorite of insects, such as hawk moths. Many of them produce an attractive scent. The berries are popular with birds.

Hong Kong, British Crown colony on the coast of southeast China, about 90 mi (145 km) from Canton, consisting of mainland territories and numerous offshore islands. Hong Kong island was ceded to the British after the Opium War in 1842. Mainland Hong Kong includes Kowloon, acquired in 1860, and the New Territories, leased to Britain for 99 years in 1898. In 1985 an agreement was reached between the United Kingdom and the People's Republic of China regarding the turnover of Hong Kong to Chinese sovereignty in 1997. Of the rocky land surface, 75% is unsuitable for building, and a mere 14% is urbanized, accommodating 90% of the population. Since the early 1900s refugees from China's political upheavals have swelled the colony's population. During Japanese wartime occupation (1941–45) the trend was briefly reversed, but since then the population has increased rapidly. Hong Kong is a free trade area and one of the world's principal ports. It has much light industry, particularly textiles and electrical goods. The colony depends on China for most of its food and water. In 1997 Hong Kong was turned over to China. In 1998 a new airport came into use, situated in the sea.

Honiara (pop. 35,300), capital of the Solomon Islands, an independent state (and member of the British Commonwealth) in the southwest Pacific Ocean. Honiara is located on the island of Guadalcanal. It was the site of a World War II U.S. military base and earlier of a Japanese military base.
See also: Solomon Islands.

Honolulu (pop. 371,300), capital and chief seaport of Hawaii, seat of Honolulu County, located on the southeast coast of Oahu Island. Honolulu grew from a fishing village in 1820 to the capital of independent Hawaii (1845) and then the territorial capital when Hawaii was annexed by the U.S. (1898). It is important as a shipping center, for sugar and pineapple processing, and as the tourist hub of Hawaii.
See also: Hawaii.

Honorius I (d. 638), pope of the Roman Catholic Church, elected 625. An aristocrat from southern Italy, he oversaw missionary activities in Britain and negotiated a peace settlement with the German Lombard tribe. He apparently supported monotheletism, a theological trend that argued that Christ had a dual nature but a single will. This idea was declared heretical at the third Council of Constantinople (680).

Honorius III (d. 1227), pope of the Roman Catholic Church, elected 1216. He inaugurated campaigns for new Crusades in Spain and France and sanctioned new religious orders (the Dominicans, the Franciscans, and the Carmelites).

Hood, John Bell (1831-79), Confederate general in the U.S. Civil War, a commander in the second Battle of Bull Run, the battle of Gettysburg, and in the resistance to General William Sherman's drive on Atlanta (1864). Disastrously defeated at the battle of Nashville (Dec. 1864), he was relieved of his command at his own request.
See also: Civil War, U.S.

Hood, Thomas (1799-1845), English humorist and editor, known for his *Comic Annuals* (1830-39, 1842). He is also regarded as a poet of protest against industrial conditions, e.g. "Song of the Shirt" (1843).

Hoof, enlarged, heavy toenail developed by many herbivorous animals. Since speed is a large herbivore's best defense against a predator, it is an advantage to be able to run on the tips of the toes, as this adds length to the stride. Hooves give stability to this tiptoe stance. Animals with hooves include horses, rhinoceroses, antelopes, goats, sheep, hogs, hippopotamuses, camels, and cattle.

Hoof-and-mouth disease *See:* Foot-and-mouth disease.

Hooke, Robert (1635-1703), English experimental scientist and one of the greatest inventors of his age. Hooke entered his most creative period in 1662, when he became the Royal Society of London's first curator of experiments. He invented the compound microscope, the universal joint, the spiral spring for watches, and a type of telescope. His microscopic researches were published in the beautifully illustrated *Micrographia* (1665), a work that also introduced the term *cell* to biology. He is best remembered for Hooke's law (1678) that the deformation occurring in an elastic body under stress is proportional to the applied stress. He also theorized a precursor to Newton's law of universal gravitation.
See also: Microscope.

Hooker, Joseph (1814-79), U.S. general during the Civil War. Appointed commander of the Army of the Potomac (1863), he was defeated by General Robert E. Lee at Chancellorsville and relieved as army commander.
See also: Civil War, U.S.

Hooker, Richard (1554-1600), English theologian whose 8-volume work *Of the Laws of Ecclesiastical Polity*, a landmark of Anglican theology, defended the Elizabethan religious settlement against both Roman Catholics and Puritans.
See also: Theology.

Hooker, Thomas (1586-1647), early American Puritan clergyman. A religious exile from England, he came to Massachusetts via Holland (1633) and became minister at the New Town (now Cambridge) settlement. Conflicts with the Massachusetts leaders drove him and his congregation to Connecticut (1635-36), and he and his followers founded Hartford.
See also: Puritans.

Hooks, Benjamin Lawson (1925-), U.S. lawyer, minister, and leader of the African-American community. President Nixon appointed him to the Federal Communications Commission in 1972. In 1977 Hooks succeeded Roy Wilkins as executive director of the National Association for the Advancement of Colored People.

Hookworm, any of various intestinal parasites (order Strongiloidae) of humans and domesticated animal. The life cycle involves a free-living larval stage followed by direct infection of the host, with no intermediate host. The parasitic adults are blood feeders and attach themselves to vessels in the wall of the intestine. Each worm may cause the loss of up to 0.25 ml of blood a day.

Hooper, William (1742-90), colonial lawyer and politician from North Carolina. He was a representative in the provincial congresses of North Carolina and in the Continental Congress (1774-77) and was a signer of the Declaration of Independence (1776).

Hoopoe (*Upupa epops*), large bird of Europe, Asia, and Africa, named for its call. Since recorded time hoopoes have been prized for their pink plumage, black and white barred wings, and large crest.

Hoosac tunnel, rock tunnel in western Massachusetts, in the Berkshire Hills. Completed in 1876, it was the first tunnel to be blasted out with nitroglycerin and drilled through with a power tool powered by compressed air. A total of 136 lives were lost during the construction of the 4 mi (6 km) tunnel.

Hoosier Poet *See:* Riley, James Whitcomb.

Hoosier State *See:* Indiana.

Hooton, Earnest Albert (1887-1954), U.S. physical anthropologist known for his attempts to relate behavior to physical or racial type. His books include *Up From the Ape* (1931) and *The American Criminal* (1939).
See also: Anthropology.

Hoover, Herbert Clark (1874-1964), 31st president of the United States, who held office during the onset of the Great Depression of the 1930s. Hoover's measures against the Depression were widely criticized as being too little and too late. He did, however, to a limited degree, try to use the powers of the government to restore prosperity.
Early life. Hoover entered Stanford University in 1891 and received his A.B. in 1895, after specializing in geology and engineering. For the next two decades he traveled throughout the world as a mining engineer and executive.

By 1914, when World War I broke out in Europe, he had become a millionaire.

Relief work. Hoover, who was living in London when the war started, helped organize the return of 120,000 Americans then in Europe. He also became active in relief efforts, heading an organization that sent food, clothing, and medical supplies to people in German-occupied Belgium and northern France. Returning home in 1917, he was appointed head of the U.S. Food Administration.

Political career. By 1920, Hoover was an internationally known figure. In 1921, President Harding appointed him as secretary of commerce, and he continued to serve under President Coolidge. In 1928, the Republican party nominated him to run for president. He won the election easily, defeating Democrat Alfred E. Smith by a huge margin.

President. After a good-will tour of Latin America, Hoover took office on March 4, 1929. He embarked on a program of economic reform, encouraging Congress to pass laws providing financial support to farmers and higher tariffs. Hoover was optimistic about the nation's economic future; however, in October 1929, barely eight months into his term, the stock market crashed and the Great Depression began. Stocks dropped some 40% in value overnight. Millions of people became unemployed. Families lost their life savings and thousands of businesses failed.

Hoover hoped to remedy the crisis by restoring business confidence, paring back government expenditures, and balancing the budget. But the Depression continued to worsen.

The president was reluctant to involve the federal government in direct relief measures. He felt that states and localities should initiate public works and relief programs. However, he did ask Congress to create the Reconstruction Finance Corporation (RFC), which lent money to banks, railways and other businesses. Eventually, it lent money to the states to help jobless workers. Hoover also supported a number of federal flood control and navigation projects, which helped to create jobs.

In June 1932, an "army" of 15,000 unemployed World War I veterans came to Washington. They were hoping Congress would agree to immediate payment of bonuses due them in 1945. Hoover had the army eject the veterans by force, which had a damaging effect on his reputation.

Although Hoover won the Republican nomination again in 1932, no one expected him to win the election. He was defeated by Democrat Franklin Delano Roosevelt, who would eventually lead the nation out of the Depression and through the years of World War II.

Herbert Clark Hoover

31st U.S. President

Born:	West Branch, Iowa; Aug. 10, 1874
Term of office:	March 1929-March 1933
Vice president:	Charles Curtis
Party:	Republican
Spouse:	Lou Henry Hoover
Children:	Two
Died:	New York, N.Y.; Oct. 20, 1964

Hoover lived for more than 30 years after leaving the presidency. After a long illness, he died in his sleep in New York City on Oct. 24, 1964.

Hoover, J(ohn) Edgar (1895-1972), director of the Federal Bureau of Investigation (FBI) from 1924 until his death. Hoover made the FBI an efficient apparatus to fight organized crime. After World War II, at Hoover's direction, the FBI began a crusade against "subversives," targeting leftist activists. By the 1960s and 1970s Hoover's conservative political views and the FBI's violation of the civil rights of its opponents made him the center of controversy. He published a number of books, including Masters of Deceit (1958) and J. Edgar Hoover on Communism (1969).
See also: Federal Bureau of Investigation.

Hoover Commission, common name for Commission on Organization of the Executive Branch of the Government, an advisory commission to prepare improvements in the efficiency of the executive branch of government. The first such commission (1947-49) submitted 273 proposals and was responsible for the establishment of the Department of Health, Education and Welfare. A second commission (1953-55) made 314 recommendations, more than half of which were adopted.

Hoover Dam, formerly Boulder Dam (1933-47), on the Colorado River between Nevada and Arizona. It is 736 ft (244 m) high and 1,244 ft (379 m) long. The dam impounds Lake Mead and has a hydroelectric capacity of 1.3 Mw. Built in 1931-35, it began operating in 1936.

Hop, tall prickly perennial vine (*Homulus lupulus*) of the mulberry family whose dried female flowers, called hops, contain *lupullin*, a substance that gives beer its bitter flavor and is used as a preservative. Hops were first grown by the Greeks, who ate the young shoots. They were first used for flavoring beer by the Germans in the 8th century.

Hope, Bob (Leslie Townes Hope; 1903-), English-born U.S. comedian, born in Eltham, England. He emigrated to the United States as a child and began his career in vaudeville, becoming famous in the 1930s through radio and motion pictures, notably in the "Road" series of movies with Bing Crosby. Since World War II he has made regular overseas tours to entertain U.S. troops and has specialized in topical political humor.

Hope, John (1868-1936), U.S. educator and civil rights leader. Son of a black mother and white father, he advocated advanced education at a time when Booker T. Washington was inclined to restrict black education to the purely technological. The first African American president of Morehouse College in Atlanta, Ga., in 1906, he became first president of Atlanta University in 1929.
See also: Civil rights.

HOPE Project, or Health Opportunity for People Everywhere, independent, non-profit organization established in 1958 by Washington, D.C., physician William B. Walsh to promote the teaching of new techniques to medical personnel in developing nations. In 1960 Project HOPE sent medical educators aboard the world's first peacetime hospital ship, the S.S. HOPE. Today Project HOPE has training programs in over 15 countries.

Hopewell *See:* Mound Builders.

Hopi, Pueblo Native American tribe of northeast Arizona. The Hopi have a complex society based on clans organized around matrilineal extended households. Since the 1820s there have been territorial conflicts between the Hopi and Navajo. In 1975 the federal government redrew territorial boundaries, making several thousand Navajo move. The Hopi are known for their elaborate religious ceremonies, which feature dancing and the kachina figure.

Hopkins, Gerard Manley (1844-1889), English poet and Jesuit priest. Hopkins's work was experimental, using natural speech and "sprung rhythm" rather than syllable counts. Unappreciated in his lifetime, his poetry has had great influence in the 20th century. "The Windhover" and "God's Grandeur" are two of his major poems. His work was published posthumously in 1918.

Hopkins, Harry Lloyd (1890-1946), U.S. politician. He was administrator of the Federal Emergency Relief Administration (1933), director of the Works Project Administration (1935), secretary of commerce (1938), and U.S. Lend Lease administrator (1941). As President Franklin D. Roosevelt's aide throughout World War II, he carried out important negotiations with Russia for both Roosevelt and President Harry S. Truman.

Hopkins, Johns (1795-1873), U.S. financier and philanthropist. A Quaker, he made his fortune as a wholesale grocer. He bequeathed $7 million to endow Johns Hopkins University and Johns Hopkins Hospital in Baltimore.

Hopkins, Stephen (1707-85), cultural and political leader in colonial Rhode Island. A signer of the Declaration of Independence, he was a delegate to the Continental Congress (1774-80).

Hopkinson, Francis (1737-91), American composer, delegate to the Continental Congress, and signer of the Declaration of Independence. His 1788 song collection was dedicated to George Washington. His son **Joseph Hopkinson** (1770-1842) wrote the words to "Hail Columbia."

Hopper, Edward (1882-1967), U.S. painter and engraver. First recognized for his etchings, he returned to painting late in life and became known for large, quiet urban studies of subtle composition, often reflecting loneliness and alienation.

Hopper, Grace Murray (1906-), U.S. computer scientist whose belief that computer languages should be more like everyday language led, in the 1950s, to the invention of COBOL (Common Business Oriented Language), a widely used computer language. After graduating from Vassar in 1928, Hopper went on to earn a Ph.D in mathematics from Yale. In 1943 Hopper joined the Navy, where she attained the rank of rear admiral.

Hoppner, John (1758-1810), English portraitist to the Prince of Wales (1789), elected to the Royal Academy (1795). His portraits include studies of Nelson, Wellington, and Sir Walter Scott.

Horace (Quintus Horatius Flaccus; 65-8 B.C.), Roman lyric poet and satirist. At first supported by a rich patron, Maecenas, he later became the favored poet of the emperor Augustus. Horace's surviving works include four books of *Odes*, two of *Satires*, two of *Epistles*, and his *Episodes*, These and the *Art of Poetry* have had deep influence on European literature.
See also: Rome, Ancient.

Horatius (Publius Horatius Cocles), legendary Roman hero. He and two companions are said to have held off an invading Etruscan army at the Sublician Bridge across the Tiber River. The Romans cut the bridge behind him, blocking the Etruscan advance, and Horatius escaped by swimming across the river.
See also: Rome, Ancient.

Horehound (*Marrubium vulgare*), aromatic plant in the mint family, with wrinkled leaves and clusters of small flowers found growing in waste places. It was once popular as a flavoring in candies and cough medicines.

Horizon, apparent line where the sky meets the land or sea. At sea, its distance varies in proportion to the square root of the height of the observer's eyes above sea level. The celestial horizon is the great circle on the celestial sphere at 90° from the zenith (the point immediately above the observer).

Hormone, chemical substance produced in living organisms by the endocrine system. Hormones act to regulate many biological processes, including growth, metabolism, digestion and reproduction. They are "messengers," usually acting at a distance from their site of origin. Hormones are carried from ductless glands through the bloodstream to their point of action.
See also: Endocrine system.

Hormuz, Strait of, 30-50 mi (48-80km) wide waterway leading out of the Persian Gulf to the Gulf of Oman and the Indian Ocean. Most Middle East oil tankers pass through the strait, which is commanded by Qishm Island (Iran) and three other islands—Greater Tunb, Lesser Tunb, and Abu Musa—currently held by Iran but claimed by the United Arab Emirates.

Horn, in music, brass wind instrument. Horns are derived from the animal horns used by primitive societies. Metal was found to produce a better tone, and horns became increasingly sophisticated and complex. Horns were introduced into orchestral music in the early 18th centrury. Valved horns (such as the trumpet) were developed in the 19th century.

Horn, bony extension, usually elongated and pointed, growing from the heads of some mammals, including cattle, sheep, and goats. The antlers of deer are not true horns. Both males and females may grow horns, which consist of a central core of bone-like material encased by a layer of the skin protein keratin. Animals use their horns for protection, either by fighting with them or by displaying them in a threatening manner.

Hornbill, any of various birds of the family Bucerotidae noted for their huge bills, which in some species bear an additional growth called a casque. Hornbills are found in most of Africa and southern Asia as far east as the Philippines. Most live in forests, but the large ground hornbill lives in open country. They feed mainly on fruit, but some hornbills eat insects or lizards. Their nesting habits are unusual. The eggs are laid in a hole in a tree trunk, and the female walls herself in with mud; while incubating the eggs, she is fed by the male through a slit in the mud wall.

Hornblende, dark green or black mineral of varied composition, usually including silicates of aluminum and other abundant elements. It forms vitreous glassy rocks. Often found in igneous and metamorphic rock, hornblende is a major constituent of the amphibole group of minerals.

Hornbook, children's primer used before printed books became cheap and widely available. Hornbooks consisted of printed sheets showing the alphabet and numerals; the sheets were pasted to a wooden, short-handled tablet and covered with a thin, transparent layer of horn for protection.

Horne, Lena (1917-), U.S. actress and blues singer. Horne began her career as a 16-year-old chorus dancer in New York City's Cotton Club and made her movie debut in *The Duke Is Tops* (1938). Horne gained widespread recognition for her singing in the movie *Stormy Weather* (1943) and went on to be a popular nightclub singer in Europe and the United States.

Horne, Marilyn (1934-), U.S. mezzo-soprano. A pupil of Lotte Lehmann, she is known for her mastery of bel canto roles in Bellini and Rossini operas. She made her Metropolitan Opera debut in 1970 as Adalgisa in Bellini's *Norma*.

Horned lizard, name for several species of lizards (genus *Phrynosoma*) native to North America, from Canada to Mexico. Because of their shape, they are often called horned toads. The body is covered with spiny scales that are particularly long on the head. Horned lizards live in dry regions, where they can bury themselves in the sand by rapid sidewise movements. They feed on insects, especially ants.

Hornet, any of several kinds of large social wasps (family Vespidae), that, unlike the more common yellow jackets, build their nests in trees or in human dwellings. The nest, enclosed in a paperlike shell, consists of a series of horizontal combs. Hornets make the papery material by chewing woody plant matters. Female hornets can inflict an extremely painful sting.

Horney, Karen (1885-1952), German-born U.S. psychoanalyst, founder of the American Institute of Psychoanalysis (1941). She stressed the importance of environmental and cultural factors in character development, rejecting many of the basic principles of Freud's psychoanalytic theory, especially his stress on the libido as the root of personality and behavior. Her best known work is *Neurosis and Human Growth* (1950).

Hornsby, Rogers (1896-1963), U.S. baseball player and manager. Hornsby, a second baseman, is considered one of the greatest right-handed batters in the game's history. His achievements include 7 National League batting titles (consecutively from 1920-25, 1928), hitting .424—the single season record (1924), and a lifetime batting average of .358, second only to Ty Cobb's .367. Hornsby played for the St. Louis Cardinals (1915-26, and 1933), New York Giants (1927), Boston Braves (1928), Chicago Cubs (1929-32), and the St. Louis Browns (1933-37). He went on to manage after his 1937 season and was inducted into the National Baseball Hall of Fame (1942).

Hornwort, any one of a group of plants related to liverworts and mosses and growing world-wide, but most commonly in warm, moist regions. A hornwort reproduces in a cycle known as the *alternation of generations*. It forms a gametophyte in the first stage of its life and a sporophyte in the second stage. The gametophyte is a small plant body called a *thallus*. The sporophyte is from 3/16-4 3/4 in (0.5-12 cm) high and resembles the horns of a cow.

Horowitz, Vladimir (1904-89), Russian-born U.S. virtuoso pianist. After a brilliant debut in Kiev (1922), he toured the USSR and Europe (1924) and the United States (1928). He became a U.S. citizen in 1944.

Horse, hoofed, herbivorous mammal (genus *Equus*). This is the only living genus of the family Equidae; the donkey and the zebra are different species of the same genus. Wild horses occurred in prehistoric times over most of Eurasia. Today, the only surviving true wild horse is the Przewalski horse of Siberia, Mongolia, and western China. Domestic horses (*E. caballus*) can be grouped as ponies, heavy draft horses, lightweight draft, and riding horses; they originated from North African stock. Thoroughbreds are descended from Arabian stock. The fossil record of the horse family provides a classic example of evolution in action. The earliest animal that can be placed in the family was Eohippus, which was the size of a fox terrier and had 3 toes of equal size on each hindfoot and 4 toes on each forefoot. The development of the single-toed foot of modern horses was an adaptation to running on hard dry grassland. The changes in tooth pattern allowed the animal to eat abrasive grasses. The increase in size may be followed through a continuous series of intermediate stages to the present day. The various species of the genus *Equus* can often interbreed (e.g., horses and donkeys), but the offspring (e.g., mules) are generally sterile.

Horse brier *See:* Greenbrier.

Horse chestnut, popular name for various trees and shrubs (genus *Aesculus*) of the family Hippcastanaceae. In winter the twigs bear sticky buds that develop into conspicuous leaves and big flowers. In the fall large, shiny seeds similar to chestnuts are released from fleshy coats. The Ohio buckeye (*A. glabra*) is the state tree. Horse chestnut wood is light and strong and is used for boxes and coffins.

Horsefly, any of various two-winged flies (family Tabanidae), so called because they bite horses, as well as other mammals. Only the females bite, piercing the skin with specialized mouthparts and sucking blood. Female horseflies require a blood-meal before laying eggs. They transmit a few diseases, but their main significance as pests is in the sting of their bite.

Horsehair worm, hair snake, or hairworm, any of about 200 types of long, thin worms making up the phylum Nematomorpha. They may grow to 28 in (70 cm). The young are hatched from eggs and form cysts, which may be eaten by insects. The larva then leave the cysts and live in the insects as parasites. The worms leave the insects' bodies when they reach adulthood.

Horse latitudes, regions of calm, quiet winds situated on either side of the equator, between 30°N and S latitudes. In early colonial days, ships bound for the Americas were often becalmed in these latitudes. The horses died from lack of fresh water and were cast overboard. This gave the regions their name.
See also: Calms, Regions of.

Horse nettle *See:* Solanum.

Horsepower,, unit of power used to indicate the rate at which work is done. In the 18th century inventor James Watt experimentally determined that a strong horse can lift up to 33,000 foot-pounds 1 foot per minute. This has become the definition of 1 horsepower. In electrical units 1 horsepower is equivalent to 746 watts; the heat equivalent is 2, 545 BTU (British thermal units) per hour.

Horse Racing, sport involving trials of speed between horses, watched by millions of people in many countries. Its interest as a spectator sport is largely based on the practice of on-and off-track betting. The oldest stake race is the English St. Leger, first run in 1776. In the United States, the most famous race is the Kentucky Derby, first run in 1875. Besides flat racing, there are steeplechasing and harness racing.

Horseradish, common name for a perennial herb (*Armoracia rusticana*), of the mustard family. Native to Eurasia, it is widely cultivated for its white, edible, pungent roots, which grow to a length of 12 in (30 cm) and are used to make a popular relish with a sharp flavor.

Horseshoe crab, or king crab, any of several marine arthropods of the order Xiphosura, "living fossils" whose almost identical ancestors have been found in rocks 175 million years old. King crabs are not true crabs but are more closely related to spiders. If the dome-shaped shell is turned over it shows a horseshoe outline and a series of jointed legs. King crabs live near sheltered shores on the Atlantic coast of the United States and around the coast of Asia. In some places king crabs are fished for pig and chicken feed, and fertilizer. They are pests in clam beds.

Horseshoe Falls *See:* Niagara Falls.

Horseshoe pitching, game played on a court by 2 or more people, in which players attempt to throw horseshoes to encircle an iron stake. The court, usually out-of-doors, is 50 ft (15.2 m) long and 10 ft (3m) wide. The iron stakes, set at either end of the court, are 1 ft (0.3m) high. Scoring is based on a system of point values placed on how close a horseshoe is to a stake. Encircling the stake, called a *ringer*, is the highest point-scoring throw, with a value of 3. A horseshoe that is only touching the stake is called a *leaner* and has a value of 2. The game originated in Roman army camps c.100 A.D.

Horsetail, primitive plant (genus *Equisetum*) related to the fern that once dominated the plant world and was important in the formation of coal. One fossil horsetail was 100 ft (30 m) high, but living species are rarely more than 2 to 3 feet (0.6 to 0.9 m) high. Each horsetail plant lasts several years. It has an underground stem that sends up hollow vertical stems each year. Each vertical stem is jointed and at each joint there is a ring of small leaves. The plant is coated with gritty silica, thus it has been called scouring rush and has been used for cleaning pans. Some horsetails have 2 kinds of stems. The first bears a spore-producing organ at the tip. The spores are released and drift away to produce small sexual plants as in ferns. These stems then die down and are replaced by taller green stems that last all season.

Horthy de Nagybanya, Miklós (1868-1957), Hungarian admiral and politician who led the counter-revolutionary army that overthrew the Communist and socialist coalition under Béla Kun (1919). From 1920 he acted as regent. He joined the Axis powers in World War II, but after trying to make peace with the USSR in 1944, he was imprisoned in Germany. Freed by U.S. forces, he settled in Portugal (1949).
See also: Hungary.

Horticultural grafting, technique of propagating plants by attaching the stem or bud of one plant (the scion) to the stem or roots of another (the stock, or rootstock). Only closely related species can be grafted. Roses and fruit trees are often grafted so that good flowering or fruiting varieties have the benefit of strong roots.

Horticulture, branch of agriculture concerned with producing fruits, flowers, and vegetables. It can be divided into *pomology* (growing fruit), *olericulture* (growing vegetables), and *floriculture* (growing shrubs and ornamental plants). About 3% of U.S. cropland is devoted to horticulture. It was originally practiced on a small scale, but crops such as the potato and tomato are now often grown in vast fields.

Horus, ancient Egyptian god. Originally a sky god, depicted as a falcon or as falcon-headed, he became thought of as the son of Isis and Osiris. He avenged his father's murder by defeating Set, the spirit of evil, and succeeded Osiris as king.
See also: Mythology.

Hosea, Book of, first of the Old Testament Minor Prophets. Its material originated in the prophecies of Hosea, delivered in Israel in the 8th century B.C. It compares God's abiding love for idolatrous Israel to Hosea's love for his prostitute wife, whom he divorced but remarried.
See also: Bible; Old Testament.

Hospice, facility for the care of terminally ill patients. Its professional staff seeks to provide alleviation of pain (rather than life-prolonging medical services), supportive psychological and spiritual counseling, and easy access for family and friends in a dignified and noninstitutional environment. The first hospice was opened in England in 1967 by Dr. Cecily Saunders. In the United States the cost of hospice care is now reimbursable under both Medicaid and Medicare.

Hospital, institution for the care of the sick or injured. Simple hospitals were first set up in Babylonian, Egyptian, Greek, and Roman communities, and in India hospitals had been established before A.D. 400. The early Christians did much to help the sick, and established the first charity hospitals, but medical knowledge was far from adequate, and death rates in hospitals were very high. Little had changed by the year 1123, when St. Bartholomew's Hospital was established in London. The majority of people admitted were either homeless or had little hope of recovery. Most physicians, apothecaries, and surgeons rendered their services at home or in an office rather than at a hospital. The first general hospital built in the United States was the Pennsylvania Hospital in Philadelphia, established in 1751. Others were built soon afterward, and medical technology improved rapidly during this period. but it was only when men like Joseph Lister obtained an understanding of the nature of infection and the importance of aseptic surgery that hospitals became safe places for treatment. Until then, a patient admitted to a hospital was more likely to die than one who remained at home. Today there are more than 9,500 hospitals in the United States, with over 2,100,000 beds, admitting over 35,000,000 patients each year. The average duration of a stay is just over 1 week.

Hostage, traditionally, a person delivered as a token of good faith; now hostages are more often kidnapped and tortured by political dissidents demanding concessions. Iran's taking of U.S. hostages (1979), with demands for the return of their deposed Shah, resulted in a major crisis for President Jimmy Carter's administration. A UN treaty outlawing the taking of hostages went into effect in 1983.

Hostel *See:* Youth hostel.

Hotel, a building that provides the public with overnight lodging. Although the basic purpose is to provide rooms for travelers to sleep in, many hotels also provide meals, entertainment, and other personal services. There are 4 major types of hotel: commercial hotels, residential hotels, resort hotels, and motor hotels (motels). Hotels date from ancient times, and can be found in almost any country in the world.

Hot Line, direct White House-Kremlin emergency communications link, established in 1963. It aims to reduce the risk of war occurring by mistake or misunderstanding. Telegraphic and radio circuits run via London, Copenhagen, Stockholm, and Helsinki.

Hot rod, automobile with improved engine or body design, giving greater acceleration and speed. Following World War II a cult of street racing developed in the United States, consisting of acceleration races between traffic lights. In the 1950s "drag racing" on special tracks was encouraged by police departments to try to prevent this. The term "hot rod" now includes recognized "stock" sedans and specially designed "dragsters."

Hot Springs (pop. 32,462), city in central-western Arkansas, 47 mi (76 km) west and southwest of Little Rock. The city was founded in 1807 by Manuel Prudhomme, a trapper. It is the site of Hot Springs National Park (designated in 1921), which encompasses almost the entire city.
See also: Arkansas.

Hot springs, or thermal springs, natural discharges of heated water from within the earth. Most hot springs originate when water passes close to or through hot, igneous rock. They can form as streams, calm pools, geysers, fumaroles, or mudpots. Modern energy concerns have aroused interest in the possible uses of geothermal energy to generate electrical power.

Hot Springs National Park, park in the Ouachita Mts., Arkansas. It is a popular tourist and health resort noted for its 47 thermal springs. The park, created in 1921, comprises 5,826 acres (2,358 hectares).

Hottentot *See:* Khoikhoi.

Houdini, Harry (Erich Weiss; 1874-1926), U.S. magician and escapologist. He was world famous for his escapes from seemingly impossible situations, as from a sealed chest underwater. He also pursued a campaign of exposing fake mediums and spiritualists.

Houdon, Jean-Antoine (1741-1828), French sculptor famous for his portraits. His sitters included Catherine the Great (1773), Voltaire (1781), and Benjamin Franklin (1791). The best known of his mythological works is *Diana* (1777).

Hound, group of dogs that hunt by sight or by following scent. Sight hounds chase quarry, overtake it, then kill or capture it. They include the greyhound, Afghan hound, Saluki, and Irish wolfhound. Scent hounds, or tailing hounds, follow the scent of their quarry and flush it out. They include the beagle, bloodhound, bassett hound, and dachshund. In general, hounds are strong, alert, and loyal dogs.

Houphouët-Boigny, Félix (1905-93), president of the Ivory Coast since it gained independence (1960) until his death in 1993. In 1946 he helped found the Rassemblement Democratique Africain (RDA), which paved the way for independence of the French West African colonies. He was a French minister of state from 1956 to 1957.
See also: Ivory Coast.

Hour, one twenty-fourth of a day. In one hour the earth rotates through 15°. Therefore an event such as sunrise occurs one hour later for every 15° west on the earth's surface. Each hour contains 60 minutes and 3,600 seconds. In astronomy, degrees of longitude are not used for measuring star positions. Astronomers instead talk of *hours of right ascension*. Each hour of right ascension corresponds to 15° on the celestial sphere. The hour as a unit of timekeeping has been in use only since the invention of clocks.

Hourglass, ancient instrument to measure the passage of time. A quantity of fine, dry sand is contained in a bulb constricted at its center to a narrow neck. The device is turned so that all the sand is in the upper chamber. The time taken for the sand to trickle into the lower chamber depends on the amount of sand and on the diameter of the neck. Small hourglasses are used in the home as egg timers.
See also: Time.

Housatonic River, river rising in the Berkshire Hills of western Massachusetts. An important source of hydroelectric power in the New England area, the Housatonic River is about 148 mi (238 km) long. It flows southward from Pittsfield, Mass., through Connecticut, and enters Long Island Sound just outside of Bridgeport.

House, building in which one or a few families live. It may be built of wood, brick, or stone. It usually consists of several rooms, which are heated by a furnace and wired for electricity. Most modern houses also contain plumbing to supply water and carry away waste. They may vary in design, size, and in their number of rooms. The housing industry actually consists of a number of related professions and involves banks, real estate and insurance companies, architects, carpenters, plumbers, and electricians.

House, Edward Mandell (1858-1938), U.S. diplomat and adviser to President Woodrow Wilson. During World War I he acted for Wilson in Europe and was responsible for arranging the peace conference and acceptance of Wilson's Fourteen Points. In 1919 his conciliatory approach during the Treaty of Versailles negotiations led to a rift with Wilson.
See also: World War I.

House Committee on Un-American Activities *See:* Un-American Activities Committee.

House of Burgesses, the first representative legislative body in colonial America, formed at Jamestown on July 30, 1619. Two burgesses represented each of the 11 boroughs of Virginia. The House of Burgesses, which was neither approved nor disapproved of by England, conformed to English law and managed all affairs of the colony. The House was dissolved in 1774, and many of the delegates were then elected to the First Continental Congress.

House of Commons, lower house of the British parliament. It consists of 635 members elected by simple majority in single-member constituencies. It is the assembly to which the government is ultimately responsible; it legitimizes legislation, votes money, and acts as a body in which complaints can be raised. Proceedings are regulated by the speaker, and a majority of members must assent before a bill becomes law.
See also: Parliament.

House of Lords, upper house of the British parliament. Members consist of the Lords Temporal: hereditary peers, life peers, and ex-officio law lords; and Lords Spiritual: the 2 archbishops and 24 most senior bishops.
See also: Parliament.

House of Representatives, one of 2 chambers of the U.S. Congress, the legislative branch of the federal government. It consists of 435 members apportioned from each state according to population. Representatives serve 2-year terms. To be elected, they must be at least 25 years of age, a U.S. citizen for at least 7 years, and a resident of the state from which he or she is chosen. The House is presided over by the Speaker of the House, who is elected by consensus of the majority party. He or she appoints joint committees and gives representatives permission to debate. Representatives serve

on 4 committees: standing (permanent), select, conference, and joint. The committee system has the power to control proposed bills.
See also: Congress of the United States.

Housing, any building, or group of buildings, that provide shelter for people. In the United States people live in more than 80 million housing units, which may include single-family homes, condominiums, apartments, hotels, motels, motor homes (trailers), and shelters for the homeless. The production of housing has grown in complexity with the enlarging population and with the advent of city planning, transportation needs, commuter demands, community services, and the desire for safe dwellings.

Housing and Urban Development, U.S. Department of (**HUD**), executive department of the federal government established 1965 to coordinate programs relating to housing problems. It took over the Housing and Home Finance Agency (HHFA). The department supervises the federal aid programs.

Housman, A(lfred) E(dward) (1859-1936), English poet and classical scholar. His poetry, at its best intensely felt and always well crafted, is collected in *A Shropshire Lad* (1896), *Last Poems* (1922), and *More Poems* (1936).

Houston (pop. 1,690,200), city and seat of Harris County in southeastern Texas and a major U.S. seaport. It is situated about 25 mi (40 km) southwest of Galveston Bay on the Houston Ship Channel. Founded in 1836 and named for Sam Houston, it remained relatively unimportant until 1901 when oil was discovered in the area. It is now a prosperous industrial, manufacturing, and wholesale distribution center.
See also: Texas.

Houston, Sam(uel) (1793-1863), U.S. frontiersman and politician, leader in the struggle against Mexico to create an independent Texas. He commanded a force of fewer than 800 settlers in a decisive battle at San Jacinto (1836) and went on to become the first president of the Republic of Texas (1836-38). During a second term as president (1841-44) he worked to bring Texas into the Union (1845). Houston served as U.S. senator (1846-59) and was governor of Texas (1859-61). He was deposed after refusing to support the Confederacy.
See also: Texas.

Hovercraft *See:* Air cushion vehicle.

Hovhaness, Alan (1911-), U.S. composer of Armenian descent, noted for his innovative use of Eastern musical materials. Among his best-known works are *Mysterious Mountain* (1955) and *Magnificat* (1957).

Howard, John (1726-90), English public official and noted reformer. Serving as high sheriff of Bedfordshire, Howard had access to Bedford jail, where the conditions in which prisoners were kept appalled him. His subsequent efforts led to an act of Parliament (1774) to improve sanitation in prisons and abolish the systems of discharge fees. He visited prisons throughout Britain and Europe and published *The State of Prisons in England and Wales* (1777), a study that inspired further reform.

Howard, Sidney (1891-1939), U.S. playwright whose work is noted for its realism. He won the 1925 Pulitzer Prize with *They Knew What They Wanted* (1924). Other well-known plays include *Lucky Sam McCarver* (1925) and *The Silver Cord* (1926).

Howard University, private, coeducational institution in Washington, D.C., established in 1867 to educate newly freed slaves. The university includes 17 schools and colleges and 12 research centers and institutes and maintains the most extensive library collection of materials on African American life in the United States. Howard admits all students, but has a special responsibility, dating to its founding, to educate black students.

Howe, Elias (1819-1867), U.S. inventor of the first viable sewing machine (patented 1846). His early machines were sold in Britain, as in the United States there was at first no interest. Later Howe fought a protracted legal battle (1849-54) to protect his patent rights from infringement in the United States.
See also: Sewing machine.

Howe, Gordie (1928-), record-setting U.S. ice hockey player. He played 26 seasons in the National Hockey League (NHL) with the Detroit Red Wings (1946-71) and Hartford Whalers (1979-80) and was named the league's most valuable player 6 times (1952, 53, 57, 58, 60, 63). Howe holds career records for most games played (1,767), most goals scored (801) and was selected as an all-star 22 times. He played for the Houston Aeros (1973-77) of the World Hockey Association (WHA) and was named its most valuable player (1974). Howe was inducted into the Hockey Hall of Fame in 1972.

Howe, Richars and William, name of 2 brothers who were British commanders in the American Revolutionary War. **Richard, Earl Howe** (1726-99) commanded the British fleet in America (1776-8) but is best known for his victory over the French off Ushant (1794) as commander of the Channel Fleet. **William, 5th Viscount Howe** (1729-1814) was a commander in the British army (1775-8). He won 2 major victories in 1777 at Brandywine and Germantown.
See also: Revolutionary War in America.

Howe, Samuel and Julia, name of a U.S. husband and wife who were prominent social reformers. The physician and teacher **Samuel Gridley Howe** (1801-76) ran a school for the blind in Boston (later the Perkins School for the Blind), where he achieved outstanding successes, most notably in teaching the deaf-blind child Laura Bridgman. He was also an active abolitionist and published the antislavery journal *Commonwealth*. **Julia Ward Howe** (1819-1910), an author, is best known for her words to the "Battle Hymn of the Republic" (1862). She was coeditor of *Commonwealth* and a campaigner for women's rights.

Howells, William Dean (1837-1920), U.S. author, critic, and chief editor of the *Atlantic Monthly* (1871-81). He was a pioneer of U.S. social fiction.

His finest and most famous novel is *The Rise of Silas Lapham* (1855). Among those influenced by his work were Stephen Crane and Theodore Dreiser.

Howler, monkey (genus *Alouatta*) named for its low, carrying call. Troops of howler monkeys set up a chorus of howls when they spot another troop near their territory. To produce this call they have a large bony box in the throat, which is a resonating chamber. Howlers are found in forests from southern Mexico to northern Argentina.

Hoxha, Enver (1908-85), Albanian leader. He helped found the Albanian Communist party in 1941 and was the first premier of the new communist government (1944-54). Continuing as party secretary after 1954, he remained a Stalinist and fell out with the USSR during the latter's de-Stalinization phase. Hoxha became allied with Communist China in the early 1960s. Later this friendship cooled when China moved toward closer ties with the West.
See also: Albania.

Hoyle, Edmond (1672-1769), English authority on card and board games, especially whist. He wrote *A Short Treatise on the Game of Whist* (1742), as well as treatises on other games, including chess and backgammon. The expression "according to Hoyle," meaning according to the rules, derives from his name.

Hrdlicka, Ales (1869-1943), Bohemian-born U.S. physical anthropologist. He expounded the generally accepted theory that the Amerinds (Native Americans or Eskimos) are of Asiatic origin. Among his works are *Old Americans* (1925) and *Alaska Diary 1926-1931* (1943).
See also: Anthropology.

Hsi Chiang *See:* Xi Jiang.

Hsun-tzu *See:* Xunzi.

Hua Kuo-Feng (Hua Guofeng; 1920-), Chinese political leader. Achieving swift promotion during the Cultural Revolution, he was made premier following Chou En-Lai's death and then succeeded Mao Tse-Tung as Communist party chairman in 1976. As China turned toward more pragmatic policies, Hua's close identification with Mao proved a handicap, and he fell from power in 1981.
See also: China.

Huang He, or Huang Ho, river in north-central and eastern China. The Huang He rises in Amne Machin Shan, Qinghai Province, and flows through Inner Mongolia, emptying into the Yellow Sea. At 2,903 mi (4,673 km), it is China's second longest river, but it is unused by ships due to its alternately swift and shallow composition. Due to years of flooding, the river is also called "China's Sorrow."

Huang Ho *See:* Huang He.

Hubble, Edwin Powell (1889-1953), U.S. astronomer who first showed (1923) that certain nebulae are in fact galaxies outside the Milky Way. By

examining the red shifts in their spectra, he showed that they are receding at rates proportional to their distances.
See also: Astronomy.

Hubble Space Telescope, orbiting reflecting telescope built to send data from space to astronomers on earth via radio waves. It was released into space on April 25, 1990 from the space shuttle *Discovery*. It orbits about 360 mi (580 km) above the earth's surface. With information sent to earth from the Hubble Telescope, astronomers hope to learn more about the cosmos, particularly "dark matter," areas in space that emit little or no light. Unfortunately, the telescope malfunctioned in space due to manufacturing flaws. In 1993 improvements were made, and as a result there has been a constant outpour of useful data. It is expected that the telescope will be able to function until 2005.
See also: Hubble, Edwin Powell; Telescope.

Huckleberry, shrub (genus *Gaylussacia*) related to the blueberry and cranberry that produces dark berry fruits. There are several species growing in the eastern United States, including the blue huckleberry (*G. frondosa*). The fruits are used to make jams and preserves.

Hudson, Henry (d. 1611), English navigator and explorer who gave his name to the Hudson River, Hudson Strait, and Hudson Bay. After voyages for the English Muscovy Company to find a northeast passage to China (1607 and 1608), Hudson turned to the west where, with Dutch and then once more English backing (1609 and 1610), he made his most successful voyages. He reached the river known as the Hudson in 1609 and the following year entered Hudson Strait and Hudson Bay, establishing an English claim to the area. After the bitter winter, he was set adrift by a mutinous crew and left to die.
See also: Exploration.

Hudson, William Henry (1841-1922), English author and naturalist, born in Argentina of American parents. *Green Mansions* (1904), his best-known novel, is set in the South American pampas. He also wrote studies of bird life and books on the English countryside, such as *A Shepherd's Life* (1910).

Hudson Bay, shallow, epicontinental sea in the northern part of Canada, named for Henry Hudson. Up to about 850 mi (1,370 km) long and 600 mi (970 km) wide, it is linked to the Atlantic Ocean by Foxe Channel. James Bay, the largest inlet, extends southward between Ontario and Quebec provinces. Hudson Bay shipping is restricted because the bay freezes over in winter.
See also: Hudson, Henry.

Hudson River, U.S. river rising in the Adirondacks, flowing generally south for 315 mi (507 km) through New York, and emptying into the Atlantic at New York City. It was discovered in 1524, but only explored fully by Henry Hudson in 1609. It is an important commercial waterway, being navigable by ocean ships as far upstream as Albany. A canal system links it to the Great Lakes. A major program was begun in 1975 to prevent further pollution and make the river safe for fishing and swimming.
See also: Hudson, Henry.

Hudson River School, group of 19th-century U.S. landscape painters. The founders were Thomas Cole, Thomas Doughty, and Asher Durand, who were especially interested in the Hudson River Valley and New England. The school later included artists who took their inspiration from other parts of the United States.

Hudson River tunnels, 7 underwater commuter tunnels extending under the Hudson River and linking New York City's Manhattan Island and New Jersey. The Port Authority Trans-Hudson Corporation (PATH) operates 4 rapid transit tunnels, all over 5,000 ft (1,500 m) long. Passenger trains pass through Amtrak's Hudson River Tunnel, and motor vehicles travel via the Holland or Lincoln tunnels. Before 1900, when the first tunnels were built, people traveling between Manhattan and New Jersey were required to ferry across the Hudson River.

Hudson's Bay Company, mercantile corporation established by the British in 1670 for trading in the Hudson Bay region. The original intention was also to colonize the area and seek a northwest passage, but the company's major activity was fur trading with the Native Americans. It played an important part during the next 2 centuries in opening up Canada. Although its vast lands were sold to the Dominion in 1870, it is still a major fur-trading company and one of Canada's chief business firms, with holdings in metal ores, oil, gas, and timber.

Hue (pop. 260,500), third largest city in Vietnam, located in central Vietnam, near the eastern coast. Founded in the 3rd century, Hue was capital of Vietnam during the rule of the Nguyen dynasty, beginning in the 16th century. The city was occupied by the French in 1883. It became a part of South Vietnam in 1954. Much of the city was destroyed during the Tet offensive in the Vietnam War, but it is under reconstruction.
See also: Vietnam.

Huerta, Victoriano (1854-1916), Mexican general and dictator (1913-14). After first supporting President Porifiro Diaz and then Francisco Madero, he rebelled, proclaiming himself president in February 1913, and had Madero and his vice-president murdered. Revolution at home and U.S. hostility combined to force him into exile.
See also: Mexico.

Hufstedler, Shirley Mount (1925-), U.S. jurist and first secretary of education (1979-81), appointed by President Jimmy Carter. Hufstedler was a county and state judge in California (1961-68) and was appointed a federal judge in the U.S. Court of Appeals in San Francisco (1968-79) by President Lyndon B. Johnson, at which time she became the nation's highest ranking female judge.

Hugh Capet (c.938-996 A.D.), king of France (987-996), founder of the Capetian dynasty. The son of Hugh the Great, the duke of the Franks, he was elected king in the place of the legitimate Carolingian heir, Charles of Lower Lorraine.
See also: Capetians.

Hughes, Charles Evans (1862-1948), U.S. jurist and statesman. He was Republican governor of New York (1906-10) and narrowly missed in his run

for the U.S. presidency in 1916 when Woodrow Wilson was elected. He served as secretary of state (1921-25) and as chief justice (1930-41) during the New Deal.
See also: Dawes Plan.

Hughes, Howard Robard (1905-76), U.S. industrialist, aviator, and film producer. President of the Hughes Aircraft Company and of the Hughes Tool Company, he was a billionaire who in his later years became an eccentric recluse. Years of litigation over his will followed his death.
See also: Aviation.

Hughes, (James) Langston (1902-67), African-American poet and writer. He is best known for adapting the rhythms of African-American music to his poetry. His works include the poetry collections *The Weary Blues* (1926), and *One-Way Ticket* (1949), and the prose *Not Without Laughter* (1930).

Hughes, Ted (1930-), English poet whose work is noted for its brutal, often violent animal imagery. Among his many collections are *The Hawk in the Rain* (1957), *Lupercal* (1960), *Crow* (1970), *Selected Poems: 1957-1967* (1972), *Moortown* (1980), *Wolfwatching* (1989), and *New Selected Poems* (1995). He was married to the poet Sylvia Plath.

Hughes, Thomas (1822-96), English jurist, reformer, and author of *Tom Brown's School Days* (1857) which, through its emphasis on Christian virtues and athletic ability, helped shape the popular image of the English public school.

Hugo, Victor Marle (1802-85), French novelist, playwright, and poet. He is best known for his historical novel *The Hunchback of Notre Dame* (1831). Among his several important collections of verse are *Les Feuilles d'Automne* (1831) and *Les Châtiments* (1853). Hugo went into exile when Napoleon III became emperor (1851), and during this period produced his famous, socially committed novel *Les Misérables* (1862). He spent his last years in France, recognized as one of his country's greatest writers and republicans.

Huguenots, French Protestants, followers of John Calvin's teaching. The Huguenot movement originated in the 16th century as part of the Reformation and found support among all segments of French society, despite constant and severe persecution. Some respite was provided by Henry IV's Edict of Nantes (1598), but this was revoked in 1685, and many thousands of Huguenots were forced into exile in America and elsewhere. Full civil and religious liberty was not granted to Huguenots until 1789.
See also: Calvin, John.

Huizinga, Johan (1872-1945), Dutch historian and writer, noted for his writings about the cultural history of the Middle Ages, which portrayed the spirit of the entire age. Huizinga's works include The Waning of the Middle Ages (1919), In the Shadow of Tomorrow (1935), and Homo Ludens (1938). During World War II, he was imprisoned by the Nazis and died shortly after his release.

Huizong, or Hui Tsung (1082-1135), last Chinese emperor of the northern Sung dynasty (r. 1101-25). He founded the first imperial Chinese academy of painting. An accomplished painter himself, Huizong urged other artists to be "true to color and form," as his realistic paintings of birds and flowers show. He spent his final decade in captivity and died in exile in Manchuria, after being overthrown by the Tartars.
See also: China.

Hukbalahap, or Huks (full name: Hukbong Magpapalayang Bayan, "People's Liberation Army"), Communist guerilla movement that posed a serious threat to the Philippine government from 1945 to 1954. Growing out of the wartime resistance movement against Japanese occupation, the Huks were chiefly disaffected peasants. Eventually the Huks were largely won over by a program of land reforms and settlement schemes. Much of the credit for the rehabilitation of the Huks goes to Ramón Magsaysay, who, mainly on the strength of the achievement, was elected president of the Philippines in 1953.
See also: Philippines.

Hull, Bobby (Robert Marvin Hull; 1939-), Canadian ice hockey player. Thought to be the greatest left wing in the history of the sport, he ranks as the fifth highest goal scorer (610) in National Hockey League (NHL) history and was selected as an all-star 9 times. Hull was nicknamed the "Golden Jet" because of his blond hair, his speed, and the power of his shots, which at times traveled at 110 mph (177 kph). In 1974-75 Hull set a World Hockey Association (WHA) single season record by scoring 77 goals while playing for the Winnipeg Jets (1972-78). He starred for the Chicago Black Hawks (1957-72) and Hartford Whalers (1980) of the NHL. Hull retired in 1981, and in 1983 was inducted into the Hockey Hall of Fame.

Hull, Clark Leonard (1884-1952), U.S. psychologist whose research on the learning process and mathematical approach to theories strengthened the scientific character of the field of psychology. Hull studied human behavior in a scientific manner. He is best known for his mathematical theory of learning, based on the relationship between habit (learning) and drive (motivation).
See also: Psychology.

Hull, Cordell (1871-1955), U.S. statesman, secretary of state (1933-44) under F.D. Roosevelt. He was a congressman (1907-21 and 1923-30) and senator (1931-33). As secretary of state he developed the "Good Neighbor" policy in relations with South American states and helped maintain relations with the USSR in World War II. After the war he was a major force behind U.S. acceptance of the UN, for which he was awarded the 1945 Nobel Peace Prize.

Hull, Isaac (1773-1843), U.S. naval officer. He was commander, during the War of 1812, of the frigate *Constitution* ("Old Ironsides"), which defeated the British frigate *Guerrière*. He later commanded the Pacific Squadron (1824-27) and the Mediterranean Squadron (1838-41).
See also: War of 1812.

Hull, William (1753-1825), army officer in the American Revolutionary War and the War of 1812. On Aug. 16, 1812, Hull surrendered Detroit, without resistance, to the British. He was prosecuted for treason by Martin Van Buren. Hull was court-martialed and condemned to death, but was reprieved by President James Madison.
See also: Revolutionary War in America; War of 1812.

Hull House, one of the first U.S. social settlement houses. Founded in Chicago in 1889 by Jane Addams and Ellen Gates Starr, it provided community services and recreational facilities to a poor community.
See also: Addams, Jane.

Human being (*Homo sapiens*), extremely adaptable mammal with highly-developed brain and nervous system, and ability to speak. Related to monkeys and apes, human beings differ from them physically by having the ability to stand and walk upright and by having a larger and more fully developed brain. Humans also use language, a trait that significantly distinguishes them from every other animal. Most scientists believe that the first recognizably human-like beings appeared in what is now Africa some 2 million years ago. This prehistoric human, referred to as *Homo habilis*, later developed into *Homo erectus*, who lived throughout Africa, Asia, and Europe and probably learned how to make and use fire. *Homo erectus* also hunted and used tools. The physical form humans have today began to appear about 40,000 years ago. Generally, humans seem to have begun as hunters and gatherers of food and to have gradually developed agricultural and industrial societies.

Human body, complex organism consisting of some 50 trillion cells, organized into tissues, organs, and structures. The body can best be studied as a complex of systems.
(1) The skeletal system, the body's framework, consists of more than 200 bones tied together with strong yet elastic ligaments. It accounts for about 18% of the body's weight.
(2) The muscular system consists of more than 650 distinct muscles that, by pulling on bones and bending joints, cause the body to move. Also part of this system are the visceral muscles, which cause movement in internal organs. The muscular system accounts for about 40% of body weight.
(3) The skin covers the whole body, allowing the maintenance of a constant internal environment. The sweat glands play an important part in excretion. Nerve endings in the skin provide the sense of touch and warn the body of external danger. The skin serves as a barrier against destructive organisms and foreign bodies.
(4) The circulatory system, consisting of the heart and thousands of miles of blood vessels and lymphatics, carries blood to all parts of the body, supplying every cell with oxygen and food and carrying from it carbon dioxide, water, and other wastes. The blood also carries hormones (the body's chemical messengers), which attack invading microorganisms, and help repair wounds by clotting.
(5) The respiratory system-including the lungs and the respiratory passages-allows the interchange of oxygen and carbon dioxide with the blood.
(6) The digestive system takes in food and breaks it down into a usable form that can be absorbed into the bloodstream. Basically, it consists of a tube

extending from mouth to anus, with various organs, such as the stomach and accessory glands (including liver and pancreas) attached.
(7) The main organs of the urinary system are the kidneys, which remove waste from the blood, and the bladder, which stores and then expels that waste in the form of urine. (8) The reproductive system ensures the continuation of the species and the passing along of traits that may be necessary for survival.
(9) The nervous system consists of the central nervous system (CNS), comprising the brain and spinal cord, and the peripheral nervous system, the nerves that carry messages to and from the CNS.
(10) The endocrine system, consisting of the hormone-producing glands, responds to nervous commands or to other hormones and along with the nervous system, coordinates the activities of other organs and adjusts their functioning in relation to the external and internal environment.
(11) The body possesses a number of specialized senses, including sight, hearing, balance, and the visceral sensations such as hunger.

Human Development Services, Office of, section of the U.S. Department of Health and Human Services, established in 1973 to govern various government social and rehabilitation programs. The Office of Human Development Services supports and funds groups with special needs, such as Native Americans, children, the elderly, the developmentally disabled, and low-income families. The agency has 4 main divisions: the Administration on Aging, the Administration for Native Americans, the Administration on Developmental Disabilities, and the Administration for Children, Youth and Families.

Humane society, organization whose purpose is to protect children and animals from mistreatment. Local humane societies in the United States fused in 1877 to become the American Humane Association.

Humanism, originally, Renaissance revival of the study of classical (Latin, Greek, and Hebrew) literature following the scholasticism of the Middle Ages, more broadly, philosophy centered on humankind and human values, exalting human free will and superiority to the rest of nature. Renaissance thinkers such as Petrarch began a trend toward humanism that embraced such diverse figures as Boccaccio, Machiavelli, Thomas More, and Erasmus and that led to much subsequent secular thought and literature, as well as to the Reformation. Modern humanism tends to be nontheistic, emphasizing the need for people to work out their own solutions to life's problems, but has a strong ethic similar to that of Christianity. Both Roman Catholic and Protestant theologians have sought to show that Christian beliefs embody true humanism.
See also: Renaissance.

Human relations, study of group behavior and how the individual, as an inherently social being with personal needs, may achieve desired goals without losing, or causing others in the general population to lose, the basic rights of dignity, respect, and self-determination. Experts in the field of human relations must understand conflict, human needs, human nature, and how individuals and groups respond to one another.

Human Rights, Declaration of, United Nations document outlining the civil, economic, political, and social rights and freedoms for all the people

of the world. Adopted by the General Assembly on Dec. 10, 1948, it declares all people to be free and to have equal rights and dignity.
See also: United Nations.

Humber, River, river in Humberside county, England, flowing eastward into the North Sea. The river's length is about 40 mi (64 km); its width is 1-7 mi (1.6-11 km). Two important tributaries are the Ouse and Trent rivers. The cities of Hull and Grimsby lie on the Humber's banks. The Humber Bridge has the longest main span (4,626 ft/1,410 m) of any suspension bridge in the world.

Humboldt, Friedrich Heinrich Alexander, Baron von (1769-1859), German naturalist. With the botanist Aimé Jacques Alexandre Bonpland he traveled for 5 years through much of South America (1799-1804), collecting plant, animal, and rock specimens and making geomagnetic and meteorologic observations. Humboldt published their data in 30 volumes over the next 23 years. In his most important work, *Kosmos* (1845-62), he sought to show a fundamental unity of all natural phenomena.

Humboldt Current *See:* Peru Current.

Hume, David (1711-76), Scottish Enlightenment philosopher, economist, and historian. His *Treatise of Human Nature* (1739-40) is one of the key works in the tradition of British empiricism, but it was his shorter *Enquiry Concerning Human Understanding* (1748) that prompted Immanuel Kant to his most radical labors. His influential *Dialogues Concerning Natural Religion* were published posthumously in 1779, long after their composition. In epistemology Hume argued that people had no logical reason to associate distinct impressions as cause and effect; if they did so, it was only on the basis of custom or psychological habit. His skepticism in this respect has always been controversial. In his own day, Hume's most popular work was his *History of England* (1754-63).
See also: Philosophy.

Humidity, amount of water vapor in the air. *Absolute humidity* measures mass of water per unit volume of air. Saturation of the air, or *dew point*, occurs when the water vapor pressure reaches the vapor pressure of liquid water at the temperature concerned; this rises rapidly with temperature. *Relative humidity*, expressed as a percentage, is the amount of water in the air at any given time compared with the amount the air could hold at that temperature before becoming saturated. The physiologically tolerable humidity level falls rapidly as temperature rises, since humidity inhibits body cooling by impeding the evaporation of sweat.

Hummingbird, tiny nectar-feeding bird of the family Trochilidae. It takes its name from the noise of its rapid wingbeats—up to 70 a second in smaller species—as it hovers at flowers to feed. Hummingbirds are colorful, with a body size in most species 2 in (5 cm) or less. With their small size and fierce activity, hummingbirds must feed about once every 10-15 min. Highly adapted to flight, hummingbirds have short legs and little feet, used only for perching. They can hover in one place and are the only birds capable of flying backward.

Hummingbird moth *See:* Hawk moth.

Humor, according to the ancients, any of the 4 bodily elements: phlegm, blood, choler, and black bile, corresponding to the 4 natural elements: earth, air, fire, and water. In the well-adjusted person, the 4 humors are in balance. If one preponderates, the person is of unequal temper: If phlegm preponderates then the person is phlegmatic; if blood, the person is sanguine; if choler, the person is choleric; if black bile, the person is melancholic. The person not in "good humor" behaves eccentrically, and is thus an object of ridicule. The word "humor" thus came to mean mocking laughter.

Humperdinck, Engelbert (1854-1921), German composer. He was much influenced by Richard Wagner, whom he assisted at the Bayreuth Festival. He wrote several operas; only *Hansel and Gretel* (1893) is widely performed today, although *The Royal Children* (1910) is revived from time to time.

Humphrey, Doris (1895-1958), U.S. modern dancer and choreographer. Influenced by Ruth St. Denis and Ted Shawn, she set up a school and company with Charles Weidman (1928) to develop her own expressive style, based upon her innovative theories of movement. Humphrey founded (with Martha Graham) the U.S. modern-dance form.

Humphrey, Hubert Horatio (1911-78), U.S. political leader, vice president from 1965 to 1969. A Democrat, he was mayor of Minneapolis, then was elected senator from Minnesota in 1948. Identified with many liberal causes, as vice president under Lyndon Johnson he nonetheless supported U.S. Vietnam policy. Unsuccessful as the Democratic candidate for president (1968), he returned to the Senate (1970).

Humus, organic substance formed in soil when microorganisms, bacteria, and fungi decompose plant and animal material. Humus is soft, spongy, and dark brown. It affects the soil's structure, water retention, nutritional value to plants, and erosion resistance.

Hun, nomadic, probably Mongolian, race that invaded southeastern Europe during the 4th and 5th centuries. They crossed the Volga River in c.372 A.D. and attacked the Germanic Goth tribes. By 432 they had invaded the Eastern Empire. Under their great leader Attila, they threatened the Roman Empire, unsuccessfully invading Gaul in 451. In 452 their Italian invasion was halted at Lake Garda. After Attila's death in 453, the Hun empire gradually disintegrated.
See also: Attila.

Hunchback, or kyphosis, deformity of the spine causing bent posture with or without twisting (scoliosis) and abnormal bony prominences. Tuberculosis of the spine may cause sharp angulation, while congenital diseases, ankylosing spondylitis, vertebral collapse, and spinal tumors cause smooth kyphosis.

Hundred Days, in French history, period between Napoleon's return to Paris from exile on Elba and the second Bourbon restoration (Mar. 20-June 28, 1815). During this time Napoleon attempted to reinstate himself as ruler

of France on a more liberal basis. He was defeated at Waterloo, and Louis XVIII was restored to the French Throne.
See also: Napoleon II.

Hundred Years War, sporadic series of wars fought mainly between England and France from 1337 to 1453. They originated in disputes over English possessions in France, and the claims of Edward III of England to the throne of France. In 1337 he invaded Gascony and won the battles of Sluis (1340), Crécy (1346), and Poitiers (1356), and seized Calais, gaining important concessions at the Treaty of Brétigny (1360). The French under Charles V retained much of their lost territory (1369-75) and attacked the English coast. Henry V of England destroyed the resulting uneasy truce when he invaded France in 1415, in pursuit of a dream of establishing himself as monarch of Britain and France; he captured Harfleur and defeated a superior French force at Agincourt. At the Treaty of Troyes (1420) Henry V was recognized as heir to the French throne, and from 1422 his infant son, Henry VI, ruled the dual monarchy, with John, Duke of Bedford, as French regent. His able rule won French support, and only the resurgence led by Joan of Arc in 1429 halted English gains. Although the dauphin (French heir to the throne, son of Charles VI) was crowned Charles VII at Reims in 1429, the English position was not assailed until 1435, when Philip the Good of Burgundy recognized Charles VII as king of France. After 1444 the English were driven back until they held only Calais (until 1448) and the Channel Islands.

Hungarian, or Magyar, one of the Ungro-Finnic languages in the Uralic group. It is spoken mainly in Hungary, but also by groups in Czechoslovakia, Romania, and Yugoslavia. Its 6 dialects do not differ widely. Standard Hungarian is the speech of the Budapest area.

Hungarian pointer *See:* Vizsla.

Hungary, country in east-central Europe, bordered by Slovakia, Ukraine, Romania, Slovenia, Croatia, the Federal Republic of Yugoslavia, and Austria. The capital is Budapest, where nearly 20% of the population lives.
Land. Hungary is basically a fertile plain, drained by the Danube River, which forms part of the border with Slovakia and then turns south through the country. The Dráva, which forms part of Hungary's border with Croatia, is the only other important river. Most of the country has black, very fertile soil. Lake Balaton, the largest lake in Europe (48 mi/77 km long), begins southwest of Budapest and extends southwest toward the Croatian border. The country is rich in game, including deer, fox, wild boar, and hare.
People. The official language is Hungarian. About two-thirds of the population is Roman Catholic, and one-third Calvinist.
Economy. Hungary was traditionally agricultural, but there has been significant industrialization since World War II. There are important electrical, chemical, food-processing and textile plants. Leading crops include corn, wheat, oats, rye, potatoes, sunflowers, and sugar beets. Apricots, grapes, paprika, and tobacco are also grown, and hogs, sheep, and cattle are raised.
History. The area that is now Hungary was conquered by the Magyars c.896 and Christianized in the 900s. A feudal system flourished until the Ottoman Turkish invasion defeated King Lewis II at Mohács (1526). Most of the country was divided between the Ottoman Empire and Austria, the west and

Hungary

Capital:	Budapest
Area:	35,920 sq mi (93,033 sq km)
Population:	10,208,000
Language:	Hungarian, Magyar
Government:	Republic
Independent:	1918
Head of gov.:	Prime minister
Per capita:	U.S. $4,120
Mon. unit:	1 Forint = 100 fillér

north coming under Habsburg rule in 1687. A bid for independence led by Lajos Kossuth (1848) failed but led to the establishment of the Dual Monarchy (1867): the Austrian Emperor Francis Joseph I was crowned King of Hungary, and the Austro-Hungarian empire was born. That empire was destroyed in World War I, and an independent Hungarian state was proclaimed in 1918. A Communist revolution in 1919 was put down by Romanian intervention, and in 1920 Admiral Nicholas Horthy de Nagybanya, a right-wing dictator, came to power. Hungary was an ally of Nazi Germany during World War II. Occupied by the USSR (1945), it became a "people's republic" in 1949. An uprising against the repressive regime was crushed by Soviet intervention (1956), and a puppet government under János Kádar was set up. Kádar introduced cultural and economic reforms in the 1960s that temporarily improved Hungarians' living standards, but his refusal to introduce further reforms during the economic decline of the 1970s led to his replacement in 1988.The Communist regime collapsed in 1989 during the general upheaval that swept Eastern Europe. In 1997 Hungary was invited to join NATO. It also wanted entry into the European Union.

Hunger, appetite (impulse, drive) for food, often referring also to the mass of uneasy sensations from the gut and particularly from hunger contractions in the stomach, which accompany the appetite; also used to describe sexual appetite.

Hunt, H(aroldson) L(afayette) (1889-1974), U.S. oil magnate. In the 1920s he invested in Arkansas oil fields. The Hunt Oil Company, founded in 1936, became one of the largest independent U.S. oil and natural gas corporations.

Hunt, (James Henry) Leigh (1784-1859), English critic, journalist, and poet. He was editor of the liberal *Examiner* (1808-22) and other journals. Hunt was a friend of the leading literary figures of his day, notably Keats and Shelley, whose poetic careers he furthered; Lamb; Hazlitt; Byron; and eventually Carlyle. His most highly regarded works are *Lord Byron and Some of His Contemporaries* (1828), *Autobiography* (1850), and the short lyric poems "Abou Ben Adhem" (1834) and "Jenny Kissed Me" (1844).

Hunt, Richard Morris (1828-95), U.S. architect. He trained and worked in Europe (1843-54), and his style in the United States was historically eclectic. He built the Statue of Liberty base and the 1893 Chicago Exposition administrative building.
See also: Architecture.

Hunt, William Holman (1827-1910), English painter who helped found the Pre-Raphaelite movement. His work is noted for its brilliant color and accurate details. *The Light of the World* (1853) is his best-known painting.

Hunting, pursuit and killing of wild animals for subsistence, profit, or sport. In Western Europe hunting means the pursuit and capture of a wild animal with the aid of hounds. In the United States and elsewhere the term means the field sport of shooting large and small game.
Hunting was an important source of food, clothing, and sometimes shelter for primitive people. Cave paintings in France and Spain indicate that these people hunted wild horses, prehistoric cattle, reindeer, and mammoths, often with the bow and arrow. Hunting as a sport was practiced by the earliest known civilizations, such as those in Babylonia and Egypt. Hunts full of pageantry and splendor were popular with kings and princes, who often gained status according to the number of animals they had killed.
With the exception of the Native Americans of the Southwest, the Southeast, and adjoining regions, the North American tribes lived almost exclusively by hunting. With the arrival of European colonists, hunting became important for the fur trade. As white settlers occupied increasing amounts of land, however, the wild game gradually disappeared; thus, in most areas of the present-day United States, game animals, especially the larger ones, exist in relatively small numbers and sometimes are even brought into a region to provide quarry for hunters. Game is also limited in variety, with rabbits and deer probably the most plentiful overall.
Western and northern Canada and Alaska are exceptions to this general scarcity; wildlife of many sorts still abounds there. Regulatory measures and the vigilant efforts of conservationists help to save game animals threatened with extinction through indiscriminate hunting. Certain African countries, mostly in East and South Africa, have also made ambitious efforts to save their often unique wildlife by establishing and patrolling enormous animal sanctuaries where the camera is the only "weapon" permitted.

Huntington (pop. 312,529), largest city in West Virginia, located on the Ohio River. It was founded in 1871 as the western terminus for the Chesapeake and Ohio Railroad and was named for Collis P. Huntington, the president of that railroad. Numerous and varied industries produce such important commercial goods as nickel and nickel alloys, furniture, railroad equipment, shoes, and glass. Huntington suffered many serious floods before the construction of an 11-mi long (18-km) flood wall that now protects the city. Marshall University is located there.
See also: West Virginia.

Huntington, Collis Potter (1821-1900), U.S. railroad tycoon. He was the chief promoter of the West's first railroad company, the Central Pacific

(1861), and he established the Southern Pacific (1884). He left most of his fortune to his nephew, Henry E. Huntington.
See also: Railroad.

Huntington, Henry Edwards (1850-1927), U.S. financier; nephew and heir of Collis P. Huntington. He formed and endowed a world-class art collection and research library at San Marino, Calif., that specializes in Anglo-American legal documents, Western Americana, and English 18th-century art and literature.

Huntington, Samuel (1731-96), Connecticut political figure who signed the Declaration of Independence. He served as a governor's council member (1755-83) and Continental Congress representative (1776-81) before becoming a Connecticut delegate to the Confederation Congress (1781-84). After being appointed chief justice of the Connecticut Supreme Court (1784), he served as lieutenant governor (1785) and governor (1786-96).

Huntington's disease (Huntington's chorea), disease marked by progressive degeneration of the central nervous system. An inherited, ultimately fatal disease that breaks out in adulthood, its symptoms are involuntary, jerky body movements and mental disturbances. It was first identified in 1871 by the American neurologist Dr. George Huntington.

Huntsman's-cup *See:* Pitcher plant.

Huntsville (pop. 238,912), city in northeastern Alabama. Founded in 1805, Huntsville was the site of the state constitutional convention in 1819, which resulted in statehood for Alabama. In the 1950s, with the establishment of the U.S. Redstone Arsenal as a research base, the city became an important center for the aerospace industry and is now known as "Rocket City, USA."
See also: Alabama.

Hunza, district in northern Kashmir controlled by Pakistan. The largest city is Karimabad. Woolen cloth and handicrafts are leading industries. Burushaski is the spoken language, but there is no written language. Most of the people are Muslims.
See also: Pakistan.

Hurdling, track and field sport in which runners jump over obstacles called hurdles, which stand at specific heights and are set equal distances apart on the track. Runners adjust their stride and bring one leg over the hurdle at a time to clear hurdles without breaking stride. Hurdles may be knocked down, but disqualification occurs if done so by runner's hand.

Huron, league of 4 Native North American tribes, approximately 20,000 strong, who lived in South Ontario in the 1600s. Members of the Iroquoian language group, they were an agrarian society who were attacked and nearly destroyed by the Iroquois (1650). Small numbers of Hurons remain in Quebec and in Oklahoma.

Hurricane, tropical cyclone of great intensity. High-speed winds spiral in toward a low-pressure core of warm, calm air (the eye). Winds of over 185 mph (298 kmph) have been measured. The direction of spiral is clockwise in the southern hemisphere and counterclockwise in the northern hemisphere. Hurricanes form over water when there is an existing convergence of air near sea level. The air ascends, losing moisture as precipitation as it does so. If this happens rapidly enough, the upper air is warmed by the water's latent heat of vaporization. This reduces the surface pressure and thus accelerates air convergence. Since they require large quantities of moist warm air, hurricanes rarely penetrate far inland. Hurricanes of the North Pacific are often called typhoons.

Hurston, Zora Neale (1901-60), U.S. author known for her literary interpretations of African-American folklore of the southern United States and the Caribbean. Her novels were *Jonah's Gourd Vine* (1934) and *Their Eyes Were Watching God* (1937). *Mules and Men* (1935) and *Tell My Horse* (1938) are collections of retold folktales.

Hus, Jan (1370-1415), Bohemian religious reformer and Czech national hero. Influenced by John Wycliffe, Hus attacked Church and papal abuses. He defended his ideas at the Council of Constance in 1414, where he was arrested, tried, and burned at the stake as a heretic. His followers, the Hussites, demanded many reforms in the Roman Catholic Church, with which they were involved in a series of wars in Bohemia in the 15th century.
See also: Bohemia.

Husák, Gustav (1913-91), Czechoslovakian Communist leader. Taking a pro-Moscow line after 1968, he replaced Secretary Dubek as leader of the Communist Party in 1969 He served as president of Czechoslovakia from 1975 to 1987.
See also: Czechoslovakia.

Husein Ibn Ali (1854-1931), sharif of Mecca (1908-16) and king of Hejaz (1916-24). In 1916 he led the World War I Arab revolt against the Turks and proclaimed himself king of all Arabia. Assisted by T. E. Lawrence, he drove the Turks from Syria, northern Arabia, and Transjordan. In 1924 Ibn Saud forced him to abdicate, and he died in exile.

Husky *See:* Siberian husky.

Hussar, European soldier who was a member of light cavalry units used for scouting. The Hussar uniform included a high, cloth cap (busby), a loose cape (dolman), and a heavily braided jacket. Napoleon perfected the efficiency of these soldiers, who became known for their fighting abilities. Hussars were no longer used after World War I.

Hussein I (1935-), king of Jordan since 1953. His policies are generally pro-Western, and he is a spokesperson for moderation in the conflict between the Arab nations and Israel. Jordan's loss of the West Bank in the 1967 Arab-Israeli war led to civil war in 1970, when King Hussein gained firmer control over the country. He declined to endorse the Camp David agreements between Israel and Egypt. His fourth wife, Elizabeth Halaby, an American, whom he married in 1978, became Queen Noor.
See also: Jordan.

Hussein, Saddam (1937-), Arab nationalist leader, president and dictator of Iraq from 1979. As chair of the Revolutionary Command Council of the Arab Ba'ath Socialist Party, a pan-Arab organization that controls all facets of Iraqi society, he established a regime marked by widespread repression, imprisonment, and fear. At the same time, the government made significant progress in industrialization. The Ba'ath took power in Iraq in 1963. Hussein, though formally second in command, was the de facto ruler as early as 1969. In 1980 he launched an attack on Iran that led to the 8-year-long Iran-Iraq war. On Aug. 2, 1990 the Iraq army invaded Kuwait. The pretext for the invasions was Iraq's territorial claim to Kuwait. Shortly after the invasion, the United States and a combined allied military force established a military presence in Saudi Arabia. After 6 months of United Nations' diplomatic efforts at peace failed, the allied forces declared war on Iraq. On Jan. 16, 1991 hostilities commenced and a ceasefire was announced on Feb. 21, 1991. Following the Gulf War, a trade boycot was inflicted upon Iraq. As a result, resistance in Iraq seems to grow. In 1995 two of Husseins sons in law fled to Jordan, they returned in 1996 and were killed within a few days. The UN closely watches the Iraqi weapons industry.
See also: Iraq; Persian Gulf War.

Husserl, Edmund (1859-1938), Czech-born German philosopher who founded phenomenology. Professor at Göttingen and Freiburg universities, he was concerned with what constitutes acts of consciousness and how they relate to experience. He held that consciousness is "intentional" in that it is always "conscious of" an object. Husserl's investigations influenced Heidegger, Sartre, and other thinkers of 20th-century existentialism.
See also: Phenomenology.

Huston, name of 3 film personalities. **Walter Huston** (1884-1950), Canadian-born U.S. actor, is best known for his roles in the play *Dodsworth* (1936), the musical comedy *Knickerbocker Holiday* (1938), and the film *The Treasure of Sierra Madre* (1947) directed by his son **John Huston** (1906-87), Hollywood writer, then director, whose other films include *The Maltese Falcon* (1941), *The Asphalt Jungle* (1950), *The African Queen* (1951), *Moby Dick* (1956), and *The Dead* (1987). John Huston's daughter **Anjelica Huston** (1951-) won the Academy Award for best supporting actress in *Prizzi's Honor* (1985).

Hutchins, Robert Maynard (1899-1977), U.S. educator, president (1929-45) and chancellor (1945-51) of the University of Chicago. He advocated the integration and synthesis of academic disciplines. In 1959 he founded the Center for the Study of Democratic Institutions as an ideal "Community of Scholars." His books include *The Higher Learning in America* (1936) and *University of Utopia* (1953).

Hutchinson, Anne Marbury (1591-1643), English Puritan religious leader, one of the founders of Rhode Island. She emigrated to Massachusetts in 1634, where she preached that faith alone could achieve salvation. She opposed obedience to the strict laws of the Puritan community. In 1638 she and her followers were banished, and they established a settlement on Aquidneck Island (now Rhode Island). She later moved to New York, where she was killed by Native Americans.
See also: Puritans.

Hutchinson, Thomas (1711-80), American colonial governor of Massachusetts, 1770-74. A political enemy of Samuel Adams, he opposed American independence, and enforced the Stamp Act (1765) although considering the act unwise. In 1773 he insisted that duty be paid on tea cargoes in Boston, which led to the Boston Tea Party. In 1774 he went to England, where he served George III as an adviser.

Hutterites, or Hutterlan Brethren, Protestant sect found primarily in South Dakota, and Canada. Like the Mennonites, they believe in common ownership of goods and are pacifists. The sect originated in 1533 as a branch of the Anabaptists and takes its name from Jacob Hutter, martyred in 1536.
See also: Anabaptism.

Hutton, James (1726-97), Scottish geologist who proposed, in *Theory of the Earth* (1795), that the earth's natural features result from continual processes, occurring now at the same rate as they have in the past. These views were little regarded until Charles Lyell's work some decades later.

Huxley, British family of writers and scientists. **Thomas Henry Huxley** (1825-95), biologist, is best known for his support of Darwin's theory of evolution, without which acceptance of the theory might have been long delayed. Most of his own contributions to paleontology and zoology (especially taxonomy), botany, geology, and anthropology were related to this. He also coined the word "agnostic." His son **Leonard Huxley** (1860-1933), writer, wrote *The Life and Letters of Thomas Henry Huxley* (1900). Of his children, 3 earned fame. **Sir Julian Sorell Huxley** (1887-1975) is best known as a biologist and ecologist. His early interests were in development and growth, genetics, and embryology. Later he made important studies of bird behavior, studied evolution, and wrote many popular scientific books. **Aldous Leonard Huxley** (1894-1963) was one of the 20th century's foremost novelists. Important works include *Crome Yellow* (1921), *Antic Hay* (1923), and *Point Counter Point* (1928), characterized by their wit and attitude toward lofty pretensions, and the famous *Brave New World* (1932) and *Eyeless in Gaza* (1936). After experimenting with hallucinogenic drugs he became interested in mysticism. Later works include *The Devils of London* (1952), *the Doors of Perception* (1954), and *Island* (1962). **Andrew Field Huxley** (1917-) shared the 1963 Nobel Prize for physiology or medicine with A.L. Hodgkin and Sir J. Eccles for his work with Hodgkin on the chemical basis of nerve impulse transmission.

Hu Yaobang (1915-89), general secretary of the Chinese Communist Party (1981-87). A friend and associate of Deng Xioping, he was removed as chairman of the party in January 1987 in the face of student demonstrations for freedom of expression.
See also: China.

Huygens, Christiaan (1629-95), Dutch scientist. He formulated a wave theory of light, first applied the pendulum to the regulation of clocks, and discovered the surface markings of Mars and the rings of Saturn. In his optical studies he stated Huygens's Principle, that all points on a wave front may at any instant be considered sources of secondary waves that, taken together, represent the wave front at any later instant. Huygens' theory of light states

that light is a disturbance traveling through some medium, such as the ether. Thus light is due to wave motion in ether.
See also: Optics; Physics.

Hyacinth, plant (genus *Hyacinthus*, especially *H. orientalis*) of the lily family grown from a bulb that produces a head of beautifully colored and perfumed flowers. It originated in the Mediterranean region. Water hyacinths (*Eichhornia crassipes*) are unrelated plants. They float on water and have been introduced to many places where they become a nuisance by blocking waterways.

Hyaline membrane disease, or respiratory distress syndrome, lung condition that is a common cause of death in premature babies. The disease is characterized by underdeveloped lungs that lack pulmonary surfactant, a substance that prevents the collapse of air sacs after breathing has begun. Immature lungs produce a glassy membrane that covers open bronchioles. Breathing becomes strained and death frequently occcurs from lack of oxygen.

Hybrid, crossbred animal or plant; an offspring of 2 different breeds, genera, or varieties. A hybrid computer system is a system that uses both analog and digital equipment. Hybrids in data communications are circuits fabricated by interconnecting smaller circuits of different technologies mounted on a single substrate.

Hyderabad (pop. 751,500), third largest city in Pakistan, located on the Indus River in Sind province. It is an important transportation and trade center, with various chemical, engineering, and milling industries.
See also: Pakistan.

Hyderabad (pop. 3,145,900), capital of the Indian state of Andhra Pradesh and historically of the region also called Hyderabad. The metropolitan area is a trade and manufacturing center producing textiles, guns, and glass products.
See also: India.

Hyderabad, region on the Deccan plateau that was once a state of south central India. Historically, Hyderabad was the site of a Hindu civilization taken over by the Muslim Mogul Empire in the 17th century. It became part of India in 1948, after a plebescite rejected independence. In 1950 it was divided among the states of Andhra Pradesh, Maharashtra, and Karnataka. Crops include cotton, rice, and grain. Mineral deposits are also present in the area.
See also: India.

Hydra, in Greek mythology, serpent with many heads, also known as Lernaean Hydra or Hydra of Lerna. Whenever a head was cut off, 2 new ones replaced it. Hercules killed the Hydra, burning the necks after decapitating it.
See also: Mythology.

Hydra, genus of freshwater animal of the phylum Coelenterata, perhaps the most familiar of the class Hydrozoa. The hydra is found in ponds, lakes, and streams throughout the world. The body is an elongated 2-in (2.5-cm) column with a mouth at one end surrounded by tentacles. Normally attached by the other end to the substrate, hydras can move by "looping" across a plane surface or by free-swimming. Hydras reproduce by asexual budding when food is abundant. When food is scarce, ovaries and testes develop on the column, and sexual reproduction gives rise to resistant, dormant embryos.

Hydrangea, genus of ornamental shrub of the saxifrage family originally from China and Japan, widely grown in pots and gardens. Its heads of small, flat-petaled flowers range from pale blue to pink, changing color in response to soil acidity.

Hydrate, any of various chemical compounds composed of water and some other substance. Common hydrates include blue vitriol ($CuSO_45H_2O$) and Glauber's salt ($Na_2CO_310H_2O$). As water evaporates, most hydrates change structure. Water that is retained by the hydrate is known as water of crystallization or hydration. Hydrates that have lost all water are called anhydrous.

Hydraulic brake *See:* Brake.

Hydraulic engine, or fluidic engine, machine that uses the motion or pressure of fluids (like oil, silicone, gas, and sometimes water) to produce power. These engines are used in jacks, hoists, hydraulic elevators, and some turbine generators.
See also: Hydraulics.

Hydraulics, branch of science concerned with the application of the properties of liquids (particularly water), at rest and in motion, to engineering problems. Since any machine or structure that uses, controls, or conserves a liquid makes use of the principles of hydraulics, the scope of this subject is very wide. It includes methods of water supply for consumption, irrigation, or navigation and the design of associated dams, canals, and pipes; hydroelectricity, the conversion of water power to electric energy using hydraulic turbines; the design and construction of ditches, culverts, and hydraulic jumps (a means of slowing down the flow of a stream by suddenly increasing its depth) for controlling and discharging flood water; and the treatment and disposal of industrial and human waste. Hydraulics applies the principles of hydrostatics and is hence a branch of fluid mechanics.

Hydrazine, chemical compound (H_2NNH_2), used in jet and rocket fuels, explosives, and corrosion inhibitors. Also known as hydronitrogen, it is a colorless liquid that absorbs water and alcohol. It has an acrid smell, burns in air, and is corrosive.

Hydriodic acid *See:* Hydrogen iodide.

Hydrobromic acid *See:* Hydrogen bromide.

Hydrocarbon, any organic compound of hydrogen and carbon. They are divided into two classes: *aliphatics*, in which the carbon atoms are arranged in chains, and *aromatics*, in which they are arranged in rings. The aliphatics are divided into various sub-groups according to the way the carbon atoms are bonded together. Hydrocarbons occur in petroleum and natural gas. Commercial products include gasoline, kerosene, airplane fuel, lubricating oils, and paraffin.

Hydrochloric acid, chemical compound (HCL) with many industrial uses. A colorless, extremely corrosive liquid that fumes when exposed to air, it is used in metallurgy and food processing. It is produced naturally in the human stomach as a digestive aid, but stomach ulcers can form if it is present in excess.

Hydroelectric power *See:* Electric power; Water power.

Hydrofluoric acid, inorganic chemical compound (HF), also called hydrogen fluoride, formed when hydrofluoric gas is dissolved in water. It is used industrially in manufacturing aluminum, in etching glass, and as a catalyst for chemical reactions.

Hydrofoil, structure that, when moved rapidly through water, generates lift in exactly the same way and for the same reasons as does the airfoil. It is usually mounted beneath a vessel (also called a hydrofoil). Much of a conventional boat's power is spent in overcoming the drag (resistance) of the water; as a hydrofoil vessel builds up speed, it lifts out of the water until only a small portion of it (struts, hydrofoils, and propeller) is in contact with the water. Thus drag is reduced to a minimum. Hydrofoils can exceed 75 mph (121 kmph) as compared with conventional craft, whose maximum speeds rarely approach 50 mph (80 kmph).

Hydrogen, chemical element, symbol H; for physical constants see Periodic Table. Hydrogen was prepared for many years before it was recognized as a distinct substance by Henry Cavendish in 1766. It is the most abundant element in the universe, making up about three quarters of the mass of the universe. On earth hydrogen occurs chiefly in combination with oxygen in water. Hydrogen is prepared commercially by the action of steam on heated carbon or iron. Hydrogen is a diatomic, colorless, explosively reactive gas, the lightest of all gases. Production of hydrogen in the United States alone amounts to hundreds of millions of cubic feet per day. Hydrogen gas is a mixture of 2 kinds of molecules, known as ortho- and para-hydrogen, which differ from one another by the spins of their electrons and nuclei. Hydrogen is used in nitrogen fixation, as rocket fuel, in reducing metallic ores, for welding, as heavy water in nuclear reactors, and as a neutron moderator. Liquid hydrogen is used in cryogenics.

Hydrogenation, chemical process that adds hydrogen to some other substance. The resulting reaction is used to change liquid oils into solid fats, powdered coal into crude oil, and nitrogen into ammonia.

Hydrogen bomb, or thermonuclear bomb, very powerful bomb whose explosive energy is produced by nuclear fusion of hydrogen isotopes, as of 2 deuterium atoms or of a deuterium and a tritium atom. The extremely high temperatures required to start the fusion reaction are produced by an atomic bomb. Lithium-6 deuteride (^{6}LiD) is the explosive; neutrons produced by

deuterium fusion react with the ^6Li to produce tritium. The end products are the isotopes of helium, ^3He and ^4He. In warfare hydrogen bombs have the advantage of being far more powerful than atomic bombs, their power being measured in megatons (millions of tons) of TNT, capable of destroying a large city. In defensive and peaceful uses they can be modified so that the radioactivity produced is reduced. Hydrogen bombs were first developed in the United States (1949-52) by Edward Teller and others, and have been tested by the USSR, Great Britain, China, and France.
See also: Fallout; Nuclear weapon.

Hydrogen bromide, chemical compound (HBr) that is a colorless, corrosive gas. If exposed to humid air it will fume; when combined with water it forms hydrobromic acid. The gas is used in various chemical reactions to make organic bromides and compounds, as a reducing agent, and as a catalyst.

Hydrogen fluoride *See:* Hydrofluoric acid.

Hydrogen iodide, chemical compound (HI) that is a colorless gas with a sharp odor. It fumes when exposed to humid air and combines easily with water to form hydriodic acid. It is used to make iodine salts, as a reducing agent, and for medical purposes in a diluted form.

Hydrogen peroxide (H_2O_2), unstable chemical compound that acts as an oxidizing agent that may cause poisoning. Hydrogen peroxide is marketed as an aqueous solution ranging from the common concentration of 3% as a topical antiseptic, 6% in hair preparations (bleaches, neutralizers, and so forth), to 30% for industrial and laboratory use and 90% for use in rocket propulsion. Decomposition of hydrogen peroxide may release large volumes of oxygen (10 times the volume for a 3% solution). Dropping a 3% solution on the eye, 3-5 times a day has been reported to be innocuous, but high-concentration hydrogen peroxide is generally feared as a cause of severe corneal damage. Ingestion of the commonly available household products (3-6%) should cause no problem other than possible mucous membrane and gastrointestinal irritation, while higher concentrations (such as 30%) are considered corrosive.
See also: Antiseptic.

Hydrogen sulfide, colorless, poisonous, flammable gas (H_2S) with an odor of rotting eggs. When combined with water it forms hydrosulfuric acid. The gas can be found around cesspools and in mines as a by-product of the decomposition of substances containing sulfur. The gas is also produced in laboratories for use as an analytical reagent.

Hydrology, branch of geophysics concerned with the hydrosphere (all the waters of the earth), with particular reference to water on and within the land. The science was born in the 17th century with the work of Pierre Perrault and Edmé Mariotte.
See also: Geophysics.

Hydrolysis, in chemistry, double decomposition effected by water, according to the general equation $XY + H_2O \rightarrow XOH + YH$. If XY is a salt of a weak acid or a weak base, the hydrolysis is reversible, and affects the pH of the solution. Reactive organic compounds such as acid chlorides and acid anhydrides are rapidly hydrolyzed by water alone, but other compounds require acids, bases, or enzymes as catalysts. Industrial hydrolysis processes include the alkaline saponification of oils and fats to glycerol and soap, and the acid hydrolysis of starch to glucose.

Hydrometer, device that measures the specific gravity of a liquid (its density relative to that of water). It is based on Archimedes' principle that states that a floating object is buoyed up by a force equal to the weight of the fluid it displaces. The instrument is a long thin glass bulb held upright by a weight at one end, allowed to float in the test liquid. The denser the liquid, the less the hydrometer sinks. The tube is calibrated in such a way that the specific gravity can be read off by comparing the level to which the bulb sinks with a scale along the side of the hydrometer. A form of hydrometer called an acidimeter is used in testing storage batteries by measuring the specific gravity, and therefore the strength, of the acid they contain.
See also: Density.

Hydrophobia *See:* Rabies.

Hydroplane, speedboat designed so that the hull rides above the surface of the water. When the boat accelerates rapidly and maintains speed, water pressure allows the flat or slightly curved bottom of the boat to skim the water.

Hydroponics, or soil-less culture, technique by which plants are grown without soil. All the minerals required for plant growth are provided by nutrient solutions in which the roots are immersed. The technique has been highly developed as a tool in botanical research, but commercial exploitation is limited primarily because of the difficulty of aerating the water and providing support for the plants. Gravel culture has overcome these problems to some extent and is used to grow some horticulture crops.

Hydrosphere, all the waters of the earth, in whatever form: solid, liquid, gaseous. It thus includes the water of the atmosphere, water on the earth's surface (e.g., oceans, rivers, ice sheets), and groundwater.

Hydrotherapy, external application of water for therapeutic purposes. The body or any of its parts may be immersed in water or water may be applied to the surface with or without the intermediary of absorbent materials. In partial baths, water may be applied by immersion, pouring, or compress to a small area of the body. For an eye wash, a hemispherical container filled to the brim with water is applied to the open eye, and as the head is tilted, the water bathes the corneal surface. The ear may be washed with a stream of water applied with a rubber bulb or syringe, usually to dislodge ear wax from the canal. The nasal passages may be bathed by sniffing water from the cupped hands, and the mouth may be washed by rinsing or irrigation.

Hydroxide, chemical compound containing the negatively charged hydroxyl ion (OH^-), used in the manufacture of detergents and medicines. Most hydroxide compounds are water soluble and can be caustic to varying degrees. Household ammonia is a familiar example of a basic hydroxide. Hydroxides are inorganic compounds; organic compounds containing the hydroxyl ion are called alcohols.

Hyena, 3 species of carnivorous mammals, family Hyaenidae, native to Asia and Africa. They are distinctive in having the shoulders considerably higher than the hindquarters and having an unusual gait, moving both limbs on one side of the body together. All 3 species have massive heads with powerful jaws. Though reviled as scavengers and carrion feeders, hyenas are active and skillful predators in their own right, hunting in packs of up to 20.

Hygiene *See:* Health.

Hygrometer, device to measure humidity (the amount of water vapor the air holds). Usually, hygrometers measure relative humidity, the amount of moisture as a percentage of the saturation level at that temperature. In the hair hygrometer, which is of limited accuracy, the length of a hair (usually human) increases with increase in relative humidity. This length change is amplified by a lever and registered by a needle on a dial. The wet- and dry-bulb hygrometer (psychrometer) has 2 thermometers mounted side by side, the bulb of one covered by a damp cloth. Air is moved across the apparatus (e.g., by a fan) and evaporation of water from the cloth draws latent heat from the bulb. Comparison of the 2 temperatures, and the use of tables, gives the relative humidity. In the dewpoint hygrometer, a polished container is cooled until the dew point is reached, giving a measure of relative humidity. The electric hygrometer measures changes in the electrical resistance of a hygroscopic (water-absorbing) strip.
See also: Humidity.

Hyksos, Asian group who invaded Egypt in the 18th century B.C. and formed the 15th and 16th dynasties of Egypt. They introduced the Asian light horse and chariot, bronze weapons, and the compound bow.

Hymn, sacred song in praise of gods or heroes, found in almost all cultures, ancient and modern. Jewish psalms, sung in the temple worship, were adopted by the early Christian Church and supplemented by distinctively Christian hymns such as the canticles. There is a continuous English hymn, tradition from the 7th century that includes 16th-century carols such as "Hark, the Herald Angels Sing." Modern hymns were developed by Isaac Watts, John Wesley, and many others in the 1700s. There are over 400,000 hymns, ranging from Gregorian chants (plainsongs) to rousing gospel music.

Hyperactive child, excessively active child who cannot concentrate on any one task for more than a few minutes. Hyperacitivity is called hyperkinesis by physicians. Symptoms exhibited by a hyperactive child range from persistent yelling and moving about to disobedience and an inability to socialize. Once thought to be mentally deficient, hyperactive children are now known to be generally of average to above-average intelligence. New teaching methods and family counseling have become part of the treatment of the condition. Stimulants and tranquilizers may also be prescribed, though drug therapy has become less popular in recent years, because its long-term effects are unknown.

Hyperbola, in geometry, curve consisting of 2 separate branches opening out in opposite directions. The hyperbola is one of the conic sections, formed when a right circular cone is intersected by a plane. It may be expressed in analytic geometry by the equation $y = 1/x$.
See also: Geometry.

Hyperkinesis *See:* Hyperactive child.

Hyperopia *See:* Farsightedness.

Hypertension, abnormally high blood pressure. Blood pressure is the pressure that the heart and arteries apply in order to squeeze the blood around the body. In a normal person, when sitting or lying quietly, the blood pressure stays at a steady, or resting, level. In moments of exercise, excitement, anger, or anxiety, the level of blood pressure is raised by te release of adrenaline and other hormones to increase the blood flow to the brain and muscles. In the hypertensive individual, blood pressure remains high; although there may be no immediate symptoms, long-term effects can be serious or fatal, and may include damage to the heart and brain. Causes include diet, kidney disorders, stress, and hereditary factors. Hypertension is treated with diet and medication.
See also: Blood pressure.

Hyperventilation, abnormal, deep and rapid breathing, frequently caused by anxiety. The level of carbon dioxide in the blood decreases, which restricts arteries, lowers blood pressure, and may result in dizziness or fainting.

Hypnos, in Greek mythology, the god of sleep. His mother was the goddess of the night, and his twin brother was Thantos, or Death. Among his sons was Morpheus, the Greek god of dreams.
See also: Mythology.

Hypnosis, artificially induced mental state characterized by an individual's loss of critical powers and consequent openness to suggestion. It may be induced by an external agency or self-induced (autohypnosis). Hypnotism has been widely used in medicine (usually to induce analgesia) and especially in psychiatry and psychotherapy. Here, the particular value of hypnosis is that while in trance, the individual may be encouraged to recall deeply repressed memories that may be at the heart of an emotional conflict; once such causes have been elucidated, therapy may proceed. Hypnosis seems to be as old as human society. However, the first definite information comes from the late 18th century with the work of Franz Mesmer, who held that disease was the result of imbalance in a patient's "animal magnetism," and hence attempted to cure this by the use of magnets. Some of his patients were cured, presumably by suggestion; the term mesmerism is still used for hypnotism.

Hypochlorous acid, weak inorganic acid (HOCl) used in bleaches and disinfectants. It is formed when chlorine is combined with water. Used to disinfect public drinking water and swimming pools, hypochlorous acid is also a strong oxidant.

Hypochondria, or hypochondriasis, mental condition involving undue anxiety about real or supposed ailments, usually in the belief that these are incurable. The source of hypochondria was once thought to be the hypochondrium, that part of the abdomen containing the spleen and liver.
See also: Neurosis.

Hypoglycemia, abnormally low level of glucose in the blood. Symptoms are tremulousness, sweating, irritability and restlessness, feeling of extreme hunger, headache and nausea, chronic fatigue and weakness. With severe hypoglycemia, the person may lose consciousness. Another form of hypoglycemia occurs in people who have had a large amount of alcohol to drink, either without eating or along with very high quantities of sugar-containing mixes.

Hypothalamus, central part of the base of the brain, closely related to the pituitary gland. It contains vital centers for controlling the autonomic nervous system, body temperature, and water and food intake, and is the center for primitive physical and emotional behavior. It also produces hormones for regulating pituitary secretion and systemic hormones including vasopressin and oxytocin.
See also: Brain.

Hypothermia, subnormal temperature of the body. Initial symptoms are weakness, slurred speech, confusion, shivering, and clumsiness. If the condition progresses, the weakness is replaced by stiff muscles, the person feels unable to move, and drowsiness and sleepiness occur. The body is no longer able to conserve heat, and the body temperature falls rapidly. Eventually, if nothing is done to return the temperature to normal, breathing will cease and the heart will stop. Activities that involve a high risk of hypothermia are swimming or other water activities; mountain climbing, skiing, and other activities that couple cold, wetness, and wind with exertion and sweating; and being out in the cold weather without proper clothing to provide warmth and protection from wetness. Special precautions must be taken with the very young and the elderly, who are the principal victims of hypothermia.
Drunkenness, exhaustion, hunger, disease, and illness all put people at greater risk of hypothermia. It is critical to stop the process immediately. Remove all wet clothing (it retains the cold and wetness); if possible, rewarm the body with whatever is available (dry clothing, towels, blankets, jackets, sweaters, even paper), and in an emergency, use the warmth (body heat) of others; a warm (not hot) bath is helpful. The person should be seen by a doctor as soon as possible.

Hyrax, or cony, rabbit-sized mammal of Africa and South Asia, of the order Hyracoidea, closely related to the elephant. The hyrax resembles the guinea pig, with short legs, ears, and tail. Some species are tree-dwelling and others, called dassies, live among rocks. They feed on plants and fruits.

Hyssop, herb (*Hyssopus officinalis*) of the mint family. Once used as a household remedy for sore throat, hyssop is now used primarily as a seasoning for meats and vegetables. The oil from its evergreen leaves has been used in the manufacture of perfumes. Grown throughout southern Europe and in parts of the United States, the hyssop plant may reach 2 ft (61 cm) in height.

Hysterectomy, surgical removal of the womb, with or without the ovaries and fallopian tubes. It may be performed via either the abdomen or the vagina and is most often used for fibroid tumors (benign tumors of womb muscle), cancer of the cervix or body of the womb, endometriosis, or other diseases causing heavy menstruation. If the ovaries are preserved, hormone secretion remains intact, though menstrual periods cease and infertility is inevitable. Recent controversy has questioned the overuse of the procedure because of the negative effects on general health.

Hysteria, or conversion disorder, medical diagnostic term for illness characterized by physical complaints without physical cause. The word "hysteria" derives from the ancient Greeks, who applied the term solely to diseases of women, which were explained as being due to malfunctioning of the uterus (hystera).

I

I, ninth letter of the English alphabet. It originated in the ancient Semitic alphabet, where it may have derived from an early symbol for "hand." It later passed into the Greek alphabet and was called *iota*. The original letter was probably a consonant representing our *y* sound, but in most Greek and Latin, as well as in many modern European languages, its sound is that of the vowel in *meet*. In English it may be short, as in *fit*, or long, as in *fine*, or it may combine with other letters for a great variety of sounds. The dot over the lowercase *i* first appeared in the 11th century. In chemistry, *I* is the symbol for iodine.

Iacocca, Lee (1924-), U.S. businessman and automobile executive; chairman and chief executive of the Chrysler Corporation. Originally an engineer and salesman with the Ford Motor Company, he rose to vice president and helped develop the Ford Mustang, a popular sports car. Beginning in 1970, he served as Ford's president, until a disagreement with Henry Ford II caused Iacocca to join the Chrysler Corporation in 1978. In 1980 he secured a U.S. government guarantee for $1.5 billion in private loans, a move that saved Chrysler from bankruptcy. The loans were repaid in 1983.

Ibadan (pop. 1,060,000), second largest city in Nigeria. Founded in the 1830s, Ibadan is located in the rich agricultural region of southwest Nigeria, and is a major commercial and industrial center. Ibadan's industries and products include brewing, producing canned goods, paint, plastics, furniture, and soap. Ibadan came under British protection in 1893. It is the capital of Nigeria's Oyo state.
See also: Nigeria.

Ibáñez, Vicente Blasco *See:* Blasco Ibáñez, Vicente.

Iberian Peninsula, landmass in southwestern Europe, occupied by Spain and Portugal. It is mostly surrounded by the waters of the Mediterranean Sea (east) and the Atlantic Ocean (west) and separated from North Africa by the

Strait of Gibraltar. The Pyrenees Mountains to the north form a natural barrier between the peninsula and the rest of Europe.

Ibert, Jacques (1890-1962), French composer of piano pieces, orchestral works, symphonic poems, and operas. Among his well-known works are a cantata, *Le Poète et la Fée* (1919), a ballet based on Oscar Wilde's *Ballad of Reading Gaol* (1922), the orchestral suites *Escales* (1922) and *Divertissement* (1930), and the light opera for radio *Barbe-bleue* (1943).

Iberville, Sieur d' (1661-1706), French-Canadian fur trader and explorer, founder of Louisiana. In 1699 he began exploring the mouths of the Mississippi River; he built a fort on Biloxi Bay and established a post at the site of Mobile, Ala.
See also: Louisiana.

Ibex, 7 species of wild goats (genus *Capra*) of the Eastern Hemisphere that differ from true goats in their flattened foreheads and usually broad-fronted horns. Always found in mountainous areas, ibex live for most of the year in separate-sex herds, with the males forming harems only during the 7- to 10-day rut.

Ibis, heronlike wading bird (family Threskiornithidae) of moderate size, characterized by a long, thin, downward-curving bill. Ibises have a worldwide distribution in tropical, subtropical, and temperate regions, and are usually found near fresh water, feeding on small aquatic animals. Ibises are gregarious and frequently raucous. Species include the sacred ibis (*Threskiornis aethiopica*), honored in ancient Egypt, and the Eastern glossy ibis (*Plegadis Falcinellus falcinellus*), common in the United States.

Ibizan hound, rare dog breed from Ibiza, an island off the eastern coast of Spain. A modern relative of an ancient Egyptian hunting dog, it is similar to the greyhound, with a slender build, a long snout, upright ears, and a long neck. It has amber eyes and a pink nose, and its coat may be long or short and red, white, brown, or a mixture of colors. It stands up to 27 in (69 cm) high and weighs up to 50 lb (23 kg).

Ibn Batuta (1304?-78?), greatest Arab traveler of the Middle Ages. He spent about 25 years traveling in Africa, Asia, and Europe. His notes (the *Rihlah*, or *Travels*) provide a priceless account of life before the rise of Europe.

Ibn Khaldun (1332-1406), Arab historian and sociologist. *Muqaddama*, the first volume of Ibn Khaldun's *Universal History*, contains the first attempt to interpret the patterns of history in the purely secular terms of geography, sociology, and allied subjects.
See also: Sociology.

Ibn Saud (1880-1953), creator of the kingdom of Saudi Arabia. Inheriting the leadership of the orthodox Wahabi movement, in 1900 he and a small band of followers captured the city of Riyadh, from which his family had been exiled, and by 1912 had conquered the Nejd from Turkey. During World War I the British favored his rival, King Husein ibn-Ali of Hejaz, in their campaign against the Turks, but in 1924-25 ibn-Saud defeated Husein,

combining Hejaz and the Nejd to form the kingdom of Saudi Arabia. He imposed order and religious orthodoxy. In the 1930s he awarded oil concessions to U.S. companies from which his family began to derive enormous wealth. Neutral in World War II, ibn-Saud took little part in the Arab-Israeli war of 1948.
See also: Saudi Arabia.

Ibn-Sina *See:* Avicenna.

Ibo *See:* Igbo.

Ibsen, Henrik (1828-1906), Norwegian playwright and poet. The pioneer of modern drama, his work developed from national Romanticism (*The Vikings at Helgoland*, 1858) to the realistic and effective presentation of contemporary social problems and moral dilemmas in such plays as *A Doll's House* (1879), *Ghosts* (1881), *The Wild Duck* (1884), and *Hedda Gabler* (1890). Very different, but as important to his philosophy, are his verse-dramas *Brand* (1866) and *Peer Gynt* (1867).

Ibuprofen, drug used for the relief of headaches, muscle aches, pain, and for the reduction of fever. Familiar trade names for ibuprofen include Advil, Motrin, and Nuprin. An anti-inflammatory agent and pain reliever, ibuprofen is also used to treat arthritis. Of a group of drugs called *propionic acid derivatives* developed in the 1960s and early 70s, ibuprofen is today the most widely used. Since 1984, ibuprofen has been available for sale without a prescription.
See also: Drug.

Icarus, in Greek mythology, son of Daedalus, with whom he was imprisoned in the labyrinth by King Minos of Crete. To escape Minos's wrath, they attached feathered wings to their shoulders with wax and flew away. Icarus, however, flew too high; the sun melted the wax, and he plunged into the sea and was drowned.
See also: Mythology.

ICBM *See:* Guided missile.

Ice, frozen water; colorless crystalline solid in which the strong, directional hydrogen bonding produces a structure with much space between the molecules. Thus ice is less dense than water and floats on it. The expansion of water on freezing may crack pipes and automobile radiators. Seawater freezes at about 28°F (–2°C). Ice has a very low coefficient of friction, and some fast-moving sports (ice hockey and ice skating) are played on it; slippery, icy roads are dangerous. Ice deposited on airplane wings reduces lift. Ice is used as a refrigerant and to cool some beverages.
See also: Water.

Ice age, any of several periods in geologic time when thick ice caps and glaciers covered large areas of the earth that now have temperate or warm climates. In 1837 Louis Agassiz, a Swiss-U.S. naturalist, was one of the first to argue that a great ice age in the past explained land features associated with glaciation hundreds of miles from permanent ice. Geologists later established that there have been several ice ages. Ice ages occurred in Australia, Canada, China, India, South Africa, and other places more than 700 million years ago, but little is known about them. Another great ice age affected the Southern Hemisphere during the early Permian period, which began c.275 million years ago. The ice ages about which most is known occurred in the Northern Hemisphere during the Pleistocene epoch in the past million years. There were 4 main glacial ages when the ice advanced: the Nebraskan (which began c.600,000 years ago), the Kansan (which began 476,000 years ago), the Illinoian (which began 230,000 years ago), and the Wisconsin (which began 115,000 years ago and ended c.10,000 years ago). The European names for these glacial ages are the Günz, Mindel, Riss, and Würm. These were separated by 3 interglacial ages during which the weather became warmer and the ice retreated. In North America the interglacials are named the Aftonian, the Yarmouth, and the Sangamon. Geologists do not know whether the close of the Wisconsin glacial age marked the end of the recent ice ages, or whether the present time is the fourth interglacial, preceding a fifth glacial age.

Iceberg, large floating mass of ice. In the Southern Hemisphere, the Antarctic ice sheet overflows its land support to form shelves of ice on the sea; huge pieces, as much as 150 mi (240 km) across, break off to form icebergs. In the Northern Hemisphere, icebergs are generally not over 175 yds (160 m) across. Most are "calved" from some 20 glaciers on Greenland's west coast. Small icebergs (*growlers*) may calve from larger ones. Some 75% of the height and over 85% of the mass of an iceberg lies below water. Northern icebergs usually float for some months to the Grand Banks, off Newfoundland, there melting in a few days. They endanger shipping, the most famous tragedy being the sinking of the *Titanic* (1912). The International Ice Patrol now keeps a constant watch on the area.
See also: Ice.

Icebreaker, vessel designed to break channels through ice for other ships, chiefly in harbors and rivers. They are of special importance in Canada, the former USSR, and Scandinavia. An icebreaker has a very strong reinforced hull and is equipped with high-powered engines that transmit power to the rugged propeller by electrical means. This enables the vessel to develop maximum power from a standing start. When breaking thin ice, the ship rams its way forward, sometimes assisted by turbulence created by a propeller at the bow. For breaking thick ice the vessel moves fast enough to ride up onto the ice, which then breaks under its weight. The shape of the hull makes icebreakers roll heavily in open water, but this also helps to break the ice. Special canting tanks containing water can also induce rolling and prevent the ship from getting trapped. The U.S. Coast Guard has a number of these vessels, with their distinctive, sharp, upward-slanting bows. The world's first atomic-powered icebreaker, the 16,000-ton (7,258 kg) *Lenin*, was launched by the USSR in 1957.

Icecap, extensive perennial cover of ice and snow, covering huge sections of the earth's polar regions. The Antarctic icecap has an area of 5 million sq mi (13 million sq km) and an average thickness of 7,000 ft (2,100 m). The majority of Greenland is covered by an icecap.
See also: Ice.

Ice cream, frozen dairy food whose main ingredients are sugar, cream or butterfat, water, flavorings, and air. Ice cream has a high caloric value and a very high vitamin A content, as well as being protein- and calcium-rich. It is also a source of smaller quantitites of iron, phosphorus, riboflavin, and thiamin. Water ices, which contain no milk products, have been known since ancient times in Europe and Asia. Ice cream probably reached the United States in the 17th century, and was first commercially manufactured by Jacob Fussel (1851). Today, the United States is the world's largest producer and consumer.

Ice hockey *See:* Hockey.

Iceland (Icelandic: *Island*), nation located on second-largest island of Europe, situated in the North Atlantic Ocean just south of the Arctic Circle, 200 mi (320 km) southeast of Greenland, 650 mi (1,050 km) west of Norway, and 500 mi (800 km) northwest of Scotland.

Land and climate. Iceland has more than 100 volcanic peaks with varying degrees of activity. Enormous ice explosions sometimes take place due to eruptions of volcanoes beneath ice fields, flooding large areas. Iceland's numerous hot springs and geysers are also of volcanic origin. Water from the springs is widely used for heating purposes. Lava fields account for more than a tenth of Iceland's surface. There are also enormous glaciers. The coastline is highly irregular, indented with numerous fjords and navigable bays, including the large Faxa Bay on the southwest coast, where Reykjavík, the nation's capital, stands. A plateau at an altitude of 2,000 ft (610 m) covers a large portion of the interior of the country. There are numerous rivers, but none is navigable. There are also many lakes. Iceland's marine climate is modified by the warm North Atlantic Drift. The average winter temperature in Reykjavík, in the south, is 30°F (–1°C) and the average summer temperature is 52°F (11°C), but the north is much colder. Only about a quarter of Iceland's surface bears natural vegetation, often a thick moss carpet found in areas not covered with snow. Only in areas protected by a winter snow cover is vegetation more dense. The lowlands have large areas of grass and, in sheltered regions, even some trees, the most common being dwarf willows, birches, and mountain ash. Native animals include the Arctic fox and various birds, of which the eider duck is valued for its down. The reindeer and mink were imported to the island.

People. Except for some blending of Irish blood, most of the people of Iceland are directly descended from the Vikings or other Scandinavians. In the second half of the 19th century, due to the country's poor economic situation, about 25,000 emigrated, mainly to Canada. Three-quarters of the population is centered in urban areas along the coast, over one-third of the population living in Reykjavík, the cultural center, with its own university (founded 1911). The Icelandic language is of the Scandinavian group. It has undergone very few changes since the 12th and 13th centuries, an era in which the famous Icelandic sagas and prose narratives were written, so that this literature is still understandable to modern readers. Iceland was almost entirely free of illiteracy by the beginning of the 19th century. Education is compulsory and free from ages 7 to 15. The university of Reykjavik is one of the institutions for higher education. Christianity was established in Iceland about a thousand years ago. By far the most prominent church today is the Evangelical Lutheran Church.

Iceland

Capital:	Reykjavík
Area:	39,769 sq mi (103,000 sq km)
Population:	271,000
Language:	Icelandic
Government:	Republic
Independent:	1944
Head of gov.:	Prime minister
Per capita:	U.S. $24,950
Mon. unit:	1 Icelandic krona = 100 aurar

Economy. Fishing (especially cod, haddock, and herring) and fish-processing are the mainstay industries and provide two-thirds of Iceland's exports. A long dispute with Great Britain over fishing rights in the waters off Iceland led to a series of "cod wars." In 1975 Iceland extended its "economic" sea limits to 200 mi (322 km) and the next year broke diplomatic relations with Britain for 4 months. There is some small-scale agriculture and manufacturing. Iceland's vast resources of natural energy in its rivers, hot streams, and geysers, as well as its important volcanic mineral potential, are only beginning to be exploited for industrial and commercial purposes.
History. Discovered by the Norse c.A.D. 870, Iceland was under Norwegian rule from 1262 and then under the Danes from 1380. The tradition of democratic government dates from A.D. 930, when the Althing, the world's oldest parliament, was established. Iceland has been entirely self-governing since 1918, and it became a fully independent republic on June 17, 1944. In 1970 Iceland joined the European Free Trade Association.

Ice skating, winter sport in the United States, Canada, and the countries of northern Europe. Originally confined to natural settings and conditions, such as frozen lakes and rivers, the sport has been widely popularized by the introduction of artificial rinks. Competitive skating, which requires many years of intensive practice, consists of figure skating and speed skating. Figure skating is a highly technical and demanding form of body control. The skater must master a large number of school figures (including turns, brackets, rockers, and loops) based on a figure eight, and must develop striking routines of individual free skating (including jumps, spins, spirals, and free movements performed to music). In competition, school figures account for 60% of the skater's score and free skating for 40%. Speed skating takes place over distances from as little as 50 yd (46 m) to as much as 5 mi (8 km). In the United States, skaters generally race against each other directly whereas in European and Olympic events they race against the clock, 2 at a time. Good speed skaters can average 20 mph (32 kmph) or more. Ice skating dates back at least as far as the 8th century and attained its first national popularity in the Netherlands in the 15th century. Metal blades first appeared in the 16th century. The first U.S. skating club was formed in Philadelphia in 1849, but it is only in the present century that skating has become a major North American sport.

I Ching, or Book of Changes, ancient Chinese philosophical and literary classic dating to c.12th century B.C. Its set of symbols and texts are used for divination. The *I Ching* was a major influence on Confucianism and Taoism. There has been a revival of interest in the *I Ching* in recent years.
See also: Confucianism; Taoism.

Ichneumon wasp, parasitic wasp (family Ichneumonidae) equipped with a long egg-laying organ, the *ovipositor*, like a hypodermic needle. It lays its eggs in the larvae of other insects and when its own larvae hatch they feed on the tissues of host or hosts. The host, such as a caterpillar, continues to live with the ichneumon larva inside it until pupation. Then the parasite kills its host and pupates itself. Some species of ichneumon wasps can penetrate 2 in (5 cm) of wood with their ovipositors to lay eggs on the larvae of horntails (large sawflies that are pests in timber plantations). These ichneumon wasps have been specially introduced into plantations to keep down the numbers of horntails.

Ickes, Harold Le Claire (1874-1952), U.S. government official. Ickes was secretary of the interior (1933-46) under Presidents Franklin D. Roosevelt and Harry S. Truman, and he also served as head of the Public Works Administration (1933-39). An able and responsible administrator, Ickes was a central figure in Roosevelt's New Deal.

Icon (Greek, "image"), religious image in the Eastern and Russian Orthodox churches. Icons play an important part in liturgy. The Virgin Mary and Jesus were traditional icon figures; by the 7th century icon worship was an officially encouraged cult in the Byzantine Christian Church.
See also: Eastern Orthodox Church.

Iconoclast (Greek *eikon*, "image" + *klastes*, "breaker"), person who practices iconoclasm, opposition to the religious use of images. Although religious pictures and statues have long been an important part of Christian worship, iconoclasts claim they lead to idolatry. Historically, the use of images in religious worship has been in dispute. In A.D. 843 the Eastern Church reached a settlement that permitted pictures but not complete images or statues.

Id *See:* Psychoanalysis.

Idaho, state in the Rocky Mountain region of the United States; bordered on the east by Montana and Wyoming, on the south by Utah and Nevada, on the west by Oregon and Washington, and on the north by British Columbia.
Land and climate. Idaho is dominated by the Rockies, including the Bitterroot, Salmon River, and Sawtooth ranges. About 50 of the state's peaks are over 10,000 ft (3,000 m) high. The Snake River (1,038 mi/1,671 km) flows across southern Idaho and curves north to form part of the western boundary of the state. The irrigated Snake River Plain is Idaho's major agricultural region. The high mountains have cool summers and severe winters, while the summers are hot on the Snake River Plain. Principal cities are Boise, Pocatello, and Idaho Falls.

Idaho

Capital:	Boise
Statehood:	July 3, 1890 (43rd state)
Familiar name:	Gem State
Area:	83,564 sq mi (216,432 sq km; ranks 13th)
Population:	1,210,000 (1997; ranks 42nd)
Elevation:	Highest—12,662 ft (3,859 m), Borah Peak
	Lowest—710 ft (216 m), Snake River at Lewiston
Motto:	Esto Perpetua (It Is Perpetual)
State flower:	Syringa (mock orange)
State bird:	Mountain bluebird
State tree:	Western white pine
State song:	"Here We Have Idaho"

Economy. Unlike many of the other western states, Idaho has vast water resources, and its dams provide hydroelectric power and water for irrigation. Idaho's chief agricultural products are cattle and dairy goods, and it is the leading producer of potatoes in the United States. Lumber and wood products are major manufactures of the heavily forested state, as are processed foods. The Sunshine Mine is the largest silver-producing mine in the country. Tourism is also important.

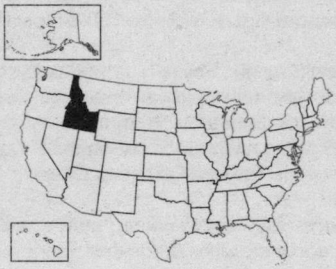

Government. Idaho's constitution, adopted in 1889, provides for a governor, serving a 4-year term. The legislature consists of a 42-member senate and an 84-member house elected to 2-year terms. The state sends 2 senators and 2 representatives to the U.S. Congress.

History. The area was inhabited by Native Americans more than 10,000 years ago. The first European Americans to explore the Idaho region were Meriwether Lewis and William Clark in 1805. At that time local tribes included the Nez Percé, Shoshone, Coeur d'Alene, and others. David Thompson, a British fur trader, set up Idaho's first trading post in 1809, and Mormons founded Franklin, Idaho's first permanent settlement, in 1860. That same year, gold was discovered, attracting scores of settlers. In 1863, the Idaho Territory was established. The U.S. Army defeated the Nez Percé Indians in 1877. Agriculture expanded during the early 20th century with the development of irrigation projects. Increasing demands for hydroelectric power led to the construction of a series of dams on the Snake River in the 1950s and 1960s. Agriculture remains an important sector of Idaho's economy, although other industries, including tourism, continue to grow.

Idaho Falls (pop. 39,734), third largest city in Idaho, located in the southeastern portion of the state, on the Snake River. Population growth in Idaho Falls flourished during the early 1900s when flour mills and sugar factories

sprung up. In 1949 the U.S. Atomic Energy Commission constructed a nuclear reactor testing station 30 mi (48 km) west of Idaho Falls. Today, Idaho Falls serves as a commercial and processing center for the farm, livestock, and dairy area of upper Snake Valley.
See also: Idaho.

Idealism, any one of a variety of systems of philosophical thought that would make the ultimate reality of the universe expressible or intelligible only in terms of ideas rather than in terms of matter or space.
See also: Berkeley, George; Hegel, Georg Wilhelm Friedrich; Kant, Immanuel.

Ideology, set of beliefs based on related political, social, and economic assumptions. People who hold to a particular ideology often rely on its system of thought in forming decisions about the way they live or work. Ideologies may be religious, such as Catholicism, or artistic, such as Impressionism. Communism, socialism, democracy, fascism, and totalitarianism are different kinds of political ideologies. For example, until 1989 the government of West Germany adhered to a form of democracy, whereas the government of East Germany adhered to a form of communism: both democracy and communism are political ideologies.

Ides, 15th day of Mar. in the ancient Roman calendar and the day in 44 B.C. on which Julius Caesar was assassinated in the Roman senate. In the Roman calendar, the 15th of Mar., May, July, and Oct. and the 13th of the other months were called the ides.

Idolatry, in religion, worship of an image or statue representing a god or spirit. Overt forms of idolatry consist of explicit acts of reverence addressed to a person or object, such as dancing to the sun. Idols are generally found in animal or human form, and may be cared for as if they were alive. Christians, Jews, and Muslims consider the worship of images a sin, and the use of lifelike images has been prohibited in Islamic and Jewish art since ancient times.
See also: Icon.

Idyl (Greek, "little picture"), short poem that deals with rural scenery, beauty, and tranquility. Idyl is often used as a synonym for pastoral. The 10 famous idyls by the Greek Theocritus became the models for idyls written in later centuries. Selections from the Bible, such as the Song of Songs, are considered idyls. Many British poets of the 16th and 17th centuries wrote pastoral poems; John Milton's *Lycidas* is an example of one of the finest idyls from this time period.

Ife, town in the Oyo province in southwestern Nigeria. Ife is the oldest town of the Yoruba tribe. Beginning about A.D. 1000, Ife was an important center of black African culture. The Yoruba people created sculptures of terra cotta and bronze. Never having achieved great political or military power, Ife declined in the early 1800s. The current city of Ife is a major collecting point for cacao and cotton, palm oil and kernels, yams, cassava, maize, pumpkins, and kola nuts. Most of its inhabitants are town-dwelling farmers.
See also: Nigeria.

Igbo, or Ibo, large ethnic group in Nigeria. Although the origin of the Igbo people is not precisely known, recent archeological evidence suggests that the Igbo's artistic culture was supported by both agriculture and flourishing trade. Located near the Nigerian coast, the early Igbo civilization participated in the slave trade, which lasted from the 1400s to the 1800s. During the 1800s and 1900s Nigeria fell under British rule, and in 1967 the Igbo homeland, along with the entire Eastern Region of Nigeria, proclaimed itself the independent republic of Biafra. Today, many Igbo occupy villages of dispersed homesteads in rain-forest country and are subsistence farmers.

Igloo, shelter or hunting ground dwelling for the Canadian Eskimos. Traditionally made of snow, sod, or stone, the best-known igloo was made of hard-packed snow cut into blocks from 2 to 3 ft (61 to 91 cm) long and 1 to 2 ft (30 to 61 cm) wide. After a first row of these blocks were laid down in a circle, the top surfaces of the blocks were shaved off in a sloping angle to form the first rung of a spiral. Additional blocks were added to draw it inward in a dome shape. One hole was left in the top for ventilation, and the igloo was kept warm mainly by a sealskin flap fit over the main entrance and seal oil lamps. Prefabricated houses have replaced igloos.
See also: Eskimo.

Ignatius Loyola, Saint *See:* Loyola, Saint Ignatius.

Ignatius of Antioch, Saint (d. c.A.D. 100), Christian bishop of Antioch, condemned to death in Trajan's reign. Ignatius wrote 7 letters (now precious early church documents) in which "Catholic Church" was first used to denote Christians everywhere, and in which he tried to prove that Docetism, a doctrine that held that Jesus' bodily sufferings were only "appearance," was heresy.
See also: Christianity.

Igneous rock, one of the 3 main classes of rocks, that whose origin is the solidification of molten material, or detrital volcanic material. It crystallizes from lava at the earth's surface (extrusion) or from magma beneath (intrusion). There are 2 main classes: *Volcanic* rocks are extruded, typical examples being lava and pyroclastic rocks. *Plutonic* rocks are intruded into the rocks of the earth's crust at depth, a typical example being granite; those forming near to the surface are sometimes called hypabyssal rocks. Types of intrusions include batholiths, dikes, sills, and laccoliths. As plutonic rocks cool more slowly than volcanic, they have a coarser texture, more time being allowed for crystal formation.
See also: Basalt; Granite.

Ignition, system used to start an engine. In an internal combustion engine the ignition system sets fire to a mixture of fuel and air to generate power. Most automobiles use spark ignition systems, in which spark plugs create electric sparks to set fire to fuel. When a spark ignition system is turned on, an electric current flows from a battery to the ignition coil, where it is increased in voltage and then sent to a distributor. In the distributor, a rotor directs the current to the automobile's set of spark plugs. At this point, the spark plugs produce the electric sparks that ignite the fuel and air mixture to start the engine.
See also: Engine.

Iguana, family of lizards, the largest and most elaborately marked lizards of the New World. It includes insectivorous, carnivorous, and herbivorous species. Many species are territorial. Iguanas characteristically show ornamental scales and a dorsal fringe, and bear tubercles on the head and body. Some species have an erectile throat fan. There are 2 major groups: ground iguanas and green iguanas; there is also 1 species of marine iguana. All species are hunted for food, although this is greatly depleting their numbers.

Ikhnaton *See:* Akhenaton.

Ileitis, inflammation of the ileum, a section of the small intestine. Crohn's disease, also known as regional ileitis or regional enteritis, is the most frequently occurring form of ileitis and is characterized by sporadic attacks, which include abdominal cramps, fever, and diarrhea. These attacks are caused by a periodic swelling of the ileum, which prevents the passage of food and may eventually cause starvation. It is not known what causes ileitis, and there is no cure, although it can be treated with special diet, intravenous feeding, and surgery, which is successful 50% of the time.
See also: Intestine.

Iliad, ancient Greek epic poem of 24 books in hexameter verse, attributed to Homer; internal references suggest it was composed in the mid-8th century B.C. It describes a quarrel during the siege of Troy between the Greek warrior-hero Achilles and King Agamemnon, which results in Achilles' brutal slaying of Hector, the Trojan warrior-prince. A companion to the *Odyssey*, the *Iliad* is one of the world's greatest tragic works of literature.
See also: Homer.

Illegal alien, person living in a country where he or she is not a citizen and without the government's consent. There are between 3 and 6 million illegal aliens in the United States, half of whom are assumed to be from Mexico. Most illegal aliens have jobs; about half work in the manufacturing or service fields. They are called undocumented workers because they have no immigration papers and therefore cannot legally be employed. In 1986, the Immigration Reform and Control Act was passed in Congress. It set a ceiling on the number of undocumented workers allowed to come to the United States and set severe penalties for employers who hired illegal aliens. The act also granted amnesty to approximately 2 million illegal immigrants.

Illicium, sole genus of plant belonging to the family Illiciales, of the illiciales order. Comprised of 42 species, illicium is a group of trees and shrubs with evergreen leaves and bisexual flowers. The inner petals of the illicium flowers grade into stamens, or male, structures, while the female portion of the flower is usually located at its base and consists of 7 to 15 carpels (ovule-bearing structures). The name *illicium* means *allurement* in Latin, and probably alludes to the pleasant aroma of the illicium flower.

Illinois, state in the north central United States; bordered by Lake Michigan in the northeast, Indiana in the east, Kentucky in the southeast, Missouri in the southwest, Iowa in the northwest, and Wisconsin in the north.
Land and climate. Illinois consists almost entirely of a rolling plain that slopes gradually from north to south. Much of the north and central portions

Illinois

Capital:	Springfield
Statehood:	Dec. 3, 1818 (21st state)
Familiar names:	Land of Lincoln, the Prairie State
Area:	56,345 sq mi (145,934 sq km); ranks 24th
Population:	11,896,000 (1997); ranks 6th
Elevation:	Highest—1,235 ft (376 m), Charles Mound
	Lowest—269 ft (82 m), Mississippi River
Motto:	State Sovereignty, National Union
State flower:	Native violet
State bird:	Cardinal
State tree:	Oak
State song:	"Illinois"

of the state are covered by dark prairie soils and loams, which are especially rich and productive. The Shawnee Hills cross the southern part of the state in a band varying from 5 to 40 mi (8 to 64 km) wide. Illinois possesses an extensive river system. The Mississippi River, which forms the state's western border, is linked with Lake Michigan by the Illinois Waterway, which includes the Chicago, Des Plaines, and Illinois rivers. The Illinois (273 mi/439 km), the largest river lying wholly within Illinois, drains about half the state. Illinois has a continental climate, with cold winters and hot summers. Chicago is the state's and region's leading city and is the third largest city in the nation. Other major cities include Springfield, Peoria, and Rockford.

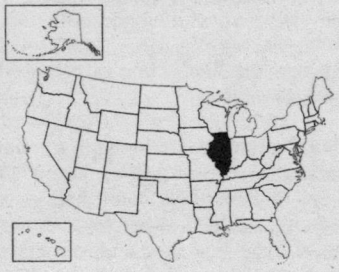

Economy. A leading agricultural state, Illinois produces corn, hogs, cattle, and soybeans. Industry includes the manufacture of machinery, electrical and electronic equipment, processed foods, metal products, and chemicals. Illinois is a leading coal producer and also has significant oil resources.

Government. The state's government is based on the constitution of 1970. The governor serves a 4-year term. The General Assembly consists of 59 senators serving 2- and 4-year terms and 177 representatives serving 2-year terms. Illinois sends 22 representatives and 2 senators to the U.S. Congress.

History. A prehistoric Native American people, the mound builders, were the first known inhabitants of what is now Illinois. By the 17th century, the principal inhabitants of the region were the Illinois, a confederation of Algonquian-speaking tribes. The first Europeans known to have visited the region were Louis Jolliet and Jacques Marquette, in 1673. In 1763, at the end of the French and Indian War, Illinois was ceded to the British. After the American Revolution the region became part of the Northwest Territory of the United States. It was made a separate territory in 1809. With the defeat of the Sauk and Fox in the Black Hawk War of 1832, the last barrier to European American settlement of the state was removed. The debates between Abraham Lincoln and Stephen A. Douglas in the senatorial race of 1858 brought Lincoln to national attention. After the Civil War, industry made great progress as immigrants poured in on the newly completed railroads. Decades of labor unrest reached their climax in the Haymarket Riot of 1886 in Chicago. Agriculture suffered a serious depression through the 1920s, to be joined by the rest of the economy during the Great Depression of the 1930s. Today Illinois continues to attract hundreds of new factories, and space age industries and atomic research facilities are thriving.

Illinois, tribal confederation of Native Americans belonging to the Algonquian linguistic group and related to Ojibwas and Miamis. Their territory originally included Illinois and parts of Iowa, Wisconsin, and Missouri. After tribal wars with the Iroquois and other northern tribes, the few survivors moved to Kansas (1832) and later to an Oklahoma reservation (1867).

Illinois River, major waterway linking the Mississippi River with Lake Michigan. Formed by the confluence of the Des Plaines and Kankakee rivers, about 45 mi (72 km) southwest of Chicago, the Illinois River flows west and southwest for about 275 mi (443 km). It joins the Mississippi about 16 mi (26 km) above Alton, Ill.

Illiteracy, inability to read and write at least simple messages. Illiteracy is therefore the absence of such ability. As civilization grows more complex, mathematical literacy also becomes an important factor, mathematics also being a kind of language.

Illumination, the decoration of a handwritten text with ornamental design, letters, and paintings, often using silver and gold leaf. Illumination flourished between the 5th and 16th centuries A.D. The art was highly developed in the Middle East, the Orient, and in Christian Europe, where monks and others skilled in calligraphy and painting often devoted their lifetimes to embellishing manuscripts of all kinds, particularly religious. Among the most celebrated manuscripts are the Irish *Book of Kells*, the Carolingian *Utrecht Psalter*, and the *Très riches heures* commissioned by Jean, duc de Berry, from the Limbourg brothers.

Illusion *See:* Optical illusion.

Illyria, ancient country in the northwestern part of the Balkan peninsula. It was settled in the 10th century B.C. by Illyrians, an Indo-European-speaking people who extended their influence from the Danube River to the Adriatic Sea in modern-day Yugoslavia and Albania. It became the Roman province of Illyricum (168 B.C.).

Ilmenite, heavy black metallic oxide mineral that is a source of titanium. Formed at high temperatures and containing 36.8% iron and 31.6% titanium, ilmenite is not widely used as iron ore because of difficulties in *smelting*, or separating the metallic constituents. The chemical formula for ilmenite is $FeTiO_3$.

Iloilo (pop. 309,500), major port of the Philippines located on the island of Panay, one of the Visayan Islands. It is also the main cultural location for the region.
See also: Philippines.

Imagists, group of poets writing in the early 20th century in the United States and England who rebelled against the artificiality and sentimentality of much 19th-century poetry. Free, idiomatic verse, unusual rhythms, and sharp, clear imagery were characteristics of their work, which was influenced by French symbolism. The movement embraced Ezra Pound, Hilda Doolittle (H.D.), Amy Lowell, D.H. Lawrence, and James Joyce.

Imago, psychoanalytic term for the unconscious, idealized representation of oneself or of an important figure from childhood, often a parent.
See also: Psychoanalysis.

Imam (Arabic, "leader") term used in Islam to denote a religious leader. In the Sunnite branch of Islam any devout Muslim may perform the services of imam in leading public worship. In the Shi'te branch the imam is a caliph, or ruler, and must be appointed by God in the line of descent from Muhammad. The term is also applied by some Muslims to any religious teacher or scholar.
See also: Islam.

Imhotep (fl.c.2980-2950 B.C.), Egyptian architect of the Step Pyramid at Saqqara. Chief minister, priest, and scribe to Pharaoh Zoser, Imhotep's fame spread and after his death he became a god of medicine. He is considered the first doctor known to history by name.
See also: Egypt, Ancient.

Immaculate Conception, Roman Catholic dogma, officially defined in 1854, that the Virgin Mary was conceived free from original sin, owing to a special act of redemptive grace. The feast of the Immaculate Conception is celebrated Dec. 8.
See also: Roman Catholic Church.

Immigration, movement of people into a country to establish a new permanent residence. People become immigrants primarily for economic, political, or religious reasons. The United States is a nation of immigrants. It has received more immigrants from more places than any other country—about 38 million from the 1820s to the 1930s—and is thus known as a "melting pot" of the world's nations. Its growth and prosperity were stimulated by great waves of immigrants in the 19th and 20th centuries. Immigration accelerated economic development by providing an abundant labor supply, while for the newcomers America offered hope of a freer and more prosperous life. Until World War I the United States maintained, more or less, an open-door policy toward immigrants, but social and economic conflicts between various ethnic groups and between the older and newer immigrants led to a major policy reversal. Restrictions had been placed on Asians (Chinese and Japanese) and other so-called undesirables even before World War I. In 1917 a literacy test was made compulsory for all immigrants. In 1921 and 1924 quotas were fixed, favoring immigration from northern

Europe, especially the United Kingdom, but imposing an overall limit of 150,000 European immigrants a year. In 1952 the McCarran-Walter Act banned communists and other subversives, removed racial exclusions, and strengthened the quota system's ethnic and national system. A 1965 act abolished the quotas discriminating among nationalities, substituting professional qualifications and skills and kinship with U.S. citizens or resident aliens as criteria. Provision also was made for political refugees. The collapse of U.S-supported regimes in Southeast Asia brought in new waves of immigrants in the 1970s. In the same decade, Mexicans, seeking relief from poverty, arrived in large numbers. South America received large numbers of immigrants before the 1930s. Since World War II an entirely new phase of immigration has taken place within Europe itself. West Indians, Asian Indians, and Pakistanis have settled in the United Kingdom, claiming their rights as members of the Commonwealth. Since 1962, the British government has introduced new laws reducing this trend. Western and northern Europe have admitted large numbers of immigrants from the less-developed parts of southern Europe. The European Community requires all its member countries to allow free movement of labor across their borders.

Immortelle (*Xeranthemum annuun*), any of several species of flower belonging to the composite family and related to the asters. The largest of what is known as everlasting flowers, the immortelle has flower heads composed of many small flowers, called florets. The yellow immortelle is characterized as an everlasting flower because it retains its natural form and color even after it has been dried.

Immunity, system of defense in animals protecting against foreign materials, specifically, infectious microorganisms, parasites, and their products. For many diseases, *humoral immunity*, exposure to the causative organism in disease itself or by vaccination, provides acquired resistance to that organism, making further infection with it unlikely or less severe. The antigen (foreign microorganism or other substance) provokes the formation of an antibody specific to that antigen. The antibody tends to neutralize viruses or to bind to antigens, encouraging destruction of bacteria by white blood cells. A number of diseases are due to the systemic effects of immune complexes (antibodies linked to antigens) that arise in the appropriate response to an infection or in serum sickness, and these especially affect the kidneys, skin, and joints. In *autoimmunity* antibodies are produced to antigens of the body's own tissues, for reasons that are not always clear; secondary tissue destruction may occur. The second major type of immunity, *cell-mediated immunity*, only occurs with certain types of infection (tuberculosis, histoplasmosis, and fungal diseases) and in certain probable autoimmune diseases. It is also important in the immunity of transplants. Lymphocytes, primed by infection or by the autoimmune or graft reaction, produce substances that affect both lymphocytes and the source of infection and result in a type of inflammation with much tissue damage. Investigation of the role of immunity and its disorders in the causation and manifestations of many diseases has led to the development of immunosuppressive drugs and other agents that are able to interfere with abnormal or destructive immune responses. Immune deficiency diseases have provided models for the separate parts of the immune system, and have led to methods of replacement of absent components of immunity. The epidemic of acquired immune deficiency syndrome (AIDS) has added some urgency to research. Passive immunity, the transfer of antibody-rich substances from an immune subject to a non-immune subject who is susceptible to disease, is important in infancy, where maternal antibodies protect the child until its own immune responses have matured. In certain diseases, such as tetanus and rabies, immune serum gives valuable immediate passive protection in non-immune subjects.

Immunization, process of becoming, or rendering a body, resistant to a particular disease. Immunization occurs naturally when disease antibodies develop through exposure or are passed from mother to fetus or nursing child, but the term generally refers to the medical procedure of administering vaccines or serums. *Vaccines* activate the production of antibodies by introduction into the bloodstream of germs, toxins, etc. (*active immunization*). *Serums* contain antibodies produced by another body (*passive immunization*) and provide only temporary immunity. The first method of immunization was Edward Jenner's smallpox vaccine (1796). Immunization should be performed in children for at least 5 dangerous diseases: whooping cough (pertussis), diphtheria, tetanus, poliomyelitis, and measles. Due to immunization, many serious diseases are now rare.
See also: Immunity.

Impala (*Aepyceros melampus*), one of the most abundant African antelopes. Impala are about 40 in (102 cm) high and red-brown in color. Males have long, black, lyre-shaped horns. Animals of the woodland edge, impala live in big herds in the dry season, breaking up into single-male harems in the wetter months for breeding. Impala herds of 10 associate with baboons for protection against predators.

Impeachment, formal accusation of a crime or other serious misconduct brought against a public official by a legislature. The term sometimes includes the trial by the legislature that follows. Impeachment began in England as a way of putting officials on trial who were derelict in their duties. Under U.S. constitutional procedure the House of Representatives has the power to impeach; the Senate tries the impeached officials. Grounds for impeachment are: "Treason, Bribery or other High Crimes and Misdemeanors," generally interpreted as being limited to demonstrably criminal acts in the United States. Conviction requires a two-thirds vote of all senators present and voting, providing there is a quorum, and entails automatic removal from office. The chief justice of the United States presides. In U.S. history Congress has impeached 11 officials and convicted 4. President Andrew Johnson was impeached but later acquitted in the Senate by one vote. In 1974, after the House Judiciary Committee recommended his impeachment, Richard M. Nixon resigned as president of the United States.

Imperialism, policy of one country or people, usually "developed," to extend its control or influence over other territories or peoples, usually "underdeveloped." There are many different kinds of imperialism—political, financial, economic, military, and cultural. The justification for imperialism has been that backward countries are advanced technologically, economically, and culturally by the influence of more developed nations. However, imperialist policies have also restricted individual and national freedoms and have often exploited undeveloped natural resources and native populations.

Imperial Valley, agricultural area in the low-lying Colorado Desert of southeastern California, extending into Mexico, called the "Winter Garden" of America. Since the construction of the 80-mi (129-km) All-American Canal irrigation and soil reclamation projects in the 1940s and 1950s, the valley has become a highly fertile farm region producing alfalfa, melons, tomatoes, lettuce, and sugar beets. Even the January temperature averages 53°F (12°C).

Impetigo, superficial skin infection, usually of the face, caused by streptococcus or staphylococcus. It starts with small vesicles that burst and leave a characteristic yellow crust. It is easily spread by fingers from a single vesicle to affect several large areas and may be transmitted to other people. It is common in children and requires antibiotic cream or sometimes systemic penicillin.

Import *See:* Exports and imports.

Impressionism, dominant artistic movement in France from the mid-1860s to 1890, characterized by the use of brushstrokes of contrasting colors to convey the impression of objects by the light they reflect. The impressionist painters, who include Edouard Manet, Claude Monet, Camille Pissarro, and others, painted landscapes and scenes of leisure in contemporary Paris. They usually worked outdoors, recording the scenes before them spontaneously and directly. The term "impressionist" was first used as a criticism of Monet's *Impression: Soleil levant* (1874). The artists organized 8 independent exhibitions for their pictures. The U.S. painters Mary Cassatt and Childe Hassam were influenced by the impressionists. The term "impressionism" is also applied to other art forms, notably literature that uses symbolic imagery and music that expresses mood and feeling.

Inca, Native American empire in the western region of South America which, at the time of the Spanish conquest, occupied what is now Peru, parts of Ecuador, Chile, Bolivia, and Argentina. It extended some 3,000 mi (4,800 km) from north to south, stretching back between 150 and 250 mi (240 and 400 km) from the narrow Pacific coastal plain into the high Andes. The name "Inca" refers to the people of the empire and is also the title of the ruler. Communications were maintained along brilliantly engineered and extensive roads, carried over the sheer Andean gorges by fiber cable suspension bridges. Trained relay runners carried messages 150 mi (240 km) a day and the army had quick access to trouble spots. Restive subject tribes were resettled near Cuzco, the capital. Detailed surveys of new conquests were recorded by *quipu*, a mnemonic device using knotted cords. Writing, like draft animals and wheeled transport, was unknown; so too was monetary currency. Taxation and tribute were levied in the form of labor services. In other respects the culture was highly advanced. At sites such as Machu Picchu, Inca architects raised some of the world's finest stone structures; precious metals from government-controlled mines were worked by skilled goldsmiths; bronze was also used; ceramic and textile design was outstanding. Agriculture was based on elaborate irrigation and hillside terracing. The

Spanish domination of the Incas began with the arrival (1532) of Francisco Pizarro, who executed the Incan emperor and conquered their cities.

Incandescent lamp *See:* Electric light.

Inchon (pop. 1,817,900), Yellow River port city located in the northwestern part of South Korea. In ancient times Inchon relied mainly upon fishing, but after foreign nations forced Korea to open up to international trade in the 1880s, it developed into a major port. In 1950, during the Korean war, the U.S. made a surprise landing at Inchon, turning back the invading North Koreans. Located about 20 mi (32 km) from the capital city of Seoul, Inchon has been a major industrial center since the late 1960s. It produces chemicals, iron, steel, and textiles, in addition to thriving in the areas of fishing and shipping.
See also: Korea; Korean War.

Inchworm *See:* Measuring worm.

Incisor *See:* Teeth.

Income, payment, whether money (pecuniary, cash, or monetary income) or as goods and services (real income), received in return for goods and services. For most people cash income takes the form of a wage or salary, usually expressed as so much per week or month. Cash income is also derived from stock dividends and from rent paid for the use of property. Many people in developing countries depend largely on noncash incomes. Even in industrialized countries some people get at least a part of their income in the form of goods rather than cash, for example, farmers who use some of their own produce. Income is distinguished from assets. For example, say that a person spends $8,000 in the course of a year but earns only $6,000, drawing the remaining $2,000 from savings. That person's income is only $6,000. The remaining $2,000 has been spent by consuming assets. Equally, if a person borrows money or receives a gift of cash, such sums are not rated as part of income, since they do not stem from productive work or investment. People regularly spend more than their income, borrowing cash and buying on credit. Businesses, too, regularly look to borrowed funds to pay for their expansion. This presupposes that borrowed money can be repaid from future income.

Income tax, the major source of government revenue. As opposed to excise taxes levied on goods, it is a tax on the incomes of individuals, proportionate to their incomes, or on corporations. At first imposed only to meet extraordinary expenditures such as war financing, income tax became permanent in Britain in 1874. In the United States it was levied during the Civil War, but an attempt to make it a permanent federal tax was ruled unconstitutional. The 16th Amendment (1913) authorized the federal government to levy the tax, and since 1919 most states have also adopted this mode of revenue raising. It is assessed on net income after allowances have been deducted for family dependents, contributions to charities, and certain other expenditures. Incomes below a certain level are entirely tax exempt; above this level the rate rises progressively to about one-third of a person's earnings.
See also: Internal Revenue Service; Taxation.

Incubation, method of keeping microorganisms such as bacteria or viruses warm and in an appropriate medium to promote their growth (e.g., in identification of the organisms causing disease); also, period during which an organism is present in the body before causing disease. Infectious disease is contracted from a source of infective microorganisms. Once these have entered the body they divide and spread to different parts, and it may be some time before they cause symptoms due to local or systemic effects. This incubation period may be helpful in diagnosis and in determining length of quarantine periods.

Indentured servant, person bound to labor for a stated period, usually 5 to 7 years. In the 17th and 18th centuries, people often agreed to indenture in return for passage to the American colonies. Others were enticed or kidnapped into indentured service. Convicts were sometimes sentenced and deported to indentured labor. With the use of slave labor, the practice of indenture disappeared.

Independence (pop. 111,806), city in Missouri, seat of Jackson County. Located about 10 mi (16 km) east of Kansas City, Independence is largely a residential suburb. Its industries include oil refining and the manufacture of cement, plastics, and farm machinery. Founded in 1827, it was the site of a Mormon colony from 1831 to 1834, and is now the headquarters of the Reorganized Church of Jesus Christ of Latter-Day Saints. The home of former President Harry S. Truman, it is the site of the Harry S. Truman Library.
See also: Missouri.

Independence, Declaration of *See:* Declaration of Independence.

Independence, War for *See:* Revolutionary War in America.

Independence Day, or Fourth of July, the principal nonreligious holiday in the United States. It commemorates the signing of the Declaration of Independence (July 4, 1776).
See also: Declaration of Independence.

Independence Hall, old state house of Philadelphia, Pa., where the Declaration of Independence was proclaimed and the Constitutional Convention of 1787 met. It now houses the Liberty Bell and a small museum.
See also: Declaration of Independence.

Index, reference list of the topics, subjects, or names in a printed work and where they may be found. There are 2 types of indexes: alphabetical, in which the entries are listed from A to Z, and analytical, in which subtopics are listed under major subject headings.

Index of Forbidden Books (*Index Librorum Prohibitorum*), official list of books banned by the Roman Catholic Church as being in doctrinal or moral error. A book could be removed from the index by expurgation of offending passages, and special permission could be given to read prohibited books. The index ceased publication in 1966.

India

Capital:	New Delhi
Area:	1,269,219 sq mi (3,287,263 sq km)
Population:	984,004,000
Language:	Hindi
Government:	Federal republic
Independent:	1947
Head of gov.:	Prime minister
Per capita:	U.S. $340
Mon. unit:	1 Indian rupee = 100 paisa

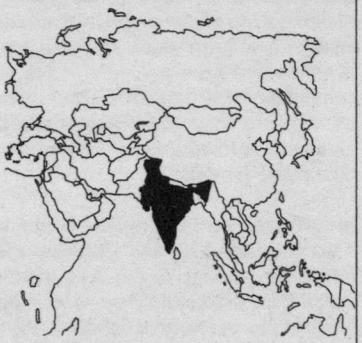

India, union of 25 states and 7 territories, the world's seventh-largest country, occupying most of the Indian subcontinent, the land mass of south central Asia that tapers southward from the Himalayan mountain system to Cape Comorin and Sri Lanka. India shares the subcontinent with Pakistan, Bangladesh, and the Himalayan states of Nepal, and Bhutan, with Sri Lanka off its coast. Only the People's Republic of China has a greater population than India.

Land and climate. The chief geographical regions of North India are the Thar Desert along the Pakistan border, the mountain valleys of Kashmir (disputed with Pakistan), the fertile plains of the Ganges and Brahmaputra rivers, and the Himalaya Mountains, which shield India from the cold winter winds of central Asia. The Deccan plateau, bordered by the western and eastern Ghats mountain ranges, occupies most of South India. The rich volcanic soil is used mainly for cotton growing, though there are also important mineral deposits. Most of the country has a tropical monsoon climate, temperatures reaching 120°F (48.8°C) in the hot season on the northern plains and, in the cool seasons, falling below freezing in the mountains. The monsoon rains are especially heavy on the western Ghats and in northeast India; some places average more than 426 in (1,082 cm) of rain a year.

People. The majority of the population lives in small villages, though the towns are growing fast. The chief cities are the seaports of Bombay, Calcutta, and Madras and the capital, New Delhi. The dominant religion is Hinduism, which, through its caste system, profoundly affects the nation's social structures. Islam, Christianity, Buddhism, Sikhism, and Jainism are also found. Education is free for ages 6-14.

Economy. Two-thirds of the labor force is engaged in agriculture. Rice, beans, peas, tea, sugarcane, jute, pepper, and timber are the main agricultural products. Output remains relatively low overall. Improvements are being sought by irrigation, land reclamation projects, and the introduction of improved strains of crops and fertilizers. About 45% of the industrial labor force works in the jute, cotton, and other textile mills. Mineral resources include oil, iron ore, coal, natural gas, copper, bauxite, and mica but are poorly exploited.

History. The Indus Valley civilization, in modern Pakistan, was the first great culture on the subcontinent. It succumbed in 1500 B.C. to Aryan peoples invading through the northwestern mountain passes; they brought the Sanskrit language and Hinduism to India. The Maurya Empire and Gupta dynasties represented high points of Buddhist and Hindu rule, but India was never united, and from the 10th century Muslim invaders added to the conflicts. In the 14th century the Delhi Muslim sultanate and the Hindu kingdom of Vijayanagar in the south were dominant. In the 1520s the Muslim empire of the Moguls was founded. Europeans also began to exert influence in the Indian subcontinent. In 1510 the Portuguese took Goa, and soon the Dutch, British, and French were vying for Indian trade. In the 18th century English and French interests contested for control of the moribund empire. Victory went to the British East India Company. After the Sepoy Rebellion (1857-58), the British government took over rule of much of the country, and the remaining independent princes, both Muslim and Hindu, recognized British primacy. In 1885 the Indian National Congress Party was set up; under Mohandas Gandhi and Jawaharlal Nehru it led the movement for independence. Muhammad Ali Jinnah led the Muslim League, urging partition into India and Pakistan on religious grounds. Many thousands died in fierce communal riots following partition in 1947.India achieved sovereign status in 1948. The constitution (1949) provided for a bicameral, democratically elected parliament and a cabinet government, with a prime minister and a president. Domestic politics has been concerned with the problem of food supply, the drive toward industrialization, the mitigation of the worst injustices of the caste system, and, since the late 1960s, tension between the central and provincial governments. The dispute with Pakistan over Kashmir flared into war in 1965. A frontier war in 1962 also emphasized the strained relations between India and China. Sikkim became an Indian state in 1975, the same year Indira Gandhi, Nehru's daughter and successor as prime minister, was convicted of election irregularities. She declared a state of emergency, jailed her opponents, and began to rule by decree. Her party was defeated in the general election in 1977. The new government dismantled the state of emergency, but the coalition that had defeated Mrs. Gandhi began to disintegrate, and in 1980 she again became prime minister. In 1984, after she had ordered attacks on Sikh separatists that left more than 1,000 Sikhs dead, she was assassinated by Sikhs in her bodyguard. Her son, Rajiv Gandhi, became her successor and prime minister (1984-89). In 1991, he was murdered while campaigning for his re-election. Gandhi was succeeded by P.V. Narasimha Rao. In 1998 India carried out several nuclear tests, which increased tensions between India and Pakistan.

Indiana, state of the north-central United States; bordered by Michigan and Lake Michigan (north), Ohio (east), Kentucky (south), and Illinois (west).
Land and climate. Indiana's Great Lakes Plains are characterized by rich, black soils and many small lakes, the result of Ice Age glaciers. Along the state's Lake Michigan shorelines lie great sand dunes. The Till Plains of central Indiana are a part of the Midwestern Corn Belt. The southern third of the state, not reached by the glaciers, is marked by gorges and steep hills called knobs. The Wabash River and its many tributaries drain about two-thirds of the state. Indiana has a humid, continental climate, with warm summers and cold winters. Principal cities are Indianapolis, Fort Wayne, and Gary.
Economy. Steel and other metal production are Indiana's principal industries. Other industries produce transportation and electrical equipment and

Indiana

Capital:	Indianapolis
Statehood:	Dec. 11, 1816 (19th state)
Familiar name:	Hoosier State
Area:	36,185 sq mi (93,720 sq km; ranks 38th)
Population:	5,864,000 (1997; ranks 14th)
Elevation:	Highest—1,257 ft (383 m), WayneCounty
	Lowest—320 ft (98 m), Ohio River
Motto:	The Crossroads of America
State flower:	Peony
State bird:	Cardinal
State tree:	Tulip (poplar)
State song:	"On the Banks of the Wabash, Far Away"

chemicals. About three-quarters of Indiana is covered by farmland. The state is a leading producer of corn, soybeans, and hogs. Bituminous coal is the state's most important mineral, and about two-thirds of the nation's limestone comes from Indiana.

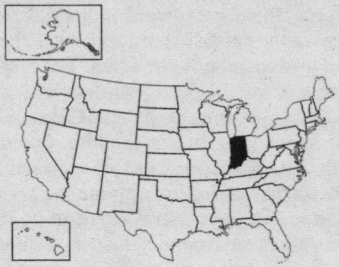

Government. Indiana is governed by the constitution of 1851. The governor serves a 4-year term. The General Assembly is composed of 50 senators serving 4-year terms and 100 representatives serving 2-year terms. Indiana sends 10 representatives and 2 senators to the U.S. Congress.

History. Indiana's earliest known inhabitants were the prehistoric Mound Builders. The area was occupied mainly by the Miami tribe when French fur traders explored it in the 17th century. After the French and Indian Wars, the area passed to the British (1763) and, after the American Revolution, to the United States. The region became part of the Northwest Territory in 1787, and in 1800 the Indiana Territory was created. Native American resistance to European American settlement ended after the battles of Fallen Timbers (1794) and Tippecanoe (1811). Indiana's automobile and steel industries grew rapidly during the late 19th and 20th centuries, but in recent years the state has been hard hit by the general decline in industry in the Midwest.

Indian, American *See:* Native Americans.

Indian Affairs, Bureau of, U.S. federal agency, part of the Department of the Interior, set up in 1824 to safeguard the welfare of Native Americans. It acts as trustee for tribal lands and funds, supervises the reservations, and provides welfare and educational facilities.

Indianapolis (pop. 746,500), capital and largest city of Indiana, located near the center of the state. The city is one of the largest in the world not situated

on a navigable waterway. This deficiency made its growth slow from around 1819, when the first settlers arrived, until 1847, when the first railroad reached the town. Additional railroads and roads made it a leading transport terminus. Modern Indianapolis contains the state's main airport (Weir Cook), and is a vital highway center, actually chosen to be the junction of more interstate highways than any other U.S. city. The capital is the marketing and distribution center for much of Indiana's agriculture and industry. Its major industries include transportation equipment, chemicals, and electrical machinery. Others are livestock sales, printing and publishing, and telephones and hardware. Just outside the city is the famous Indianapolis Speedway, site of the yearly Memorial Day 500-mi (800-km) race.
See also: Indiana.

Indianapolis 500 *See:* Automobile racing.

Indian art and architecture, classical tradition dates from the fall of the Indus Valley civilization (1500 B.C.) and the establishment of the Indo-Aryan culture based on Hinduism. The naturalistic Aryan pantheon assimilated local deities and concepts to produce a complex system, celebrated in the sacred Hindu texts, the Vedas. Statues, paintings, and ornate temples symbolize and embody the gods and their attributes or powers. With the spread of Buddhism under Asoka (d.232 B.C.), the stupa, a round brick- or stone-faced earth mound, containing a relic or tomb and surrounded by a square stone railing, was the favored religious architectural form. Painting and sculpture, notably in the Ajanta caves and the art of Gandhara, portray episodes in the physical and spiritual life of the Buddha. The golden age of Indian culture came during the Gupta dynasty (A.D. 320-500). Resurgent Hinduism soon adapted the Buddhist styles in the classic porch, pillared hall, and cella of the Hindu temple, often surmounted by massive conical spires. In the 13th century southern India perfected the Dravidian pyramidal temple and produced superb bronze sculptures, such as the famous dancing Siva. Indian Muslim art reached its peak under the Moguls.

Indian bean *See:* Catalpa.

Indian Desert *See:* Thar Desert.

Indian fig *See:* Prickly pear.

Indian hemp *See:* Dogbane.

Indian mallow (*Abutilon theophrastii*), weed of the mallow family, a group of dicotyledonous flowering plants. The Indian mallow grows from under 1 ft (30 cm) to over 6 ft (1.8 m) tall, and has orange-yellow flowers. The Indian mallow was given its common name because it originally grew in India, but has also been called *velvet leaf* and *stump weed*, the latter because it was once used to stamp designs onto butter.

Indian Mutiny *See:* Sepoy Rebellion.

Indian Ocean, world's third largest ocean (28,350,000 sq mi/73,426,500 sq km), bounded by Antarctica to the south, Africa to the west, and Australia and Indonesia to the east. The Indian subcontinent divides the northern part of the ocean into 2 great arms, the Arabian Sea to the west and the Bay of Bengal to the east. Largest of its many islands are Madagascar and Sri Lanka.

Indian paintbrush, any of about 200 species (genus *Castilleja*) of wildflower in the figwort or snapdragon family of flowering plants. Also called *painted cup*, the Indian paintbrush gives forth tiny flowers that are mostly green, while its leaves are brightly colored—commonly red, pink, yellow, or lavender. A species (*C. linariaefolia*) of Indian paintbrush is the state flower of Wyoming.

Indian pipe (*Monotropa uniflora*), low, flowering plant of the family Ericaceae. Often mistaken for fungus, which actually serves as food for it, the indian pipe grows in moist woods in eastern Asia and North America. Its scaly stem grows 6 to 10 in (15 to 25 cm) tall. The Indian pipe got its name because it resembles a group of clay pipes.

Indian reservation, land set aside by the U.S. government for use by Native Americans. The first Indian reservation was established for a Delaware Indian tribe in the New Jersey colony in 1758. During the early and middle 19th century, as white settlers claimed more Indian land in the eastern U.S., the government established Indian reservations west of the Mississippi River. In 1823 the Bureau of Indian Affairs, an agency of the Department of the Interior, was formed to oversee affairs on these reservations. Since 1970, when President Nixon called for a new era of Indian self-determination, the tribes have had increased authority over all aspects of their welfare. There are now approximately 285 federal and state Indian reservations, covering 50 million acres in about 30 states.
See also: Native Americans.

Indian root *See:* Spikenard.

Indians *See:* Native Americans.

Indian Territory, region west of Arkansas, into which the Cherokee, Creek, Seminole, Choctaw, and Chickasaw tribes were forcibly moved under the 1830 Indian Removal Act. In 1866 they were penalized for supporting the South in the Civil War by having other tribes resettled in the western part of this territory. Massive white settlement of other portions after 1889 led to disorder and the collapse of tribal government; by 1906 white settlers outnumbered Native Americans six to one, and the territory was incorporated into the state of Oklahoma.

Indian tobacco *See:* Lobelia.

Indian turnip *See:* Jack-in-the-pulpit.

Indian wars, struggle in North America between the Native Americans and European colonizers from the earliest colonial times to the late 19th century. Despite peaceful trade under Powhatan, hostilities between Native Americans and the English settlers of Jamestown, Va., began in 1622, and by 1644 the native tribes had been crushed. In New England, war with the Pequot tribe (1636) resulted in their massacre. With the end of King Philip's War in 1678, Native American resistance in New England was broken. During the Revolutionary War trade regulations were introduced to protect Native Americans from exploitation. Trade and land companies continued to cheat them, however, provoking uprisings. In 1811 an alliance of southern and western tribes under the Shawnee chieftain Tecumseh was defeated at the Tippecanoe River; Tecumseh's death in 1813 ended tribal resistance in this area. The Seminole in Florida, however, continued hostilities until 1816. In 1830 the Indian Removal Act, passed by President Andrew Jackson, authorized the transfer of southeastern tribes to land west of the Mississippi. Native American resistance was met by illegal force; Jackson even ignored a Supreme Court order upholding the land rights of the Cherokees. In 1855 the defeated Nez Percé tribes were given land in the northwestern states, but when gold was found in the area they were again forced to move. Chief Joseph led an unsuccessful revolt against this in 1877. The second half of the 19th century saw the final suppression of the Native Americans. The Navaho, holding the land between the Rio Grande and California, were defeated by Kit Carson in 1863 and transferred to northwestern Arizona. After the Civil War attempts were made to restrict the Apaches, though Cochise and others resisted; their last war chief, Geronimo, surrendered in 1886. In 1871 the government ceased to recognize tribes as independent nations. The Great Plains, home of the Sioux, Apache, and Cheyenne, were subdued in 1870-90 by a combination of military force and the depletion of buffalo herds. The Native American victory at the battle of Little Bighorn only hastened their defeat. Crazy Horse surrendered in 1877, and there was a final massacre at Wounded Knee, S. Dak., in 1890.

Indies *See:* East Indies; West Indies.

Indigo bunting (*Passerina cyanea*), North American songbird of the family Emberizidae, which includes the bunting, finches, grosbeaks, and sparrows. The male bunting of this species has a deep indigo blue head and blackish wings and tail, while the female is brown with darker wings and lighter underparts. Helping farmers by feeding on insects and weed seeds, the indigo bunting ranges from Ontario and New Brunswick to as far south as the Gulf states.

Indium, chemical element, symbol In; for physical constants see Periodic Table. Indium was discovered spectroscopically by Ferdinand Reich and H.T. Richter (1863). The element is most frequently associated with zinc minerals, but is also found in iron, lead, and copper ores. It is prepared as a byproduct in the smelting of zinc. Indium is a silvery-white, soft, low-melting metal. Indium and its compounds are used in making dental alloys, bearing alloys, transistors, solar batteries, and other semiconductor devices.

Indochina, political term for peninsular Southeast Asia between China and India. It was formerly French Indochina, and is now divided into Vietnam, Laos, and Kampuchea (Cambodia). The area contains two densely peopled, rice-rich deltas (Red River in the North, Mekong River in the south), separated by the Annamite mountain chain. Thais, Laos, and Annamese (Vietnamese) settled Indochina from the north. From the second century A.D., many states and cultures affected by India and China rose and fell there, including Funan, the Khmer Empire, Champa, and Annam. European penetration began in the 16th century. France concluded a treaty with Annam in 1787, annexed Cochin China in 1862, and by 1900 had welded separate states into the single political unit of French Indochina. World War II and militant nationalism destroyed France's authority and in 1949 Cambodia and Laos gained independence. The communist Vietminh drove the French out of Vietnam; the United States continued France's anticommunist role in the long Vietnam War, but by 1976 Indochina was effectively under communist control.

Indo-European languages, large family of language spoken throughout most of Europe and much of Asia, and descended from a hypothetical common ancestor, Proto-Indo-European, extant more than 5,000 years ago. There are 2 main branches: the Eastern, with 6 main groups, and Western, with 4. The Eastern branch includes the extinct Anatolian and Tocharian groups, as well as Albanian, Armenian, Balto-Slavic, and Indo-Iranian (with its important sub-group, the Indo-Aryan languages). The Western branch includes Celtic, Greek, Romance or Italic (Latin and the languages derived from it), and Teutonic or Germanic (one of which is English). Until the beginning of the 20th century it was thought that Sanskrit inscriptions represented the oldest written form of any of the family; however, both ancient Hittite and Linear B, which have since been deciphered, are older.

Indonesia, republic of southeast Asia occupying most of the Malay archipelago, the world's largest archipelago, consisting of more than 13,000 islands and islets strung out along the equator from Sumatra facing the Indian Ocean in the west to New Guinea in the east. These were the Indies sought by Christopher Columbus and other explorers. The Moluccas, part of Indonesia, were the Spice Islands of the merchant venturers.
Land and climate. Extending for more than 3,000 mi (4,828 km) from west to east, Indonesia's islands range in size from small deserted reefs to large islands like Sumatra (182,860 sq mi/473,607 sq km), the world's sixth-largest island. About half of New Guinea, the world's second-largest island, and about three-quarters of Borneo, third-largest island, belong to Indonesia. More than 6,000 of Indonesia's islands are inhabited. Many of the islands have luxuriant tropical rain forests containing valuable hardwoods. Although some have areas of low-lying plain or swamp, most are mountainous. Java, Sumatra, and the Little Sunda group have a great line of volcanic peaks. The eruption in 1883 of Krakatoa, in the strait between Java and Sumatra, resulted in the loss of 30,000 lives. There are few large rivers. Rivers flowing into the comparatively shallow South China, Java, and Arafura seas build up deltas, often at a remarkably rapid rate. Coastal scenery ranges from coral reefs, sandy beaches, and mangrove forests to cliffs. Vegetation and wildlife are varied. Some islands, like Java and Borneo, have distinctly Asiatic types, while New Guinea has Australian types, both types being blended in the islands in between. The rain forests contain teak, ebony, and other hardwoods, giant creepers, and shade-loving plants. Along the coasts there are casuarina trees, coconut, and other palms and, where it is muddy, extensive mangrove forests. Wildlife includes elephants, tigers, rhinoceros, orangutans, and, in the eastern islands, pouched animals like the opossum, wallaby, and cuscus. There are many beautiful and brightly colored birds. Snakes and crocodiles abound, but Indonesia's most famous reptile is the Komodo

Indonesia

Capital:	Jakarta
Area:	741,101 sq mi (1,919,443 sq km)
Population:	212,942,000
Language:	Bahasa Indonesia
Government:	Presidential republic
Independent:	1949
Head of gov.:	President
Per capita:	U.S. $980
Mon. unit:	1 Indonesian rupiah = 100 sen

dragon, the giant lizard of the small island of Komodo east of Sumatra. The main islands fall into 3 groups: (1) the Greater Sunda Islands: Java, Sumatra, Indonesian Borneo (Kalimantan), and Celebes (Sulawesi); (2) the Lesser Sunda Islands, including Bali, Flores, Lombok, Sumba, Sumbawa, and Indonesian Timor; (3) the Moluccas (Maluku), including Ambon, Aru Islands, Banda Islands, Buru, Ceram, Halmahera, and the Tanimbor Islands. Including West Irian (formerly Netherlands New Guinea), Indonesia has a total area of more than 741,101 sq mi (1,919,443 sq km). Its most important islands, in terms of population density and economic and cultural activity, are Java, Bali, and Sumatra. Indonesia has a hot, rainy, equatorial climate that is modified by monsoonal winds. From mid-June to Oct. the southeast monsoon brings dry air from Australia. From Nov. to Mar. a north or northeast monsoon blows from mainland Asia across the South China Sea, where it collects much moisture and brings heavy rains. Violent tropical thunderstorms occur almost daily.

People. Two-thirds of the population lives on Java, site of the capital and chief port, Jakarta. The population can be broadly divided into Malays and Papuans, with Chinese, Arabs, and others. Bahasa Indonesia is the official language, but over 250 other languages are spoken. Education is compulsory, and most Indonesians are literate. There are more than 50 universities and technological institutes.

Economy. Some 55% of the population is in farming, producing rice, coconuts, cassava, corn, peanuts, sweet potatoes, spices, and coffee, and raising cattle, goats, hogs, and chickens. The economy rests largely on agriculture, forestry, and fisheries, but mineral resources are being increasingly exploited. Coal, bauxite, copper, manganese, nickel, and precious metals are mined. Indonesia's most important products are oil, its chief export, and tin, of which it is one of the world's major producers. There is some light manufacturing, mostly centered on Java.

History. Hominids lived on Java 1 million years ago. Civilization grew under Indian influence after the 4th century A.D.; several kingdoms flourished from the 12th to 14th centuries. Islam spread swiftly in the 15th century. European impact began in 1511, when the Portuguese captured Malacca. But Portugal eventually kept only East Timor, losing control to the English and Dutch. The Dutch East India Company founded Batavia (Jakarta) in 1619 and dominated the so-called Dutch East Indies until the Netherlands assumed control in 1798. Britain occupied the islands (1811-16) during the Napoleonic Wars, then returned them to the Dutch, who greatly expanded cash-crop exports during the 19th century. Nationalist movements emerged in the early 1900s, and after Indonesia's occupation by Japanese forces in World War II, Sukarno proclaimed Indonesia an independent republic. The Dutch were forced to grant independence in 1949. President Sukarno's dictatorial, anti-Western regime and extravagant spending damaged the economy. General Suharto deposed Sukarno in 1968. He suppressed left-wing groups, severed links with Communist China, and restored relations with the West, seeking to stabilize the economy. In 1975, after Portugal withdrew from East Timor, Indonesian troops invaded, and in 1976 the region was proclaimed a province of Indonesia, a move not recognized by the UN. Popular unrest, caused by economic crisis and a call for democratic reform, led to Sukarno's resignation in 1998. He was succeeded by B.J. Habibie. Large forest fires on Borneo and Sumatra caused heavy smoke production which endangered public health in Indonesia and Malaya (1997-98).

Induction, electric, name of the phenomenon whereby an electrically charged object charges another object without touching it. As distinct from electromagnetic induction, which is the force produced on an electrically charged particle by a changing magnetic field, electric induction is caused by the attraction that opposite electrical charges have for each other (electrostatic attraction). In electric induction if a body is positively charged electrons in the uncharged body will be attracted to it; if the opposite end of the body is then grounded, electrons will flow into it to replace those drawn to the other end. Therefore, the body acquires a negative charge after the ground connection is broken. The Van de Graaff generator, used in nuclear physics experiments, utilizes electric induction.
See also: Van de Graaff generator.

Inductive method, logical process which starts from the particular and goes to the general. For example, a person may experience several rainy days while staying in a particular area and generalize that the area has a rainy climate; it is a method that leads to probabilities, not certainties. Francis Bacon proposed induction as the logic of scientific discovery, but the empirical sciences use both induction and deduction, which involves drawing particular conclusions by reasoning from general premises.
See also: Deductive method.

Indulgence, in the Roman Catholic Church, remission of the temporal punishment (on earth or in purgatory) that remains due for sin even after confession, absolution, and doing penance. In consideration of prayers and good works, the Church may grant plenary (full) or partial indulgences by administering the merits of Jesus and the saints. Sale of indulgences was denounced by the Protestant reformers, and the abuse was abolished by the Council of Trent.
See also: Trent, Council of.

Indus River, river rising in the Himalayas of western Tibet and flowing 1,800 mi (2,900 km) through Kashmir and Pakistan to its 75-mi-(121-km) long delta on the North Arabian Sea. Cradle of the ancient Indus Valley civilization, it is now a source of hydroelectric power and irrigation.

Industrial arts, area of general education that includes automobile mechanics, electronics, graphic arts, industrial crafts, industrial drawing, metalworking, plastics, photography, and woodworking. Also known as *technology education*, industrial arts began as a curriculum area in the U.S. during the late 1800s. Until the 1970s most industrial arts programs enrolled only boys, but today most programs are coeducational. Industrial arts courses may focus on one skill in depth, or several skills in a broader way. Among the goals of industrial arts programs are to teach the use of tools and machines and to encourage creativity.

Industrial design, expression of the special relationship between the artist, the consumer, and the manufacturer in a developed, industrialized society. Its origins lie in the Industrial Revolution of the late 18th century, which began to link mass production with a powerful new form of distribution, the steam train, and with a growing consumer-oriented community. Its full expression is everywhere present—from the mass-produced automobile to the mass-produced ready-to-wear suit. Slowly but certainly, the craftsperson, whose products were based on an individual relationship with the consumer, has all but disappeared.

Industrialism *See:* Industrial Revolution.

Industrial pollution *See:* Environmental pollution.

Industrial relations, conduct of relations between organized labor and management and the relations between individual workers and their supervisors. Wage rates, work conditions, and productivity are among potential sources of conflict between the 2 sides. Unresolved conflicts can result in strikes and lockouts that cut output and profits and thus harm employees and employer alike. In the United States the federal government helps to settle major industrial disputes, the National Labor Relations Board serving as adjudicator. U.S. industrial relations are largely governed by the Wagner Act of 1935 and the Taft-Hartley Act of 1947.

Industrial Revolution, period of rapid transition from an agrarian to an industrial society; specifically, the prototype of such periods, the late 18th and early 19th centuries in the United Kingdom. This period saw Britain transformed from a predominantly agricultural society into the world's first industrial nation. In the 18th century, British imperialism, technology, economic development, and natural resources combined to provide unique opportunities for building business fortunes. The growth of capitalism developed the factory system to harness new inventions that cheaply mass-produced textiles to exploit the expanding world market for British cloth. Key inventions in textile production included John Kay's flying shuttle (c.1733), James Hargreaves's spinning jenny (c.1764), Richard Arkwright's water frame (1769), and Edmund Cartwright's powered loom (1785). In 1709 Abraham Darby had learned to smelt iron with coke; in 1781, James Watt patented a steam engine producing rotary motion. Soon many factories were using steam-powered iron machinery. Canals and, from the 1830s, railroads and steamships provided a transportation network linking new industrial cities with sources of supply and markets. The urban masses were supported by increasingly efficient agriculture, due to scientific advances and the stimulus to self-sufficiency of the Napoleonic Wars. Largely through improvements in food supply, sanitation, and medicine Britain's population rose from under 7 million in 1750 to over 20 million in 1850, creating an increased labor force while escalating consumer demand. Factory workers endured appalling working and living conditions before legislation brought improvements. The wealth they had created, however, made possible a more general prosperity.

Industrial Workers of the World (IWW), U.S. labor organization, founded in 1905 by revolutionary socialists to radicalize the labor movement. It reached its greatest influence 1912-17, and at its peak it had almost 100,000 members. Unlike the American Federation of Labor (AFL), it aimed not at improving labor conditions but at revolution. It lost support by attempting to exploit World War I; its strikes were considered treasonable. IWW leaders were imprisoned and the movement almost wholly suppressed.
See also: Labor movement.

Indus Valley civilization, centered around the Indus River in India and Pakistan, the earliest known urban culture of the Indian subcontinent. Superimposed on earlier stone- and bronze-using cultures dating from 4000 B.C., the Indus Valley civilization, with its main cities Harappa and Mohenjo-Daro, lasted from 2500 to 1750 B.C. About 100 of its towns and villages, some with citadels, have been identified.
See also: Indus River.

Inert gas *See:* Noble gas.

Inertia, in physics, tendency of a body to persist in its state of rest or motion. The term is sometimes used in psychology to describe latency or resistance to change.
See also: Newton, Sir Isaac.

Inertial guidance, method by which a vehicle is guided without contact with a ground base. Used primarily to guide missiles, airplanes, and submarines, inertial guidance provides navigation information through use of an *inertial navigator*. This device consists of a *gyroscope*, which indicates direction, and an *accelerometer*, which measures changes in speed and direction. Then a computer processes this information to calculate the vehicle's position and guide it. The inertial guidance system is based upon the ancient navigational technique by which speed and direction were used to calculate a vehicle's direction.
See also: Navigation.

Infant *See:* Baby.

Infantry, body of soldiers who fight on foot using light weaponry, such as rifles, machine guns, bazookas, mortars, and grenades. Despite the mechanization of warfare, infantry units still form the largest combat branch of most armies. In the U.S. army an infantry division consists of about 15,000

infantry members and normally includes 8 armored battalions equipped with tanks and heavy weapons.
See also: Army.

Infection, state or condition in which the body or a part of it is invaded by a pathogenic (disease-causing) microorganism or virus that, under favorable conditions, multiplies and produces effects that are injurious. Localized infection is usually accompanied by inflammation, but inflammation may occur without infection.
The 5 classical symptoms of infection listed by early medical writers are: (1) *dolor*—pain; (2) *calor*—heat; (3) *rubor*—redness; (4) *tumor*—swelling; (5) *functio laesa*—disordered function.
Pain is especially prominent when the infection is confined within closed cavities and is in proportion to the virulence and extent of the infection. Redness and swelling are not evident when infection is within some rigid tissue or deep within some cavity; they are more apparent when superficial structures are involved. In fact, "discoloration" would be a better term than "redness," for the color is more blue, or purple in advanced infections, while tuberculosis infections have long been called "white swellings." Heat may be evident on the surface, but there may be considerable elevation of body temperature even with small infections. "Disordered function" depends upon the part affected as well as upon the virulence. With almost all acute infections, there is either an absolute or relative increase of polymorphonuclear leukocytes in the blood.

Infertility, inability or diminished ability to produce offspring. Infertility affects about 15% of couples in the United States and the United Kingdom. Male fertility depends on adequate production of sperm by the testicles, unobstructed transit of sperm through the seminal tract, and satisfactory depositing of it within the vagina. Causes of impaired spermatogenesis include certain environmental poisons, undescended testicles, injury- or infection-related testicular atrophy, drug effects, prolonged fever, and endocrine disorders. Obstruction of the seminal tract may result from congenital defects and from inflammation of the testicles, epididymis, vas deferens, and prostate gland, and seminal surgical division of both vasa deferens (vasectomy). Defective delivery of sperm into the vagina may result from surgery of the bladder neck, removal of the prostate gland, hypospadias, premature ejaculation, functional or organic impotence, or structural abnormalities of the female genital tract.
Female infertility first of all depends on the ability to develop ova (eggs) in the ovaries. These eggs must be able to leave the ovaries and travel into and down the fallopian tubes. For sperm to be able to reach them, the structure of the vagina, cervix, and the main body of the uterus must not impair them, and the mucus surrounding the cervix must be abundant, clear, and elastic. The fallopian tubes must be clear, from the uterus up to the place where the sperm meet the eggs. In addition, after conception has occurred, the lining (endometrium) of the uterus must be able to take the implantation of the fertilized egg; otherwise, there will be an early miscarriage. Infertility in women can result from disease, disturbance, or deformity of any of these structures or functions. The most common reason for infertility is hormonal imbalance that affects the woman's ability to produce viable eggs or the type of cervical mucus that she produces. The fallopian tubes can become blocked

by scars due to inflammation. There also may be some abnormality of the vulva, cervix, or uterus.
See also: Reproduction.

Infinity (∞), quantity greater than any finite quantity. In modern mathematics infinity is viewed in 2 ways. In one, the word has a definite meaning; and with transfinite cardinal numbers, for example, it may have a plurality of meanings. In the other, infinity is seen as a limit: to say that parallel lines intersect at infinity, for example, means merely that the point of intersection of 2 lines may be made to recede indefinitely by making the lines more and more nearly parallel. Similarly, in $f(x)=1/x$ it is meaningful to say that $f(x)$ tends to infinity as x tends to zero; again, the sequence $1,2,3,....n$ tends to infinity because, however large n is chosen, there is an $(n+1)$ greater than it. In advanced set theory an infinite set is defined as one whose elements can be put in a one-to-one correspondence with those of a proper subset of the set (i.e., a subset that is not the whole set).
See also: Set theory.

Inflation, in economics, decline in the value of money, which implies a general increase in the prices of commodities and services. Deflation means the opposite—generally falling prices, usually accompanied by lower profits and fewer jobs. Times of mild inflation are usually characterized by high employment, with factories producing near their capacities to capture the increased amount of currency available. Once full employment has been reached and factories begin operating at or near capacity, however, additional increases in national spending drive prices higher at a rapidly increasing rate. The reason for this is that a relatively static amount of goods and services is being "chased" by an increased number of dollars. Further increases in spending or shortages in goods and services lead to rapid inflation. Industries raise prices because their costs are going up. In turn, labor asks for higher wages to offset the increase in the cost of living. Extreme inflation can lead to major disruption in the social order. People buy property, stock, or commodities, expecting a rapid increase in value. Prices can rise out of proportion to real value. In the United States, inflation averaged less than 1% yearly during the 1950s and about 3% in the 1960s. Since then, inflation has been considerably greater, averaging over 6% for 1970-77, with periods of double-digit (10% or greater) inflation at the end of the decade and into the 1980s. Government attempts to limit the impact of runaway inflation through monetary and fiscal policies, as well as "jawboning," that is, making public speeches to apply political pressure to corporations and labor unions to act in the public interest. Similar tactics, as well as the limited power of the presidential veto, can be used against congressional spending proposals that are deemed inflationary.
See also: Economics.

Inflection, in grammar, changes in form that words undergo with each change in grammatical function. For example, the English verb *write* becomes *writes* in the third person singular of the present tense. *Write* has 3 additional forms: *wrote*, *written*, and *writing*. This set of inflections for a verb is called *conjugation*. The set of inflections for a noun or pronoun is called *declension*. For example, the English noun *dog* has 4 forms: *dog*, *dogs*, *dog's*, and *dogs'*.
See also: Grammar.

Inflorescence, arrangement of flowers on the stem of a plant. Tulips and anemones, among other plants, carry single flowers at the tops of their stems. Most plants, however, carry their flowers in clusters called *inflorescences*. This is especially true of those species whose individual flowers are small. The inflorescence is thought to be more attractive to pollinating insects than a single flower would be. The commonest type of inflorescence is the *raceme*, in which numerous flowers are borne on one or more sides of the main stem. The oldest flowers are always at the bottom. The individual flowers normally have short stalks. If they are stalkless the inflorescence is often called a *spike*. The foxglove is a typical raceme. In the *corymb* the individual flower stalks on the lower part of the stem are longer than those higher up. The result is that all the flowers are brought to more or less the same level and make a conspicuous display. In the *umbel*, which looks similar to the corymb, the main stem stops growing after a while and all the flower stalks come from one point. The oldest flowers are on the outside. Umbels are characteristic of the carrot family. The *cyme* is an inflorescence in which the main stem produces only 1 or 2 side shoots before ending in a flower. Each of the side shoots then does the same. Where 2 branches are formed each time, there is a continued forking of the stem, with a flower in the center of each fork. There are several other kinds of inflorescence. The dandelion or daisy head, for example, is a very condensed inflorescence called a *capitulum*. Very often the flowering shoot will produce several branches, and each branch may then form a raceme, a corymb, or an umbel. Branched inflorescences of this kind are called *panicles*.

Influenza, specific acute respiratory disease caused by viruses and characterized by fever, head cold, cough, headache, malaise, and inflamed mucous membranes of the respiratory tract. It usually occurs as an epidemic in the winter. Hemorrhage, bronchitis, pneumonia, and sometimes death occur in severe cases. Acute epidemics occur about every 3 years. Persons at high risk of developing severe diseases are those with chronic lung disease, heart valve disease, or congestive heart failure; pregnant women in the third trimester; and elderly persons who are confined to bed. The antiviral drug amantadine has a beneficial effect on fever and respiratory symptoms if given early in uncomplicated influenza. It is of no benefit when the illness is complicated with pneumonia, but might improve recovery from a lung infection. The basic treatment otherwise is the relief of symptoms. Aspirin, paracetamol, and other drugs to lower the temperature and relieve pain are helpful. Vaccines that include the prevalent strains of influenza viruses have a 60% chance of reducing the incidence of infection for 1 to 2 years after vaccination. The immunity is less when the virus changes appreciably (antigenic drift) and when a major viral mutation occurs (antigenic shift). No significant protection is afforded unless the new strain is incorporated into the vaccine. Vaccination is especially important for the aged and for those with heart, lung, or other chronic diseases.

Information Agency, U.S. (USIA), independent, U.S. government agency that conducts international communication, education, cultural, and exchange programs to foster understanding between the citizens of the United States and those of other nations. It performs a variety of communication activities, using academic and cultural exhibits, newspapers, and films. Founded in 1953 and headquartered in Washington, D.C., the USIA brings worldwide leaders in politics, social welfare, and other fields to meet with their colleagues in the United States.

Information theory, or communication theory, mathematical discipline that aims to maximize the information that can be conveyed by communications systems and minimize the errors that arise in the course of transmission. The information content of a message is conventionally quantified in terms of bits (binary digits). Each bit represents a simple alternative: in terms of a message, a yes or no; in terms of the components in an electrical circuit, that a switch is open or closed. Mathematically the bit is usually represented as 0 or 1. Complex messages can be represented as a series of bit alternatives. Five bits of information only are needed to specify any letter of the alphabet, given an appropriate code. Thus able to quantify information, the theory employs statistical methods to analyze practical communications problems. The errors that arise in the transmission of signals, often termed *noise*, can be minimized by the incorporation of redundancy, wherein more bits of information than are strictly necessary to encode a message are transmitted so that if some are altered in transmission there is still enough information to allow the signal to be correctly interpreted. The handling of redundant information costs something in reduced speed of or capacity for transmission, but the reduction in message errors compensates for this loss. Information theoreticians often point to an analogy between the thermodynamic concept of entropy and the degree of misinformation in a signal.
See also: Mathematics.

Infrared rays, rays resembling light rays, but undetectable by the human eye. Also called *heat rays*, infrared rays are given off by objects in relation to their temperature. Emission of infrared rays increases as an object gets hotter. The British astronomer Sir William Herschel discovered infrared rays in 1800 by observing the effect of the heat they produced. The *sniperscope* is an instrument that perceives infrared rays from objects that are warmer than their surroundings. The military utilizes infrared radiation and the sniperscope in missile detection, guidance systems, and night-vision apparatus.
See also: Electromagnetic waves.

Inge, William (1913-73), U.S. playwright. He was noted for psychological studies of life in small Midwestern towns, in such plays as *Come Back, Little Sheba* (1950), *Picnic* (1953), which won a Pulitzer Prize, *Bus Stop* (1955), and *A Loss of Roses* (1959).

Ingres, Jean Auguste Dominique (1780-1867), French neoclassical painter. He is known for his mastery of line and superb draftsmanship. *The Vow of Louis XII* (1824) won him acclaim as the foremost classicist of his time, but today he is better known for portraits and nude studies such as the *Odalisque* (1814). A disciple of Raphael, he was a determined opponent of the romantic movement and an inspiration to many later artists, including Edgar Degas, Pierre-Auguste Renoir, and Pablo Picasso.

Inheritance tax, assessment on property bequeathed by a deceased person to a specific legatee. It thus differs from an estate tax, levied on a deceased person's estate as a whole. In the United States most states levy both estate

and inheritance taxes; since 1916 the federal government has levied only an estate tax.
See also: Taxation.

Inititive, referendum, and recall, methods by which voters may directly intervene to influence government policy between elections. Initiative, provided for in most U.S. states, is a procedure whereby a new law is proposed in a petition, then submitted to a vote by the legislature or electorate or both. Laws so passed are generally not subject to veto. Referendum allows citizens a direct vote on proposed laws and policies. A referendum may be demanded by petition, but in most U.S. states it is mandatory for measures such as constitutional amendments and bond issues. Recall, adopted by many cities and some states, provides for the removal of an elected official by calling a special election. Such an election must usually be demanded in a petition whose signers number at least 25% of the votes originally received by the official. Recall has rarely succeeded at state level.

Injunction, formal written court order commanding or prohibiting any act. An injunction may be temporary, pending the outcome of a court action, or permanent, if the court's decision confirms the injunction's validity. Such writs are widely applied to prevent, for example, the misuse of property; the wrongful denial of, or cancellation of membership in, a union or other organization; the infringement of copyrights or patents; violent action in labor-management disputes; or the removal of a child from the care of a parent. Violation of an injunction is punishable as contempt of court. In Topeka, Kans., in 1954, an injunction forbade the exclusion of a black student from a segregated school.

Ink, liquid or paste used for writing or printing. Writing inks were used as early as c.2500 B.C. by Egyptians and Chinese, who created ink from natural materials such as berries, bark, linseed oil, and soot. Today, there are thousands of kinds of inks, used both in the printing industry and in ballpoint and fountain pens for writing. Most printing inks contain pigments, as opposed to dyes. Vehicles, which carry the pigment and help bind it to the paper, vary greatly in printing. Thick, sticky inks are used in the printing of books and magazines, and many contain *driers* to speed up the chemical reaction of oxidation and help the ink dry faster. Most writing ink consists of dyes and resins dissolved in a solvent, such as water and *glycol*, an alcohol.

Inness, George (1825-94), U.S. landscape painter. His best-known works, such as *The Lackawanna Valley* (1855), show the influence of Jean-Baptiste Camille Corot and the Barbizon school. Another principal work is *June* (1882). His later work, such as *The Home of the Heron* (1893), is less realistic and more atmospheric.

Innocence *See:* Bluet.

Innocent, name of 13 popes. **Saint Innocent I** (d.417) was pope from 401. He championed papal supremacy, but failed to prevent the sack of Rome by Alaric in 410. **Innocent II** (Gregorio Papareschi; d.1143) was pope from 1130. He convened the Second Lateral Council (1139). **Innocent III** (Giovanni Lotario de'Conti; 1161-1216) was pope from 1198. Under him the medieval papacy reached the summit of its power and influence. In an assertion of temporal power he forced King John of England to become his vassal and had Holy Roman Emperor Otto deposed in favor of Frederick II. He initiated the Fourth Crusade (1202) and supported the crusade against the Albigenses (1208). He presided over the Fourth Lateran Council (1215), the culmination of the entire medieval papacy. **Innocent IV** (Sinibaldo de'Fieschi; c.1190-1254), pope from 1243, clashed with Emperor Frederick II over the temporal power of the papacy, and was forced to flee to Lyons, France, until Frederick's death. He worked for the unification of the Christian churches. **Innocent VIII** (Giovanni Battista Cibo; 1432-92), pope from 1484, was worldly and unscrupulous. He fomented the witchcraft hysteria and meddled in Italian politics. For a fee he kept the brother and rival of Sultan Bayazid II imprisoned. **Innocent XI** (Benedetto Odescalchi; 1611-89) was pope from 1676. An opponent of quietism, he favored toleration of Protestantism, and over this and the issue of papal power clashed with Louis XIV of France. **Innocent XII** (Antonio Pignatelli; 1615-1700) was pope from 1691. A stern reformer, he abolished nepotism and was renowned for his piety and charity. **Innocent XIII** (Michelangelo Conti; 1655-1724) was pope from 1721. He bestowed Naples and Sicily on their de facto possessor, the Emperor Charles VI, and recognized the claims of James, the Old Pretender, to the British throne in the hope of a Catholic revival.

Innsbruck (pop. 118,100), capital of the Austrian Tyrol province, located on the Inn River, at an altitude of 1,880 ft (573 m) between steep Alpine ranges. Innsbruck became a prosperous town mainly because of its position near the Brenner Pass. Modern manufactures include textiles, chemicals, metal goods, and mosaics. There are many notable medieval castles in the city, including the 15th-century castle Fürstenburg. Innsbruck University was founded in the 17th century. The city is noted for the scenic beauty of its surroundings and is a popular tourist center in both winter and summer.
See also: Austria.

Inoculation, introduction of a germ, a poison produced by a germ, or serum into the body to set up the production of antibodies that will subsequently protect the individual from an attack of the disease, rendering the individual immune.
See also: Immunization.

Inouye, Daniel Ken (1924-), U.S. senator from Hawaii (1962-). A member of the Watergate committee (1972-74), Inouye was chairman of the 1987 congressional committee that investigated the Iran-Contra Affair.

Input-output analysis, method of studying the relationship between various parts of the economy, developed by U.S. economist Wassily Leontif. It relies upon the use of complex numerical tables.
See also: Economics.

Inquest, formal legal inquiry to ascertain a fact. It is most commonly used to investigate death under circumstances where violence is suspected. The coroner, or in some cases a medical examiner, invites the jury to view the body. Then, depending on the evidence presented, the jury decides whether to order a post-mortem examination. It may recommend that a suspect be detained for trial. Inquests are also held to determine damages in cases where the defendant has not appeared in court. The institution is rooted in early English law.

Inquisition, medieval agency of the Roman Catholic Church to combat heresy, first made official in 1231 when Pope Gregory IX appointed a commission of Dominicans to investigate heresy among the Albigensians of southern France. It aimed to save the heretic's soul, but a refusal to recant was punished by fines, penance, or imprisonment, and often by confiscation of land by the secular authorities. Later the penalty was death by burning. Torture, condemned by the former popes, was permitted in heresy trials by Innocent IV (d. 1254). The accused were not told the name of their accusers but could name their known enemies so that hostile testimony might be discounted. Often the Inquisition was subject to political manipulation. In 1524 it was reconstituted to counter Protestantism in Italy; its modern descendant is the Congregation of the Doctrine of the Faith.
The Spanish Inquisition, founded in 1478 by Ferdinand and Isabella, was a branch of government and was distinct from the papal institution. Its first commission was to investigate Jews and Muslims who had publicly embraced Christianity but secretly held to Judaism or Islam. Under the grand inquisitor Torquemada, it became an agency of official terror—even St. Ignatius Loyola was investigated. It was extended to Portugal and South America and not dissolved until 1820.
In January 1998 the archives of the papal Inquisition, until 1902, were made accessible to researchers.
See also: Torquemada, Tomás de.

Insect, member of the class Insecta, phylum Arthropoda, or invertebrate animals with jointed legs. There are about 750,000 known species of insects, and more are being discovered every year.
Anatomy. The body of an insect, like that of other arthropods, is covered by a hard, waterproof "shell" that forms an external skeleton to which the muscles are attached. The head bears jaws and other structures for dealing with food. It also carries several sense organs, including the compound eyes made up of clusters of separate units. The antennae, or feelers, are organs of touch, smell, and occasionally of hearing. Sense organs are also found on other parts of the body: Grasshoppers and crickets have ears on the legs or thorax, and houseflies have tastebuds on their feet. The middle section, or thorax, bears the limbs. It consists of 3 parts, each of which carries a pair of jointed legs ending in hooks that allow the insect to hang on walls or ceilings. Two pairs of wings sprout from the back of the thorax. Some insects have no wings, and the flies have turned one pair into balancing organs. The abdomen is the largest section of the body and has no visible external organs except those concerned with reproduction and occasionally a pair of short sense organs, such as antennae called cerci (for example, in earwigs). Insects do not have a closed system of blood vessels. The heart simply pumps blood through the arteries to the extremities, where it washes around the organs and slowly drains back to the heart. Nor do insects have lungs. Air is carried into the body down minute tubes, called tracheae, which run from openings in the skin into each organ.

Life cycles. Most insects lay eggs, but some give birth to live young. The mother usually abandons her eggs, but the social insects, including bees and wasps, have elaborate systems of caring for their young. The eggs hatch into larvae, such as the maggots of flies, the caterpillars of butterflies and moths, and the nymphs of dragonflies. The development into an adult insect is accomplished in one of two ways. (1) Incomplete metamorphosis: In dragonflies, grasshoppers, and others, the newly hatched larva looks rather like the adult. It molts several times, shedding its skin each time and growing a little larger. Adult features such as wings become more apparent at each molt until, at the final molt, the adult insect crawls out of the old skin. (2) Complete metamorphosis: The larva is very different from the adult. After growing for some time, it changes into the adult in one drastic step. To do this it forms a pupa or chrysalis in which it can reorganize its structure. In this way a sausage-shaped caterpillar turns into a butterfly. A single insect is able to exploit 2 very different ways of life. Thus a caterpillar feeds on leaves and a butterfly drinks nectar.
Habitat. Insects vary in size from almost microscopic wasps to the huge extinct dragonflies with wingspans of over 2 ft (61 cm). They live in many different environments, boring into wood, burrowing underground, living in other animals, and swimming underwater. They are found in the hottest deserts, on the coasts of Antarctica, in hot springs, and in the saltiest lakes (such as Salt Lake, Utah); the petroleum fly lives in pools of crude petroleum oil in California. They may also exist in huge numbers. Locust swarms may contain 1 billion individuals, and springtails form dense carpets on the ground.

Insecticide, any substance toxic to insects and used to control them in situations where they cause economic damage or endanger the health of humans and their domestic animals. There are 3 main types: stomach insecticides, which are ingested by the insects with their food; contact insecticides, which penetrate the cuticle (exterior covering); and fumigant insecticides, which are inhaled. Stomach insecticides are often used to control chewing insects like caterpillars and sucking insects like aphids. They may be applied to a plant prior to attack and remain active in or on the plant for a considerable time. They must be used with considerable caution on food plants or animal forage. Examples include arsenic compounds, which remain on the leaf, and organic compounds, which are absorbed by the plant and transported to all its parts (systemic insecticides). Contact insecticides include the plant products nicotine, derris, and pyrethrum, which are quickly broken down, and synthetic compounds such as DDT (and other chlorinated hydrocarbons), organophosphates (malathion, parathion), and carbamates. Polychlorinated biphenyls (PCBs) are added to some insecticides to increase their effectiveness and persistence. Highly persistent insecticides may be concentrated in food chains and exert harmful effects on other animals such as birds and fish.
See also: Insect.

Insectivore, order (Insectivora) of small insect-eating mammals, regarded as the most primitive group of placental mammals, having diverged little from the ancestral form. The skull is generally long and narrow, with a primitively large complement of unspecialized teeth in the jaw. Ears and eyes are small and often hidden in fur or skin. The group includes shrews, hedgehogs, and moles.

Insectivorous plant *See:* Carnivorous plant.

Installment plan, system of credit by which merchandise is paid for over a fixed period of time in installments known as deferred payments. Normally, part of the purchase price must be paid at the time of the sale. Goods generally bought using an installment plan are automobiles, farm machinery, and homes.

Instinct, in biology and psychology, behaviors in reaction to external stimuli that have not been consciously learned. It is in fact difficult to separate such inherited genetic behaviors from those stemming from learned and environmental factors, since higher animals placed from birth in artificial environments display some, but not all, instinctive reactions characteristic of their species. It has been further suggested that embryos may have some learning ability—that is, that some learning before birth is possible. Numbered among the instincts are the sex drive, aggression, territoriality, and the food urge, but much debate surrounds such classification. In psychology, "instinct" (sometimes called "drive") is studied particularly with regard to the frustration of or conflict between the existence of two fundamental instincts: the life instinct, akin to the libido, and its opposite, the death instinct.
See also: Biology; Psychology.

Insulation, inhibiting or limiting the conduction of electricity or heat through the use of specific materials. An electric current or voltage is contained by materials (insulators) that offer a high resistance to current flow, will withstand high voltages without breaking down, and will not deteriorate with age. The mechanical properties desired vary with the application: Cables require flexible coatings, such as polyvinyl chloride, while glass or porcelain is used for rigid mountings, such as the insulators used to support power cables. In thermal insulation, there is a reduction of transfer of heat from a hot area to a cold. Thermal insulation is used to keep something hot, to keep something cold, or maintain something at a roughly steady temperature. Heat is transferred through conduction, convection, and radiation. The vacuum bottle thus uses 3 techniques to reduce heat transfers: a vacuum between the walls to combat conduction and convection; silvered walls to minimize the transmission of radiant heat from one wall and maximize its reflection from the other; and supports for the inner bottle made of cork, a poor thermal conductor.

Insulin, protein hormone manufactured in the pancreas by minute areas of tissue called the islets of Langerhans, and then secreted into the blood, where it controls the digestion of carbohydrates. A lack of insulin or a disturbance of its use by the cells is the cause of diabetes.
See also: Diabetes; Hormone.

Insull, Samuel (1859-1938), English-born U.S. financier. Secretary to Thomas Edison in the 1880s, he became head of the Chicago Edison Co. and built a huge conglomerate supplying electricity throughout Illinois and other states. It collapsed in 1932. Later he was tried for fraud and acquitted.

Insurance, method of financial protection by which one party undertakes to indemnify another against certain forms of loss. An insurance company pools the payments for this service and invests them to earn further funds. Each insured person pays a relatively small amount, the premium, for a stated period of coverage. In return the company will, subject to an assessment of a claim, reimburse the insured for loss caused by an event covered in the policy. Forms of insurance have existed since the earliest civilizations. Modern insurance began with the medieval guilds, which sometimes insured members against trade losses. The specialized fields of fire and maritime insurance developed in the 17th and 18th centuries. The development of probability theory allowed the statistical likelihood of damage to be calculated, making insurance as a business possible.

Integrated circuit, combination of interconnected circuit elements and amplifying devices inseparately associated on or within a continuous layer of semiconductor material, called a substrate.

Integration, in U.S. history, right to equal access for people of all races to such facilities as schools, churches, housing, and public accommodations. It became an issue of public importance in the United States after the Civil War and the pasage of the 13th, 14th, and 15th amendments to the Constitution, 1864-70, which declared the African American free and equal, and the Civil Rights Act of 1866. Although slavery was ended as a legal institution, state laws were passed during the reaction against Reconstruction to enforce the physical segregation of blacks and whites.

Tennessee adopted the first "Jim Crow" law in 1875, segregating public transportation. In 1896 the Supreme Court approved "separate but equal" accommodations for blacks, following which segregation laws proliferated. In the North segregation in housing created the black slum ghettos; while less common than in the South, segregation still continued in factories, unions, and restaurants. In 1910 the National Association for the Advancement of Colored People (NAACP) was founded in New York, followed by the National Urban League in 1911. Several activist groups were formed in the 1940s, including the Congress of Racial Equality (CORE).

The NAACP won its greatest legal victories in 1954 and 1955, when the Supreme Court outlawed segregation in the public schools and ordered that integration be implemented "with all deliberate speed." Among black leaders advocating passive resistance to discriminatory local laws was Martin Luther King, Jr. His Southern Christian Leadership Conference and the more radical Student Non-Violent Coordinating Committee exerted political pressure to enact the Civil Rights Act of 1964 and the Voting Rights Act of 1965. Integration was more generally accepted during the 1970s, although serious unrest occurred over busing practices to end school segregation in many cities.

Intelligence, mental ability, including learning ability, problem-solving ability, and the capacity for abstract thinking. There has been much debate as to whether intelligence is inherited or a product of the environment. The fact is that physical constitution may contain developmental potentialities, but the environment decides to what extent and in what ways these potentialities are realized. Heredity and environment interact to such a degree that a clear distinction between their contributions is often impossible.

Intelligence quotient
(IQ), index of intelligence determined through a subject's answers to arbitrarily chosen questions. The IQ is merely a standard score that places an individual in reference to the scores of others within his or her age group. Mental age represents the age level corresponding to the score reached on the test. Thus, if a child 10 years old gives a test score appropriate to that of the average 12year-old child, his or her mental age would be 12 and his or her IQ is 120. This method works reasonably well for younger children but has grave disadvantages when applied to older children or adults. In psychological literature, the following classification is found:

Above 140	"Near" genius or genius
120-140	Very superior intelligence
110-120	Superior intelligence
90-110	Average intelligence
80-90	Dull normal
70-80	Borderline deficiency
50-70	Educable mentally retarded
30-50	Trainable
20-30	Severely mentally retarded

See also: Binet, Alfred.

Intelligence service, institution of a national government that gathers information; particularly about clandestine activities of other countries or enemies, for the purpose of protecting national security. Such functions were once performed chiefly by foreign ambassadors. Under Elizabeth I, England was among the first Western countries to set up an elaborate intelligence service, privately financed by Sir Francis Walsingham. Joseph Fouché established an equally vital network for Napoleonic France. Britain's intelligence service reached its highest point during World War II, with the brilliant amateurs of MI-5.
In the United States, military espionage first assumed great importance during the Civil War, in which it was employed extensively by both sides. During World War I the U.S. intelligence service was organized largely by the Office of Strategic Services (OSS). It was given its present form in 1947 with the creation of the Central Intelligence Agency (CIA).
The CIA, which came under investigation and some censure in the late 1970s, coordinates the intelligence functions of all government departments and agencies. All the armed services have their own intelligence branches.

Intelligence test *See:* Intelligence quotient; Testing.

Inter-American conferences *See:* Pan-American conferences.

Intercontinental ballistic missile *See:* Guided missile.

Interest, money paid for the use of money loaned. It is generally expressed as a percentage of the principal (sum loaned) per period (usually per year or per month). In simple interest, interest is calculated on the basis of the sum loaned. In compound interest, interest is paid on the principal plus the accumulated interest, recalculated periodically. Actual payments for compound interest are thus higher (and more complex to calculate).

Discount interest is subtracted from the principal before the money is given to the borrower.

Interference, in physics, mutual action of waves of any kind upon each other, by which their vibrations and effects are increased, diminished, or neutralized. In information science the term is used to denote the occurence of unwanted signals that degrade the quality of wanted signals.
See also: Physics.

Interferometer, any instrument of measurement employing interference effects of waves. Interferometers are used for measuring the wavelengths of light, radio, sound, or other wave phenomena or the refractive index of gases. Some interferometers measure very small distances using radiation of known wavelength. In acoustics and radio astronomy, they are used for determining the direction of an energy source. In most interferometers the beam of incoming radiation is divided in two, led along paths of different but accurately adjustable lengths, and then recombined to give an interference pattern. Perhaps the best-known optical instrument is the Michelson interferometer devised in 1881. More accurate for wavelength measurements is the Fabry-Perot interferometer, in which the radiation is recombined after multiple partial reflections between parallel, lightly silvered glass plates.
See also: Interference.

Interferon, class of small soluble proteins produced and released by cells invaded by a virus, that inhibits viral multiplication. Interferon production may also be induced by certain bacteria and specifically sensitized lymphocytes. There are indications that interferon may be useful in the treatment of certain types of cancer. A nasal spray containing interferon produced in the laboratory prevented between 78% and 84% of colds caused by rhinoviruses in families participating in 2 independent studies published in January 1986 in the *New England Journal of Medicine*.
See also: Cancer.

Interior, Department of the, department of the executive branch of the federal government, headed by the secretary of the interior. Founded in 1849, its original task was to administer the census and Indian affairs and to regulate the exploitation of natural resources. Today it has 5 major areas of responsibility, each in the charge of an assistant secretary: Fish, Wildlife, Parks, and Marine Resources; Mineral Resources; Water and Power Development; Water Quality and Research; and Public Land Management (which includes the Office of the Territories, and the Bureau of Indian Affairs).

Interior decoration, design and arrangement of decorative elements in a home or public building. Until relatively recently, architectural and interior styles were almost inseparable and the names used to characterize each period applied both to the architecture of buildings and their interior decor.

Interleukin, generic term for a group of proteins, formed in white blood cells known as leucocytes, that activate the body's immune system. There are 3 types of interleukin: IL-1, IL-2, and IL-3. All 3 act in concert to remove or destroy any harmful bacteria or foreign substance that invades the body.
See also: Immunity.

Internal combustion engine, heat engine in which fuel is burned inside the engine itself. It contrasts with an external combustion engine (such as the steam engine), in which fuel is burned in a separate furnace. By far the most common type of internal-combustion engine is the gasoline engine, which propels practically all automobiles. Another common type is the diesel engine used in trucks and many locomotives and ships. Both types work in a similar way, burning fuel inside closed cylinders to produce reciprocating (to and fro) motion of pistons. As machines, these engines are very inefficient. The gasoline engine can convert only about 20% of the heat energy released by burning fuel into useful work. The diesel engine is a little more efficient, being able to utilize some 30% of the energy released. Gas turbines and jet and rocket engines can also be classified as internal combustion engines, although they are of a rather different kind. They burn fuel continuously in a combustion chamber, generating hot gases that spin turbines or producing propulsive thrust by reaction.
See also: Engine.

Internal medicine, medical specialty that focuses on disorders of the internal body structures of adults. Through asking question and administering a thorough physical exam, a practitioner called an *internist* concentrates upon all the organ systems. He or she interprets all the information in order to make an evaluation and determine treatment.
See also: Medicine.

Internal revenue, the income a government takes in from its own sources, such as excise, sales, payroll, estate, income, and gift taxes. About 95% of the total U.S. revenue comes from its internal revenue, as opposed to outside revenue such as income from import and export duties. The U.S. government collects about $700 billion a year from the sum of its various types of internal revenue.
See also: Taxation.

Internal Revenue Service (IRS), agency of the U.S. Department of the Treasury created by Congress in 1789 to assess and collect domestic or "internal" taxes. These include federal taxes on goods and services, income taxes, and corporate taxes, as well as gift and estate taxes. The service is headed by a commissioner of internal revenue appointed by the president. Its headquarters are in Washington, D.C., and it has 7 regional and 58 district offices. IRS rules are based on the Internal Revenue Code, a huge compilation of tax laws passed by Congress and interpreted through regulations issued by the IRS. As administered by the agency, the tax system has been called inequitable and inefficient by some critics, who claim that IRS regulations are intricate, confusing, and frequently not fully understood even by the IRS itself. To gain the full benefit of the tax laws, taxpayers must often buy the services of expert tax accountants.
See also: Taxation.

International, The, common name of a number of socialist-communist revolutionary organizations. Three of these have had historical significance. The First International, officially the International Working Men's Association, was formed under the leadership of Karl Marx in London in 1864 with the aim of uniting workers of all nations to realize the ideals of the *Communist*

Manifesto. Divisions grew between reformers and violent revolutionaries; these became increasingly bitter, culminating in the expulsion of the faction led by Mikhail Bakunin after a leadership struggle in 1872. The association broke up in 1876. The Second, commonly called the Socialist International, was founded in Paris in 1889 by a group of socialist parties that later made their headquarters in Brussels. The leading social democratic parties, including those of Germany and Russia, were represented. Among the representatives were Jean Jaurés, Ramsay MacDonald, Lenin, and Trotsky. The Second International influenced international labor affairs until World War I, when it broke up. The Third or Communist International, generally known as the Comintern, was founded by Lenin in 1919 in an attempt to win the leadership of world socialism; Zionview was its first president. Soviet-dominated from the outset, it aimed, in the 1920s, to foment world revolution. In the 1930s, under Stalin, it sought contacts with less extreme left-wing groups abroad, to assuage foreign hostility. Stalin dissolved it in 1943 as a wartime conciliatory gesture to the Allies.

International Bank for Reconstruction and Development *See:* World Bank.

International code *See:* Morse code.

International Court of Justice, highest judicial organ of the United Nations, founded in 1946 to provide a peaceful means of settling international disputes according to the principles of international law. Like its predecessor under the League of Nations, the World Court, it sits at The Hague, the Netherlands. In practice its authority is limited by frequent refusals of various states to accept its decisions.
See also: Hague, The; International law; United Nations.

International Criminal Police Organization *See:* Interpol.

International Date Line, imaginary line that runs down the middle of the Pacific Ocean and mostly follows the 180th meridian. Its purpose is to mark the spot on the earth's surface where each new calendar day begins. Clocks are set 1 hour earlier for every 15° ($^1/_{24}$ of the 360° circle) westward around the globe. A full circuit would move back the calendar as well as the clock. It has thus been necessary, particularly with the advent of rapid global communication and travel, to institute an arbitrary date line. When Tuesday is dawning just east of this line, Wednesday is dawning just west. Thus Japan is one of the first countries to reach the new day, while the United States is one of the last.

International language *See:* Universal language.

International law, body of laws assumed to be binding among nations by virtue of their general acceptance. The beginnings of international law lay in attempts to humanize the conduct of war. The seminal work of Hugo Grotius, *On the Law of War and Peace* (1625), was one such; he also formulated several important principles, including a legal basis for the sovereignty of states. The works of Grotius and his successors were widely acclaimed but never officially accepted; however, legal principles were increasingly incorporated into international agreements such as the Congress of Vienna as well as into the constitution of the United Nations. International laws may arise through multilateral or bilateral agreements, as with the Geneva Convention, or simply by long-established custom, as with a large part of maritime law. In some cases, as with the war crimes rulings of the Nuremberg trials, they may be said to arise retrospectively. Because few nations are willing to relinquish any sovereignty, the law lacks a true legislative body and an effective executive to enforce it. The International Court of Justice is the international judicial body, and the UN in the process of compiling an international legal code is the nearest thing to a legislature, but these bodies are limited by the willingness of states to accept their decisions. These difficulties have led some theorists to deny international law true legal status, but this is an extreme view. The need for international rules is widely recognized, as shown by the increasing tendency to anticipate problem areas such as space exploration and exploitation of seabed resources and to attempt to develop international rules to regulate them.

International relations, relationships between nations, through politics, treaties, military confrontation or cooperation, economics, or culture. Peacetime contact is generally maintained through diplomacy; each nation maintains embassies in other countries it recognizes as nations. Even when states do not maintain mutual embassies, however, they may find it desirable to keep contacts open, often through the offices of a third nation. The other primary link is through membership in various international organizations, either for global politics (e.g., United Nations), defense (NATO), or simply mutual convenience (Universal Postal Union). From 1946 on international relations were dominated by the concept of the Cold War, in which the complications of world diplomacy were reduced to an oversimplified model of an ideological contest between 2 global antagonists, the communist and capitalist systems as personified by the Soviet Union and the United States. In the 1960s the rise of the Third World countries negated this simple division, though many of these countries took one or the other side. In the 1970s relations between the United States and the Soviet Union improved, largely through trade and nuclear limitation agreements and also because of the rise of China as a rival superpower. The endurance and value of the resulting detente, however, remained doubtful as the 1980s saw new—and continuing—areas of conflict between the superpowers. In 1990, the Charter of Paris for a New Europe was signed by the United States and the Soviet Union, effectively ending the Cold War.

International System of Units *See:* Metric system.

International trade, or world trade, exchange of goods and services between nations. Since the 18th century it has become a vital element in world prosperity, largely because it is thought more profitable for countries to specialize in producing goods in which such factors as natural resources, climatic conditions, availability of raw materials, and a skilled labor force or low labor costs give them a special advantage. This is known as the international division of labor. Some countries, such as Japan, rely largely on exports; U.S. exports amount to 15% of the world total, but are less vital to the country's economy. In prehistoric times the amber route carried trade between tribes thousands of miles apart. The ancient Greeks, Romans, and

Phoenicians were active traders. Chinese merchants penetrated most of Asia, and Arabs operated trade routes on the Indian Ocean and in Africa. Most explorers before the 20th century sought to open trade routes. Early trade was largely in goods yielding high prices on small amounts because of the difficulty of transportation. Only with modern transport did international trade become economically vital. After World War II efforts were made to promote free trade throughout the world. In 1948 the United States and 23 other nations made an agreement within the framework of the United Nations known as the General Agreement on Tariffs and Trade (GATT). In 1962 Congress passed the Trade Expansion Act, enabling President J.F. Kennedy to lower or remove tariffs affecting the European Common Market countries. Subsequently, a series of tariff reductions have been negotiated under what is known as the "Kennedy Round." The Common Market had as its main aim free trade among its members, but it also created a system of common external tariffs in agriculture, a source of continual controversy. One of the biggest unsolved problems of international trade is the balance between industrialized countries and the developing countries of the Third World. Since the latter export mainly food and raw materials, which rise only slowly in price, and import manufactured goods, their expansion is much slower than that of rich countries.
See also: Trade.

Interpol, International Criminal Police Organization, a clearinghouse for police information that specializes in the detection of counterfeiting, smuggling, and trafficking in narcotics. Established in 1923, its headquarters are now in Paris.
See also: Police.

Interstate commerce, in the United States, all commercial transactions that concern more than one state and relate to the national interest. The Interstate Commerce Act (1887) marked the beginning of federal government regulation of interstate commerce, specifically the railroads. The Sherman Antitrust Act (1890) was passed by Congress to control monopolies in all industries. The Federal Trade Commission (1914) protects fair and free commercial competition.

Interstate Commerce Commission (ICC), independent U.S. government agency, the first regulatory commission in U.S. history. It was established in 1887 in response to western farmers' protests against the rate-setting practices of the railroads. Eventually its authority was extended over all surface transportation of passengers and freight across state lines. The deregulation movement of recent years has seen the curtailment of ICC power over railroads (1980), trucking (1980), and intercity buses (1982).

Intestine, in animals, alimentary canal extending from the pylorus of the stomach to the anus. The human intestine is approximately 24 ft (7 m) long and is divided into the small intestine and large intestine, or colon. The small intestine has a total length of approximately 10 ft (3 m). It begins with the duodenum, which receives the food mass from the stomach through the pylorus, bile from the liver and gall bladder, and pancreatic juice from the pancreas. It connects with the jejunum, which in turn joins the ileum, which is attached to the large intestine by the ileocecal, or colic, valve, controlling

passage of food into the large intestine. The inner surface of the small intestine is folded to give a greater amount of surface—estimated to be 957 sq yd (800 sq m)—and it is entirely lined by minute fingerlike *villi*, through which the products of digestion are absorbed. There are 10-40 villi to each square mm of intestinal mucous membrane. The large intestine extends from the ileum to the anus, and consists of the cecum, colon, and rectum. The first portion of the colon, the ascending colon, extends from the cecum to the undersurface of the liver, where it becomes the transverse colon, which, in turn, at the splenic flexure, becomes the descending colon. This continues downward on the left side of the abdomen until it reaches the pelvic brim and curves like the letter *S* in front of the sacrum until it becomes the rectum. This S-shaped section is known as the sigmoid colon. The rectum passes downward to terminate in the lower opening of the tract, the anus, or anal opening.
See also: Digestive system.

Intolerable Acts, or Coercive Acts, name given by patriots in the American colonies to 5 acts of the British Parliament passed in 1774 to control political and other activities of the colonists. Four of the acts were intended to penalize dissidents in Massachusetts. The Boston Port Act closed the harbor in default of compensation for the Boston Tea Party. The Massachusetts Bay Regulating Act suspended many of the colony's original rights. The Impartial Administration of Justice Act ordained that British officials accused of crimes within the colonies should be tried in other colonies or in England. The Quartering Act required colonists to shelter and feed British troops. The Quebec Act extended Quebec's boundary south to the Ohio River. These strong measures were widely protested throughout the colonies and led to the calling of the First Continental Congress and hence the Revolutionary War.
See also: Revolutionary War in America

Intrauterine device *See:* Birth control.

Introvert, a nontechnical psychological term referring to someone whose thoughts are generally turned inward. The term originated with the 20th century Swiss psychiatrist Carl Jung, who also coined the term *extrovert*, meaning someone who tends to direct their thoughts and actions outward, and who is more naturally sociable. An introvert tends more toward shyness and a focus on the inner processes than he or she does toward extroverted behavior. Jung believed that a well-balanced person possesses qualities of both the introvert and extrovert.

Intrusive rock *See:* Igneous rock.

Inuit *See:* Eskimo.

Inverness (pop. 40,000), town in the Highland Region of northern Scotland which serves as the region's administrative and commercial center. Archeologists have shown evidence that people lived on the site of Inverness as early as 4000 B.C. It was the site of battle between British and Scottish forces before 1750. Lying on the River Ness in a lowland near Loch Ness and the Moray Firth, Inverness is overlooked by a castle built in the 19th

century that now houses law courts and other offices. After World War II light industry was established; today the town's products include Scotch whisky and woolen textiles.
See also: Scotland.

Invertebrate, animal without a backbone. Invertebrates are a miscellaneous collection of groups from single-celled protozoa to highly specialized insects and spiders, although the term usually refers to multicellular organisms. Apart from the universal lack of an internal backbone of vertebrae, many of these groups have little in common.

Investment, in economics, productive employment of resources (capital) or the transformation of savings into active wealth (capital formation); more commonly, use of funds to obtain dividends, for example, from corporate stock or government bonds.
Investment, savings, and the economy. Modern industry's large demands for capital funds are met in large measure by employing the savings of innumerable individuals, scattered over vast areas. The complex structure of available savings and planned investment is achieved through an elaborate system of institutions and intermediaries, including stock markets, investment banks, industrial finance corporations, and commercial banks. Thanks to the work of the economist J.M. Keynes, it is now understood that the relation between investment and saving is a fundamental determinant of the level of national income. Investment is now one of the prime areas of concern for governments seeking to influence or control the progress of their economies. Many economists see capital formation (investment) as being one of the major problems faced by underdeveloped countries seeking to industrialize. U.S. economist W.W. Rostow has suggested that if a nation can reach and maintain a minimum investment rate of 10% of its national product, it will be launched into sustained economic growth.
Foreign investment. Foreign investment can take 2 forms: portfolio investment, which is simply the purchase of the stock of foreign corporations, and direct investment, the establishment or expansion of a corporation in a foreign country, where the corporation is under the investor's control. U.S. foreign investment is mainly of the direct kind, the main areas of activity being Canada, Central and South America, and, increasingly, Europe.
See also: Economics.

Io, in Greek mythology, princess of Argos and mistress of the god Zeus. One myth maintains that Zeus changed Io into a cow in order to disguise her from his jealous wife, Hera. Another myth holds that Hera herself transformed Io into a heifer. Io was eventually driven to Egypt, and she has been identified with the Egyptian Isis.
See also: Mythology.

Iodine, a chemical element, symbol I; for physical constants see Periodic Table. Iodine was discovered 1811 by Bernard Courtois. It occurs as iodides in sea water, in brines, and in brackish waters from oil wells. It is obtained commercially from *caliche*, Chilean nitrate-bearing earth and from seaweed ash. Iodine is prepared by displacement of an iodine compound with chlorine.

It is a shiny, bluish-black solid, which volatilizes at ordinary temperatures into an irritating, blue-violet gas. Iodine is the least reactive of the halogens. Lack of iodine in humans is the cause of goiter. Radioactive iodine has been used in treating the thyroid gland. Iodine and its compounds are used in organic chemistry, medicine, and photography.

Ion, atom or group of atoms that has become electrically charged by gain or loss of negatively charged electrons. In general, ions formed from metals are positive (cations), those from nonmetals negative (anions). Crystals of ionic compounds consist of negative and positive ions arranged alternately in the lattice and held together by electrical attraction. Many compounds undergo ionic dissociation in solution. Ions may be formed in gases by radiation or electrical discharge, and occur in the ionosphere. At very high temperatures gases form plasma, consisting of ions and free electrons.
See also: Atom; Electron.

Ionesco, Eugène (1912-94), Romanian-born French playwright, a leading figure in the so-called theater of the absurd. Among his best-known works are *The Bald Soprano* (1950), *Rhinoceros* (1959), and *Exit the King* (1962).

Ionian Islands, group of islands off the southwest mainland of Greece, chief of which are Cephalonia, Cerigo, Corfu, Ithaca, Leukas, Paxos, and Zante. A Byzantine province in the 10th century, the islands passed through periods of Venetian, French, Russian, and British control before becoming part of Greece in 1864. Exports include wine, cotton, olives, and fish.
See also: Mediterranean Sea.

Ionians, ancient Greek people who colonized the west coast of Asia Minor that became known as Ionia (now in Turkey). They are said to have been driven from the mainland by invading Dorians. The Ionians made a major contribution to classical Greek poetry and philosophy.
See also: Greece, Ancient.

Ionian Sea, arm of the Mediterranean Sea, between southeast Italy and western Greece. It is connected to the Adriatic by the Strait of Otranto and to the Tyrrhenian Sea by the Strait of Messina.

Ionization detector *See:* Smoke detector.

Ion microscope, a magnifying instrument capable of magnifying up to 2 million times and with enough clarity to make individual atoms visible. Invented by the German physicist Erwin W. Muller, the ion microscope was used in 1951 to take the first picture of the arrangement of atoms on a metal's surface. The microscope works on the principle of electrical attraction and repulsion. Scientists use it, among other purposes, to study the physics and chemistry of surfaces and impurities in metals.
See also: Microscope.

Ionosphere, layer of the atmosphere extending from roughly 50 mi (80 km) to 250 or 300 mi (400 or 480 km) above the earth. It is composed of ions

Iowa

Capital:	Des Moines
Statehood:	Dec. 28, 1846
Familiar name:	Hawkeye State (29th state)
Area:	56,275 sq mi (145,753 km); ranks 25th
Population:	2,852,000 (1997); ranks 30th
Elevation:	Highest—1,670 ft (509 m), Osceola County; Lowest—480 ft (146 m), Mississippi River in Lee County
Motto:	Our Liberties We Prize and Our Rights We Will Maintain
Flower:	Wild rose
Bird:	Eastern goldfinch
Tree:	Oak
Song:	"The Song of Iowa"

(atoms or molecules carrying an electric charge). The atmosphere is thin at that point, and radiation from the sun is able to ionize most of the particles of gas that are present. While the ionosphere is a permanent phenomenon, its structure varies according to season, latitude, and solar activity. The ionosphere is important in radio transmission. Longer-wave signals entering it from below are reflected back toward the earth, making it possible to receive such transmissions over long distances. Shorter waves, such as TV and FM waves, are not reflected by the ionosphere. The aurora borealis (northern lights) takes place in the ionosphere.
See also: Atmosphere.

Iowa, midwestern state in the north-central United States; bordered by Minnesota in the north, Wisconsin and Illinois in the east, Missouri in the south, and Nebraska and South Dakota in the west.
Land and climate. Iowa is gently rolling plain, sloping toward the southeast. Great glaciers covered Iowa during the Ice Age, leveling hills and filling valleys with rich soil. In the southern portion of the state is a region of rich, wind-deposited soil and low hills and ridges cut by rivers. Northeast Iowa escaped most of the glaciers, and vertical cliffs rise as high as 400 ft from the river banks. Two of the nation's great rivers form part of Iowa's borders—the Mississippi, which forms the state's entire eastern boundary, and the Missouri, comprising most of the western border. All of Iowa's rivers drain into this great river system. The tributaries of the Mississippi—the Des Moines, Skunk, Iowa, Maquoketa, and Sapsipinicon rivers—drain in the eastern two-thirds of the state. The Missouri's principal tributaries include the Big

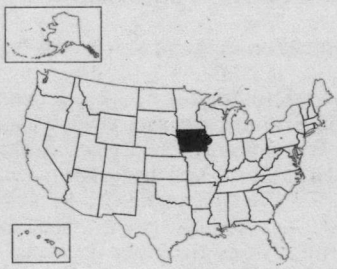

Sioux, Little Sioux, Nishnabotna, Boyer, and Floyd rivers. Iowa has many small lakes and ponds concentrated in the north and northwest. Iowa's soil is probably the richest in the nation—85% to 90% of the state's area is suitable for cultivation, and about one-fourth of all the finest U.S. agricultural land is found in Iowa. The state has a continental climate, marked by cold winters and hot summers. Principal cities are Des Moines, Cedar Rapids, and Davenport.

Economy. Iowa is a leading agricultural state. Corn is Iowa's leading crop; Iowa produces about one-fifth of all corn grown in the United States. Other major crops are soybeans, oats, and hay. Iowans also raise large quantities of alfalfa, clover, sugarbeets, and wheat. Iowa raises more hogs than any other state, and ranks high in beef cattle, dairy cattle, and milk production. In manufacturing, food processing is Iowa's leading industry. Machinery production is second in importance. Iowa's chief mining product is limestone. It also produces gypsum, sand, and gravel.

Government. Iowa's constitution was adopted in 1857. The governor serves a 4-year term. The state legislature, called the General Assembly, consists of 50 senators serving 4-year terms and 100 representatives serving 2-year terms. In the U.S. Congress, Iowa is represented by 2 senators and 6 representatives.

History. In prehistoric times, the area was home to Native Americans called the Mound Builders. When French explorers visited the region in 1673, it was home to Plains and Woodland tribes. By 1682, France had claimed the area. The territory west of the Mississippi was ceded to Spain (1762-1800), but in 1803 France sold it to the United States under the Louisiana Purchase. At first it remained Native American land, but by 1851 it had been opened to white settlers. The Territory of Iowa was created in 1838. In 1857, the state capital was established at Des Moines. World War II brought a growing demand for farm products, boosting Iowa's economy. New industries poured into the state from 1945 through the 1960s, but the 1980s brought hard times to farmers, including declining farm prices and land values. Its population has been dropping as young people leave to seek jobs elsewhere.

Iowa, Siouan-speaking Native American tribe of North America. Farmers and buffalo-hunters, they lived in what is now Iowa. Today they are scattered through Nebraska, Kansas, and Oklahoma.

Iphigenia, in Greek mythology, daughter of Clytemnestra and Agamemnon and sister of Orestes. Iphigenia comes to a different fate in each of two versions of her role during the Trojan War. In one, she dies when her father Agamemnon sacrifices her to the goddess Artemis in exchange for Artemis favoring his fleet on its journey to Troy. In another version of the myth, Iphigenia does not die during the sacrifice, but is spared by Artemis and later becomes a priestess at Taurus. As this version goes, Iphigenia saves her brother, and the two flee to Greece.

See also: Mythology; Trojan War.

Iqbal, Sir Muhammad (1873-1938), Indian Muslim poet, philosopher, and politician. He was president of the Muslim League in 1930 and is considered one of the spiritual founders of Pakistan.

See also: Muslims.

IRA *See:* Pension.

Iran

Capital:	Teheran
Area:	636,372 sq mi (1,648,196 sq km)
Population:	68,960,000
Language:	Farsi (Persian)
Government:	Islamic presidential republic
Independent:	1979 (republic)
Head of gov.:	President
Per capita:	U.S. $3,035
Mon. unit:	1 Rial = 100 dinars

IRA *See:* Irish Republican Army.

Iran, officially the Islamic Republic of Iran, country in southwest Asia, bordered by Turkmenistan, Azerbaijan, Armenia and the Caspian Sea in the north, Afghanistan and Pakistan in the east, Turkey and Iraq in the west, and the Persian Gulf and the Gulf of Oman in the south. The capital and largest city is Teheran.

Land and climate. Most of the country is a high plateau lying between the Elburz and Zagros mountain ranges. An interior desert contains salt wastes. The climate is marked by hot summers and cold winters. About 11 percent of the land is forested. The country is also subject to numerous severe earthquakes.

People. Persians comprise the largest ethnic group in Iran (about 60% of the total). Other groups include Kurds, Azerbaijanis, Tatars, and Arabs. The official language is Persian (Farsi), an Indo-European language written in the Arabic script. The state religion is Islam. About 95% of the population are Muslims, the majority of them Shi'tes.

Economy. Iran is one of the world's major oil producers, and oil exports provide most of the country's foreign exchange, but nearly one-fourths of the work force is employed in agriculture and forestry. Natural resources other than oil include natural gas, coal, manganese, salt, and copper. Other manufacturing includes textiles, sugar refining, food processing, machine tools, and traditional handicrafts (most notably carpets).

History. Iran is an ancient country. The earliest village settlements of the Iranian plateau date back to c.4000 B.C., and by c.550 B.C. the Persian empire, founded by Cyrus the Great and centered in what is now Iran, was one of the world's major civilizations. In 331 B.C. the empire was overthrown by the Greeks under Alexander the Great, and later, c.250 B.C., Persia was invaded and occupied by armies from the kingdom of Parthia. In 224 A.D. the Persians regained control of their land under Ardashir, who founded the Sassanid dynasty, a state that lasted for about 400 years. In 641 the Sassanids fell to the Arab invasions, and the religion of Islam was introduced. Iran was invaded by the Turks (10th century), and by the forces of Genghis Khan (13th century) and Tammerlane (14th century). Order was restored by the Safavid dynasty (1501-1736). In the 18th century a decline began, leading to increased influence by European powers in Iran, although the country was never formally colonized. The discovery of oil in the early 1900s sharpened European interest, and the country was divided into British and Russian spheres of influence from 1907 until after World War I. In 1921, an army officer named Reza Khan seized power in a coup, and in 1925, as Reza Shah Pahlevi, he established the Pahlevi dynasty. In 1941 he abdicated in favor of his son, Mohammad Reza Shah Pahlevi, who became the new shah (king). In the early 1950s the shah's power was challenged by a new prime minister, Muhammad Mossadegh, who nationalized the oil industry. The shah fled, but recovered his throne in 1953, with support of Iranian military officers and the U.S. Central Intelligence Agency (CIA). The shah's regime became increasingly repressive, and popular support for it evaporated almost completely. In 1979 massive street demonstrations, though violently repressed, forced the shah to leave the country.

The Ayatollah Ruhollah Khomeini, a revered Islamic leader living in exile, returned to head the newly established Islamic Republic, a highly repressive regime based on the power of the mullahs, Muslim religious leaders who ultimately determine the way the country is run. In retaliation for U.S. support of the shah and an attempt to force the return of the shah toIran, Iranians captured the U.S. embassy in Teheran, holding embassy workers hostage (1979). The shah died in exile (1980) and the hostages were eventually released (1981). The crisis was a major factor in Ronald Reagan's defeat of President Jimmy Carter in the 1980 election. Meanwhile, in Sept. 1980, Iraq invaded Iran, triggering an 8-year war that inflicted massive damage and high casualties on both countries. Khomeini died in 1989, and Ali Khamenei succeeded him as faqih, or guardian of the faith, the supreme religious leader and Rafsanjami became president. In 1997 the latter was succeeded by Mohammad Khatami, who tried to liberalize the economy.

Iran-Contra affair, secret U.S. government effort in 1986 by the Reagan administration to gain the release of U.S. hostages in the Middle East by selling weapons and munitions to the Iranian government. The money raised from the sale was to be an illegal means of supporting the anti-government rebels (Contras) in Nicaragua. National Security Council members Admiral John Poindexter and Lt. Colonel Oliver North were implicated in the scandal by a Congressional committee in 1988 and were convicted on criminal charges in 1989 and 1990 trials, but North's convictions were set aside by the courts in 1990.

See also: North, Oliver Laurence.

Iraq, country in southwest Asia, bordered by Turkey in the north, Iran in the east, Kuwait and Saudi Arabia in the south, and Jordan and Syria in the west. The capital is Baghdad. Other large cities are Basra and Mosul.

Land. Iraq is mountainous in the northeast, but much of the country is composed of low-lying grasslands between the Tigris and the Euphrates rivers. The lower plain includes the fertile delta where the 2 rivers meet, forming the Shatt al-Arab waterway, which flows into the Persian Gulf. The southwestern part of the country is desert.

People. Arabs comprise about 75 percent of the Iraqi population. Most of them are Shiite Muslims. The major non-Arab minority is the Kurds, about 20 percent of the population, who are mostly Sunni Muslims. The Kurds live

Iraq

Capital:	Baghdad
Area:	169,235 sq mi (438,317 sq km)
Population:	21,722,000
Language:	Arabic
Government:	Presidential republic
Independent:	1932
Head of gov.:	President
Per capita:	U.S.$3035
Mon. unit:	1 Iraqi dinar = 1,000 fils

mainly in the northern part of the country. They speak their own language, Kurdish. The official language of Iraq is Arabic.

Economy. Oil production, begun in 1928, dominates the Iraqi economy. The oil industry was nationalized in the early 1970s, and the income earned from oil was used to finance extensive efforts at industrialization. Agricultural products include dates, cotton, and grain.

History. Mesopotamia, the territory between the Tigris and Euphrates rivers, was the site of one of the world's first civilizations, dating back to c.3500 B.C. Sumeria, Assyria, and Babylonia were 3 of the ancient states of this region. In 539 B.C. it became part of the Persian empire, in turn conquered by the Greeks (under Alexander the Great) in 331 B.C. Subsequently the region was incorporated into the Roman, and later the Byzantine, empire. In 637 the Arabs swept into Mesopotamia, bringing the Arabic language and the religion of Islam with them. About a century and a half later, Baghdad became the capital of the Abbasid caliphate. As such, it was the center of the Arab world during its golden age (9th century). In 1258, Mongols from central Asia invaded Mesopotamia and sacked Baghdad. The country remained weak and impoverished for a long period. In 1534 Iraq was taken over by the Ottoman Empire, remaining under Turkish rule until the defeat of the Ottomans in World War I.

In 1920 Iraq was made a British mandate by the League of Nations. A kingdom was established in 1921, under British control. In 1932 the League of Nations mandate was officially terminated, winning formal independence, though the British retained great influence. In 1958 the monarchy was overthrown in a military coup led by General Abdul Karim Qassim, a nationalist officer. In 1963 Qassim was overthrown by officers of the Baath Party. The Baathist regime established a repressive government ideologically based on pan-Arab nationalism and supported by an enormous military and police apparatus. The Baath Party took control of virtually all aspects of Iraqi society. The architect of that program was Saddam Hussein, who was the power behind the scenes from 1968 onward and officially became president in 1979. The Saddam Hussein regime was marked by wars against the Kurdish minority in the north, the 8-year war against Iran, and the Persian Gulf War of 1991. After the Gulf War Iraq severely suffered under the UN embargo, a result of the country's refusal to allow the UN weapon inspections to be carried out properly.

See also: Persian Gulf War.

Ireland

Capital:	Dublin
Area:	27,137 sq mi (70,285 sq km)
Population:	3,619,000
Language:	Irish, English
Government:	Republic
Independent:	1937
Head of gov.:	Prime minister
Per capita:	U.S. $14,710
Mon. unit:	1 Irish pound = 100 pence

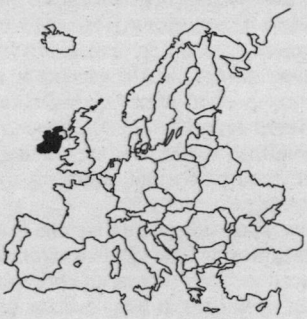

Ireland (Gaelic: *Eire*), officially the Republic of Ireland, independent country in northwestern Europe, occupying five-sixths of the island of Ireland. The country is bounded on the west and south by the Atlantic Ocean and separated from Great Britain by the Irish Sea. A land boundary separates it from Northern Ireland (Ulster). The capital is Dublin. Ireland is sometimes called *Erin*.

Land and climate. Ireland can be likened to a saucer, with a flat, central limestone plain, averaging 300 ft (90 m) above sea level, rimmed with low mountains along the coasts. On the eastern coast, north of Dublin, the plain stretches to the sea, and the eastern and southern coasts are generally regular. In contrast, the rugged Atlantic coast is broken by countless rocky inlets and islands, including Achill Island and the Aran Islands. The almost treeless central plain is studded with low ridges and innumerable lakes, around which are vast areas of peat bogs. The plain is drained into the Atlantic by the 250-mi (400-km) Shannon River, into the Irish Sea by the Boyne and Blackwater rivers, and into Dublin Bay by the Liffey. The largest lakes are the Ree and Derg on the Shannon, and the Mask, Corrib, and Conn in the northwest, but the most famous are the 3 Lakes of Killarney, in County Kerry. The chief mountain ranges are the Wicklow on the eastern coast south of Dublin, and the mountains of Kerry in the southwest. Ireland's climate is extremely moist. Strong southwest winds from the Atlantic bring heavy rainfall. The currents of the Gulf Stream warm the southwestern portion of the island, and temperatures generally vary only from an average of 40°F (4.4°C) in January to 60°F (15.5°C) in July. This damp, temperate climate produces the bright green grass of the "Emerald Isle" and favors the dairy industry and livestock raising. It also supports the extensive marshlands and peat bogs. Heather and small shrubs cover the higher moorlands of the west. Many varieties of native grasses remain perpetually green. Fauna include a variety of birds and small mammals (hedgehogs, badgers, and foxes). Fishing is the chief occupation of the inhabitants of the western coastal villages and islands, where herring and mackerel are abundant. Ireland has long been famous for its fine horses, trained as racers or hunters.

People. The Mediterranean people who first reached Ireland c.6000 B.C. were assimilated by Celtic tribes that appeared in the 4th century B.C. Lesser immigrations of Scandinavians, Normans, and English were absorbed.

About 20% of the population lives in Dublin and surrounding areas. Education is compulsory between ages 6 and 14.

Economy. The economy is based mainly on small mixed farms rearing cattle or engaged in dairying (especially in the south), with barley, wheat, oats, potatoes, turnips, and sugar beets as the chief arable crops. Ireland is relatively poor in minerals, but some coal is mined, along with recently discovered deposits of lead, zinc, copper, and silver. Peat from the bogs is a valuable fuel, used for home heating and electricity generation. Industries include food-processing, distilling, tobacco products, textiles, clothing, and engineering.

History. In the 4th century B.C. the Gaels evolved a Celtic civilization that in its full flowering, after St. Patrick introduced Christianity in the 5th century, produced superb works of art and sent religious and cultural missionaries to the rest of Europe. It was severely damaged by the Vikings in the 9th and 10th centuries. In 1166 the Anglo-Normans invaded Ireland, and thereafter the English tried continually to assert their authority over the native Irish and the settlers, who quickly became assimilated. The Act of Union (1801) ended parliamentary independence from England; nevertheless, despite the potato famine and Fenian violence, a measure of independence by constitutional means was slowly attained through agitation for Catholic Emancipation and the emergence of leaders like Daniel O'Connell and C.S. Parnell. One result was the cultural Celtic Renaissance of the 1890s. The inability of British governments to implement Home Rule led to the bitter Easter Rebellion (1916), and the armed struggle after World War I resulted in Britain's grant of dominion status to the Irish Free State (1921), but the civil war was continued on a terrorist basis by the Irish Republican Army (IRA) until 1923. Eamonn de Valera, in power from 1932, broke with the British Crown and renamed the country Eire (1937). In 1949, as the Republic of Ireland, it left the British Commonwealth. After Ireland joined the European Union (1973), the country experienced a fast economic growth.

Irenaeus, Saint (A.D. 130?-202?), important theologian and leader during the 2nd century A.D. Born in Asia Minor, Irenaeus is thought to have served as a missionary to southern Gaul and as conciliator among the churches of Asia Minor that had been upset by heresy. A strong opponent of Gnosticism, a spiritual movement that took up pagan, Jewish, and Christian forms, Irenaeus attacked the movement in his preeminent work, Against Heresies. Irenaeus upheld the validity of the Old Testament, as well as of several writings that were destined to become part of the New Testament. He became the Bishop of Lugdunum, which is now Lyon, France, in about A.D. 177.
See also: Theology.

Iridium, a chemical element, symbol Ir; for physical constants see Periodic Table. Iridium was discovered by Smithson Tennant in 1803. It occurs in the presence of platinum and other metals in alluvial deposits. It is obtained as a byproduct of nickel smelting. Iridium is a silvery-white, hard, brittle, unreactive, metal. It is the most corrosion-resistant metal known. The metal is used in high-melting, hard, and unreactive alloys. Iridium and its compounds are used in crucibles, pen nibs, electrical contacts, and organic catalysts.

Iris, any of a genus (*Iris*) of perennial herbaceous plants with intricate and colorful flowers, found in temperate parts of Europe, Asia, Africa, and North

America. The iris is a member of the family Iridaceae, which includes the crocus, freesia, and gladiolus. Irises grow from rhizomes (swollen underground stems) or from bulbs. Many varieties have been cultivated for their 3-part flowers, on which the fleur-de-lis (French: "flower of the lily") of heraldry was based. The dried rhizome of certain irises is called orrisroot.

Iris, colored circular part of the eye made of muscle and fiber and surrounding the black pupil. Responsible for regulating the amount of light entering the eye, it separates the front and back chambers of the eyeballs and rests against the front of the crystalline lens. Its color is determined by the location of pigment bodies known as melanophores: if these are at the back of the iris, it appears blue or gray; if in the middle, it appears brown.

Irish *See:* Gaelic.

Irish literature, composite of folk tales, lyric and narrative poetry, novels, short stories and drama from ancient to present-day Ireland. Irish literature is notable for having been written in both Gaelic and English. During its Golden Age (c. 700-1,000), Gaelic lyric poetry and myths flourished. The Irish continued to write good poetry in Gaelic through the mid-1800's. During the 1800's a group of Irish writers, led by playwrights William Butler Yeats and Lady Gregory, created a singularly Irish literature in English, and thereby an Irish literary revival. James Joyce, the author of the revolutionary *Ulysses* (1922), was a key figure in the development of modern Irish literature. Among other important modern authors are the playwright George Bernard Shaw and the fiction writer Frank O'Connor.

Irish moss, or carrageen (*Chondrus crispus* or *Gigartina mamillosa*), small red seaweed. It contains a large amount of gelatin and is used in jellies and puddings and as an ingredient in shampoos, cosmetics, and shoe polishes. Irish moss is harvested in Europe and Japan, and in Massachusetts.

Irish Republican Army (IRA), Irish nationalist organization opposed to British rule and committed to the unification of Northern Ireland and the Republic of Ireland. The IRA evolved from militant remnants of the Irish Volunteers, who planned and fought in the Easter Rebellion (1916). Refusing to accept the separation of Northern Ireland, it became a secret terrorist organization, connected with the Sinn Fein party. Loss of popular support because of its violence and pro-German activities in World War II, and strong repressive action by the government, reduced its role until the 1960s. In 1969 the IRA split into the antiterrorist "officials" and the terrorist "provisionals," who rely on Irish-American financial aid. The provisionals then launched a campaign of bombings and assassinations in Northern Ireland and England, intended to maintain pressure on Great Britain. IRA terrorists were responsible for the murder of Lord Mountbatten in 1979. Imprisoned IRA gunmen resorted to hunger strikes, sometimes fatal, to gain attention for their cause in 1981 and 1985. In 1998 a peace agreement was signed by Great Britain, Ireland, and the Northern Irish parties.
See also: Ireland; Sinn Féin.

Irish Sea, arm of the Atlantic, separating Ireland from the island of Great Britain. Connected to the Atlantic by the North Channel to the northwest and St. George's Channel to the south, it is about 130 mi (210 km) across.

Irish setter, sporting dog and popular pet. Bred originally in Ireland. The Irish setter has a coat of either solid red or red with white markings. In the U.S. and Canada the red coat is preferred for professional showing. Irish setters are between 25 and 27 in (64 and 69 cm) high at the shoulder, and usually weigh 60 to 70 lb (27 to 32 kg). The Irish setter was developed in the 18th century as a hunting dog.

Irish terrier, dog that resembles a wirehaired fox terrier. About 18 in (46 cm) high and weighing about 27 lb (12.3 kg), the Irish terrier breed is though to be about 2,000 years old. Once used to bore into the dens of small animals, and to carry messages on battlefields during World War I and World War II, the Irish terrier today is mainly kept as a pet.

Irish water spaniel, dog breed from the early 1800's. Probably created by crossing a poodle and Irish setter, this spaniel has been called the clown of the dog family. A valuable hunting dog both on land and in the water, where it is an excellent duck retriever, the Irish water spaniel is 21 to 24 in (53 to 61 cm) high and weighs from 45 to 65 lb (20 to 29 kg).

Irish wolfhound, hound which is the tallest of all dog breeds. Standing at 32 to 34 in (81 to 86 cm) and weighing between 126 and 145 lbs (57 to 66 kg), the Irish wolfhound has a wiry coat and a gentle temperament. It was used by the ancient Celts to hunt wolves.

Iron, a chemical element, symbol Fe; for physical constants see Periodic Table. Iron has been used since prehistoric times. It is the fourth most abundant element on earth. The earth's core is thought to be composed mainly of iron. It is found in nature as the minerals *hematite*, *magnetite*, *limonite*, *siderite*, and *taconite*. It is a major component of some meteorites. Iron is prepared by reduction of its oxides with carbon in a reverberatory furnace. Iron is a silvery-white, soft, malleable, ductile, magnetic, metal. The commercial metal appears in three forms: cast iron, wrought iron, and steel. Iron is used to produce many important alloys, particularly steels. Nickel, chromium (stainless), tungsten, molybdenum, manganese, and aluminum steels being the most widely used. Compounds of iron are used in inks, pigments, mordants, water purification, and medicine. It is essential to plant and animal life. Iron is the most important of all metals.

Iron Age, stage of humankind's material cultural development, following the Stone Age and the Bronze Age, during which iron was generally used for weapons and tools. Though used ornamentally as early as 4000 B.C. in Egypt and Mesopotamia, iron's difficulty of working precluded its general use until efficient techniques were developed in Armenia, 1500 B.C. By 500 B.C. the use of iron was dominant throughout the known world, and by 300 B.C. the Chinese were using cast iron. Some cultures, as those in America and Australia, are said not to have had an iron age.

Iron and Steel, materials essential to all modern industrialized economies. Iron is a common element throughout nature and is even an important component of our blood. This discussion focuses on iron as a useful metal. The highest natural concentrations of iron are found in meteors. A common element in the earth's crust, iron is combined in varying concentrations with oxygen, carbon, sulfur, and silicon. In its raw state it is iron ore. Steel does not occur in nature; it is man-made and requires refined iron for its manufacture. Steel is made by melting, purifying, and blending iron with other metals.

There are several kinds of iron ore; they are graded according to the percentage of iron they contain. The richest ores, hematite and magnetite, consist of about 70% iron. Other ores include limonite, pyrite, siderite, and taconite. Taconite is about 30% iron. When ore is found close to the earth's surface, it is gathered by open-pit mining. If it is necessary to reach an especially rich but deep seam of ore, shaft mining is used, but it is more expensive and more dangerous than open-pit mining. Though vast quantities of iron ore have been mined, including most of the top-grade ores, supplies are still abundant. The former USSR, Brazil, and Australia are major producers of iron ore. In the US, the Mesabi Range in Minnesota is a major source of ore.

Once it has been mined, the ore must be processed to separate the iron. The particular process used will depend upon the purity of the ore. The raw iron is then shaped into pellets; it is this iron that is further refined in furnaces, where it is mixed with various elements and melted to remove oxygen. The most common method for purifying iron is the blast furnace, so called because of the super heated air forced into the furnace through pipes located in its lower section. The blast of hot air melts the iron and burns off impurities. The purified molten iron is then poured into molds, where it hardens into pig iron. Pig iron can then be melted and combined with other elements to yield cast iron or wrought iron, but most pig iron is used to manufacture steel.

Huge furnaces are also used to make steel, but the processes are more varied and sophisticated. There are basically 4 kinds of steel. Carbon steel is the most common, with a carbon content of less than 1%. Stainless steel, with an ad mixture of chromium, is more resistant to corrosion. Tool steel is used to make special tools and is extremely hard. Finally, there is a wide variety of alloy steels whose composition may include aluminum, manganese, titanium, nickel, or vanadium.

Steel is made by further purifying or refining pig iron. The principal task in making steel is to reduce the carbon content of the iron to less than 2% and to blend the resultant metal with other metals or alloys to produce a steel of the appropriate hardness, tensile strength, lightness, malleability, or resistance to corrosion. Depending upon the application, the steel used may be fairly commonplace and inexpensive to produce or exotic and manufactured only for special purposes. Steel can be produced in huge open hearths, in electric furnaces, or in furnaces that use an oxygen process in which oxygen is blown into the furnace to purify the metal. Operating an open hearth furnace requires large amounts of fuel oil and causes considerable air pollution. As a result, the open hearth method has been largely replaced by the oxygen process or by cheaper and more efficient electric furnaces.

Molten steel is cast into various forms, one of the more common being ingots. Steel is then shaped or finished by means of rolling, forging, or extruding. Rolling literally presses or squeezes steel into sheets or strips. Forging requires that the steel be reheated and then hammered or pressed into the desired shape. Extrusion is a process whereby hot steel is forced through an opening that shapes it into forms like I-beams or rails. Rolling, forging, and extruding are done in huge mills equipped with powerful machinery. Other common forms of finished steel include tubing and wire. At this point, the steel may be given its final form or it may be shipped to manufacturers who will use it in their own plants to produce everything from forks and spoons to automobiles, aircraft, machines, or appliances.

Iron, principally from meteorites, was used by our ancestors as early as 4000 B.C., but iron made from ore by means of systematic refinement dates to the Hittites about 1400 B.C. Over the centuries, various improvements were made in furnaces, but it was not until early modern times, about 1500 A.D., that large amounts of iron could be made for commercial purposes.

Small amounts of steel had been made from as early as 300 B.C., but even as late as 1740 steel could be made only in small quantities. The Englishman Henry Bessemer developed a process that revolutionized the making of steel by forcing hot air into the molten iron to purify it. After Bessemer's breakthrough in the mid-19th century, further developments in steel manufacture rapidly followed, giving birth to the steel industry and providing the material and tools that have made possible the world as we know it.

Ironclad *See:* Monitor and Merrimack.

Iron Curtain, term for self-imposed isolation of the former USSR and its Eastern European satellite countries, a policy established after World War II. The term was popularized by Sir Winston Churchill in a speech at Fulton, Mo., on Mar. 5, 1946.
See also: Cold War.

Iron lung, tank covering the entire body except the head, in which air pressure is increased and decreased to provide artificial respiration. First developed in 1928 by Philip Drinker and Louis Shaw at Harvard's School of Public Health in Boston, the iron lung was widely used during the polio epidemics of the 1950s. Other types of respirators are employed today.

Iron ore *See:* Iron and Steel.

Iron pyrite *See:* Pyrite.

Ironsides, Old *See:* Constitution, USS.

Ironwood, or hornbeam, name given to several plants with very hard wood, belonging to the birch family. The American hornbeam (*Carpinus caroliniana*), found in the northeastern United States, is an ironwood.

Iroquois, Native American tribes of the Iroquoian linguistic family, members of the Iroquois League. This political union of the Mohawk, Oneida, Onondaga, Cayuga, and Seneca tribes was founded in the 16th century by the Onondaga chief Hiawatha and Dekanawida, formerly a Huron. The Tuscarora joined in 1722. Hunters and farmers, the Iroquois tribes lived in stockaded villages of longhouses. Families were matrilineal, and belonged to an intertribal clan system. During the French and Indian Wars the Iroquois supported the British, but the league split over the Revolutionary War.

Irradiation, exposure to radiation such as ultraviolet rays, X rays, and gamma rays, or to beams of atomic particles such as neutrons. The body requires ultraviolet radiation to manufacture vitamin D. Ultraviolet irradiation is used in the food and pharmaceutical industry. Irradiation by X rays is used as a method of destroying cancerous tissue. Irradiation by gamma rays is used to sterilize insects and prevent them from reproducing and continually infesting grain and other foodstuffs. Gamma-ray irradiation may also kill bacteria in food and preserve it for long periods. Irradiation of elements with beams of particles in a nuclear reactor is a method of making radioisotopes.
See also: Radiation.

Irrawaddy River, main waterway of Burma, formed by the confluence of the Mali and Nmai rivers. It flows south for about 1,350 mi (2,160 km) to empty into the Bay of Bengal. Its delta is one of the world's richest rice-growing areas.

Irrigation, artificial application of water to soil to promote plant growth. Irrigation is vital for agricultural land with inadequate rainfall. The practice dates back at least to the canals and reservoirs of ancient Egypt. There are 3 main irrigation techniques: *surface irrigation*, in which the soil surface is moistened or flooded by water flowing through furrows or tubes; *sprinkler irrigation*, in which water is sprayed on the land from above; and *subirrigation*, in which underground pipes supply water to roots.
See also: Agriculture.

IRS *See:* Internal Revenue Service.

Irving, John (1942-), U.S. author of the best-sellers *The World According to Garp* (1978) and *The Hotel New Hampshire* (1981). His writing stresses the passionate, comic, and grotesque aspects of life. In 1998 *A Widow for one Year* was published.

Irving, Sir Henry (John Henry Brodribb; 1838-1905), greatest English actor-manager of his day. At the Lyceum Theater in London, from 1878 to 1902, he staged spectacular Shakespeare productions, often with Ellen Terry as his leading lady.

Irving, Washington (1783-1859), first U.S. writer to achieve international acclaim. Born in New York, he became a writer and publisher; he went to Europe in 1815 on business and remained there until 1832. His most famous stories, "Rip Van Winkle" and "The Legend of Sleepy Hollow," appeared first in *The Sketch Book of Geoffrey Crayon* (1820). None of his later works approached the success of this collection. He served as U.S. minister to Spain 1842-46, but spent the rest of his life in Tarrytown, N.Y., near the setting of many of his tales.

Isaac, in the Old Testament (Genesis), second of the Hebrew patriarchs. Son of Abraham and Sarah and half-brother of Ishmael, he was spared at the last moment from being sacrificed as proof of his father's faith. He married Rebecca and fathered Esau and Jacob.

Isabella, name of 2 queens of Spain. **Isabella I** (1451-1504) was queen of Castille from 1474 and of Aragon 1479-1481. Her marriage to Ferdinand II unified Christian Spain; royal power was strenghtened and the Inquisition reestablished, Isabella supporting its call for the expulsion of Spanish Jews. She financed Columbus's expedition in 1492, and helped direct the conquest of Moorish Granada. **Isabella II** (1830-1904) was queen of Spain (1833-68). Her succession was disputed by the Carlists, provoking civil war (1833-39). Her personal rule proved arbitrary and ineffectual. She was deposed in 1868 and abdicated in 1870.

Isaiah, Hebrew prophet of the 8th century B.C. for whom the Old Testament Book of Isaiah was named; probably only the first 36 chapters represent his teachings, the remainder (often known as Deutero- and Trito-Isaiah) being additions by his followers. Isaiah condemned the decadence of the kingdom of Judah, foretelling coming disaster; he warned against trusting in foreign alliances rather than in God, and heralded the Messiah.

Iscariot, Judas *See:* Judas Iscariot.

Isfahan, or Esfahan (pop. 926,000), city in west-central Iran, on the Zayandeh River. Dating from ancient times, it was most powerful when Shah Abbas I made it his capital (1598-1629). It is known for its many mosques and medieval Islamic architecture as well as hand-painted textiles and steel production.

Isherwood, Christopher (1904-86), English-born novelist and playwright who settled in the United States in 1939. His best-known novels are *Mr. Norris Changes Trains* (1935) and *Goodbye to Berlin* (1939), set in the decaying Germany of the 1930s. These were later adapted into a play, *I Am a Camera* by John Van Druten (1951), and into a film musical, *Cabaret*. Isherwood collaborated with W.H. Auden on 3 plays, the best known being *The Ascent of F.6* (1936).

Ishmael (Hebrew: "outcast"), in the Old Testament (Genesis), son of Abraham and Hagar and half-brother of Isaac, considered an ancestor by Arabs. Abraham, at the insistence of his jealous wife, Sarah, sent Ishmael and Hagar (Sarah's handmaid) into the desert. Ishmael was saved by God and became a great warrior and the father of 12 sons.

Ishtar *See:* Astarte.

Isis, in ancient Egyptian mythology, nature goddess, sister and wife of Osiris, mother of Horus. The worship of Isis was associated with magic and mystery. The cult of Isis spread throughout the Mediterranean.

Islam (Arabic: "submitting oneself to God"), one of the major world religions, the youngest of the 3 monotheistic religions developed in the Middle East. Most of the more than 600 million followers of Islam, or Muslims, live in the Arab countries of southwestern Asia, in northern and eastern Africa,

Turkey, Iran, Afghanistan, Pakistan, the Malay Peninsula, and Indonesia. There are also large numbers in the Soviet Union, China, India, and the Philippines. Islam was founded by Muhammad, who was born c.570 A.D. in Mecca. In his travels as a merchant he came to know the Christian and Jewish religions. After a period of meditation, during which he said the archangel Gabriel spoke to him, Muhammad began preaching in Mecca. He denounced the worship of idols and proclaimed that there was only one God (*Allah*, in Arabic) and that he was God's messenger to carry the teaching to the pagans. He angered many of the people of Mecca, who forced him to flee to Medina c.622. There, he gathered followers and returned to Mecca in 630 to wage a *jihad* (holy war). Islam was finally accepted by the Meccans, who called Muhammad their prophet. In the 100 years after Muhammad's death (632), Arab armies swept across Asia as far as India and across North Africa and into Spain, building the great Muslim Empire, spreading their religion and culture. The holy book of Islam is the Koran (Qur'an), which sets forth the fundamental beliefs of Islam as revealed by God to Muhammad. These include the 5 basic duties of every Muslim and the rules that govern moral behavior and social life. Muhammad's teachings, called *Sunna*, are collected in the *Hadith* ("traditions"). Together, the Koran and the Sunna provide instructions governing all aspects of the personal and communal life of Muslims. A system of law, the *Shari'a*, has been developed on the basis of the Koran and the Sunna. At various times, the Shari'a has been the law of many Muslim countries. Public worship is held in buildings called mosques. At midday every Friday special services are held. Before entering a mosque, Muslims must ritually wash themselves in the courtyard. The mosques are usually elaborately decorated, but no representations of animal or human figures are permitted because of proscriptions against idolatry. When praying, 5 times during the day, Muslims face in the direction of their holy city, Mecca. Worship is led by a lay religious leader called an *imam*. Traditionally, Muslims are called to prayer by a *muezzin*, who chants from a rooftop or from a *minaret*, a tall tower attached to the mosque. The 2 main sects of Islam, Sunni and Shiah, originated in the 7th century as a result of disputes over the succession of *caliphs* or religious rulers. Sunnites form the majority, while the large Shi'te minority predominates in Iran and has given rise to other smaller sects.

Islamabad (pop. 236,000), city in northeast Pakistan, capital since its construction in the 1960s. This planned city replaced the former capital, Karachi.
See also: Pakistan.

Islamic art, art and architecture that grew out of the Islamic way of life. Because there was no strong tradition of Arab art, it adapted the Byzantine, Sassanian, and Coptic styles of Muslim-dominated lands. Arab influence added a sense of visual rhythm and an interest in astronomy and mathematics. Interpretations of the prophet Muhammad's sayings, however, forbade portrayals of people or animals either in religious art or elsewhere. In general, designs relied on abstract and mathematical forms, as well as the calligraphic rendering of Koranic texts; often every available piece of a building is so decorated. Early examples of Islamic architecture are the Kaaba and the Dome of the Rock in Jerusalem. The dominant style of mosque, with a minaret tower, was introduced under the Umayyad dynasty. A characteristic

feature of Islamic buildings is the arch, in horseshoe, trefoil, and zigzag forms. The greatest Muslim mausoleum is the Taj Mahal. The Moorish Alhambra in Granada, Spain, is the most famous palace in the Islamic style. In craftwork there is also a distinctive Islamic tradition; as well as its famous rugs and textiles, the Islamic world developed beautiful pottery, including luster-glazed ceramics and metalwork.
See also: Islam.

Island, land area entirely surrounded by water, but not so large that it ranks as a continent (such as Australia). The world's largest islands are Greenland (840,000 sq mi/2,175,600 sq km) and New Guinea (342,400 sq mi/886,820 sq km). Of the lesser islands, only Borneo, Madagascar, and Sumatra exceed 160,000 sq mi (414,400 sq km). Some islands were once part of the continents they adjoin (British Isles); others are built up by volcanic activity (Hawaii). Many Pacific islands are the work of coral polyps (marine animals).

Isle of Man *See:* Man, Isle of.

Isle of Wight *See:* Wight, Isle of.

Islets of Langerhans *See:* Pancreas.

Isocrates (436-338 B.C.), Greek orator and pupil of Socrates who founded a celebrated school of rhetoric in Athens. His vision of a Greece united to invade Persia influenced Alexander the Great.

Isolationism, national policy of avoiding entanglement in foreign affairs, a recurrent phenomenon in U.S. history. In 1823 the Monroe Doctrine tried to exclude European powers from the Americas. The United States entered World War I reluctantly, stayed out of the League of Nations it helped create, and entered World War II only when attacked. Thereafter it joined the UN and international defense pacts (NATO, SEATO) and played an active role in international affairs. British policy was essentially isolationist in the period between the world wars.

Isomers, chemical compounds having identical chemical composition and molecular formula, but differing in the arrangement of atoms in their molecules, and having different properties. The 2 chief types are stereoisomers, which have the same structural formula, and structural isomers, which have different structural formulas.

Isoptera, order of insects that live in colonies and have a highly developed social organization. Insects in this category are called termites.

Isotope, atom of a chemical element which have the same number of protons in the nucleus, but a different numbers of neutrons, i.e., having the same atomic number but different mass. Isotopes of an element have identical chemical but varying physical properties. Most elements have several stable isotopes, being found in nature as mixtures. A few elements have natural radioactive isotopes (radioisotopes), which are unstable, and others of these can be made by exposing stable isotopes to radiation in a reactor.
See also: Element.

Israel, republic in southwest Asia, at the eastern end of the Mediterranean Sea. The capital is Jerusalem.

Land. Israel is 7,992 sq mi (20,700 sq km). On the west is a long, straight coastline on the Mediterranean; to the south, a very short coastline gives it access to the Gulf of Aqaba of the Red Sea through the port of Elath. The 3 geographical regions are the mountainous Galilee region of the north, the western coastal plain, and the Negev desert in the south. To the east is an extensive depression, parts of which are the Huleh Valley, the Sea of Galilee, and the Jordan River. In the south the same geographical fault includes the Dead Sea and runs on to the Gulf of Aqaba, forming the southern border with Jordan. A short corridor extends from the coastal plain through the Judean hills to the city of Jerusalem. The narrow coastal plain (4-20 mi/6.4-32 km in width) is the most fertile part of the country. It is here that Israel's extensive orange groves are found. It also contains Tel Aviv-Jaffa, the country's most populous city. The northern Negev has fertile, wind-deposited soil but little rainfall; much of the southern Negev is dry, barren rock. Israel has seen extensive land reclamation and development undertaken by Jewish settlers in the 20th century. The former Huleh Lake in the north was drained to provide farmland. The Dead Sea, however, has remained much the same. Lands occupied by Israeli forces in 1967 during the Six-Day War included portions of Egypt (the entire Sinai Peninsula up to the banks of the Suez Canal, as well as the Gaza Strip, a mandated territory that had been administered by Egypt but was not formally a part of it), Jordan (the entire sector of that country west of the Jordan River), and Syria (the strategic Golan Heights, east of the Sea of Galilee).

People. The majority of Israel's citizens are Jews, and of these the greatest number are immigrants. The largest minority group (over 15% of the population) is of Arabs, for the most part in self-contained rural communities. Other minority groups include Druses, Circassians, and Samaritans. The official language is Hebrew, but because of the high percentage of immigrants, many Israelis remain more literate in languages other than Hebrew. The second most dominant language is Arabic, and many native-born Israeli Jews speak it. English is also widely spoken, along with French, German, and Yiddish. Elementary schooling is free and compulsory, and there are reduced fees and special grants for promising students in secondary schools. A large minority of pupils attend state-supported religious schools. Arab pupils generally attend their own schools. There are also schools run by Christian communities and missionary groups. Universities and institutions of higher learning include the Hebrew University in Jerusalem, Tel Aviv University, Bar Ilan University in Ramat Gan, the Technion in Haifa, and the Weizmann Institute of Science in Rehovot. The majority of Israel's population is urban, but its rural population is highly important. There are over 200 agrarian settlements known as *kibbutzim*, in which the members share all goods and receive no wages; all meals are eaten together, important decisions are made by a general meeting of all the members, and children are raised in special houses, away from their parents. Other agricultural settlements also practice cooperative or communal living to some degree, such as common ownership of land or cooperative purchasing and marketing.

Economy. Land reclamation and irrigation have nearly tripled the cultivated area since 1955. Major crops include citrus fruit, grains, olives, melons, and grapes. Mineral resources include gypsum, natural gas, oil, and phosphates; potash, magnesium, and bromine come from the Dead Sea. Light industry is

Israel

Capital:	Jerusalem
Area:	7,992 sq mi (20,700 sq km)
Population:	5,644,000
Language:	Hebrew, Arabic
Government:	Republic
Independent:	1948
Head of gov.:	Prime minister
Per capita:	U.S. $15,920
Mon. unit:	1 New shekel = 100 agorot

developing, and manufactures include chemicals, textiles, and paper. Tourism is a major industry. Because of heavy defense spending and reliance on imported oil, Israel suffers from severe payments deficits and one of the world's highest inflation rates—exceeding 100% per year.

History. In 1947 the UN voted to divide Palestine (then under British mandate) into Jewish and Arab states. After the subsequent British withdrawal, Palestine Arabs and Arab troops from neighboring countries immediately tried to eradicate Israel by force, but the Israelis defeated them, capturing almost all of Palestine. Arab refugees, settled in southern Lebanon, the West Bank, and Gaza Strip in UN-administered camps, are a continuing social and political problem. Refugee camps have proved a fruitful recruiting area and cover for Palestinian guerrilla groups. When Egypt nationalized the Suez Canal in 1956 and closed it to Israeli shipping, Israeli troops overran Gaza and Sinai, winning the right of passage from Elath to the Red Sea. In the Six-Day War (1967) Israel acquired large tracts of its neighbors' territories, including the West Bank and East Jerusalem; these it refused to return without a firm peace settlement. It lost some of these in the Yom Kippur War (1973). In 1978 Egypt and Israel reached the so-called Camp David accords, and Israel began returning the Sinai to Egypt. In 1978 and 1981 Israeli troops invaded south Lebanon in retaliation for Palestinian attacks in Israel, and Israeli bombers destroyed an alleged atomic bomb plant in Iraq in 1981. In 1982 Israeli forces invading Lebanon besieged Beirut; in time Palestinian guerrillas left the city and the Israelis partially withdrew from Lebanon. In 1985 Israeli forces left Lebanon except for a small strip of land in the south. Israel's continued occupation of the West Bank and Gaza remained a problem for Arabs and was a factor in making the country a target of Iraqi missiles in the War in the Persian Gulf (1991). In the early 1990s negotiations regarding the occupied territories improved, and the Jericho district on the West Bank and the Gaza Strip attained some form of autonomy in 1994. During the peace proces prime minister Rabin was killed (Nov. 1995). Execution of the Oslo agreements (1993 and 1995) was difficult under Rabin's successor Netanyahu. In October 1998 Netanyahu and Arafat reached an interim agreement.

See also: Palestine; Palestine Liberation Organization; Zionism.

Israel, Kingdom of, Hebrew kingdom, first as united under Saul, David, and Solomon (1020-922 B.C.), and then the breakaway state in the north founded by Jeroboam I in the territory of the 10 tribes. In 722 B.C. this was overrun by the Assyrians; the tribes were killed, enslaved, or scattered.

Israelites *See:* Jews.

Istanbul (pop. 6,620,200), city in northwest Turkey, lying on the Sea of Marmara and divided by the Bosporus (strait). Until 1930 its official name was Constantinople, of which Istanbul was originally a contraction. Built in A.D. 330 on the site of a former Greek town, Byzantium, it reached its cultural height under Justinian I in the 6th century. After years of decay it was taken by the Ottoman Turks in 1453, and was rebuilt as the Turkish capital, which it remained until 1923 when the capital was moved to Ankara. It is still the economic and cultural heart of Turkey, a port, transport hub, and manufacturing center.
See also: Turkey.

Isthmus, narrow strip of land connecting 2 large land masses. Examples are the Isthmus of Panama, linking North and South America, and the Isthmus of Suez, linking Africa and Asia.

Italian, one of the Romance languages, spoken in Italy and in parts of Switzerland, France, and Yugoslavia. It derives from colloquial Latin. The Tuscan dialect established in the late Middle Ages as a literary language by Dante, Petrarch, and Boccaccio became the foundation of modern Italian. Since the Renaissance, words from other Romance languages have been added. Many of the regional dialects of Italy are still spoken.

Italian literature, literature dated to Francis of Assissi's *Canticle of the Sun* (1226), written not in Latin but the vernacular. The love theme was expressed in Dante's *The Divine Comedy* (1321). Petrarch combined Christian living with classical ethics in *Il Canzoniere* (The Book of Songs) in the mid 1300s and Boccaccio's masterpiece, *The Decameron* (1349-1353), depicted characters of his time with humor. Machiavelli's *The Prince* appeared in 1513. Important works of the late Renaissance include Giorgio Vasari's *Lives of the Artists* (1550), Benvenuto Cellini's autobiography (1558-62), and the pastoral dramas of Torquato Tasso (1544-95) and Battista Guarini (1536-1612). The baroque period (1600s) gave rise to Marino's Adonis, Galileo's scientific prose and Camparella's *The City of the Sun*. The Age of Reason (1700s) was characterized by a less elaborate poetic style. Among the most significant works were the opera libretti (texts) by Pietro Metastasio (1698-1782) and plays of Carlo Goldoni (1707-93), which drew heavily on the tradition of improvised comic theater called *commedia dell'arte*. Romanticism (1800s) celebrated sentiment over reason. A major figure was the poet, novelist, and playwright Alessandro Manzoni (1785-1873). A major movement in Italian literature and theater of the late 19th century was *verismo*, in which the harsh realities of the lives of the poor were portrayed. The futurism movement, typified by the writings of Filippo Tommaso Marinetti (1876-1944), employed language glorifying the violence of the machine age. Luigi Pirandello (1876-1936), who won the 1934 Nobel Prize for literature, wrote

novels but was best known for such ironic and philosophical plays as *Six Characters in Search of an Author* (1921).
The post-World War II neorealists include Alberto Moravia (1907-90) and Cesare Parese (1908-). Recently the novelist Italo Calvino (1923-85) and the playwright Dario Fo (1926-) have achieved international fame.

Italian Somaliland *See:* Somalia.

Italo-Ethiopian War (1935-36), Fascist Italy's conquest of Ethiopia, launched from Italian-held Eritrea and Somalia. Refusing to accept the League of Nations proposals for settling border disputes, Benito Mussolini used planes, guns, and poison gas to overwhelm the ill-equipped Ethiopians, and to forge a new empire. Too weak to halt aggression, the League merely voted economic sanctions against Italy, which simply left the League.
See also: Mussolini, Benito.

Italy, republic in southern Europe, mainly a long, narrow, boot-shaped peninsula that extends into the Mediterranean Sea. It is bounded on the north by France, Switzerland, Austria, and Slovenia; on the west by the Ligurian and Tyrrhenian seas; on the east by the Adriatic Sea; and to the south by the Ionian Sea. The islands of Sicily and Sardinia and numerous smaller islands are parts of its territory. Within its borders are 2 separate, sovereign states: the Republic of San Marino and the Vatican City. The capital is Rome.
Land and climate. A predominantly mountainous country, Italy is divided by a number of natural barriers into distinct regions. In the north is the great curve of the Alps, along which lie Italy's borders with its northern neighbors. In north-central and northeastern Italy are the lakes of Como, Maggiore, and Garda. The Apennine chain runs the length of the peninsula, extending in an easterly direction from Genoa to central Italy and then in a westerly direction into Calabria, the "toe" of the Italian "boot." There are a number of crater lakes in these regions, and the volcanoes of Vesuvius near Naples, Etna in Sicily, and Stromboli in the Lipari Islands are still active. The mountains of Sicily are a continuation of the Apennines, and Sardinia is also mountainous. Italy's single large plain lies in the Po Valley, which crosses the country from west to east just below the Alps. There are narrow coastal plains on either side of the Apennines, and a low, relatively small plateau lies below the Gargano spur. These alluvial plains constitute Italy's most fertile soil. The mountainous areas are largely unproductive. The Po River is Italy's largest and most important river. The Tiber flows through Rome to the Tyrrhenian Sea, and the Arno passes through Florence and Pisa to empty into the Ligurian Sea. Both rivers rise in the Apennines. Most other rivers in Italy are seasonal, and their volume is greatly diminished during the summer. In the Alps, the Po Valley, and the high ranges of the Apennines, winters are cold and summers can be rainy and variable. The rest of the peninsula has a Mediterranean climate: hot, dry summers and mild, rainy winters. Southern Italy and Sicily are especially arid, and irrigation is essential for successful cultivation. Remnants of great forests are found in the Alps, where fir and pine trees grow, and in the remote areas of the Apennines, where there are stands of chestnut, pine, oak, and beech trees. In central and southern Italy olive groves cover much of the land, while the southern regions also produce cacti, citrus trees, and palm trees. With the exception of bears, chamois, deer,

Italy

Capital:	Rome
Area:	116,324 sq mi (301,277 sq km)
Population:	56,783,000
Language:	Italian
Government:	Republic
Independent:	1946 (republic)
Head of gov.:	Prime minister
Per capita:	U.S. $19,020
Mon. unit:	1 Lira = 100 centesimi

and wolves in some remote mountain regions, Italy has few large mammals. Tuna, anchovies, and sardines are plentiful in offshore waters.

Rome contains imposing ruins of its past glory as capital of the western world and is of commercial and cultural importance. The cities of Milan, Turin, and Genoa in the north form the so-called industrial triangle, Milan leading in finance and commerce, Turin in heavy industry, and Genoa in international shipping. Italy's art cities—Venice, Verona, Bologna, Ravenna, Florence, and Siena—bear witness to the significance of Italian culture. Naples, the south's principal city and an international port, is a center for excursions to nearby Sorrento, the islands of Capri and Ischia, and the ruins of Pompeii and Herculaneum. Palermo, the capital of Sicily, has medieval relics of the Norman occupation.

People. Italy is a densely populated country (on average 192 inh./sq km). The highest concentrations are in the industrial cities of the north, the Po Valley, and the areas around Rome and Naples, more than half of the population being urban. Italian, which is derived from Latin, is the official language and is spoken by most citizens, along with a number of regional dialects. Roman Catholicism is the state religion and is taught in the public schools, but freedom of religion is guaranteed.

Economy. Foreign aid and founder membership in the European Common Market boosted postwar economy before the oil crises of the 1970s damaged it. Increased industrial output (steel, chemicals, automobiles, typewriters, machinery, textiles, and shoes) enriched the north, but a faltering agriculture kept the south poor. The main farm products are grapes, citrus fruits, olives, grains, vegetables, and cattle. Mineral resources are limited, but Italy has hydroelectric power, natural gas, and oil. There are also a few nuclear power stations. Tourism helps the trade balance.

History. The Romans, a Latin people of central Italy, held most of the peninsula by 200 B.C., absorbing the Etruscan civilization in the north and Greek colonies (dating from the 8th century B.C.) in the south. In the 5th-6th centuries A.D., barbarian tribes (Visigoths, Ostrogoths, and Lombards) overran Italy, forming Germanic kingdoms. These kingdoms were disputed by the Byzantine Empire, whose lands in Italy became the core of the Papal States. Italy was to remain divided for over 1,000 years, although nominally part of Charlemagne's empire from 774 and part of the Holy Roman Empire from 962. In the Middle Ages the south came under Norman rule. Powerful rival city-states emerged in the center and north, from the late Middle Ages under the Medici and other dynasties. Italy pioneered the Renaissance, but Spain (from the late 1400s) and Austria (from the early 1700s) controlled much of the land until the nationalistic Risorgimento culminated in unity and independence under King Victor Emmanuel II (1861). Italy gained Eritrea, Italian Somaliland, and Libya in Africa, and fought alongside the Allies in World War I. In 1922 the fascist dictator Benito Mussolini seized power, later conquering Ethiopia and siding with Nazi Germany in World War II. Defeated Italy emerged from the war as a republic shorn of its overseas colonies and firmly allied with the West. Since the beginning of the 1990s, Italy is trying to eliminate corruption and organized crime.

Iturbide, Agustín de (1783-1824), Mexican revolutionary and emperor of Mexico (1822-23). As a royalist officer, he united the revolutionaries with his Plan of Iguala (1821), which proclaimed Mexican independence. Exploiting political divisions, he became emperor of independent Mexico. But opposition to his capricious rule brought abdication, exile, and (on his return) execution.

Ivan, name of 6 Russian rulers. **Ivan I** (c.1304-40) was grand prince of Moscow 1328-40. **Ivan II** (1326-59) was grand prince of Moscow 1353-59. **Ivan III**, Ivan the Great (1440-1505), was grand duke of Moscow 1462-1505. He paved the way for a unified Russia by annexing land, repelling the Tatars, strengthening central authority over the Church and nobility, and revising the law code. **Ivan IV**, Ivan the Terrible (1530-84), was grand prince from 1533 and the first tsar of Russia (1547-84). He annexed Siberia, consolidated control of the Volga River, and established diplomatic and trading relations with Europe. He strengthened the law and administration, but was notoriously cruel. **Ivan V** (1666-96) was co-tsar (with Peter I) 1682-90. **Ivan VI** (1740-64) was tsar 1740-41.

Ivan V *See:* Peter I, the Great.

Ives, Charles Edward (1874-1954), U.S. composer. Ives was a major 20th-century innovator. His music (mostly pre-1915) incorporated popular songs and hymn tunes, and exploited dissonance, polytonality, and polymetric construction. Ignored by his contemporaries, he influenced later composers. His best known works include *Three Places in New England* (1908-14) and *Piano Sonata No. 2* (*Concord, Mass., 1840-1860*) (1909-15). His *Symphony No. 3* (1904-11) won a 1947 Pulitzer Prize.

Ives, James Merritt *See:* Currier & Ives.

Ivory, hard white dentine substance making up the tusks of elephants, walruses, and other tusked mammals. Ivory has been greatly prized as a material for carving decorative objects for centuries. The poaching of elephants for their tusks threatens their existence in Africa.

Ivory Coast, republic in West Africa. The capital is Yamoussoukro.

Ivory Coast

Capital:	Yamoussoukro
Area:	124,503 sq mi (322,462 sq km)
Population:	15,466,000
Language:	French
Government:	Presidential republic
Independent:	1960
Head of gov.:	Prime minister
Per capita:	US $660
Mon. unit:	1 CFA franc = 100 centimes

Land and climate. The Ivory Coast occupies about 124,503 sq mi (322,462 sq km) on the northern coast of the Gulf of Guinea and is bordered on the east by Ghana, on the west by Liberia and Guinea, and on the north by Mali and Upper Volta. Behind the sand spits, navigable lagoons, and surf beaches of the 315-mi (507-km) coastline, a dense rain forest extends northward over more than a third of the country. Beyond the forest the ground rises to a plateau, with grass and woodland savannas and isolated granitic masses. The northwest is mountainous. The Sassandra, Bandama, Comoé, Cavally, and other rivers flow southward to the Gulf of Guinea, but only short distances are navigable owing to the many rapids. The climate is hot. The rainy season lengthens and the amount of rain increases the farther one goes south. The extreme south has 2 distinct rainy seasons.

People. The population contains many ethnic and tribal groups, the most important being the Baoulé, Agnis-Ashantis, Kroumen, Mandé, Dan-Gouro, and Koua. Nearly a million Africans from Upper Volta, Guinea, and Mali live in the Ivory Coast, and there are some 35,000 French, Lebanese, and others. Around 40% of the population lives in the towns, the largest of which is Abidjan, chief port, and university center. Over 60% of the population is animist; 25% (mainly in the north) is Muslim, and nearly 13% is Christian. Some 60 tribal languages are spoken, but French is used officially and in commerce and education. The republic devotes more than 25% of its annual budget to education.

Economy. The Ivory Coast was one of the most prosperous countries in West Africa. Farming, forestry, and fisheries provide most of the gross national product. Major cash crops are coffee, and cocoa. Palm oil, pineapples, and bananas are also exported, as are hardwoods, including mahogany, iroko, satinwood, and teak. Diamonds and petroleum are mined. Trade is chiefly with European Community (EC) countries and the United States. The Ivory Coast is an associated state of the EC.

History. Once a French colony, the Ivory Coast became autonomous within the French Community in 1958, but soon opted for full independence (1960). Close economic, cultural, and defense ties with France were retained. Its attitude has tended to be pro-Western, but so far as East-West relations were concerned its official line was neutrality. From 1960 until 1993 Félix Houphouet-Boigny dominated politics. The matter of his succession caused severe political and social unrest.

Ivory palm, or ivory nut palm (Phytelephas macrocarpa), slow-growing palm with a short trunk, native to South America. Plants are male or female. Female flowers form a cluster of seeds that ripen and fall to the ground. Hard and white, the seeds are easy to carve and are used for buttons, chess pieces, and small ornaments.

Ivy, hardy, evergreen plant (genus *Hedera*) of the family Araliaceae. The English ivy (*H. helix*) is a popular house plant, coming in a number of dwarf, climbing, and variegated varieties. Several other plants that have ivylike leaves are also called ivy, for example ground ivy (*Glectoma hederacea*) and Boston or grape ivy (*Parthenocissus tricuspidata*).

Iwo Jima, Japanese island in the western Pacific, scene of a fierce battle in World War II. Largest of the Volcano islands (about 8 sq mi/21 sq km), it was annexed by Japan in 1891 and captured by U.S. marines in Feb.-Mar. 1945 at the cost of over 21,000 U.S. casualties. U.S. administration ended in 1968.
See also: World War II.

Ixtacihuatl, or Iztaccihuatl (Aztec: "white woman"), dormant volcano in central Mexico, about 35 mi (56 km) southeast of Mexico City. Its 3 snow-covered peaks resemble the head, breasts, and feet of a sleeping woman.

Izmir (Greek: Smyrna; pop. 1,757,400), port city on the west coast of Turkey, at the head of the Gulf of Izmir, about 45 mi (72 km) from the Aegean Sea. Founded by Ionians in the 11th century B.C., the city came under Roman rule. In the 4th century A.D. it became part of the Byzantine Empire and, in 1424, of the Ottoman Empire. The Greeks occupied the city in 1919. The Treaty of Lausanne (1923) restored Izmir to Turkey, and an exchange of populations was made. The city is rich in antiquities, including the Agora, or ancient marketplace, and remains of aqueducts.
See also: Turkey.

J

J, tenth letter of the English alphabet. One of the last letters added to the alphabet, *j* is a variant of the letter *i*, from which it became formally distinguished only with the advent of printing. Before that time, *j* was simply an elongated *i*, and the 2 characters were used interchangeably. Thus, in Roman numerals, *j* sometimes replaced *i* to signify 1. It has the sound of *y* in Latin, German, and Scandinavian languages. In Spanish it has the sound of *h*.

Jabbar, Kareem Abdul- *See:* Abdul-Jabbar, Kareem.

Jabiru, any of various large birds of the stork family found from Mexico to Argentina. Jabirus are white with dark blue and red naked skin on the head and neck. Among the largest flying birds in the world, they may reach 55 in (125 cm) in length. They nest in palm trees.

Jaçana, any of several water birds of the jaçana family with long legs and toes that enable it to walk on water lilies and other floating plants. Jaçanas are brightly colored and are found in Africa, southern Asia, Australia, and in the Americas.

Jacaranda, any of various species of flowering tree (genus *Jacaranda*) native to South America and the West Indies and grown widely in Africa, the southern United States, and other warm places. The foliage is made up of fern-like fronds of small leaves; the blue or violet flowers grow in clusters.

Jackal, carnivorous mammal (genus *Canus*) closely related to dogs and wolves. The four species are distributed throughout Africa and South Asia. Though often considered primarily scavengers, jackals will also hunt and kill birds, hares, mice, and insects. Small packs may form temporarily, but they are usually solitary animals.

Jackdaw, small crow (*Carrus monedula*) of Europe, western Asia, and North Africa. It is renowned for its inquisitive and thievish nature and its ability to imitate speech.

Jack Frost, personification of winter, depicted in many children's stories as a rosy-cheeked imp. During the night he paints the world with frost, tracing delicate patterns on window panes and leaving icicles on trees. He probably originated in Scandinavian mythology.

Jack-in-the-pulpit, any of several plants of the arum family (genus Arisaema) that flower in spring before the leaves appear. The flower is really an elaborate, colored tubular structure called a spathe. It surrounds a stem, the spadix, on which many small flowers grow. The flowers are fertilized by flies, and by autumn the spathe falls away to reveal a cluster of bright red berries which are poisonous when eaten raw.

Jack rabbit, common name for hares of the genus *Lepus*. All seven species are found in central and western North America. Jackrabbits have large ears and longer hind legs than rabbits. Found in open, comparatively arid plains, they flourish in drought-stricken, overgrazed areas. They move by jumping rather than running.

Jackson (pop. 395,396), capital and largest city of Mississippi, located on the west bank of the Pearl River. Local industries include processing of cottonseed oil, lumbering, and manufacture of agricultural machinery. There are many oil and gasfields in the region. Founded as a trading post around 1780, Jackson was incorporated in 1821 and named after Andrew Jackson. The city was nearly destroyed during the Civil War.
See also: Mississippi.

Jackson, Alexander Young (1882-1974), an original member of "The Group of Seven" Toronto landscape artists of the 1920s and 1930s. He painted in bold, fresh colors, portraying the beauty of the Canadian wilderness.
See also: Group of Seven.

Jackson, Andrew (1767-1845), 7th president of the United States. Jackson, the first person from west of the Appalachians to be elected president, transformed the presidency with his rugged frontier virtues and devotion to "the common man." His 2 terms in office coincided with a great period of democratic reforms known as "Jacksonian Democracy."

Early life. At age 13, Jackson joined the South Carolina militia, took part in battle, and was captured by the British. He was later released. Jackson studied law and was admitted to the bar in 1787. In 1788, he moved to Nashville—then part of North Carolina—to practice law. In 1791, he married Rachel Robards, a widow.

Politics and war. In 1796, Jackson helped draft a constitution for the new state of Tennessee, then served briefly in the U.S. Congress. Jackson's service in the War of 1812 made him a national hero. He defeated the Creek Indians in the Battle of Horseshoe Bend (1814) and the British in the Battle of New Orleans (1815). For his toughness, Jackson's men dubbed him "Old Hickory." His military successes, flamboyance, and aggressive patriotism made him an appealing candidate for high office. In 1824, he ran for the presidency and won the most votes, but not a majority. The decision went to the House of Representatives, which elected John Quincy Adams. In 1828, Jackson again ran against Adams in a long, bitter, vituperative campaign. Jackson won the presidency; John C. Calhoun became vice president.

President. To eliminate the closed political-caucus system and the rule of wealth and privilege, Jackson introduced a system of "rotation in office." The procedure, meant to shake up the bureaucracy and reward his friends, became known as "the spoils system."

Jackson believed in the slogan "Let the people rule," but also strengthened his power as president. His enemies organized into an opposition party called the Whigs—and the United States once more had a two-party system. Discord within Jackson's administration deepened when Vice President Calhoun opposed the high tariff acts of 1828 and 1832. Calhoun's native state, South Carolina, claimed that states had the right to nullify any federal laws they considered oppressive, and threatened to secede from the Union. To enforce the law and preserve the Union, Jackson ordered troops to Charleston. Calhoun resigned and South Carolina backed down, but this dispute over states' rights remained unsettled until the Civil War. One of the biggest conflicts of Jackson's presidency was his "Bank War." The Bank of the United States, said Jackson, was an unconstitutional and privileged monopoly that would soon control the government. He turned the 1832 presidential campaign into a vendetta against the Bank and easily defeated

Andrew Jackson

7th U.S. President

Born:	Waxhaw settlement, S.C.; Mar. 15, 1767
Term:	Mar. 1829-Mar. 1837
Vice presidents:	John C. Calhoun; Martin Van Buren
Political party:	Democratic
Spouse:	Rachel Donelson Robards Jackson
Children:	None
Died:	Nashville, Tenn.; June 8, 1845

opponent Henry Clay. In Jackson's second term, he supported the Indian Removal Act of 1830, which authorized forced removal of thousands of Indians from traditional homelands, pushed France to pay for damages to U.S. shipping during the Napoleonic Wars, and established diplomatic relations with the new Republic of Texas.
Retirement. Jackson left office in 1837 and spent the last 8 years of his life at the Hermitage, his estate near Nashville.

Jackson, Helen Hunt (1831-85), U.S. author who publicized the mistreatment of Native Americans. *A Century of Dishonor* (1881) condemned governmental malpractice; the novel *Ramona* (1884) described the plight of Native Americans in California's missions.

Jackson, Henry Martin (1912-83), U.S. political leader, Democratic representative (1941-53) and senator from Washington (1953-83). He was chair of the Senate Committee on Energy and Natural Resources, and as ranking Democrat on the Armed Forces Committee he became a major spokesperson on national defense issues. In foreign affairs he was an articulate ally of Israel. In 1972 and 1976 he sought but did not win the democratic presidential nomination.

Jackson, Jesse Louis (1941-), U.S. clergyman and political leader. An associate of Martin Luther King, Jr. during the civil rights movement in the 1960s, Jackson later founded Operation Breadbasket (1966) and People United to Save Humanity (1971). He was the first African American to wage major, though unsuccessful, campaigns for the presidential nomination, running in Democratic primaries in 1984 and 1988. Since the 1988 elections, Jackson has continued his activities as an eloquent and effective speaker on vital national and foreign issues.

Jackson, Mahalia (1911-72), African-American gospel singer whose powerful and expressive contralto voice gained her a worldwide reputation. She was active in the civil rights movement in the 1960s.

Jackson, Michael (1958-), U.S. rock singer, songwriter, and dancer. His album *Thriller* (1982) sold 40 million copies worldwide, making it the largest-selling record ever. Jackson's career began in 1966, when he was the lead singer of his family's band, The Jackson Five. He left the band in the mid-1970s, to pursue a solo career. His hits include *The Wiz* (musical film; 1978), *Off the Wall* (1980), *Bad* (1987), *Dangerous* (1994), and *HIStory* (1995).

Jackson, Robert Houghwout (1892-1954), U.S. Supreme Court justice from 1941 to 1954 and chief U.S. prosecutor at the Nuremberg Trials. A supporter of the New Deal, he served as solicitor general (1938-40) and attorney general (1940-41).
See also: Supreme Court of the United States.

Jackson, Shirley (1919-65), U.S. author. Her best-known works, such as *The Haunting of Hill House* (1959) and the short story "The Lottery" (1948), blend Gothic horror with psychological insight. Autobiographical works, such as *Raising Demons* (1957), are in a contrastingly humorous vein.

Jackson, Stonewall (Thomas Jonathan Jackson; 1824-63), Confederate general in the American Civil War. He earned his nickname for his stand against the Union forces at the first battle of Bull Run (1861). After his bold tactics in the 1862 Shenandoah Valley campaign (May-June 1862), he fought brilliantly at the battles of Richmond, the Seven Days Battles, Cedar Mountain, the second battle of Bull Run, Antietam, and Fredericksburg. At Chancellorsville he was fatally wounded by accidental fire from his own troops.
See also: Civil War, U.S.

Jackson, William Henry (1843-1942), U.S. photographer known for his documentation of the scenery of the West. His photos of Yellowstone for the U.S. Geological Survey led to its being named the first national park. After 1924, he worked as a painter.

Jackson Hole, fertile valley in northwestern Wyoming partially lying in Grand Teton National Park. Part of the Snake River valley, Jackson Hole extends along the Teton Range for about 50 mi (80 km). The valley abounds in wildlife, providing feeding grounds for moose, deer, and elk. Jackson Wildlife Range, within the park, provides an area for naturalist observation and study. The area also attracts many skiers because of its excellent ski conditions.

Jacksonville (pop. 661,200), city in Florida, seat of Duval County. It is located in the northeastern part of the state, on the St. Johns River, about 20 mi (32 km) from the Atlantic Ocean. Jacksonville is a major port and commercial center. Among its industries are the manufacture of paper, wood products, fertilizer, cigars, and machinery. It is also the site of 2 naval air stations. First settled in 1816, Jacksonville was laid out in 1822 and named for Andrew Jackson. It was incorporated in 1832.
See also: Florida.

Jack the Ripper, unknown murderer of at least seven prostitutes in London between Aug. 7 and Nov. 10, 1888. Each victim's throat was cut. Failure to solve the mystery led to the resignation of the head of Scotland Yard.

Jacob, in the Old Testament, son of Isaac and Rebecca, ancestor of the Israelites. He fled after tricking his older twin, Esau, out of his birthright. He settled in Mesopotamia, later returning to Canaan. After wrestling with an angel, he was given the name Israel. He had 2 wives, Leah and her younger sister, Rachel. (Gen. 25-50.)
See also: Bible; Old Testament.

Jacob, François (1920-), French biologist who shared with J.L. Monod and A.M. Lwoff the 1965 Nobel Prize for physiology or medicine for his work with them on regulatory gene action in bacteria.

Jacobean style, term applied to early English Renaissance architecture and furniture that flourished during the reign of James I. Decorative motifs from the late Perpendicular period were combined with crude classical details. In furniture of this period, strapwork, or forms carved in flat relief, was popular, along with Flemish-inspired classical ornament. In furnishings, the style

lasted into the late 17th century. Many examples of Jacobean style can be seen in the colleges of Oxford and Cambridge universities.
See also: Renaissance.

Jacobins, powerful political clubs during the French Revolution, named for the former Jacobin (Dominican) convent where the leaders met. Originally middle-class, they became increasingly radical advocates of terrorism. After they seized power in 1793, the extremists, led by Robespierre, instituted the Reign of Terror. In the Thermidor reaction the clubs were suppressed, to revive under the Directory and finally be put down by Napoleon.
See also: French Revolution; Robespierre, Maximilien Marie Isidore.

Jacobites, supporters of that branch of the House of Stuart exiled by the Glorious Revolution of 1688; a large number were Highland Scots. Jacobites sought to regain the English throne for James II and his descendants, notably James Edward Stuart (1688-1766), "The Old Pretender," and Charles Edward Stuart (1720-88), "Bonnie Prince Charlie." After rebellions in 1715, 1719, and 1745, they were effectively crushed at the battle of Culloden Moor (1746).
See also: England; Stuart, House of.

Jacobs, Joseph (1854-1916), English scholar and writer of children's fairy tales. His works include *Aesop's Fables* (1889), *Celtic Fairy Tales* (1891), and *More Celtic Fairy Tales* (1894), which include "Jack and the Beanstalk" and "The Three Little Pigs." He was also secretary (1882-1900) of the Russo-Jewish Committee (London), formed to improve the condition of Jews in Russia.

Jade, name for either of 2 tough, hard minerals with a compact interlocking structure, commonly green but sometimes white, mauve, or yellow. Jade is used as a gem stone to make carved jewelry and ornaments. Nephrite, the commoner form of jade, occurs in China, the former USSR, New Zealand, and the western United States. Jadeite, rarer and prized for its more intense color and translucence, is found chiefly in Burma, China, and Japan.

Jaeger, any of various large, fast-flying birds (genus *Stercoranius*) of the northern seas. Jaegers nest in the Arctic but migrate south along the coasts of the United States. They can be recognized by their slender, bent wings and their fan-shaped tails, with 2 long feathers in the center.

Jaffa, port on the coast of the Mediterranean Sea, just south of Tel Aviv, Israel, with which it was merged in 1949. Jaffa is one of the oldest cities in the world, dating back to ancient Egypt. Most of its mainly Arab population left in 1948.
See also: Israel.

Jagger, Mick *See:* Rolling Stones.

Jaguar, large cat (*Panthera onca*) found in Mexico and Central and South America. The jaguar's coat bears black spots arranged in rosettes on a background varying from white to yellow. It lives in thick cover in forests or swamps. Though they are accomplished swimmers, jaguars hunt mostly on the ground or in trees. Adult males stand about 2.5 ft (76 cm) tall at the shoulder and weigh about 200 lb (90 kg).

Jaguarundi, long-tailed, short-legged cat (*Felis jaguarondi*) that resembles a large weasel. Its fur is rusty red or gray. The jaguarundi lives in brush and grassland from the southwestern United States to Argentina. It feeds on small animals and fruit.

Jahan, Shah *See:* Shah Jahan.

Jahn, Helmut (1940-), German-born U.S. architect whose work emphasizes steel, glass, and concrete, erected straight lines and overlapping planes, as exemplified in Kemper Arena (1974) and Bartle Convention Center (1976), both in Kansas City, Mo. In 1980 he shifted to a post-modern style combining modern and historical elements.
See also: Architecture.

Jai alai, or pelota, Spanish-Basque game similar to handball, from which it evolved in the 17th century. The ball, or *pelota*, is made of hard rubber covered with goatskin. Each player is equipped with a *cesta*, a narrow, basket-shaped racket of wicker, which is strapped to the player's wrist. The jai alai court, or *cancha*, is enclosed by three walls, the fourth side consisting of a wire screen that protects spectators. The players alternately throw the ball against the front wall, catching it in the cesta either on the fly or after one bounce on the floor. A player is awarded a point if he/she served, and their opponent is unable to return the ball off the front wall. The game is extremely popular in Cuba, Mexico, and Spain. It is usually associated with betting.

Jainism, philosophy and religion with about 2 million adherents, mainly in India. It was founded in about the 6th century B.C. as a protest against the ritualism of Hinduism. The last of its succession of 24 original saints, called Mahavira or Jina, seems to have been a historical figure. He taught the doctrine of *ahimsa*, or non-injury to all living animals. Jains do not believe in a creator God, but see the universe as divided into two independent eternal categories: "life" and "non-life". They maintain that people can reach perfection only through ascetic, charitable, and monastic discipline.

Jakarta (pop. 8,222,500), capital and largest city of Indonesia, in northwestern Java. It is the country's commercial, transport, and industrial center, manufacturing automobiles, textiles, chemicals, and iron products, and processing lumber and food. Much of Indonesia's foreign trade passes through the port. The city grew out of the Dutch East India Company settlement of Batavia (1619). With independence in 1949 it was made the capital and renamed Djakarta, now officially spelled Jakarta.
See also: Indonesia.

Jakes, Milos (1922-), former president of Czechoslovakia (1987-89). A politcally active communist since 1945 who studied in Moscow, Jakes was appointed secretary-general of the communist party and president in 1987. The weakening of the communist party in 1989 and the growth of a reform movement led to his resignation that year.
See also: Czechoslovakia.

Jamaica

Capital: Kingston
Area: 4,244 sq mi (10,991 sq km)
Population: 2,635,000
Language: English
Government: Parliamentary monarchy in the British Commonwealth
Independent: 1962
Head of gov.: Prime minister
Per capita: U.S. $1,510

Jamaica, third-largest island in the West Indies, situated in the Caribbean Sea, 90 mi (145 km) south of Cuba and 100 mi (161 km) west of Haiti. The name Jamaica is derived from the Arawak Indian name *Xaymaca* (isle of woods and water).

Land and climate. Jamaica's surface is largely a limestone plateau, with a backbone of mountains and volcanic hills running east and west. In the east, Blue Mountain has an elevation of 7,402 ft (2,256 m), the highest point on the island. Sugar, bananas, allspice, coffee, ginger, and citrus fruits are grown on the warm mountain slopes. Rain forests in the north and northeast supply bamboo, mahogany, and ebony. Vegetation is generally richly tropical or subtropical, with over 3,000 species of flowering plants. Jamaica is generally rainy, with the heaviest falls occurring in May and Oct. Kingston, the capital, is fairly dry, with only 30 to 35 in (76 to 89 cm) per year. Hurricanes may occur between Aug. and Nov.

People. Most Jamaicans are of African descent. The others are East Indians, Chinese, and Europeans, mainly British. English is spoken throughout the island, and a local patois (a mixture of African and archaic English words) is also used. Most people are Protestants, either Anglican or Baptist. There are over 800 schools on the island, but people in remote rural areas are often illiterate. The principal campuses of the University of the West Indies are located in Jamaica. Over 30% of the people live in rural areas, but in recent years the population of the two major towns, Kingston and Montego Bay, has increased. The birthrate is high, and the density of population (564 persons per sq mi) creates serious problems.

Economy. Jamaica is predominantly agricultural. Sugar refining and the manufacture of molasses and rum are the principal industries. The island also has a thriving tourist industry. In 1942 deposits of bauxite were discovered, and today Jamaica is one of the world's chief suppliers of this aluminum ore. Gypsum is another important export commodity.

History. In 1494, Christopher Columbus discovered Jamaica, which was thinly settled by the Spaniards in 1509 and remained a Spanish colony until it was ceded to the British in 1670. By the 18th century the original inhabitants, the Arawak Indians, had been killed off by disease and the harsh treatment of their colonial rulers. From 1660 African slaves were imported to work in the lucrative sugar industry. Jamaica was particularly prosperous under Sir Henry

Morgan, a buccaneer who served as lieutenant-governor from 1674 to 1683. By the 18th century the island was a leading slave trading center.
When slavery was abolished in 1834, the sugar industry declined. Thereafter unemployment, poverty, and overpopulation caused tension, and riots occurred, especially in the 19th and early 20th centuries. To improve conditions, crop diversification was encouraged, including the cultivation of bananas, and substantial governmental changes were made between 1930 and 1940. In 1962, after 3 centuries as a British colony, Jamaica became an independent nation within the Commonwealth of Nations.

James, name of 6 kings of Scotland. **James I** (1394-1437) technically became king in 1406, but he was held prisoner in England 1406-24. After being ransomed by Scottish nobles, he returned to Scotland and suppressed a turbulent aristocracy; he was assassinated during an abortive aristocratic revolt. **James II** (1430-60) reigned 1437-60. His son, **James III** (1451-88), reigned 1460-88. His son, **James IV** (1473-1513), king from 1488 to his death, was the great Renaissance king of Scotland. He reformed law and administration, extended royal authority, built a powerful navy, and was a patron of the arts and sciences. He married Margaret, daughter of Henry VII of England. He was killed at the battle of Flodden Field during an attempted Scottish invasion of England. **James V** (1512-1542), his son, was king from 1513, but actually reigned 1528-42, during the beginnings of the Reformation. He supported Catholicism for financial and political reasons. His daughter was Mary Queen of Scots. He died soon after his army was defeated by the English at Solway Moss. **James VI**, king of Scotland from 1567, became James I of England.
See also: Scotland.

James, name of 2 kings of England, Scotland, and Ireland, both belonging to the House of Stuart. **James I** (1566-1625), became king of Scotland in 1567, when his mother, Mary Queen of Scots, was forced to abdicate. Until 1583, when James turned 17, the country was ruled by regents. James supported Elizabeth I of England and in 1587 accepted the execution of his mother. In 1603 he succeeded Elizabeth, becoming king of England. His early popularity waned as he sought autocratic control over Parliament, bolstered by his belief in the divine right of kings. He sponsored the translation of the Authorized Version of the Bible (1611), also known as the King James Version. His strict anti-Puritan views caused many Puritans to flee to America, where they founded Plymouth Colony (1620). **James II** (1633-1701), reigned 1685-88. He was the second son of Charles I, successor of James I. During the English civil war he fled to France (1648). He returned to England in 1660, at the time of the Restoration. A Roman Catholic, James II acceded to the throne in 1685, after the death of Charles II. His autocratic methods and pro-Catholic appointments made him unpopular, and in 1688 James II was ousted by William of Orange, his Protestant son-in-law, in what became known as the Glorious Revolution. In 1689 James tried to restore his rule from his base, Ireland, but his forces were defeated in the battle of the Boyne (1690).
See also: England.

James, Epistle of, 20th book of the New Testament, traditionally attributed to St. James, the Less. One of the Catholic (general) Epistles, it is primarily a homily on Christian ethics.
See also: Bible; New Testament.

James, Henry (1843-1916), U.S.-born novelist and critic, brother of William James. He settled in London in 1876 and became a British citizen in 1915. A recurring theme in his work is the corruption of innocence, particularly as shown by the contrast between sophisticated, corrupt Europeans and brash, innocent Americans. James's most famous works, distinguished by subtle characterization and a precise, complex prose style, include *The Americans* (1877), *Daisy Miller* (1878), *The Portrait of a Lady* (1891), *The Turn of the Screw* (1898), and *The Golden Bowl* (1904).

James, Jesse (1847-82), U.S. outlaw. A member of William Quantrill's raiders during the Civil War, he and his brother Frank led the James Gang, robbing banks and trains from Arkansas to Colorado and Texas, beginning in 1866. Living as an ordinary citizen in St. Joseph, Mo., he was murdered for a $5,000 reward by gang member Robert Ford.

James, P(hyllis) D(orothy) (1920-), English mystery writer. In her novel *Cover Her Face* (1962), she created the character of Adam Dalgliesh, Scotland Yard commander. He was also the hero of *Death of an Expert Witness* (1977) and *A Taste of Death* (1986). She also introduced Cordelia Gray, a London detective, in *An Unsuitable Job for a Woman* (1972) and *The Skull Beneath the Skin* (1982). In 1997 *A Certain Justice* was published.

James, Saint, Christian leader of the 1st century A.D., referred to as the brother of Jesus in the Galatian Epistles, though theologians have disputed any blood relationship between them. James is credited as the author of the Epistle of James in the New Testament, but true authorship is uncertain. His feast day is May 3.
See also: Apostles.

James, William (1842-1910), U.S. philosopher and psychologist, considered the originator of the doctrine of pragmatism; brother of novelist Henry James. His first major work was *Principles of Psychology* (1890). Turning his attention to questions of religion, in 1902 he published *The Varieties of Religious Experience*, which has remained his best-known work. James's pragmatism, which he called "radical empiricism," argued that the truth of any proposition rested on its outcome in experience, and not on any eternal principles.
See also: Pragmatism.

James Bay, inlet of the southern part of Hudson Bay, Canada. The bay was named for Captain Thomas James, who made extensive explorations of the area in 1631. Several early Hudson's Bay Company colonies were established there.

James River, river in Virginia, formed by the confluence of the Jackson and Cowpasture rivers and flowing east and southeast past Lynchburg and Richmond to Chesapeake Bay. About 340 mi (547 km) long, it is navigable for about 150 mi (241 km) between Richmond and the bay.

James the Greater, Saint, one of the twelve apostles of Jesus along with his brother, St. John. He was the first apostle to be martyred, and he is venerated widely in Spain, as Santiago.
See also: Apostles.

James the Less, Saint, one of the twelve apostles of Jesus. He is often associated with James the Younger and James, the "brother" of Jesus, but they are probably three different people.
See also: Apostles.

Jamestown, former village in southeastern Virginia, on the James River, first permanent English settlement in North America. Founded in 1607 by colonists from the London Company, it was named for King James I. Lord De la Warr reinforced it in 1610, and John Rolfe introduced tobacco cultivation in 1612. In 1619 the House of Burgesses, first representative government of the colonies, met there. The village was destroyed during Bacon's rebellion in 1676.
See also: Virginia.

Janácek, Leo (1854-1928), Czech composer and collector of Moravian folk music, best known for his operas *Jenufa* (1904), *Katia Kabanova* (1921), and *The Makropulos Case* (1926). First professor of composition at the Prague Conservatory (1919), he wrote many songs, as well as chamber and choral works, in particular the *Glagolitic Mass* (1926).

Janissaries, elite Turkish infantry of the 14th-19th century, conscripted from prisoners of war and Christian children abducted and reared as fanatical Muslims. From 1600 Turks gradually infiltrated the highly privileged corps, which became increasingly corrupt. Unruly and rebellious, it was massacred by order of Sultan Mahmud II in 1826.
See also: Infantry.

Jansen, Cornelius (1585-1638), Dutch Roman Catholic theologian. In 1636 he was appointed bishop of Ypres, Belgium. In *Augustinus* (published posthumously, 1640), Jansen argued for a return on the part of Christians to the positions of St. Augustine on grace, free will, predestination, and salvation. Though counter to church doctrine, these ideas attracted many Catholic followers in France and the Low Countries. Early 18th-century papal bulls discredited Jansenism, but in parts of the Netherlands Jansenists still have churches.
See also: Theology.

Jansky, Karl Guthe (1905-50), U.S. radio engineer. While studying static interference for the Bell Telephone Laboratories (1931), he discovered radio waves from sources outside the earth. This led to the development of radio astronomy.

Janus, in Roman mythology, guardian of gateways and doors and god of beginnings. The first hour of each day and first day of each month was holy to him. January is named for him, and many Roman doorways and arches bear his image: a double-faced head looking in 2 directions.
See also: Mythology.

Japan (Japanese: *Nippon*), country off the east coast of Asia, an archipelago of 4 principal islands (Hokkaido, Honshu, Kyushu, and Shikoku), 500 smaller islands, and 3,000 minor ones. The capital is Tokyo.
Land. The Japanese archipelago extends 1,300 mi (2,092 km) from northeast to southwest. Most of its area of 154,883 sq mi (377,835 sq km) is accounted

Japan

Capital:	Tokyo
Area:	145,883 sq mi (377,835 sq km)
Population:	125,932,000
Language:	Japanese
Government:	Parliamentary monarchy
Independent:	1947 (constitutional monarchy)
Head of gov.:	Prime minister
Per capita:	U.S. $39,640
Mon. unit:	1 Yen = 100 sen

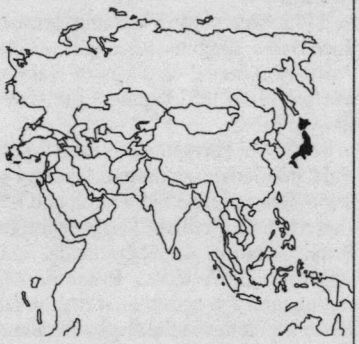

for by the 4 main islands. More than 4/5 of Japan is mountainous; the highest peak is Mount Fuji (12,385 ft/3,775 m). More than 250 Japanese peaks are higher than 6,500 ft (1,981 m); there are about 50 active volcanoes. Most Japanese live in the 1/5 of the country that is relatively flat. There are many streams and rivers; among many inland lakes, Lake Biwa is the largest.

Japan is poor in certain resources, with almost no iron ore and with petroleum that meets less than 1/10 of its requirements. Luxuriant forests cover 2/3 of the country. Large mammals include deer, monkeys, bears, wild boars, and wolves; smaller mammals are badgers, ermines, foxes, hares, mink, otters, and squirrels. About 450 species of birds have been observed.

People. One of the world's most densely populated nations, Japan has more than 124 million people. Its population density of 817 people per sq mi creates economic, social, and pollution problems.

The Japanese are basically a Mongoloid people; centuries of isolation and inbreeding have produced a homogenous racial stock. Japanese is the universal language, except among the 15,000 Ainus (a primitive people of Caucasian origin) and 707,000 foreigners (mostly Korean) living in the country. English is the main foreign language.

The 2 major religions are Buddhism and Shinto. Many Japanese observe practices of both, with a Shinto family shrine and a Buddhist family altar. Schools are crowded, but the literacy rate is 99%, Asia's highest. The higher education system includes 475 colleges and universities and 610 junior colleges.

Economy. Having moved from feudalism to capitalism in just over a century, Japan is one of the world's leading industrial nations. Products range from ships and automobiles to electronic equipment, cameras, and textiles. Imports include coal, petroleum, and industrial raw materials. Rice is the chief agricultural crop. Japan has extensive fisheries.

History. Artifacts dating from at least 4000 B.C. have been found in Japan. The first Japanese state was ruled by the Yamato clan, from whom the present imperial house is said to descend. Japan has been subject to cultural influences from China by way of Korea. Rice cultivation was introduced from China (c.250 B.C.) and Buddhism from Korea (c.A.D. 538). In the 7th century A.D., Chinese ideographic script was adapted to the Japanese language, and the administrative system of the T'ang Dynasty was adopted. Land became the

property of the emperor, who distributed it, and clan chiefs became imperial officials.
In 1192 Minamoto Yoritomo seized power as shogun (military dictator). Successive shoguns ruled absolutely, with the emperors as figureheads. Power was based on a vassal class of warrior knights, or samurai. Feudal warfare (1033-1573) paved the way for powerful lords who were free of shogun rule.
In 1543, the Portuguese visited Japan, followed by other European traders and Christian missionaries. A policy of isolation (sakoku) closed Japan to all foreigners except a few Dutch and Chinese traders until 1853-4, when U.S. Commodore Matthew Perry negotiated a trade treaty. Similar treaties with Britain, France, the Netherlands, and Russia followed. The shogunate collapsed in 1867. Under Emperor Meiji (1867-1912), Tokyo became the capital, and a program of westernization began.
Japan's victories in the Russo-Japanese War and Sino-Japanese Wars won her recognition as a world power, as did her support of the Allies in World War I. In the 1930s a militarist regime took power, built a large Asian colonial empire, and formed an alliance with Nazi Germany and Fascist Italy. Japan entered World War II with a surprise attack on Pearl Harbor (1941). The war brought economic ruin and nuclear devastation, and the Japanese surrendered in 1945. Since World War II, Japan has concentrated on economic development. The end of the 1990s was characterized by economic deterioration.

Japan, Sea of, arm of the Pacific Ocean between Japan and the eastern coast of Asia. It has an area of about 400,000 sq mi (1 million sq km) and is warmed by the Japan Current. Average depth is 4,500 ft (1,370 m), with some trenches descending to 12,000 ft (3,660 m).
See also: Pacific Ocean.

Japan clover *See:* Lespedeza.

Japan Current, or Kuroshio, warm strong ocean current running northeast along the southeastern Japanese coast. In summer, some of the current splits off, eventually reaching the Sea of Japan; most however, turns east past the Aleutians to form the North Pacific Current.

Japanese, language spoken by more than 100 million people, most of them in Japan. Japanese seems not to be related to any other language, although some linguists believe there may be a connection with Korean. Written Japanese originally used only adapted Chinese characters (*kanji*); in the 8th century phonetic characters (*kana*) were added.

Japanese beetle, metallic green beetle (*Popillia japonica*), related to the june beetle. In the United States, where it was accidentally introduced from Japan in 1917, it is an agricultural pest because none of its natural enemies was established. The larvae live underground and feed on plant roots.

Japanese chin, or Japanese spaniel, dog native to China. A favorite pet among Japanese royalty for centuries, the species was brought to the United States in the mid-1850s after Commodore Perry's expedition. The dogs have a soft white coat with uniform black or red patches around the face. They weigh about 5-9 lb (2-4 kg).

Japanese literature, one of the world's great literatures, consisting of works written in the Japanese language. Around the 6th century, largely through Korean influences, the Japanese came into contact with Chinese culture and civilization and adopted Chinese ideograms. By the early 8th century, the Japanese had begun to produce a native literature. The *Kojiki* (Record of Ancient Matters), the sacred book of Shinto, dates from 712 A.D. A work glorifying the imperial family and its divine descent, the *Kojiki* also recounts early folk tales, legends, myths, and songs. The *Nihonshoki* (The Chronicles of Japan) are the earliest Japanese historical work; they date from 720 A.D. Toward the end of the 8th century, after 771 A.D., came the *Man'yoshu*, a remarkable compendium of 4,500 poems, a wide-ranging record of lyric expression in the native language.

The Heian period (794-1185) marked the end of Japan's absorption of the Chinese influence and the emergence of its own distinct literary character and genius. The Chinese ideograms were too complex for rapidly recording running throught or quick impressions, so the Japanese developed two distinct cursive scripts, the flowing *hiragana* and the angular *katakana*. The greatest work of the Heian period and one of the great works of world literature was composed in the *hiragana* script by a prominent woman of the Heian court, Lady Murasaki Shikibu. Her *Tale of Genji*, written in the early 11th century, is an elaborate tale of the love and intrigues of a certain Prince Genji. The work is not only a skillfully told story but is also rich in its portrayal of character and deeply colored by a Buddhist sensibility.

The Heian court and its aristocracy were replaced by a military government and, from 1185 to 1587, the samurai, or soldier, class became dominant. The change was reflected in literature. *The Tale of the Heike*, Japan's greatest historical fiction, was written in the early 1300s. *Tanka* continued to be composed, but poems called *renga* were also written. *Renga* consisted of chains of poems made by several poets, usually composed as they drank. But it was also during these centuries that two great literary forms were developed. The Noh drama, powerful in its solemnity and restraint, featured a masked actor, dance, chanting, and musical accompaniment. It was perfected by the actor and playwright Zeami Motokiyo. The *kyogen* was slapstick farces which accompanied Noh performances.

The reign of the samurai was marked by frequent instability and bloody warfare. Power was finally consolidated under a single clan which gave its name to an era, the Tokugawa (1603-1867). Under the Tokugawa, the written language was standardized. The kabuki theater developed with its brilliant costumes, melodramatic tales, and energetic acting style. And, in the early 1700s, the puppet theater, or *bunraku*, was brought to a high level of refinement.

Heian literature was dominated by an aristocratic sensibility; the literature of the Tokugawa era was patronized by the bourgeoisie. In the late 1600s, Ihara Saikaku (1642-93) gave up a career as a poet to pursue a successful career writing fiction. His contemporary, Matsura Basho (1648-94) developed the *haiku*, a poetic form of 17 syllables, which challenged and eventually supplanted the *tanka*. The Tokugawas pursued a policy of strict isolation for Japan. That policy ended with the arrival of Commodore Perry in 1858. In 1867, the samurai were replaced by the Emperor Meiji. Just as early Japan had studied China, Meiji Japan set out to study the West, and the impact of those studies opened new fields for Japan's literary talents. Prominent among the Meiji writers of the 1880s who learned western languages, studied western literature, and took the first decisive steps toward mastering the new forms were Yamada Bimyo, Koyo Ozaki, Rohan Koda, Futabatei Shimei, and Tsubouchi Shoyo. Tsubouchi Shoyo was a Shakespeare scholar and urged Japanese writers to compose European-style novels. In response, Futabatei produced *Drifting Clouds* in 1889. In a remarkably short time, Japanese writers created outstanding works. Perhaps the greatest Japanese novelist was Natsume Soseki, who began his career with the now-famous *I Am a Cat* in 1905. Ryonosuke Akutagawa wrote brilliant stories and fables, including *Rashomon*. Shiga Naoya wrote *A Dark Night's Passing* in 1937. Japan's outstanding contemporary writers include Jun'ichiro Tanizaki, author of *The Makioka Sisters*; Jiro Osaragi; Osamu Dazai; Kobo Abe; Yasunari Kawabata, author of *Snow Country* and recipient of the Nobel Prize for literature in 1968; Yukio Mishima, author of *Confessions of a Mask*; and Oaka Shohei.

Virtually everyone in Japan can read. As a result, all branches of literature have benefited. Apart from numerous publications and periodicals, it has been observed that more works of the world's literature have been translated into Japanese than into any other single language.

Japanese print, fine art developed in 17th-century Japan. The artist drew a pattern onto a wood block and a carver cut the pattern, leaving only a portion of the surface raised. The design could be reproduced many times by applying ink to its surface and printing it on paper. Printmaking was originally done in black and white, but color techniques were introduced by the mid-1700s.

Japanese spaniel *See:* Japanese chin.

Jarrell, Randall (1914-65), U.S. poet and influential critic. His poetry is emotional and often pervaded with a sense of tragedy and alienation; best-known collections are *Selected Poems* (1955), *The Woman at the Washington Zoo* (1960), and *The Lost World* (1965). *Poetry and the Age* (1953) is the first of three collections of his criticism.

Jaruzelski, Wojciech (1923-), Polish general and politician, appointed both premier and Communist party leader in 1981 to resolve the crisis involving the independent trade union Solidarity. He arrested the Solidarity leaders and imposed martial law, but he was unable to remedy the country's economic difficulties. In 1985 he became president under a new system of government and resigned as premier. In Sept. 1990 he indicated his intention to step down in order that an election might take place. In 1996 he and eleven others had to appear in court for violently crushing a workers' revolt in 1970, in which 44 people were killed.

Jasmine, or jessamine, vine or shrub (genus *Jasminum*) with yellow or white star-shaped flowers, noted for their fine scent. It is found throughout Europe, Asia, and Africa and has become naturalized in the United States. In the south of France, acres of jasmine are grown and their flowers plucked for the oil, which is used in perfumes.

Jason, Greek mythological hero. Jason laid claim to the kingdom of Iolkos, which his uncle, Pelias, had seized from Jason's father, Aeson. Pelias agreed

to return the kingdom if Jason brought him the magical Golden Fleece, held by King Aeetes of Colchis. Jason assembled a force, the Argonauts, who set sail in the Argo to seek the fleece. After many adventures, they recovered the fleece, with the aid of Aeetes's daughter, Medea, who fell in love with Jason. She accompanied him back to Greece and became his queen. But when Jason tried to divorce Medea, she destroyed Creusa, his bride-to-be, as well as Creusa's father, and (in some versions of the story) her own children. The gods then caused Jason to wander aimlessly until his death.
See also: Argonauts; Mythology.

Jasper, opaque, compact, fine-grained variety of quartz used in jewelry and interior decoration. Its color varies from red, yellow, brown, and dark green to grayish blue.

Jasper National Park, park in the Canadian Rockies of western Alberta, established 1907. Covering an area of 4,200 sq mi (10,900 sq km), it is a scenic preserve of peaks, glaciers, lakes, rivers, canyons, waterfalls, and hot springs. Many vanishing species are protected, including wolves, bears, and herds of elk.

Jaspers, Karl (1883-1969), German philosopher noted for his steadfast opposition to Nazism and his acute yet controversial analyses of German society. Early work in psychopathology led him into the Heidelberg University philosophical faculty in 1913. He there became one of Germany's foremost exponents of existentialism.
See also: Existentialism.

Jaundice, abnormal yellowing of skin and the whites of the eyes caused by excess bilirubin, normally removed by the liver and excreted as bile, in the blood. Jaundice occurs with liver damage (hepatitis, late stages of cirrhosis) and when the bile ducts leading from the liver to the duodenum are obstructed by gallstones or by cancerous tumors.

Java, island in southeastern Asia, part of the Republic of Indonesia, about 600 mi by 120 mi and bounded on the south and southwest by the Indian Ocean. Java accommodates nearly two-thirds of the population of Indonesia, together with the capital, Djakarta. Other important cities include Bandung, Surabaja, and Medan.
Java is traversed from east to west by a chain of volcanic mountains, the highest of which is Mt. Semeru (12,060 ft/3,676 m). The fertile tropical plain along the northern coast is drained by the Solo and Brantas rivers, and rainfall is heavy, for Java lies just south of the equator.
The Javanese are mainly farmers (many are smallholders), producing rubber, coffee, tea, sugar, cocoa, and cichona bark (from which quinine is derived) for export. Small-scale manufacture of consumer goods was encouraged by the former Dutch administration and has been further developed by the present Indonesian government. For centuries handicrafts have been important to the economy, and Java is noted for its artistic silverwork and batik textiles. By far the most important of Java's mineral resources, oil, is found in the northeastern part of the island and is well exploited. Other mineral deposits include gold, phosphate, and manganese.
See also: Indonesia.

Java man, early human species. Fossils found on the Indonesian island of Java in 1891 gave scientists evidence to date the species from 500,000 to 1 million years ago. Java man is an instance of *Homo erectus*, a stage of human development when humans began to stand erect. Examination of skulls show large jaws and teeth.
See also: Prehistoric people.

Javelin, spear made from lightweight metal or wood with a sharp pointed tip. Javelin throwing, a track and field competition, is an Olympic sport. After a running start, the competitor throws the javelin over the shoulder, releasing it in a high arc, in an attempt to gain the greatest distance on each throw.

Javelina *See:* Peccary.

Jay, brightly colored, noisy bird of the crow family. Many jays bear crests. They are found in North and South America, Europe, and Asia. The blue jay (*Cyanocitta cristata*) lives in eastern North America, while the scrub jay (*Aphelocoma coerulescens*), Steller's jay (*C. stelleri*), and piñon (*Gymnorhinus cyanocephalus*) are found in the Rocky Mountains.

Jay, John (1745-1829), U.S. lawyer, first chief justice of the Supreme Court. He helped draft the N.Y. state constitution in 1777, and in 1778 he was elected president of the Continental Congress. In 1782, along with Benjamin Franklin and John Adams, he negotiated the Treaty of Paris (1783) which ended the Revolutionary war. As secretary for foreign affairs (1784-89) he supported the new constitution, believing in the need for a strong central government. He was chief justice of the Supreme Court (1789-95). In 1794 he negotiated the unpopular Jay Treaty. A conservative member of the Federalist Party, he served as governor of N.Y. 1795-1801.
See also: Supreme Court of the United States.

Jay Treaty, agreement between the United States and Britain negotiated by John Jay, 1794, to settle conflicts arising out of violations of the 1783 Treaty of Paris and to regulate trade and navigation in the Atlantic. The Jay Treaty provided for British evacuation of northwestern forts, compensation for confiscated U.S. shipping, U.S. repayment to Britain of prewar debts, and limited trading concessions to the United States. No mention was made of the impressment of U.S. seamen or compensation for abducted U.S. slaves. For this reason the treaty was considered a capitulation to the British.

Jazz, unique form of American music. A piece of jazz music begins with a melody and a harmonic scheme, on which the players improvise variations, typically using syncopated rhythms. The word "jazz" may derive from a slang word describing a swaying kind of walk, or it may come from the French word *jaser*, to gossip.
The origins of jazz are found in the work songs, laments, and spirituals of the slaves of the U.S. South. With the abolition of slavery and the migration of thousands of black workers to southern towns and cities, especially New Orleans, these songs and spirituals were given a new impetus. As they were

played by the street bands that accompanied weddings and funerals and by the smaller bands that played in the cafés of the Storyville district of New Orleans, such forms as the blues, ragtime, and the stomp were established.

The original New Orleans style started to change in the 1920s as blacks moved to the cities of the North. New styles emerged, such as the piano boogie woogie, and jazz began to find a wider audience, thanks to the radio and phonograph. In the 1930s and 1940s, big bands, composed mainly of white musicians, played a commercialized type of jazz called swing, which became the most popular dance music on both sides of the Atlantic. In the late 1940s a completely new jazz style, called bebop, appeared on the scene, pioneered by several brilliant black musicians. Bebop was the start of the modern jazz era. "West Coast" and "cool" jazz styles followed in the 1950s and 1960s. The latest jazz developments are almost totally removed in both form and spirit from the original New Orleans style.

One element in jazz that has not changed much is its instrumentation. The old New Orleans bands generally consisted of trumpet or cornet, trombone, clarinet, saxophone, piano, double-bass, and drums. The majority of jazz musicians still play one or another of these instruments.

Many jazz musicians figure in the history of 20th-century music. Joe "King" Oliver, Edward "Kid" Ory, Sidney Bechet, Ferdinand "Jelly Roll" Morton, Louis Armstrong, Thomas "Fats" Waller, and the first great white jazzman, Leon "Bix" Beiderbecke, were among the early masters of jazz. Fletcher Henderson, Edward "Duke" Ellington, and William "Count" Basie led some of the great bands of the 1930s and 1940s, while Glenn Miller, Benny Goodman, and Woodrow "Woody" Herman were among the band leaders of the swing era. Perhaps the most passionate jazz has come from the great blues singers, such as Bessie Smith and Billie Holiday. Modern jazz can be traced through the playing of musicians like Coleman Hawkins, Lester Young, Earl Hines, Charlie Parker, John "Dizzy" Gillespie, Miles Davis, and John Coltrane. In the 1960s a new "free form" jazz was developed by Ornette Coleman, Cecil Taylor, and others.

Jazz Age *See:* Roaring Twenties.

Jean Baptiste de la Salle, Saint (1651-1719), French Roman Catholic priest canonized in 1900. He founded the Order of the Christian Brothers, which brought religious instruction to the poor. In the 1680s he established the Institute of Brothers of the Christian School, and other schools were established by his order throughout Western Europe.

Jeanne d'Arc *See:* Joan of Arc, Saint.

Jeanneret-Gris, Charles Édouard *See:* Le Corbusier.

Jeddah *See:* Jidda.

Jeep, 4-wheel-drive vehicle used for navigating rough terrain. Popular with the army, jeeps came into widespread use during World War II. The name evolved from the initials G.P., standing for "general purpose" vehicle. They became the prototypes for civilian vehicles of the same name, which is now a registered trademark of the Chrysler Corporation.

Jeffers, Robinson (1887-1962), U.S. poet. His powerful poetry, its tone disillusioned, laments human fate and glorifies nature. *Tamar and Other Poems* (1924) is his best-known collection, but his chief success was an adaptation of Euripides' *Medea* (1946).

Jefferson, Joseph (1829-1905), U.S. actor best known for his portrayal of Rip van Winkle, a role he created in London in 1865 and played for the rest of his life.

Jefferson, State of, proposed state in the Texas Panhandle, in the northwestern part of Texas. The area was proposed for statehood by the Texas legislature in 1915, but the proposal was never enacted into law.
See also: Texas.

Jefferson, Thomas (1743-1826), third president of the United States and principal author of the Declaration of Independence. Jefferson was highly accomplished in many fields—politics, diplomacy, science, architecture, education, farming, and music, to name only a few. He was a brilliant writer and a philosopher of democracy—on behalf of the American cause in the Revolution and as the foremost advocate of popular rule in the young republic.
Early life. Jefferson attended William and Mary College, graduated in 1762, then studied law, being admitted to the bar in 1767. In 1770, he began building Monticello, the home near Charlottesville, Va., that he had designed. In 1772, he married Martha Wayles Skelton. Only 2 of their 6 children survived infancy.
The Revolution. In 1769, Jefferson entered the House of Burgesses, Virginia's colonial assembly. As relations with Britain deteriorated, he joined the revolutionaries' cause. A radical democrat, he believed men should be free to govern themselves, and opposed aristocracy of birth or wealth. His writings made him one of the leading political theorists in the colonies.
In 1776, as a delegate to the Continental Congress, Jefferson was named to a 5-man committee to prepare a declaration justifying independence; Jefferson wrote most of it. It is considered the most eloquent statement of his views on democracy and government. The Continental Congress adopted the declaration on July 4, 1776.
Jefferson returned to Virginia's legislature, then became governor in 1779. In 1783, he was elected to the new U.S. Congress.
Service to the nation. Jefferson served as the U.S. minister to France (1785-89) and as the first U.S. secretary of state (1789-93). Although President George Washington disliked the idea of political parties, 2 parties formed around Jefferson and Alexander Hamilton, secretary of the treasury. Jefferson's followers became known as Democratic-Republicans (or Republicans) and Hamilton's as Federalists. Jefferson believed in the rationality of man and saw the nation's future as an egalitarian, agricultural society of small landholders. He opposed the idea of strong, central government, believing that all governments should be kept from gaining too much power. Hamilton considered the people "a great beast" and wanted the nation to develop into a commercial and industrial one led by a strong national

Thomas Jefferson

3rd U.S. President	
Born:	Shadwell, Goochland (now Albemarle) County, Va.; Apr. 13, 1743
Term:	Mar. 1801-Mar. 1809
Vice presidents:	Aaron Burr; George Clinton
Political party:	Democratic-Republican
Spouse:	Martha Wayles Skelton Jefferson
Children:	6
Died:	Charlottesville, Va.; July 4, 1826

government and a wealthy aristocracy. Washington was unable to settle the dispute between his 2 top advisers; Jefferson resigned in 1793. Three years later, the Democratic-Republicans persuaded him to run against Federalist John Adams for the presidency. Jefferson lost by a narrow margin, thus becoming Adams's vice president. In 1800, Jefferson and running mate Aaron Burr ran against Federalists John Adams and John C. Pinckney. Jefferson and Burr received equal electoral votes, so the House of Representative had to decide who would be president. It chose Jefferson.

President. Jefferson's greatest diplomatic coup was the Louisiana Purchase (1803), which doubled the size of the nation. The following year, he sent Lewis and Clark to explore the new territory. Their expedition led to the settlement and eventual incorporation of the West into the nation.

Under Jefferson, the Democratic-Republicans balanced the budget, built a surplus, and reduced the national debt. Jefferson's personal popularity carried him and running mate George Clinton to an overwhelming victory in the 1804 presidential election, but his second term was beset by foreign-affairs problems, particularly a conflict between Britain and France. Hoping to avoid war, Jefferson established an embargo forbidding the export of U.S. products and prohibiting U.S. ships from sailing to foreign ports. The embargo, however, hurt U.S. traders far more than it did Europe. Jefferson's presidency ended under a cloud of unpopularity.

Retirement. Jefferson retired to Monticello. Active to the end, he pursued his many interests and founded the University of Virginia. He died on July 4, 1826—the 50th anniversary of the signing of the Declaration of Independence and the same day as his old friend and rival, John Adams.

Jefferson City (pop. 33,619), capital of Missouri and seat of Cole County. Located on the Missouri River, in the central part of the state, Jefferson City is the commercial center for the surrounding agricultural region. Industries include food processing, printing, and publishing. The city was laid out in 1822 and named for Thomas Jefferson.

See also: Missouri.

Jeffersonian democracy *See:* Jefferson, Thomas.

Jefferson Memorial, monument in Washington, D.C., dedicated in 1943 to the memory of Thomas Jefferson. A white marble structure in classical style, it was designed by John Russell Pope and contains a statute of Jefferson by Rudulph Evans.

Jefferson Territory, area comprising what is now the state of Colorado and parts of Utah, Nebraska, and Kansas. Thousands of settlers came to the area in 1859 after rumors that gold had been discovered there. A provisional government was established, but Congress refused to recognize the Jefferson Territory as a state.

Jeffersonville (pop. 21,220), city in southern Indiana, on the Ohio River across from Louisville, Ky. Built on the site of Fort Steuben, the community was designed by President Thomas Jefferson in 1802. The seat of Clark County, it is a river port and manufacturing center and houses the Southeast Campus of Indiana University.
See also: Indiana.

Jeffries, James Jackson (1875-1953), U.S. heavyweight boxer who won the championship from Bob Fitzsimmons in 1899. He retired undefeated in 1905; returning to the ring in 1910 he was defeated by Jack Johnson.

Jehoiakim, king of Judah (r.c.608-598 B.C.). Son of King Josiah, Jehoiakim was placed on the throne by Necho, the Egyptian pharaoh who defeated Josiah. Jehoiakim later switched his alliance from Necho to the Babylonian king, Nebuchadnezzar II, but then revolted against him. Jehoiakim died under mysterious circumstances during the Babylonian siege of Jerusalem.

Jehoshaphat, king of Judah (r.c.873-849 B.C.). An ally of King Ahab of Israel, Jehoshaphat was the first Judean king to make a treaty with Israel. He reigned during an era of relative peace and solidified his alliance with Israel by having his son, Jehoram, marry the daughter of King Ahab.

Jehovah, variant of the name of God in the Old Testament. The four Hebrew letters YHWH, referring to God, were considered sacred and unpronounceable. In reading the Hebrew Bible, the word *Adonai* (Lord) was substituted. Medieval translators believed YHWH should be read "Yahweh," and the name "Jehovah" was incorrectly derived from that.

Jehovah's Witnesses, international religious movement founded in 1872 by Charles Taze Russell in Pittsburgh, Pa. Their central doctrine is that the Second Coming of Christ is imminent. They avoid participation in secular government, which they see as diabolically inspired. Over a million members proselytize by house-to-house calls and through publications such as *The Watchtower* and *Awake*, issued by the Watchtower Bible and Tract Society.

Jehu, king of Israel (r. c.842-815 B.C.). An officer in the army of King Jehoram, Jehu was anointed king by a disciple of the prophet Elisha after Jehoram began promoting the worship of Baal. Jehu murdered Jehoram, Queen Jezebel (Jehoram's mother), King Ahaziah of Judah, and other members of the royal family. After ordering all the followers of Baal into their temple, Jehu's soldiers slaughtered them. Jehu restored traditional Jewish worship and began a dynasty that ruled for another century.
See also: Israel.

Jellicoe, Sir John (1859-1935), British admiral of the fleet (1919), commander of the British grand fleet at the battle of Jutland (1916). He was governor-general of New Zealand (1920-24).
See also: Jutland, Battle of.

Jellyfish, familiar name for the free-swimming stage of various invertebrate animals of the phylum Cnidaria. They often have a pulsating jellylike bell and trailing tentacles. Many Cnidarian classes display an alternation of generations, where a single species may be represented by a polyp form, usually asexual, and a medusoid, sexually reproductive stage. These medusoid forms are frequently referred to as jellyfish. The true jellyfish all belong to the class Scyphozoa, where the medusa is the dominant phase and the polyp or hydroid is reduced or absent. Jellyfish are radially symmetrical. Rings of muscle around the margin of the bell contract to expel water and propel the jellyfish forward.

Jenghis Khan *See:* Genghis Khan.

Jenkins, Charles Francis (1867-1934), U.S. inventor. His "phantascope" (1895) was a motion picture projector that enlarged narrow film images into life-sized figures. He also patented an airplane braking device, an altimeter, and a mechanical automobile starter.

Jenkins, Roy Harris (1920-), British political leader. Elected to the House of Commons in 1948 as a Labour Party member, he served as minister of aviation, chancellor of the exchequer, and twice held the post of home secretary. He was president of the Commission of the European Community (1977-81). In the early 1980s he helped found the Social Democratic Party, a split from the Labour Party, and in 1982 he was elected to Parliament under the party's banner. He lost his seat in 1987.
See also: Parliament; United Kingdom.

Jenne, or Djenné, city in southern Mali. Founded c.1300 in a swampy lowland between the Niger and Bani rivers, Jenne became a trade hub between the West African coastal region and the lower Sahara. In 1468 it was conquered by the Songhai Empire, and in the mid-1600s it was a focal point for black Muslim culture and learning.
See also: Mali.

Jenner, Edward (1749-1823), English physician, pioneer of vaccination. He took note of the country saying that dairy-maids who had had cowpox would not contract smallpox, and this led him, in 1796, to inoculate a boy, James Phipps, with cowpox. When the procedure made the boy immune to smallpox, the modern science of immunology was born.
See also: Immunization; Vaccination.

Jenner, Sir William (1815-98), Victorian-era British physician. Best known for his research on typhus and typhoid fever, Jenner was one of the first members of the medical profession to draw a distinction between them and prescribe appropriate treatment. Jenner was also a pioneer in the treatment of diptheria. He served as president of the Royal College of Physicians

(1881-88) and was the personal physician of Queen Victoria and other members of the royal family.
See also: Typhoid fever; Typhus.

Jenney, William Le Baron (1832-1907), U.S. architect and designer of the Home Insurance company in Chicago. He used metal columns instead of stone, which reduced the weight of the building and allowed for taller structures.
See also: Architecture.

Jensen, J. Hans (1906-73), German physicist who shared the Nobel Prize for physics (1963) with Maria Goeppert Mayer and Eugene Paul Wigner for research on the shell structure of atomic nuclei.

Jenson, Nicolas (1415?-80), 15th-century French printer who designed several important typefaces still in common use today. He was sent by the king of France to Mainz, Germany, to learn book printing from Johannes Gutenberg. In 1470 Jenson devised a system of roman type that later evolved into other practical fonts.
See also: Printing.

Jerboa, any of various small desert-living rodent (family Dipodidac) with long tails and long hind legs. Jerboas have large eyes and ears, short front legs, and move by hopping. They are common in the deserts of North Africa and Asia, where they live in holes and emerge at night to feed on leaves and seeds.

Jeremiah, book of the Old Testament, 24th in the Authorized Version, second of the Major Prophets. It tells of the prophecies of Jeremiah, who called for moral reform, threatening the population with doom otherwise. He continued prophesying in Egypt after Jerusalem fell to Babylon.
See also: Bible; Old Testament.

Jericho (pop. 5,300), ancient village in Palestine, north of the Dead Sea. Excavations have suggested that Jericho may be the site of the oldest known human permanent settlement in the world. In the Bible, it was captured from the Canaanites by Joshua. It has periodically been destroyed and rebuilt. In 1967 it was occupied by Israel. After years of negotiations the Palestinians attained some form of autonomy over Jericho district in 1994.
See also: Palestine.

Jeroboam, 2 kings of ancient Israel. **Jeroboam I** (r. 922-909 B.C.) led the rebellion of the northern tribes of Judea after King Solomon died, which resulted in Israel and Judah splitting into separate kingdoms. He restored Jewish shrines at Bethel and Dan, thus releasing the people from their obligation to make pilgrimages to the Holy Temple in Jerusalem, the capital of Judah. **Jeroboam II** (r. 785-745 B.C.) ruled during a time when Israel was a political and economic power, despite widespread corruption.
See also: Israel.

Jerome, Jerome Klapka (1859-1927), English humorist and playwright, who wrote the classic comic novel *Three Men in a Boat* (1889), a work cherished for its broad humor and sentimentality.

Jerome, Saint (Sophronius Eusebius Hieronymus; c. 340-420), biblical scholar, one of the first theologians to be called a Doctor of the Church. After being educated in classical studies, he fled to the desert as a hermit to devote himself to prayer. Subsequently papal secretary, he translated the Old Testament into Latin and wrote New Testament commentaries. His feast day is Sept. 30.
See also: Bible.

Jersey, largest and southernmost of the British Channel Islands. Its main industries are tourism and agriculture. It contains numerous remnants of prehistoric life and was known to the Romans as Caesarea.

Jersey City (pop. 224,400), city in northeastern New Jersey, seat of Hudson County. Located across the Hudson River from Manhattan, Jersey City is a major transportation center with extensive port facilities, several major railways, and tunnel and ferry connections with New York City. Its industries include shipping, oil refining, chemicals, and the manufacture of consumer products. The city is also the site of a stockyard. First settled by the Dutch in 1618, it became the town of Jersey in 1804 and was incorporated as a city in 1820.
See also: New Jersey.

Jersey Lily *See:* Langtry, Lillie.

Jerusalem (pop. 544,200), capital (since 1980) and largest city of Israel. It stands on a ridge west of the Dead Sea, 35 mi (56 km) from the Mediterranean. The city may date from the 4th millennium B.C. In c.1000 B.C. King David captured it from the Jebusites and made it his capital. The great Temple was built by David's son Solomon in 970 B.C. David's dynasty was ended in 586 B.C. by the invasion of King Nebuchadnezzar, who sacked the Temple and deported most of the Jews to Babylon. Cyrus II of Persia allowed the Jews to return and the Temple was rebuilt. Jerusalem was subsequently ruled by Syria, the Roman Empire, and the Byzantine Empire. It was taken over by the Muslims in 637 and has been part of the Muslim world ever since, except for a period of rule by the Crusaders (1099-1187). The 1947 UN resolution establishing the state of Israel made it an international city, but in the 1948 Arab-Israeli conflict it was divided, the Old City being under Jordanian administration, the New City under Israeli rule. In the 1967 Arab-Israeli War, Israel took the Old City, and all of Jerusalem was placed under unified administration. There are traditional Armenian, Christian, Jewish, and Muslim quarters in the Old City, which is also the site of three of Jerusalem's holiest places: the Wailing Wall (Jewish); the Church of the Holy Sepulcher (Christian); and the Dome of the Rock (Muslim).
See also: Israel.

Jerusalem artichoke (*Helianthus tuberosus*), North American flowering plant closely related to wild sunflowers. It produces edible tubers that have a taste similar to artichokes, hence the name. They are also a source of fructose and alcohol. The plants can grow to 12 ft (3.7 m) in height. They bear yellow flowers.

Jessamine *See:* Gelsemium.

Jesuits, name given to members of the Society of Jesus, an order of Roman Catholic priests and brothers dedicated to foreign missions, education, and studies in the humanities and sciences. Jesuit life is regulated by the constitutions written by the founder of the Society, St. Ignatius of Loyala. Vows of poverty, chastity, and obedience to the pope are taken, and training may last up to 15 years. After its founding in 1534, the order undertook missions in Asia under St. Francis Xavier and participated in the Counter-Reformation in Europe. Their influence and power led to their expulsion from many countries, and in 1773 Pope Clement XIV dissolved the Society. It was restored, however, in 1814.
See also: Roman Catholic Church.

Jesus Christ (4? B.C.-A.D. 29?), central figure of the Christian religion. Jesus is believed by Christians to be the Son of God and the Lord and Savior of mankind. The name "Jesus" is the Greek rendering of the Hebrew *Joshua* (Savior). The title "Christ" comes from *Christos*, the Greek translation of the Hebrew *Messiah* (Anointed One).
The main source for information about the life and teachings of Jesus are the 4 Gospels—Matthew, Mark, Luke, and John—and the epistles of the New Testament. From the numerous details given there, it is possible to form a vivid picture of Jesus. These details are given with an intention expressly stated by John: "These are written that you may believe that Jesus is the Christ, the Son of God, and that believing you may have life in his name" (John 20:31).
According to the Gospels, Jesus was born of the Virgin Mary, wife of Joseph, in Bethlehem, Judea. Their home was in Nazareth, Galilee. Little is known of his childhood except that, when he was 12, he went to the Temple in Jerusalem with Mary and Joseph. When Jesus was about 30 years old, his cousin John the Baptist began preaching repentance in the wilderness of Judea and baptizing penitents in the Jordan River. As Jesus was being baptized by John, a voice from heaven affirmed that Jesus was the Son of God (Mark 1:11). For some time after that Jesus traveled about the country, teaching and healing, mainly in Galilee but also in other parts of Palestine. He gathered 12 followers, or disciples, who helped spread the new ideas.
Jesus' interpretation of the Jewish law and his messianic claims alarmed the established religious authorities. On his last journey to Jerusalem for the Passover, Jesus entered the city in triumph. The authorities, threatened by his popularity, plotted against him. After the Last Supper, Jesus went to the Garden of Gethsemane to pray. One disciple, Judas Iscariot, betrayed him, and he was taken prisoner. Brought before members of the ecclesiastical court of the Jews, he was found guilty of blaspheming. He was then taken for sentencing to the Roman civil governor, Pontius Pilate, who charged him with treason against Rome and condemned him to death by crucifixion.
The resurrection of Jesus on the third day after his death and burial convinced the disciples that he was indeed the Son of God. They continued to spread Jesus' teachings, and hundreds of Jews and later Gentiles were converted to the new faith. Although the Christian Church eventually split into many parts, the accuracy of the Gospels and the divinity of Jesus are universally held Christian beliefs.
See also: Bible; Christianity; New Testament.

Jet, form of lignite coal valued for its gem-like properties. In its raw state it is hard and black and has a smooth surface. After polishing, it resembles black glass and is often used to make buttons, costume jewelry, and other decorative items.

Jet airplane *See:* Airplane; Aviation.

Jet engine *See:* Jet propulsion.

Jet lag *See:* Biological clock.

Jet propulsion, propulsion of a vehicle by reaction to the rapid expulsion of a gas backward. The reaction imparts an equal forward momentum to the vehicle. The chief use of jet propulsion is to power airplanes. The first jet engine was designed and built by Sir Frank Whittle (1937), but the first jet-engine aircraft to fly was German (Aug. 1939). Jet engines are internal-combustion engines. The turbojet is the commonest form. Air enters the inlet diffuser and is compressed in the air compressor. It then enters the combustion chamber, where the fuel is injected and ignited, and the hot, expanding exhaust gases pass through a turbine that drives the compressor and engine accessories. The gases are expelled through the jet nozzle to provide the thrust.
See also: National Aeronautics and Space Adminstration.

Jet Propulsion Laboratory, research facility in Pasadena, Calif. The laboratory, which is operated by the California Institute of Technology under the aegis of the National Aeronautics and Space Administration (NASA), pioneered the development of space probes for the United States. These included the first unmanned crafts to survey the moon and land on its surface in the 1950s and 1960s. Other probes developed there explored the solar system and flew close enough to some of the outer planets to photograph them, thus providing valuable data.
See also: Jet propulsion.

Jet stream, narrow bands of fast easterly-flowing winds, stronger in winter than in summer, found at altitudes of 7 to 8 mi (11-13 km). Speeds average about 40 mph (64 kmph) in summer and 80 mph (128 kmph) in winter, though more than 200 mph (320 kmph) has been recorded.

Jetty, man-made pier designed to aid in navigation. They are constructed primarily of wood, stone, concrete, or combinations of these materials. Breakwater jetties reduce the force of waves on a harbor or shoreline, while river jetties expedite the flow of silt through a delta. Jetties at the mouths of rivers such as the Mississippi and the Columbia funnel the water through narrow channels, thus forcing the currents to carry silt further out to sea.

Jewel Cave National Monument, national monument in western South Dakota that preserves an extensive complex of interconnected limestone caverns in the Black Hills and contains one of the longest underground cave systems in the U.S. Jewel Cave was set aside as a national monument in 1908.

Jewelry, ornaments worn by people to enhance their physical appearance, to display wealth, or to follow custom. Bracelets, rings, necklaces, and earrings are the most common types of jewelry. Made from precious metals such as gold and silver, colorful polished stones (gems), or other attractive natural materials, jewelry is an art form that has existed since earliest times. Ancient peoples wore jewelry made from such materials as feathers, shells, and teeth before they wore clothes. Jewelry found at the sites of early civilizations can yield clues to the technological development of ancient cultures.

Jewett, Sarah Orne (1849-1909), U.S. author. She wrote about late 19th century life in her native New England, often using seaports and rural towns of Maine as settings. Her best-known works are *Deephaven* (1877), *A Country Doctor* (1884), and *The Country of the Pointed Firs* (1896). She also wrote poetry and children's stories.

Jewfish (*Epinephelus itajara*), large game fish of the sea bass family. Jewfish and related species inhabit the eastern and western coastal waters of the United States and Latin America. The largest known species grows to 12 ft (3.75 m) and weighs up to 680 lb (310 kg).

Jewish community centers (JCC's), centralized facilities offering social functions for Jews. JCC's serve about 1 million people of all ages in 275 locations throughout North America and are operated by the National Jewish Welfare Board (JWB). JCC's usually feature arts and crafts, drama, recreation and sports, and educational programs.

Jewish feasts *See:* Judaism.

Jews, followers of Judaism, a group held together by a shared religion and a common history and culture more than 3,000 years old.

Jewish history begins with the patriarchs: Abraham, his son Isaac, and his grandson Jacob (also named Israel). Abraham led his family from Mesopotamia to Canaan (Palestine). The children of Israel (Joseph and his brothers, the sons of Jacob) migrated to Egypt, where a pharaoh enslaved the Israelites until Moses led them out in the Exodus.

After 40 years of wandering, the Israelites reentered Canaan (c.1200 B.C.). They united in a monarchy under King Saul. His successor, David, brought prosperity and peace, and conquered Jerusalem. David's son, Solomon, built the Temple at Jerusalem. Under Solomon's son Rehoboam, the kingdom split into Judah and Israel. The monarchies ended with the defeat of Israel by the Assyrians (721 B.C.) and the defeat of Judah and destruction of the Temple by the Babylonians (587 B.C.). Many of the inhabitants of both kingdoms were deported; those from Israel lost their identity, becoming the "Ten Lost Tribes." The term *Diaspora* is used to refer to the settling of scattered colonies of Jews outside Israel.

During the 2nd and 1st centuries B.C., the Maccabees briefly restored Jewish independence before the Romans established domination over the Jews. They rose against the Romans in A.D. 66; when the revolt was put down 4 years later, Jerusalem was destroyed.

The rise of Christianity brought increasing harassment of the Jews. During the Middle Ages in many countries they were confined to ghettos and excluded from trades, professions, and ownership of land. At the time of the Crusades, a new wave of persecution began; one by one Western European nations expelled the Jews, until they were allowed to live only in parts of Germany and Italy. The Jews found refuge in the Ottoman Empire, in the New World, and in Eastern Europe, where they became increasingly trapped in a life of poverty and persecution in lands under Russian rule.

The Enlightenment and the advent of capitalism for a time benefitted the Jews economically and socially. Prejudice against them (anti-Semitism) continued, however, and gave rise in the late 19th century to renewed Zionism, the movement for reestablishing a Jewish state in Palestine that dated from the destruction of Jerusalem in A.D. 70.

Meanwhile (1881-1914), one-third of Eastern European Jews (1 million people) emigrated; 90% settled in the United States. In 1917 the Balfour Declaration guaranteed "a national home for the Jewish people" in Palestine, but Jewish settlement there aroused the hostility of the Arab inhabitants.

In the 1930s, all other Jewish problems were overshadowed by the rise of Nazism. With the outbreak of World War II, the Nazis began murdering the Jews of Europe, eventually killing 6 million. Reaction to this catastrophe led to the establishment of the state of Israel in 1948.

Today there are 13 million Jews worldwide. The Jews of Israel number more than 4 million, and some 6 million Jews live in the United States.

See also: Israel; Judaism.

Jew's-harp, or jaw's harp, musical instrument that produces a resonant sound. It is held up to the mouth, and a thin, metal tongue between 2 prongs of a circular frame is plucked, producing vibrations. Notes are formed by the player changing the size or shape of the mouth cavity.

Jiang Qing, or Chiang Ch'ing (1914-91), Chinese Communist leader; widow of Mao Zedong. She joined the Communist Party in 1933 and married Mao in 1939. During the 1960s she led the Cultural Revolution and was elected to the Politburo in 1969. Accused by Mao's successors of leading a coup attempt, she and 3 other radicals (the "Gang of Four") were arrested and charged with treason. Jiang was condemned to death, but her sentence was commuted to life imprisonment in 1983.

See also: China; Gang of Four; Mao Zedong.

Jicama, yam bean, or Mexican turnip, vine belonging to the pea family, native to parts of Latin American and Asia. The Jicama plant is cultivated for its edible tubers.

Jidda, or Jiddah (pop. 1,500,000), city in western Saudi Arabia, situated on the Red Sea. Jidda has the country's largest airport and is the port of entry for millions of Muslims making pilgrimages to Mecca and Medina. Founded in the 7th century A.D., Jidda is a banking, oil refining, and manufacturing center.

See also: Saudi Arabia.

Jigger *See:* Chigger.

Jim Crow, name for a system of laws and customs in the southern United States to segregate African Americans from white society. The name comes from a minstrel song. The laws dated from the 1880s and applied to schools, transportation, theaters, and parks. These laws were invalidated by Supreme

Court decisions in the 1950s and 1960s and the Civil Rights Acts of 1964 and 1968.
See also: Segregation.

Jiménez, Juan Ramón (1881-1958), Spanish poet. At first influenced by symbolism, in *Diary of a Poet and the Sea* (1917) he developed a free, direct style of his own: *poesía desnuda* (Spanish "naked poetry"). After the Spanish Civil War he moved to Puerto Rico. He received the Nobel Prize for literature in 1956.

Jiménez de Quesada, Gonzalo (1500?-79?), Spanish conquistador who claimed the area around Colombia for Spain as New Granada. He settled there, doing much to improve the colonists' lot, and founded Bogotá (1538). He led a disastrous expedition in search of El Dorado (1569-71).

Jimmu Tenno, mythical Japanese military and political leader. According to legend, he conquered large areas around the Inland Sea and became Japan's first emperor in the 600s B.C., but historians dispute the dates and question his existence. Jimmu Tenno is said to be a descendant of the sun goddess, leading to popular acceptance of the divinity of the Imperial Family, whose lineage is traced to him.
See also: Japan.

Jimsonweed, or thorn apple, low shrubby plant (*Datura stramonium*) with thick leaves and white trumpet-shaped flowers. All parts of the plant are poisonous. It is named for Jamestown, Virginia, where a party of English soldiers died after eating it as a vegetable.

Jinnah, Muhammad Ali (1876-1948), Indian Muslim lawyer and political leader, founder of Pakistan. At first a member of the Indian Congress Party, he resigned in 1921, charging it with Hindu bias. From 1934, as head of the Muslim League, he campaigned for Muslim rights in an independent state. In 1947 he became Pakistan's first head of state.
See also: Pakistan.

Jinrikisha, or ricksha, 2-wheeled passenger vehicle pulled manually. The runner, or *hiki*, runs between 2 long poles extending from the body of the carriage. Used as a public vehicle in China and Japan around the turn of the century, jinrikishas carried 1 or 2 people. Jinrikishas were later considered demeaning to humans and outlawed.

Jiulong *See:* Kowloon.

Jiva *See:* Jainism.

Jívaro, South American tribe inhabiting the lower Andes mountains in eastern Ecuador and Peru. Their principal activities are fishing, hunting, pottery-making, and weaving. A people once famous for ritual head-shrinking, they fiercely resisted Spanish encroachment.

Joan of Arc, Saint (1412?-31), French heroine of the Hundred Years War. A peasant girl from Domremy, Lorraine, she heard "voices" telling her to liberate France from the English. Given command of a small force by the

Dauphin (later Charles VII), she inspired it to victory at Orléans in 1429. She stood beside the Dauphin when he was crowned Charles VII that year and joined him in his unsuccessful siege of Paris. Captured at Compiègne (1430), she was tried for heresy by an ecclesiastical court of French clerics who sympathized with the English, and burnt at the stake. The verdict was posthumously reversed in 1456, and she was canonized in 1920.
See also: Hundred Years War.

Job, Book of, book of the Old Testament, 18th in the Authoized Version. Apparently based on a folk tale in dialogue form, it is about the problem of good and evil. God permits Satan to torment the virtuous Job with the loss of family, wealth, and health. Finding small comfort in wife and friends, Job is bitter, but remains faithful. He is restored to good fortune in old age.
See also: Bible; Old Testament.

Jobs, Steven Paul (1955-), U.S. computer designer and businessman, founder with Stephen Wozniak of Apple Computer, Inc. (1976). The company's success reshaped the personal computer industry. Managerial disputes caused Jobs to leave Apple in 1985. In 1988 he unveiled a computer system aimed at the college and university market, called NeXT.
See also: Computer.

Job's Daughters, international order affiliated with the Masons. Open only to girls between 11 and 20 who are related to Master Masons, the organization has about 49,000 members in 1,600 chapters in the United States and abroad. It promotes knowledge, patriotism, parental respect, devotion to Christian principles, and aid to charitable causes.

Jodl, Alfred (1890-1946), German-Nazi officer, chief of operations in World War II. He signed the surrender at Rheims, May 7, 1945. Convicted of war crimes at the Nuremberg Trials, he was executed.
See also: Nazism.

Jodrell Bank Observatory, or Nuffield Radio Astronomy Laboratories, English space tracking station and research facility, located near Manchester. Housing one of the world's largest radio telescopes, Jodrell Bank tracked *Sputnik I*, the first satellite ever launched. It also transmitted the first photographs from a Soviet probe on the moon in 1966.
See also: Astronomy.

Joel, Book of, book of the Old Testament, 29th in the Authorized Version, second of the Minor Prophets. Messianic in nature, it forecasts the Day of the Lord in apocalyptic terms.
See also: Bible; Old Testament.

Joey *See:* Kangaroo.

Joffre, Joseph Jacques Césaire (1852-1931), commander-in-chief of the French army (1914-16). He underestimated German power at the start of World War I, but he shared credit with Gen. J.S. Gallieni for the victory on the Marne. After the mismanagement of Verdun he resigned, but he was immediately made a marshal of France.

Joffrey, Robert (1930-88), U.S. dancer and choreographer. His company, the Robert Joffrey Theater Dancers, was founded in 1954. By 1976, when it became the Joffrey Ballet, it was one of the most highly regarded of U.S. companies. The touring Joffrey II Company was formed in 1970 to develop young dancers.

Jogues, Saint Isaac (1607-46), 17th-century French Jesuit missionary. Sent to Canada and western New York to convert Native Americans and Canadians, Jogues first sighted the strait connecting Lake Superior with Lake Huron, which he named Sault de Sainte Marie. Jogues was held captive and tortured by Iroquois warriors in 1642, but he managed to escape. On Oct. 18, 1646, he was murdered while on a mission among the Mohawks in western New York. He was canonized in 1930.
See also: Jesuits.

Johanan Ben Zakkai (d. c.80), Jewish Pharisee who, after the destruction of the Temple by Rome in A.D. 70, founded the academy at Jabneh (Yibna), thus ensuring the survival of Judaism.
See also: Judaism.

Johannesburg (pop. 704,000), city in northeastern South Africa. It is the hub of a prosperous mining region, with the world's largest gold field, the Witwatersand, nearby. First settled by prospectors in 1886, Johannesburg is South Africa's largest metropolitan area and a thriving cultural, commercial, and industrial center.
See also: South Africa.

Johanson, Donald Carl (1943-), U.S. anthropologist. His discovery of fossilized remains in Africa, estimated to be between 2.5 and 3 million years old, gave scientists evidence of some of the earliest origins of the human species. In 1974 Johanson uncovered the skeleton of what is believed to be the first humanlike creature to walk erect (classified as *Australopithecus afarensis*). In 1986 he found a skull and bones of an individual of the species *Homo habilis*, enabling scientists to piece together a link between humans and their ape-like predecessors.
See also: Anthropology; Prehistoric people.

John, name of 22 popes and 2 antipopes. **Saint John I** (d.526), pope (523-26), was sent to Constantinople by Theodoric, the Ostrogoth king, to win toleration for Arianism from the emperor; Theodoric imprisoned him when he failed. **John VII** (d.882), who reigned from 872 to 882, sought political power for the papacy. He attempted (and failed) to keep the Muslims out of Italy and was forced to pay tribute in order to spare Rome. He momentarily resolved a dispute with the Eastern Church by recognizing Photius as patriarch of Constantinople (879), after the death of his enemy, St. Ignatius. He crowned emperor Charles II (the Bald, in 875) and Charles III (the Fat, in 881). He was assassinated by members of his household. **John XXII** (1249-1334) was the second pope (1316-34) at Avignon; he filled the college with French cardinals. A skillful administrator, he lost popularity when he persecuted the Franciscan Spirituals, observers of strict evangelical poverty. When he contested the election of Louis IV, the king attempted to have him declared a heretic; this prompted John to imprison Nicholas V, the antipope Louis had appointed. The name of **John XXIII** was first taken by Baldassare Cossa (c.1370-1419), a Neapolitan antipope (1410-15). As a cardinal, he supported the Council of Pisa (1409), which tried (unsuccessfully) to end the Great Schism between the popes of Rome and Avignon. Elected pope by the Council, he defended Rome against his rival, Gregory XII, and, pressured by Emperor Sigismund, convened the Council of Constance to attempt reconciliation again. He agreed to abdicate if his rivals would as well, but then reneged. The Council accepted Gregory's resignation and deposed the other two. The name **John XXIII** was next taken by Angelo Giuseppe Roncalli (1881-1963). Of peasant stock, he was elected pope in 1958 after serving as cardinal and patriarch of Venice since 1953. He made major changes in the church, promoting cooperation with other Christian churches and other religions. The encyclical *Mater et Magistra* (1961) advocated social reform in underdeveloped countries. In 1962 he convened the Second Vatican Council.

John (1167-1216), king of England, from 1199 to his death. The youngest son of Henry II, John succeeded his brother Richard I as king. John's refusal to accept a papal nominee as archbishop of Canterbury led to his excommunication in 1209. High military spending during his reign alienated the nobles, and in 1215 they forced John to sign the Magna Carta, confirming their feudal rights. John later repudiated it and waged a war against the barons, who summoned French support. John died while the issue was still in doubt.
See also: England.

John III Sobieski (1624-96), late-17th-century king of Poland. Ascending to the throne in 1674 during a time of frequent wars and civil unrest, Sobieski united the Polish people against the incursions of their warlike neighbors and led a Christian army to victory over Turks outside the gates of Vienna in 1683. Following his victory, Sobieski formed a military alliance with the pope, the Holy Roman emperor, and Venice against the Muslims.

John VI (1769-1826), early-19th-century king of Portugal. He became regent in 1792 when his mother, Maria I, was judged mentally unfit to rule. He fled to Brazil in 1807 when an invasion by Napoleon was feared. In 1816, while still in Brazil, John became Portugal's king, but he didn't return until a revolution in his favor 5 years later. In 1822 his son, Pedro I, declared Brazil independent.

John, Epistles of, three New Testament epistles (23rd-25th) ascribed to St. John the Apostle. First John is a discourse about the 2 aspects of religion, practical and mythical. Second John warns against denials of the reality of Jesus's history. Third John protests an obstinate church leader's failure to receive missionaries.
See also: Bible; New Testament.

John, Gospel of *See:* Gospel.

John, Saint, one of the Twelve Disciples, (called the Evangelist, the Divine, and the Beloved Disciple), son of Zebedee and brother of St. James the

Greater, thought to be the author of the fourth Gospel, 3 New Testament epistles and the Revelation.

John Birch Society, U.S. anti-Communist organization. Established in 1958 by Robert Welch and named after a U.S. military officer killed by Chinese Communists in 1945, the society grew to 3,000 chapters by fueling fears of Communist plots in the United States and around the world. Its controversial methods include "smear campaigns" launched against public officials they believe to be Communist sympathizers.

John Bull, personification of the typical Englishman, created by John Arbuthnot (1667-1735) in a series of pamphlets (1712) satirizing Whig policy. The character was usually portrayed as a burly, good-natured farmer or tradesman.

John Chrysostom, Saint *See:* Chrysostom, Saint John.

John Henry *See:* Henry, John.

John of Austria (1547-78), Spanish military commander, illegitimate son of Emperor Charles V. Noted for his skill and gallantry, he commanded the Christian fleet and defeated Turks at Lepanto (1571) and conquered Tunis (1573). Governor general of the Spanish Netherlands (1576-78), he fought the rebellion of William the Silent.

John of Damascus, Saint (c.675-c.749), Orthodox Syrian theological writer and antagonist of iconoclasm. He resigned an inherited post under the Saracen caliph to become a monk.

John of Gaunt (1340-99), duke of Lancaster, fourth son of Edward III of England. Through marriage to his cousin Blanche, he became the duke of Lancaster. (Their eldest son became King Henry IV.) A commander in France under his brother, Edward the Black Prince, during the Hundred Years War, he married again, in 1371. Through his second wife, Constance of Castile, he gained a claim to the kingship of Castile and Léon. He ruled England for his senile father when the Black Prince was taken ill and his nephew, Richard II, was too young to assume leadership. His economic policies made him unpopular in many quarters, as did his unsuccessful campaigns (1386-88) to claim the Castilian throne. He remained influential during Richard II's reign, helping to effect peace between Richard and his barons. In 1396 he married Catherine Swynford, his third wife. They were ancestors of the Tudors.
See also: England; Tudor, House of.

John of Leiden (c.1509-36), Dutch innkeeper who became leader of the Anabaptists in Münster and in 1534 set up a brutally corrupt theocracy, the Kingdom of Zion, with himself as "king," in which private ownership was abolished. In 1535 the bishop of Münster crushed the revolt; John was tortured and executed.

John of the Cross, Saint (1542-91), Spanish poet and mystic, founder of a reformed Carmelite order. Influenced by St. Theresa of Avila, he is remembered for such treatises as *The Dark Night of the Soul.* Canonized in 1726, he was made a Doctor of the Church in 1926.

John Paul I (Albino Luciani; 1912-78), pope (1978). A moderate traditionalist, patriarch of Venice when elected pope, he died of a heart attack 34 days after his election. His was the shortest papal reign in nearly 400 years.

John Paul II (Karol Wojtyla; 1920-), first non-Italian pope elected in 450 years (1978). A Pole who was archbishop of Krakow before becoming pope, John Paul II has maintained a theologically conservative position on such controversial issues as birth control, abortion, and liberation theology. He has been outspoken on world events, and has spent much of his time traveling to many countries around the world.

Johns, Jasper (1930-), U.S. artist. A leading exponent of pop art, he used common objects in artistic contexts in such works as *Flag* (1958), and *Painted Bronze* (1960). Johns was influenced by Marcel Duchamp.

Johnson, Andrew (1808-75), 17th president of the United States. Johnson was the only U.S. president to be impeached by the House of Representatives. The difficulties of Reconstruction demanded an outstanding president, but Johnson—an accidental chief executive facing a hostile Congress—was temperamentally unsuited for the office.

Early life. Poverty kept Johnson from receiving any formal education. At age 13, he was apprenticed to a tailor, but ran away after 2 years. He later settled in Greeneville, Tenn., and opened a tailor shop. In 1827, he married Eliza McCardle, who taught him writing and arithmetic.

Public career. Johnson became involved in local politics as a Democrat and was elected town alderman before he was 21. He became mayor, then served in the Tennessee House of Representatives, the state Senate, and the U.S. House of Representatives. After 4 years as Tennessee's governor, he was elected to the U.S. Senate in 1857.

Johnson sympathized with the poor and uneducated, and championed mountaineers and small farmers against wealthy plantation owners. A slave owner, he opposed abolition and supported the Fugitive Slave Law of 1850. But he also supported legislation that would help small farmers by opening the West to settlement—even though it meant more free states would be added to the Union.

Andrew Johnson

Born:	Raleigh, N.C.; Dec. 29, 1808
Term:	Apr. 1865-Mar. 1869
Vice president:	None
Political party:	Democratic (but elected on the "National Union" ticket with Republican Abraham Lincoln)
Spouse:	Eliza McCardle Johnson
Children:	5
Died:	Carter Station, Tenn.; July 31, 1875

Republican Abraham Lincoln won the 1860 presidential election, causing most Southern leaders to call for secession. Johnson, however, remained devoted to the Union. In 1864 the Republicans renominated Lincoln and, to win support from "War" Democrats, they made Johnson his running mate. Their ticket won. In April 1865—six weeks after the inauguration—Lincoln was assassinated, thrusting Johnson into the presidency.

President. The Civil War had just ended, and Johnson faced the difficult task of reconstructing the South—and the Union. He issued a controversial proclamation granting amnesty to most Confederates who would swear loyalty to the Constitution. Most Southern states ratified the 13th Amendment abolishing slavery. However, they also passed the first in a series of laws that severely restricted the rights of African Americans.

Johnson maintained that reconstruction was exclusively an executive function; Congress disagreed. It passed the Civil Rights Act of 1866 over Johnson's veto and put forth other measures he opposed. In 1867, the Reconstruction Act was passed; thereafter, Congress exercised unprecedented authority over national policy.

Impeachment. Johnson removed an opponent from the Cabinet without consent of Congress, violating its Tenure of Office Act. The House impeached him for this and other reasons and, in March 1868, the Senate held Johnson's trial for "high crimes and misdemeanors." Conviction required a two-thirds majority; Johnson escaped conviction by a single vote. The power of the presidency was saved and balance between the branches of government preserved.

Other than the acquisition of Alaska by Secretary of State William Seward, Johnson's administration had few successes. Johnson was not nominated to the 1868 Democratic ticket, and left the presidency a bitter and disappointed man. He twice ran for Congress, but lost. Finally, in 1874, he won an election. The only former president to become a U.S. Senator, Johnson served only a special brief session in March 1875. He died soon after.

Johnson, Charles Spurgeon (1893-1956), U.S. educator, sociologist, and first black president of Fisk University (1946-56). He also helped reorganize the Japanese educational system after World War II and was U.S. delegate to UNESCO.

Johnson, Earvin *See:* Johnson, Magic.

Johnson, Hiram Warren (1866-1945), U.S. statesman. As a prosecuting attorney in San Francisco he successfully prosecuted corrupt political bosses (1908). He was governor of Cal. (1911-17) and U.S. senator (1917-45). He was a hard-line isolationist, opposing U.S. membership in the League of Nations and any war preparations.

See also: Isolationism.

Johnson, Jack (1878-1946), U.S. boxer, first African American to win the world heavyweight championship (1908). He fled the country (1912), jumping bail after his arrest on charges of violation of the Mann Act (a law prohibiting the transportation of women across state lines for immoral purposes). Johnson's outspokenness and refusal to submit to white supremacy made him highly controversial in the United States. He lost the title to Jess Willard in Havana in 1915, in a fight that he later claimed was fixed.

Johnson, James Weldon (1871-1938), U.S. author and political leader. He was U.S. consul in Venezuela and Nicaragua (1906-12) and a founder and secretary of the National Association for the Advancement of Colored People (1916-30). His books include *The Autobiography of an Ex-Colored Man* (novel, 1912), *God's Trombones* (1927), and *Black Manhattan* (1930).

Johnson, John Harold (1918-), U.S. publisher of black-interest magazines such as *Negro Digest*, *Ebony*, and *Jet*. He founded the Johnson Publishing Co. in Chicago in 1942. Since 1962 he has also published books directed mainly to black readers.

Johnson, Lyndon Baines (1908-73), 36th president of the United States. Johnson became chief executive upon the assassination of President John F. Kennedy, then was elected to a full term by an unprecedented majority. His 5 years in office were marked by far-reaching liberal legislation, but also by mounting domestic unrest and massive escalation of the U.S. war in Vietnam.
Early life. After graduating from high school in 1924, Johnson worked at various jobs before attending college, from which he graduated in 1930. After teaching high school for 2 years, he went to Washington, D.C., as the secretary to a new member of Congress from Texas. In 1934, Johnson married Claudia Alta "Lady Bird" Taylor. The Johnsons had 2 daughters.
Political career. In 1937, Johnson was elected to the U.S. House of Representatives. He was reelected 5 times. In 1948, he was elected to the Senate; in 1955, he became Senate majority leader. Johnson became one of the most powerful figures on Capitol Hill. One of his most notable achievements was the Senate's 1957 passage of the first major civil-rights bill since Reconstruction.
In 1960, Johnson ran for the Democratic presidential nomination, but John F. Kennedy won it. Johnson accepted the vice-presidential nomination. The Kennedy-Johnson ticket narrowly defeated Republican candidates Richard M. Nixon and Henry Cabot Lodge.
As vice president, Johnson held an office with relatively little power. That changed suddenly on Nov. 22, 1963, when President Kennedy was assassinated in Dallas, Tex. Johnson took the oath of office the same afternoon.
President. Johnson promised to continue the Kennedy program, and Congress soon passed the Civil Rights Act of 1964 and a new tax law, both Kennedy measures. Johnson also proposed a "War on Poverty" and persuaded Congress to appropriate almost $950 million for anti-poverty programs. In 1964, Johnson and running mate Hubert H. Humphrey won a landslide

Lyndon Baines Johnson

36th U.S. President

Born:	Near Stonewall, Tex.; Aug. 27, 1908
Term:	Nov. 1963-Jan. 1969
Vice president:	Hubert H. Humphrey (Jan. 1965-Jan. 1969)
Political party:	Democratic
Spouse:	Claudia Alta "Lady Bird" Taylor Johnson
Children:	2
Died:	Johnson, Tex.; Jan. 22, 1973

victory over Barry Goldwater and William Miller. Now president in his own right, Johnson formulated a wide-reaching program, called "the Great Society," for improving U.S. life. At first, Johnson enjoyed unrivaled popularity and wielded tremendous influence. From 1963 to 1967, Congress enacted 226 major proposals out of 252 requests—a 92% rate of success for Johnson's administration.

But the overwhelming issue of Johnson's presidency was an unpopular and bloody war. Kennedy had sent the first U.S. troops to Vietnam, but under Johnson their advisory role became a combative one. Johnson gradually committed more troops; by mid-1966, 300,000 U.S. troops were in Vietnam and the fighting showed no signs of nearing an end, despite massive U.S. bombing of North Vietnam and heavy loss of life on both sides.

By 1966, the U.S. was deeply divided over the war. Racial unrest—including riots in the overcrowded slums of several large cities—further taxed an already strained administration. On Mar. 31, 1968, Johnson announced that he would not run for reelection.

Retirement. After leaving office in Jan. 1969, Johnson retired to his Texas ranch. He avoided involvement in politics, devoting his time to publishing his memoirs, establishing the Lyndon B. Johnson Library, and running his ranch. He died on Jan. 22, 1973.

Johnson, Magic (Earvin Johnson, Jr.; 1959-), U.S. professional basketball player. Johnson, a 6-ft 9-in (206 cm) guard, has revolutionized the role of a "big-man." His passing, shooting, and ball-handling ability are unparalleled for a player his size. After leading Michigan State University to the National Collegiate Athletic Association (NCAA) basketball championship (1979), he went on to star for the Los Angeles Lakers (1979-) and has helped them win 5 championships (1980, 82, 85, 87, 88). In 1991 Johnson became the all time NBA assist leader (9,921). His other achievements include 7 Most Valuable Player (MVP) awards—3 regular season (1987, 89, 90), 3 playoff (1980, 82, 87), and 1 All-Star MVP (1990). Only Kareem Abdul-Jabbar has won more MVP awards. Infected by the HIV-virus he had to give up playing professional basketball in 1991. In 1998 he was made a United Nations goodwill ambassador.

Johnson, Philip Cortelyou (1906-), U.S. architect and historian. Together with Henry-Russell Hitchcock, he wrote *The International Style* and became a major exponent of the new architecture. His glass house (1949) at New Canaan, Conn., won him international recognition. It is clearly influenced by Miës van der Rohe, with whom he designed the Seagram Building, New York City (1958). Johnson's later work includes the New York State Theater at Lincoln Center (1964) and the American Telephone and Telegraph Headquarters Building (1978), in New York City.

See also: Architecture.

Johnson, Richard Mentor (1780-1850), ninth vice president of the United States. He served under President Martin Van Buren from 1837 to 1841, following terms in the Kentucky state legislature, the U.S. House of Representatives, and the U.S. Senate. Johnson was the only vice president in U.S. history ever elected by the Senate, after none of the 4 candidates received a majority of the electoral votes in the 1836 election.

Johnson, Samuel (1709-84), English author, one of the major poets, critics, conversationalists, and lexicographers of his time. He wrote for various London magazines beginning in 1737, publishing the poem *London* (1738), which inaugurated his fame. From 1746 to 1755 he prepared his pioneering *Dictionary of the English Language* (1755). The moral romance *Rassalas* (1759) followed, and then the *Idler* essays (1758-60). In 1763 he met James Boswell, his biographer, who recorded much of Johnson's brilliant conversation. In 1764 he founded his Literary Club (with Joshua Reynolds), an elite circle centered around "Doctor" Johnson, which included Burke, Garrick, Boswell, and Goldsmith. In 1765, he published his edition of Shakespeare, the model for those to follow. *Lives of the Poets* (1779-81), a 10-volume work, was one of his last. Johnson's contributions were central in defining the period of English literature that came to be known as the Augustan Age.

Johnson, Sir William (1715-74), British superintendent of Indian affairs in North America (1755-74). His just and honest conduct kept the Iroquois nations, into which he was adopted, on the British side in the French and Indian War. He commanded the victorious forces at the battle of Lake George.
See also: French and Indian Wars.

Johnson, Walter (1887-1946), U.S. baseball player. Nicknamed "The Big Train," Johnson was a right-handed pitcher famous for his fastball. His achievements include winning the second most games in major league history (416) and pitching the most career shutouts (110). He played for the Washington Senators (1907-27) and was among the first group of players inducted into the National Baseball Hall of Fame (1936).

Johnson Space Center, formerly the Manned Spacecraft Center renamed in 1973 after former President Lyndon Johnson's death. Built in the early 1960s, it became the National Aeronautics and Space Administration (NASA) headquarters for all U.S. manned space missions in 1964. The center also serves as a training base for U.S. astronauts as well as a construction site for spacecraft. The center, located in Houston, Texas, covers an area of 1600 acres.
See also: National Aeronautics and Space Adminstration.

Johnston, Albert Sydney (1803-62), brilliant Confederate general, secretary of war for the Texas Republic (1838-40). Confederate second-in-command, he was driven back by superior forces on the Mississippi-Allegheny front. His daring strategy almost won the battle of Shiloh, but he was mortally wounded in the first day's fighting.
See also: Civil War, U.S.

Johnston, Joseph Eggleston (1807-91), Confederate general, credited with the victory at Bull Run in 1861. Wounded at Fair Oaks, he was relieved of command in 1864 after a feud with Jefferson Davis; he returned to command in 1865 but had to surrender to Gen. Sherman after 2 months. In 1879-81 he was a member of the U.S. House of Representatives.

Johnstown (pop. 241,247), city in southwestern Pennsylvania, in the heart of a rich coal belt on the Conemaugh River. Settled in 1770 Johnstown has

long been an important iron, steel, and coal center, especially since the Civil War. In 1889, the city suffered a disastrous flood that killed more than 2,200 people when the dam at the South Fork Reservoir broke.
See also: Pennsylvania.

John the Baptist, Saint (d. c.A.D. 30), Jewish prophet, son of Zacharias and Elizabeth, who was a relative of Mary. John preached a mission of repentance in the Jordan Valley, predicting the imminent coming of the Messiah. He baptized his followers and also baptized Jesus, whom he considered the son of God.

John the Evangelist, Saint *See:* John, Saint.

Joint, in anatomy, junction or union between two or more bones, especially one in which bones move. Generally speaking, three kinds of junctions can be distinguished. A fibrous junction consists of connective tissue; almost no movement is possible in this type of joint. A cartilaginous junction is composed of cartilage; here only moderate movement is possible. The synovial junction is the most familiar type of joint. Here the extremities of the facing bones are covered with a thin layer of smooth cartilage, separated from each other by synovial fluid. This kind of joint permits the greatest amount of movement. The type of movement possible depends on the type of joint. Some examples are the hinge (knee and elbow), the pivot (neck and skull connection), and the ball and socket (hip and shoulder).
See also: Bone.

Joint Chiefs of Staff, U.S. agency within the Dept. of Defense, meant to advise the president and secretary of defense on military matters. Set up in 1942, it has five members: a chairman, the Army and Air Force chiefs of staff, the chief of naval operations, and the Marine Corps commandant.
See also: Defense, Department of.

Joint-stock company, forerunner of the modern corporation, a form of business association in which the working capital is obtained by selling shares of stock to individuals who may transfer them without the consent of the group. The shareholders are collectively responsible for the company's debts. The most famous early joint-stock companies were the British East India Company (1600), the Dutch East India Company (1602), and the Hudson's Bay Company (1670).
See also: East India Company.

Joint tenancy, ownership of real property by 2 or more persons, each having equal rights to its use during their lifetimes. To qualify, the partners must enter into possession at the same time and hold the title in common. If one tenant dies, the property falls in its entirety to the survivor(s).

Jojoba (*Simmondsia californica* or *S. chinensis*), desert plant of northern Mexico and the U.S. Southwest. Jojoba beans yield a high-quality oil similar to sperm whale oil, which has been banned in the United States since 1971. Processed as a substitute for whale oil, jojoba is used in shampoos, cosmetics, and industrial chemicals.

Joliot-Curie, Irène (1897-1956), French physicist, daughter of Pierre and Marie Curie. She and her husband, **Frédéric Joliot-Curie** (1900-58), shared the 1935 Nobel Prize in chemistry for artificially producing radioactive materials by bombarding elements with alpha particles. In 1940 they turned their attention to the chain reaction in nuclear fission. Both helped organize the French atomic energy commission, but Frédéric was removed as first chairman in 1950 because of his leftist political views. Irène became chairwoman in 1951. Like her mother, Irène died from leukemia probably contracted as a result of prolonged exposure to radioactive materials.
See also: Nuclear energy; Radiation.

Jolliet, or **Joliet, Louis** (1645-1700), 17th-century French-Canadian explorer. He traversed and mapped out much of the upper Great Lakes and the Mississippi River. Accompanied by Father Jacques Marquette, he explored the Mississippi by canoe in 1673, beginning from what is now Wisconsin and traveling over 1,000 miles to the mouth of the Arkansas River. In later years, Jolliet explored the Hudson Bay region and the Labrador coast.

Jolson, Al (Asa Yoelson; c.1866-1950), Russian-born U.S. singer and actor. Star of the first full-length sound film, *The Jazz Singer* (1927), Jolson popularized such songs as "Sonny-Boy," "Swanee," and "Mammy."

Jonah, Book of, in the Old Testament, 32nd in the Authorized Version, 5th of the Minor Prophets. Unique in its entirely narrative form, it tells of the Hebrew prophet Jonah, who disobeyed God's command to travel to Nineveh to convert the city. Instead Jonah sailed away, and his crew threw him overboard during a storm brought on by his disobedience. Swallowed by a "great fish," Jonah was cast out of the fish's body three days later. He then returned to Ninevah to fulfill his mission.
See also: Bible; Old Testament.

Jones, Absalom (1746-1818), early African-American religious leader. He founded the St. Thomas African Episcopal Church (1794), the first black Episcopal church in the United States, and became the first black Episcopal priest (ordained 1804). Born a slave, Jones bought his freedom in 1784. Three years later, while serving as a lay preacher at a predominantly European-American church in Philadelphia, Jones and Richard Allen founded the Free African Society. They led a walkout by black congregation members, protesting segregated seating policies. The St. Thomas African Episcopal Church was formed when the Free African Society split in two.
See also: Allen, Richard.

Jones, Bobby (Robert Tyre Jones, Jr.; 1902-71), U.S. golfer. Although he was an amateur, he won the U.S. Open four times (1923, 1926, 1929, 1930) and the British Open three times (1926, 1927, 1930). In 1926 he became the only golfer ever to win both those titles in the same year. He won a total of five U.S. Amateur tournaments (1924, 1925, 1927, 1928, 1930). In 1930 he won golf's grand slam, winning the amateur and open championships in both Britain and the United States. After his retirement, he and banker Clifford Roberts founded the Augusta National Golf Club in Georgia, establishing what is now called the Masters tournament.

Jones, Casey (John Luther Jones; 1863-1900), U.S. railroad engineer and folk hero who drove the *Cannon Ball* express from Memphis, Tenn. to Canton, Miss. When it collided with a freight train on Apr. 30, 1900, Jones applied the brakes in time to save the passengers and crew, but he was killed.

Jones, Ernest (1879-1958), British physician and psychologist. A colleague of Sigmund Freud and author of a comprehensive 3-volume book on him, Jones introduced Freudian theories and principles to the United Kingdom, the United States, and Canada. His efforts led to the general acceptance of Freud by the medical and scientific communities. In 1911 Jones was one of the founders of the American Psychoanalytic Association, and 2 years later he helped establish its British counterpart.
See also: Freud, Sigmund; Psychoanalysis.

Jones, Inigo (1573-1652), English architect. After studying the works of Palladio in Italy, he designed sets and costumes for court masques and later became the king's surveyor of works (1615-44). His masterpieces include the Queen's House at Greenwich, the banquet hall at Whitehall, and St. Paul's Cathedral in Covent Garden, London. His departure from the Jacobean style marked the beginning of England's Renaissance and Georgian periods, and he is considered one of the first great architects of England.
See also: Renaissance.

Jones, James (1921-77), U.S. novelist. His first book, *From Here to Eternity* (1951), portrayed the degradation of army life on the eve of World War II. Other works include *Some Came Running* (1957), *The Pistol* (1959), and *The Thin Red Line* (1962).

Jones, James Earl (1931-), U.S. actor who achieved stardom for his portrayal of Jack Johnson in the stage productions of *The Great White Hope* (1968). He is also an acclaimed Shakespearian actor noted for his role in *Othello* (1963, 1982). Jones won a Tony Award for his performance in the Broadway production of *Fences* (1986). His distinctive voice was used as that of DarthVader, in the classic science fiction film series, *Star Wars*.

Jones, John Paul (1747-92), Scottish-born U.S. naval hero of the Revolution. He raided British ships during the war for independence, capturing the *Drake*, a British warship, and the *Serapis* (1779). During the battle with the *Serapis*, Jones was the commander of the *Bon Homme Richard*. When the *Richard* was badly damaged, Jones was asked to surrender, but told the British commander, "Sir, I have not yet begun to fight!"
See also: Revolutionary War in America.

Jones, LeRoi *See:* Baraka, Imamu Amiri.

Jones, Mary Harris (1830-1930), U.S. labor leader known as "Mother Jones." She was one of the organizers of the International Workers of the World (IWW), a radical labor group whose members were often involved in violent incidents around the turn of the century. Jones was jailed on 4 occasions between 1902 and 1914 for inciting miners to go on strike in West Virginia and Colorado.

Jonson, Ben (1572-1637), English dramatist and lyric poet. His play *Every Man in His Humour* (1598) established his reputation. That was followed by *Every Man out of His Humour* (1599) and *The Poetaster* (1601), a satire. His best-known works were biting comic plays: *Volpone* (1606), *Epicoene* (1609), *The Alchemist* (1610), and *Bartholomew Fair* (1614). His poetry includes the collections *The Forrest* (1616), containing the song "Drink to me only with thine eyes," and *Underwoods* (1640).

Joplin, Scott (1868-1917), African-American composer and pianist, the best known practitioner of the style called ragtime. His works include the "Maple Leaf Rag" (1899) and the opera *Treemonisha* (1911).

Jordan, nonnavigable river beginning in north Israel and flowing about 200 mi (320 km) south through the Sea of Galilee and the Ghor Valley into the Dead Sea. The portion of the river between the Sea of Galilee and the Dead Sea forms the border between the Kingdom of Jordan and the West Bank, occupied by Israel since the 1967 war.

Jordan, officially Hashemite Kingdom of Jordan, country in southwest Asia, bordered by Israel to the west, Syria to the north, Iraq to the northeast, and Saudi Arabia to the south and east. The capital is Amman.
Land and climate. The area east of the Jordan River, with 94% of the country's area, is mostly desert. West of this area is the Jordan Rift, which includes the Jordan River, the Dead Sea, and the Araba, a low, dry riverbed extending down to the Gulf of Aqaba. West of the Jordan River is the most fertile part of the country, the West Bank. It was incorporated into Jordan in 1950 but has been occupied by Israel since June 1967. In addition to the Old City of Jerusalem (annexed by Israel in 1967), the West Bank contains the cities of Nablus, Bethlehem, Hebron, Jericho, Jenin, Ramallah, and Tulkarm.
People. The population is mainly Arab, and about half are Palestinians, most of whom live in the urban centers. Almost 95% of the people are Sunni Muslims, the remainder Shi'te or Christians. The official language is Arabic.
Economy. Jordan's economy is largely agricultural, with wheat, barley, and fruits the principal crops. Most industry is limited to food processing and textiles, although there is some oil refining, and cement and fertilizer manufacturing. Phosphate is mined. The economy was greatly disrupted by the loss of the West Bank, and Jordan relies heavily on remittances and foreign aid, mostly from Saudi Arabia and the US.
History. The region that is now Jordan has been ruled by many different empires, including Alexander the Great's, the Roman, and the Byzantine. It was conquered by the Arabs in the 7th century and from then on was part of the various Arab dynasties, including the Umayyads and Abbasids. In 1516 the Ottoman Empire took control, and until the end of World War I Jordan was ruled by the Turks. After the war, it became part of the mandate of Palestine. The Hashemite family, driven out of Arabia by the Saudis, became the local rulers. In 1946 Jordan became an independent state, with the Emir Abdullah as king. In the 1948 war with Israel, the Jordanian army conquered the West Bank. In 1951 Abdullah, who had made a truce with Israel, was assassinated; his grandson, Hussein, was enthroned the following year. Jordan's subsequent involvement in the June 1967 Arab-Israeli War cost it the West Bank, which was occupied by Israel. In 1970 the growing power of the Palestinian guerrillas in Jordan led to a bitter civil war after which the

Jordan

Capital: Amman
Area: 37,738 sq mi (97,740 sq km)
Population: 4,435,000
Language: Arabic
Government: Parliamentary monarchy
Independent: 1946
Head of gov.: Prime mininster
Per capita: U.S. $1,510
Mon. unit: 1 Jordan dinar = 1,000 fils

Palestinian fighters were expelled from the country. In 1974, however, Hussein recognized the Palestine Liberation Organization as the sole legitimate representative of the Palestinian people, and in 1988 he renounced Jordan's claim to the West Bank. In 1994 Jordan and Israel signed a peace treaty.

Jordan, Barbara Charline (1936-), first African-American woman from a Southern state to serve in the U.S. Congress. A Democrat, Jordan represented Texas in the U.S. House of Representatives for 3 terms (1973-79). In 1974, as a member of the House Judiciary Committee, she became nationally known during the impeachment hearings for President Richard Nixon. Two years later she was the first black keynote speaker at a national Democratic Party convention.

Jordan, Ernst Pascual (1902-), German physicist. He was a pioneer in the field of quantum mechanics, a method of analyzing atomic structures and particle motion. Along with Max Born and Werner Heisenberg, Jordan contributed to the development of the first mathematical formula for quantum mechanics in 1925.
See also: Quantum mechanics.

Jordan, Michael (1963-), U.S. professional basketball player. A 6-ft 6-in (198 cm) guard and forward for the Chicago Bulls of the National Basketball Association, he is considered one of the best players of all time. His vertical-leap, athleticism, and slam-dunks, have become his trade-marks. After helping North Carolina win the National Collegiate Athletic Association championship (1982) he led the 1984 U.S. Olympic basketball team to a gold medal. Jordan was named NBA Rookie of the Year (1984-85), won the Most Valuable Player (MVP) award (1987-88, 1990-91 ,1991-92, 1995-96, 1997-98 seasons), and has led the league in scoring from 1987-1990 (averaging 34.6 points over the 4-year period).

Joseph, in the Bible, favored son of Jacob and Rachel. His brothers, jealous of his dreams and his coat of many colors, sold him into slavery. He was eventually taken to Egypt, where he became an influential member of the house of Potiphar. He was later unjustly imprisoned, on the basis of accusations made by Potiphar's wife. Joseph won his release by interpreting the pharaoh's dreams, and the pharaoh made him governor of Egypt. While holding that post, he rescued his family from famine.

Joseph, Chief (Hinmaton-Yalaktit; c.1840-1904), leader of the Nez Percé, a Native American tribe. He non-violently resisted the forced resettlement of his people under a treaty fraudulently obtained by the United States in 1863. In 1877, when fighting broke out, he led a 1,000-mi (1,609-km) mass flight from Oregon to Canada. The Nez Percé were defeated only 30 mi (48 km) from the border. Joseph lived out his life on Colville Reservation in Washington.

Joseph, Saint, in Christian tradition, husband of the Virgin Mary, a descendant of David. He is honored by Orthodox and Roman Catholics as the foster father of Jesus. His feast day is March 19.

Josephine (Marie Josèphe Rose Tascher de la Pagerie; 1763-1814), first wife of Napoleon Bonaparte; empress of France (1804-9). At 17 she married Vicomte Alexandre de Beauharnais, who was executed by the revolutionary government in 1794. Two years later, she met and married Napoleon. Josephine's inability to bear children who could succeed Napoleon resulted in an amicable divorce in 1809. She remained in love with him for the rest of her life and asked to join him in exile on Elba. He refused, but she died before his refusal reached her.
See also: Napoleon I.

Josephus Flavius (c.A.D. 37-100), Jewish historian and soldier in the Jewish revolt against the Romans (A.D. 66). After the revolt, Josephus won the favor of the Roman general Vespasian. He took Roman citizenship and became governor of Galilee. His writings include *History of the Jewish War*, *Antiquities of the Jews*, and *Against Apion* (a defense of the Jews).

Joshua, book of the Old Testament, sixth in the Authorized Version. Joshua was the successor of Moses as leader of the Israelites. The book of Joshua describes his command of the Israelite armies in their campaign of conquest of Canaan and the division of the land among the Twelve Tribes of Israel. The Battle of Jericho was one of the major victories of the conquest.

Joshua tree *See:* Yucca.

Josiah, king of ancient Judah (r. 639-609 B.C.). His reign was marked by a revival of traditional Jewish worship. Josiah reinstated religious services in the Jerusalem Temple after destroying the idols his father, King Amon, had placed there. During restoration of the Temple, the laws of Moses were found and Josiah read them to the people. Josiah declared independence from the Assyrian Empire and was killed in battle with the Egyptian Pharaoh Necho II at Megiddo.

Jouett, Jack (1754-1822), U.S. patriot. Known as the "Paul Revere of the South," he is credited with preventing the capture of Thomas Jefferson during the American Revolution. After learning of the British plan to kidnap Jefferson and members of the Virginia legislature in 1781, Jouett rode more than 40 mi (64 km) on horseback to alert them

Joule, James Prescott (1818-89), English physicist who determined the relationship between heat energy and mechanical energy and discovered the first law of thermodynamics, a version of the law of conservation of energy. The joule (a unit of work or energy) is named for him.
See also: Thermodynamics.

Journalism, preparation of information for communications media, including newspapers, magazines, radio, and television. Education to formalize journalism began in the late 19th century, and universities and colleges throughout the United States now offer degrees in journalism.

Jove *See:* Jupiter.

Joyce, James (1882-1941), Irish novelist, considered by many the leading 20th-century master of the English language. Though Joyce left his homeland at age 20, returning only infrequently for brief visits, he nevertheless was greatly influenced by his Irish roots. Dubliners, short stories written in 1914, was published in London but suppressed in Ireland because of its topical references. During World War I he worked on the autobiographical novel A Portrait of the Artist as a Young Man (1916), following his protagonist as he comes to realize the grip Irish society has on him and his need for freedom from it. Ulysses, written 1914-21, follows Homer's Odyssey in themes and allusions. It recounts a particular day—June 16, 1904—in the life of three characters, the salesman Leopold Bloom, his wife, Molly, and Stephen Dedalus (the young man in A Portrait). Publication was delayed due to charges of obscenity, and Ulysses did not appear in the United States until 1933. In Finnegans Wake (1939) Joyce develops a complex exploration of dream consciousness. The meaning of the work has been vigorously debated since its publication. Other writings include three volumes of poetry—Chamber Music (1907), Pomes Penyeach (1927), and Collected Poems (1937)—and the play Exiles (1918).

J particle *See:* Psi particle.

Juana Inés de la Cruz (1651-95), Mexican-Spanish poet and scholar. As a girl she left court to become a nun. Criticized for her "unwomanly" studies, she defended women's education in a vigorous letter to her bishop (1691). Her lyric poems, especially the sonnets, are among the finest in Spanish. She died nursing epidemic victims in Mexico City.

Juan Carlos I (1938-), king of Spain since 1975. Groomed as Gen. Francisco Franco's successor, he was so named in 1969. In 1975, when Franco died, he became the first Spanish king since the deposition of his grandfather (1931). He proved to be an unexpectedly strong force for stability and democracy and was instrumental in thwarting an attempted right-wing military coup in 1981.
See also: Spain.

Juan de Fuca, Strait of, waterway between Vancouver Island and the Olympic Peninsula of Washington state. Forming part of the boundary between the United States and Canada, the strait is about 100 mi (160 km) long and 11 to 17 mi (18 to 27 km) wide. It is an important shipping channel for the ports of Seattle, Washington, and Vancouver and Victoria, British Columbia. The passage's name comes from a Greek navigator who sailed for Spain and claimed discovery in 1592, although his claim has been disputed.

Juan Fernández, 3 small, sparsely populated Chilean islands in the Pacific Ocean. Lying 400 mi (640 km) west of Chile, they were discovered by Spanish explorer Juan Fernandez c.1563. One of the islands, Róbinson Crusoe, is believed to be the site of the self-imposed exile of Alexander Selkirk, the inspiration for Daniel Defoe's *Robinson Crusoe*. The other islands are Alejandro Selkirk and Santa Clara.

Juárez (pop. 797,700), or Ciudad Juarez, city in Mexico, situated on the Rio Grande opposite El Paso, Tex. Juarez serves as a major port of entry from the United States. Founded by Spanish colonial soldiers in 1662, the city's original name was El Paso del Norte ("North Pass"). In 1888 it was renamed in honor of Mexican leader Benito Juarez. Today Juarez is an important cotton-processing center and popular tourist destination.
See also: Mexico.

Juárez, Benito Pablo (1806-72), Mexican political leader and president (1857-65, 1867-72). He enacted major reforms within the military and the church to reduce their power and redistributed large portions of land to poor farmers (*peons*). In the mid-1850s, he overthrew the dictator, Santa Anna, and led the nation's liberal faction in the "War of Reform." Between 1864 and 1867 he fought the French and deposed their puppet emperor, Maximilian.

Judah, biblical figure of ancient Canaan. He was the ancestor of one of the 12 tribes of Israel that bears his name. As the fourth son of Jacob and Leah, Judah is credited with persuading his other brothers not to kill Joseph. During the great famine in Canaan, Judah, his brothers, Jacob, and their families settled in Egypt at Joseph's invitation. Judah's name was later given to the kingdom with Jerusalem as its center.

Judah Halevi *See:* Halevi, Judah.

Judah Maccabee (d.160-? B.C.), Jewish leader of the Hasmonean dynasty who, upon his father's death, took leadership of the revolt against the Syrian ruler Antiochus IV, who had initiated religious persecution of the Jews. Judah Maccabee's rededication of the temple of Jerusalem is commemorated by the Hanukkah.

Judaism, religion of the Jewish people, the oldest of the world's monotheistic faiths. The essence of Judaism is the belief in one God. At daily prayers and services Jews repeat the words of Deuteronomy 6:4: "Hear O Israel: The Lord our God, the Lord is One." In Jewish beliefs, Abraham, the Jewish patriarch, made a covenant with God that he and his descendants would carry the message of the one God. This covenant, the burden of special service to God, is Judaism's reason for being, and the relationship between God and the Chosen People is the subject of the Hebrew Bible, the foundation of Judaism. The Torah, the first part of the Bible (known as the Five Books of

Moses, or the Pentateuch), contains the Ten Commandments and the ritual laws and ethical precepts that form the structure of the Jewish religion. In the centuries after the Bible was completed, its text was explained and adapted by a set of traditions and interpretations known as the Oral Law. When the Temple of Jerusalem and the hereditary priesthood were destroyed in A.D. 70, the Oral Law was recorded in a work known as the Mishnah, the discussion and interpretation of which forms a commentary called the Gemara. These two works together make up the Talmud, second only to the Bible in its authority. Differences over ritual observance are the chief characteristics of the groups within Judaism today. Reform Judaism began in the 19th century in answer to the challenge of rationalism. Reform Jews believe that each generation has the right to adapt or discard traditions it finds no longer meaningful. Much of the Reform synagogue service in the United States is in English, and the compatibility of Judaism with modern secular values is emphasized. Orthodox Judaism accepts the totality of the Bible and the Oral Law as divine revelation and holds strictly to all dietary laws and codes of conduct. Religious services are conducted solely in Hebrew, men and women sitting in separate parts of the synagogue. The extremes of Reform and Orthodox Judaism have to some extent been bridged in the United States by the Conservative movement, which has attempted to combine the traditions of Orthodox observance with some of the freedom of choice and adaptability found in Reform Judaism.

Judas Iscariot, in the Bible, one of the Twelve Apostles, the one who betrayed Jesus. For 30 pieces of silver he identified Jesus to the soldiers at Gethsemane by a kiss of greeting. According to Matthew, he later repented and hanged himself.
See also: Apostles.

Judas Maccabaeus *See:* Judah Maccabee.

Judas tree *See:* Redbud.

Juddah *See:* Jidda.

Judea, ancient name for south Palestine. Originally known as Canaan, it was called Judea after the Hebrews returning from Exodus took possession of it. The name was derived from Judah, ancestral patriarch of one of the 12 tribes of Israel, and the term Jews is a shortened form of Judeans. King David was the first ruler of a united Judea, with Jerusalem as the capital. After the death of his son, King Solomon, Judea split into 2 kingdoms: Israel and Judah.

Jude, Epistle of, brief letter near the end of the New Testament. It warns against false teachers and the consequences of heresy within the church. Of unknown authorship, the 25-verse epistle is believed to have been written around A.D. 100.
See also: Bible; New Testament.

Jude, Saint, or Saint Judas, one of the Twelve Apostles, also called Lebbaeus or Thaddaeus, possibly the author of the New Testament epistle of Jude, which warns against heresy. Jude is an anglicized form of Judas, to distinguish him from Judas Iscariot. His feast day is Oct. 28.
See also: Apostles.

Judges, Book of, in the Old Testament, 7th of the Authorized Version, the sequel to Joshua. It recounts the Hebrews' successive apostasies from God and their punishment by enemy oppression. The judges were mainly military leaders sent by God to deliver the people. The main judges are Barak, Deborah, Gideon, Abimelech, Jephthah, and Samson.
See also: Old Testament.

Judgment, legal decision made by a court. A judgment is legally binding upon the parties named in it and often involves restitution imposed on a guilty party by a judge or someone acting in a legal capacity. Once a judgment is handed down, it has the force of law behind it, and violations can be punished by the court. Judgments made in criminal cases can usually be appealed to a higher court, which can either overturn or uphold a lower court ruling.

Judicial Conference of the United States, policymaking and review arm of the U.S. judicial system. It consists of 25 members and is presided over by the Chief Justice of the U.S. Supreme Court. Established in 1922, the conference meets once a year to review caseloads in all federal judicial districts and circuits and reviews complaints against federal judges. Recommendations are submitted to Congress and the U.S. Supreme Court and go into effect after 3 months unless Congress rejects them.

Judicial department *See:* Constitution of the United States; Justice, Department of; Supreme Court of the United States.

Judith, book of the Apocrypha of the Authorized Version of the Bible, present in the Old Testament of the Western canon but not in the Hebrew Bible. It tells how a young Jewish widow, Judith, saves her city, Bethulia, by seducing and murdering the Assyrian general Holofernes.
See also: Bible.

Judo, form of unarmed combat, a Japanese sport developed by Jigoro Kano in 1882 using the principles of jujitsu. It combines the use of balance, timing, and force to use one's opponent's own strength against him. Colored belts, ranging from white for beginners to black for experts, denote proficiency grades.

Judson, Adoniram (1788-1850), U.S. missionary. His 30-year work in Burma resulted in the first translation of the Bible into Burmese (1834) and an English-Burmese dictionary (1849). Judson entered the ministry and helped organize a Congregationalist missionary society, which sent him to India in 1812. Disagreements with certain Congregationalist practices led him into the Baptist ministry. He helped the Baptists organize a similar missionary society, and in 1813 he was assigned to Burma.
See also: Baptists.

Juggernaut, or Jagannatha (Sanskrit, "lord of the world"), Hindu temple and idol in Puri, India. The shrine was completed in the 12th century. Once a year, during the June-July Rathayatra festival, the huge Juggernaut and its brother and sister idols are placed on wheeled carts and rolled through the streets, requiring the work of hundreds of people to move them. The word *juggernaut* has come to mean a heavy, unstoppable force.

Juggling, art of keeping several objects in motion in the air simultaneously and catching them. Juggling was practiced by the Egyptians, Greeks, and Romans; the French equivalent was a medieval troubadour who juggled, sang, and danced. Juggling came into its own in circuses and music halls in the 19th century. The word juggling has also come to mean dishonest manipulation, especially of money.

Jugoslavia *See:* Yugoslavia.

Jugular vein, any of several veins on each side of the neck that return venous blood from the head. Their proximity to the surface makes them liable to trauma.
See also: Vein.

Juilliard, Augustus (1836-1919), wealthy U.S. patron of the performing arts. After making his fortune in the textile industry, Julliard devoted time and money toward promoting cultural endeavors. He became president of New York's Metropolitan Opera Company in 1892 and served until his death. Large sums of money bequeathed from his estate established the Julliard Musical Foundation, which supports the Julliard School, a prestigious musical education institute.

Jujitsu *See:* Judo.

Julian (A.D. 331-363), 4th-century Roman emperor, known as *The Apostate* (the traitor). He was the last ruler to oppose the spread of Christianity in the Roman Empire. The nephew of Constantine I, Julian rejected his Christian education and tried to promote worship of the Roman gods after becoming emperor in 361. He prevented Christians from teaching in Roman schools, but his death in battle against the Persians 2 years later ended the persecutions.

Juliana (1909-) queen of the Netherlands (1948-80) following the abdication of her mother, Queen Wilhelmina. She abdicated (1980) in favor of her daughter Beatrix.
See also: Netherlands.

Julian, Percy Lavon (1899-1975), U.S. chemist and chemical business executive. He developed several important soybean-based products, including a synthetic progesterone used to prevent miscarriages. He also created physostigmine, a drug used to treat glaucoma.
See also: Chemistry.

Julian calendar, system of time measurement widely used between 46 B.C. and 1582. It was named for Julius Caesar, who devised it. The Julian calendar was based on solar cycles. The year was divided into 12 alternating 30- and 31-day months, with Feb. (29 days) being the exception. The Julian year was 11 min. and 14 sec. longer than the annual solar cycle, resulting in a discrepancy of 10 days by 1582. Pope Gregory XIII corrected the problem, bringing his Gregorian calendar into synchronization with the solar year.
See also: Calendar.

Julius II (1443-1513), pope (1503-13). As Cardinal Giuliano della Rovere he went into exile (1492-1503) when his bitter enemy Borgia became pope

Alexander VI. As pope, Julius commanded the armies that reconquered the Papal States; he then led the Holy League against France (1510). The fifth Lateran Council (1512), which he assembled, attacked corruption in the church. A patron of Raphael, Michelangelo, and Bramante, Julius II laid the foundation stone of St. Peter's Cathedral.

Julius Caesar *See:* Caesar, (Gaius) Julius.

July Revolution, popular revolt in France in July 1830 against King Charles X. Middle-class opposition was aroused when the king's ultraroyalist minister, Jules Armand de Polignac, published the July Ordinances, which suspended freedom of the press, dissolved the chamber of deputies, and reduced the electorate by 75%. Rioting broke out, and though Charles repealed the Ordinances, he was forced to abdicate. His cousin the duke of Orleans became King Louis Philippe.
See also: France.

Jumna River, or Yamuna River, tributary of the Ganges, in Northern India. It begins in the Himalayas and is nearly 900 mi (1,400 km) long. Canals draining water from the Jumna irrigate about 12,000 sq mi (31,100 sq km) in central India. The cities of Delhi and New Delhi lie along the banks of the Jumna, and it flows close to Agra, site of the Taj Mahal. The Jumna joins the Ganges near Allahabad. Their confluence is considered sacred to Hindus.

Jumping *See:* Olympic Games; Track and field.

Jumping bean, seed of various Mexican shrubs, principally those of the genera *Sebastiania* and *Sapium* of the spurge family. The appearance of jumping is due to movement of the larva of the moth *Carpocapsa saltitans* contained inside.

Junco, any of several species of small North American finches (genus *Junco*), usually ashen in color but with conspicuous white lateral tail feathers. The slate-colored junco nests up to the treeline in Alaska, migrating south in winter. Some have crossed the Atlantic.

Juneau (pop. 23,300), capital of Alaska and port city in the southeast panhandle, situated at the foot of Mt. Juneau, on the Gastineau Channel. Ice free even in winter, Juneau supports fishing (especially salmon), lumbering, sawmilling, and tourism. The surrounding mountains yield asbestos, nickel ore, limestone, and marble, and the rapid mountain streams are a source of hydroelectric power. Juneau was founded by prospectors in 1880, when gold-bearing quartz was discovered nearby. It has the largest area (3,108 sq mi/8,050 sq km) of any U.S. city.
See also: Alaska.

June bug, or June beetle, any of many large flying beetles (family Melolonthidae) that feed on the leaves of trees. The white larvae live underground, feeding on the roots of grasses and plants, causing considerable damage.

Jung, Carl Gustav (1875-1961), Swiss psychiatrist, founder of analytical psychology. Jung's work on mental complexes brought him into contact with

Sigmund Freud in 1907, a relationship that lasted until 1912, when Freud broke with Jung upon the publication of Jung's *Psychology of the Unconscious*. In this book Jung argued that there were two components of the unconscious: repressed or forgotten information of an individual's life and collective information shared by all human beings or by those in particular cultural groups. In 1921 Jung expounded on introversion and extroversion in *Psychological Types*. Jung believed that harmony between the conscious and unconscious was the most important psychological goal for the individual.
See also: Psychoanalysis.

Jungfrau (German, "maiden"), mountain in the Swiss Alps. The Jungfrau is 13,642 ft (4,158 m) high and presents a formidable challenge for mountain climbers. It is also the site of the highest railroad in Europe, constructed between 1896 and 1912. The railway ends at a level pass, 11,333 ft (3,454 m) high, between the Jungfrau and its neighboring peak.

Jungle fowl, any of several wild birds (genus *Gallus*), from which domestic fowls probably descended. Found in the forests of southeast Asia, the jungle fowl is becoming rarer as its habitat is destroyed.

Junior Achievement, U.S. organization aimed at teaching students about the nation's business system. Founded in 1919, Junior Achievement has about 785,000 student members from the fifth through the 12th grades. They learn how to set up corporations, buy and sell stock, keep records, and handle payrolls. Programs are sponsored by local businesses and industries, and volunteers from those businesses often serve as advisers and teachers.

Juniper, any of several species of evergreen trees or shrub (genus *Juniperus*) of the cypress family, found in northern temperate zones. The cones of the common juniper (*J. communis*) are fleshy, like berries, and are used to flavor gin. Some junipers are used for lumber and oil; those called cedars, e.g., the American eastern red (*J. virginiana*), supply insect-repellant closets and fenceposts. Its oil is used in perfume and medicine.

Junípero Serra *See:* Serra, Junípero.

Junk, any of various Chinese sailing vessels, used in the Far East for thousands of years. Junks are wooden craft, up to 30 by 10 ft (9 by 3 m), with flat-bottoms, high sterns (rears) and square bows (fronts). They have tall, heavy masts, up to 5 in number, with sails made of cotton cloth or straw matting. They have deep rudders and little or no keel. Though some people live on junks, they are now mainly used for transporting goods on rivers and coastal waters.

Juno, in Roman mythology, queen of the gods. She was the sister and wife of Jupiter, king of the gods, and revered by Roman women as the goddess of marriage and childbirth. Representations of Juno adorned some of the most famous temples of the Roman Empire, and she played a prominent part in *The Aeneid*, Vergil's epic poem about the founding of Rome. Juno's Greek counterpart was Hera.

Jupiter, in astronomy, largest planet in the solar system (equatorial diameter of 89,400 mi/143,800 km), fifth planet from the Sun (average distance 483.6 million mi/778.3 million km). Jupiter is larger than all the other planets combined, with a mass 317.9 times that of Earth. Believed to have a solid core of rocky material, it is mostly gaseous with an atmosphere composed mostly of hydrogen and helium but including traces of ammonia and methane. Prominent cloud belts paralleling its equator are occasionally interrupted by stormlike turbulences, particularly the Great Red Spot, an elliptical area at least 300 yrs old and measuring 30,000 by 10,000 mi (48,000 by 16,000 km). Jupiter has 16 known moons, the largest and most distant of which, Callisto and Ganymede, are larger than Mercury. Io, the satellite closest to Jupiter, exhibits volcanism, probably because of tidal action resulting from its close proximity to the planet. Jupiter, also has a ring system, much fainter than that of Saturn and invisible from Earth. In 1973, 1974, and 1979, U.S. space probes (*Pioneers 10* and *11* and *Voyagers 1* and *2*) collected data on the Jovian system. Another probe, the *Galileo* collected data on Jupiter (1995).
See also: Planet; Solar System.

Jupiter, in Roman mythology, king of the gods and supreme ruler over the entire universe. Patterned after Zeus, king of the Greek gods, Jupiter overthrew his father, Saturn, and married his sister, Juno. Jupiter's other brothers and sisters were Neptune, Pluto, Ceres, and Vesta. His children were Mars, Vulcan, Apollo, Bacchus, Mercury, Diana, Hercules, and the 9 Muses of the arts. Jupiter's temple on the Capitoline Hill in Rome was the focal point of Roman polytheistic worship.
See also: Mythology.

Jura Mountains, forested mountain range in western Europe, crossed by gorges, and fertile valleys, extending from the Rhone River to the Rhine River on the Swiss-German border. The highest peak in the Juras is Cret de la Neige (5,652 ft/1,723 m).

Jurassic, the middle period of the Mesozoic era, lasting from about 195 to 140 million years ago.

Jury, in common law, body of laypeople assembled to study evidence and make judgments in legal proceedings. In England, the jury was probably an extension of the Norman practice of calling character witnesses, people who had personal knowledge of a dispute. Over time, the make-up of the jury changed: disinterested parties were presented with formally produced evidence. This system was adopted from English law into the United States in the 18th century. The sixth and seventh amendments to the U.S. Constitution provide for jury trial in most criminal and civil cases. A grand jury (12-23 people) hears evidence and decides whether a trial is justified; a petit (small) jury of 6 or 12 people sits at the trial proper. Until 1970, verdicts had to be unanimous, but certain exceptions are now permissible. A hung jury (one that is unable to reach a verdict) necessitates a new trial with a new jury.

Justice, Department of, federal executive department created by Congress (1870). Headed by the attorney general, its functions are to enforce federal laws, furnish legal counsel to the federal government and represent it in

Supreme Court cases, administer federal prisons, and supervise district attorneys and marshals. Its agencies include the Federal Bureau of Investigation, the Immigration and Naturalization Service, and the Drug Enforcement Administration. Its divisions include Antitrust, Civil, Civil Rights, Criminal, Land and Natural Resources, and Tax.

Justinian I (483-565), Byzantine emperor (527-65), nephew of Justin I. His attempts to impose heavy taxation and religious orthodoxy on the diverse peoples and sects of the empire, especially the Monophysites (a Christian minority), led to the Nika riots (532), which were quelled by Empress Theodora, aided by Justinian's generals Belisarius and Narses. Among Justinian's accomplishments are the codification of Roman law (*Digests*) and such great churches as Hagia Sophia and San Vitale.
See also: Byzantine Empire.

Justinian Code, collection of early Roman civil laws, known as *Corpus Juris Civilis* (Latin, *Body of Civil Law*). Compiled by legal scholars at the behest of the Byzantine emperor Justinian I (r. A.D. 527-565), the code formed the basis of the legal systems of many Western nations for centuries afterward. Justinian had his scholars determine which Roman laws should remain in force, be modified, or be repealed. The code also proposed new laws. The 4 parts of the code are the *Institutes*, the *Digest*, the *Codex*, and the *Novels*.
See also: Law; Rome, Ancient.

Justin the Martyr, Saint (c.100-165), Christian theologian who opened the first school of Christian studies in Rome. He was martyred under Marcus Aurelius. His *Apology* and *Dialogue* defended Christianity against charges of impiety and sedition.

Jute, annual plant (genus *Corchorus*) of the linden family, and its fiber. Cultivated in India and Bangladesh, stems of the *C. capsularis* and *C. olitorius* are cut and laid in water until the long fibers can be separated. The fibers are then dyed and spun and used for making burlap, insulation, and rope.

Jutes, Germanic people who originated in Scandinavia, probably in Jutland, the Danish peninsula. With the Angles and Saxons they invaded England in the 5th century, settling in the south and southeast. Their national identify was soon lost, although some cultural influence seems to have survived in Kent.

Jutland, Battle of, only major naval battle of World War I, fought between the British and German fleets off the coast of Jutland (Denmark) on May 31, 1916. Though greatly outnumbered the Germans performed masterfully and escaped in the fog. The British fleet under Admiral Jellicoe suffered heavy losses leading to controversy about Jellicoe's tactics.

Juvenal (Decimus Junius Juvenalis; A.D. 60?-140?), Roman poet. His 16 satires are scathing attacks on the corruption of social and political life in Rome. Many of his epigrammatic sayings ("A sound mind in a sound body") have passed into everyday use.

Juvenile court, court with special jurisdiction over young offenders (usually up to age 18). In many nations, special provisions are made in legal proceedings involving minors. Rehabilitation, rather than punishment, is normally emphasized, including removal from parental care if the home environment is thought to contribute to delinquency. In the interest of flexibility and informality, certain ordinary courtroom practices may be suspended in juvenile court.

Juvenile delinquency, term applied to violations of the law by those legally considered under the age of majority. The maximum age for juveniles varies from place to place. Most countries deal with young offenders in special juvenile courts. Many sociologists contend that criminal activities are only one expression of a disturbed life pattern, of which transiency, violence, poverty, and the failure of family relationships are also typical. The high rate of illegal activity in adolescence probably reflects the general disturbances common to this age group. Action taken by the juvenile courts is theoretically correctional rather than punitive.

K

K, 11th letter of the English alphabet, is derived from the Semitic *kaph*, representing the palm of the hand, and from the ancient Greek *kappa*. After C was given the K sound, the Romans stopped using K except as an abbreviation. K is sometimes used as an abbreviation for *knight*, as in K.C. (Knights of Columbus); for *kilo*, a prefix meaning 1,000; and in chess, for *king*. In chemistry K is the symbol for potassium.

K2, mountain peak in the Himalayas of northern Kashmir, near the China-India border, second highest in the world. Also known as Mount Godwin-Austen and Dapsang, K2 is 29,064 ft (8,859 m) high. It was first scaled in 1954 by an Italian team under the leadership of Ardito Desio. Henry Haversham Godwin Austen surveyed the mountain in 1856.

Kaaba, or Caaba, most sacred shrine of Islam, the chief goal of pilgrimage, in the courtyard of the Great Mosque at Mecca, Saudi Arabia. Pilgrims must circle this flat-roofed building 7 times, and then kiss the venerated object encased within—the Black Stone, said to have been given to Adam on his fall from paradise. The Kaaba is the center of the Muslim world, and it is in its direction that Muslims face in prayer.

Kabalevsky, Dmitri (1904-87), Russian composer and critic. His works include symphonies, ballet, chamber music, and operas, such as *Colas Breugnon* (1938) and *The Taras Family* (1949).

Kabbalah, or Cabala (from the Hebrew word for "traditional lore"), mystical Jewish interpretation of the Torah and other holy writings. Based largely on doctrines of post-biblical sages, it entails the idea that every word and letter of the holy writings contains hidden meanings whose mystery must be uncovered through constant study. Under the guidance of Isaac Luria in the late 16th and early 17th century, Kabbalism became more messianic in

orientation. Hasidism, a Jewish movement that began in the 18th century, adopted many Kabbalist beliefs.
See also: Judaism.

Kabuki, traditional Japanese popular theater that developed in the 17th century in contrast to the aristocratic Noh theater. A blending of dance, song, and mime, kabuki dramatizes both traditional stories and contemporary events in a stylized but exuberant fashion. It remains popular today and has influenced much Western theatrical thought.

Kabul (pop. 1,036,000), capital and largest city of Afghanistan. Strategically located in the Hindu Kush Mountains, Kabul has been a battleground for invading empires during much of its 3,000-year history. It became the capital of Afghanistan in 1773. It is now an economic and commercial center, as well as the site of Afghanistan's leading university. High-quality rugs and karakul sheepskins produced in Kabul are among Afghanistan's leading exports. The city has been the scene of heavy fighting at various times during the Afghan civil war; from 1979 to 1989 it was the headquarters of the Soviet occupying troops. In 1996 it was taken by the fundamentalist Taliban.
See also: Afghanistan.

Kádár, János (1912-89), Hungarian Communist leader. In the 1956 uprising, he left his position in Imre Nagy's cabinet to lead the Soviet-supported counter-government that crushed the revolt. He became premier (1956-58, 1961-65) and first secretary of the party (1956). His leadership brought a liberalization to all facets of Hungarian life.
See also: Hungary.

Kaddafi, Muammar Muhammad al- *See:* Qadhafi, Muammar Muhammad al-.

Kaesong (pop. 345,600), city in North Korea near the South Korean border, about 30 mi (48 km) northwest of Seoul. It is a key agricultural and industrial hub and the site of many historic cultural landmarks. Chosen as the first capital of a united Korean kingdom (Koryo) in the 10th century, Kaesong was the country's leading city until 1392, when the ruling dynasty fell and the capital was moved to Seoul. In 1951 it was the site of the first peace talks aimed at ending the Korean War.

Kafir (*Sorghum vulgare*), type of grain of the grass family. Commonly grown on the North American plains and used as cattle feed, kafir was imported from Africa. The plants resemble cornstalks, attaining heights of 4 to 7 ft (1.2 to 2.1 m). Kafir is closely related to the sorghum grains of Africa and Asia.

Kafka, Franz (1883-1924), German writer. Kafka was born in Prague, of Jewish parents. Kafka created stories of conflicts for isolated, guilt-ridden protagonists—conflicts that could not be resolved or escaped, no matter their personal effort. His executor ignored instructions to destroy all his work, and subsequently published his novels, including *The Trial* (1925), *The Castle* (1926), and *America* (1927), and his short stories, including "The Metamorphosis" (1915), "A Country Doctor" (1919), and "In the Penal Colony" (1920).

Kahn, Louis Isadore (1901-74), U.S. architect, noted for his work on housing projects like Carver Court (1944), Coatesville, Pa., and university buildings. His work also included the planning of the Kimbell Art Museum (Fort Worth, Tex.), and the Yale University Art Gallery. Kahn held a professorship at the University of Pennsylvania from 1957 until his death.
See also: Architecture.

Kaiser, Henry John (1882-1967), U.S. industrialist, founder of the Kaiser-Frazer Corp., automobile manufacturers. He contributed greatly to the Allied war effort during World War II by his development of faster production techniques for ships, aircraft, and military vehicles, especially the famous jeep.

Kala-azar, dumdum fever, or visceral leishmaniasis, severe infectious disease found chiefly in Asia and caused by a protozoa (*Leishmania donovani*) and transmitted by the bite of sand flies. Symptoms include fever, anemia, leukopenia, and enlargement of the spleen and liver.

Kalahari Desert, arid plain in southwest Africa, lying mainly in Botswana but extending into Namibia and South Africa. The region, 100,000 sq mi (260,000 sq km) in area, has low annual rainfall (5-20 in/13-51 cm), seasonal pasture for sheep, and a wide variety of game. It is inhabited principally by the nomadic San (Bushmen) and Khoikhoi.

Kale, edible green vegetable (*Brassica oleracea*) of the mustard family. Valued as a source of vitamins A, B-complex, and C, kale's curled leaves are usually boiled or steamed before eating. Plants may attain heights of 24 to 30 in (61 to 76 cm), while dwarf varieties range from 12 to 15 in (30 to 38 cm).

Kaleidoscope, optical device that produces colorful patterns and designs. It consists of a tube with mirrors and pieces of colored beads and glass that is held to the eye and rotated to form symmetrical color patterns. Patented in 1817, the kaleidoscope is used by designers to formulate carpet and wallpaper patterns.

Kaliningrad (pop. 406,000), port city in western Russia, on the mouth of the Pregolya River, which flows into the Baltic Sea. Formerly called Königsberg, Kaliningrad was founded in 1255 as part of East Prussia. In 1945 it was absorbed by the Soviet Union and renamed Kaliningrad. Today it is a naval base for the Baltic Fleet. Fishing, machine building, and shipbuilding are the main industries.
See also: Union of Soviet Socialist Republics.

Kalmar Union, treaty whereby Denmark, Norway, and Sweden were united under Margaret of Denmark and her heirs. It was signed at the Swedish port of Kalmar (1397), which became the Union's political center. The Union endured until 1523.

Kalmia *See:* Mountain laurel.

Kamchatka Peninsula, peninsula in northeastern Russia, extending 750 mi (1,210 km) south from the Asian mainland to separate the Sea of Okhotsk from the Bering Sea and Pacific Ocean. It is largely tundra and pine forest, with 2 volcanic ranges. Geographic features include Siberia's highest peak, Kluychevskaya Sopka (15,584 ft/4,750 m), and 22 active volcanoes, along with geysers and hot springs. Main occupations include lumbering, fur-trapping, and fishing. The peninsula's main city is Petropavlovsk-Kamchatski.
See also: Union of Soviet Socialist Republics.

Kamehameha I (1738?-1819), Hawaiian king from 1790. This benevolent despot, who conquered and ruled all the Hawaiian islands (1810), encouraged foreign contact and trading.

Kamenev, Lev Borisovich (1883-1936), Russian Bolshevik leader, active in the Russian Revolution and member of the first politburo of the Communist party. After Lenin's death (1924) he joined Stalin and Zinoviev to defeat Trotsky's bid for power. However, Stalin ousted Kamenev and Zinoviev in 1925 and they joined Trotsky's opposition movement. In 1936, Stalin had both Kamenev and Zinoviev arrested and executed for treason.
See also: Bolsheviks; Russian Revolution.

Kamikaze (Japanese, "divine wind"), Japanese force of suicide pilots in World War II. Inspired by the ancient samurai code of patriotic self-sacrifice, they deliberately crashed bomb-bearing planes onto Allied ships and installations. They inflicted particularly heavy damage at Okinawa.
See also: World War II.

Kampala (pop. 458,400), capital and largest city of Uganda, on Lake Victoria in east Africa. When Uganda became self-governing in 1962, Kampala superseded Entebbe as the capital. The city was originally constructed on six adjacent hills. Uganda's agricultural and commercial markets are concentrated in Kampala.
See also: Uganda.

Kampuchea (officially Cambodia), republic in Southeast Asia, bordered on the north by Thailand and Laos, on the east and southeast by Vietnam, on the southwest by the Gulf of Siam, and on the west and northwest by Thailand. The capital is Phnom Penh.
Land and climate. Mainly a broad plain, Kampuchea occupies 69,898 sq mi (181,035 sq km), and is separated from Thailand by the Dangrek Mountains in the north and the Cardamom Mountains in the west. The Mekong, one of the most important rivers in southern Asia, enters Kampuchea from Laos and crosses the country from north to south. A large, shallow lake, the Tônlé Sap, occupies central Kampuchea. Annual inundations caused by the overflow of the Mekong River create excellent conditions for rice cultivation. The climate is tropical and humid, with a rainy season lasting from May to Oct. Rainfall is plentiful, reaching as high as 250 in (635 cm) per year in the Cardamom Mountains. Temperatures range from 68° to 97°F (20° to 36°C). Wildlife is abundant, particularly in the forests, and includes elephants, water buffaloes, tigers, leopards, honey bears, crocodiles, and snakes. Elephants are often domesticated. There are abundant freshwater fish. Plant life is also

Kampuchea (Cambodia)

Capital:	Phnom Penh
Area:	69,898 sq mi (181,035 sq km)
Population:	10,024,000
Language:	Khmer
Government:	Constitutional monarchy
Independent:	1953
Head of gov.:	Prime minister
Per capita:	U.S. $270
Mon. unit:	1 Riel = 100 sen

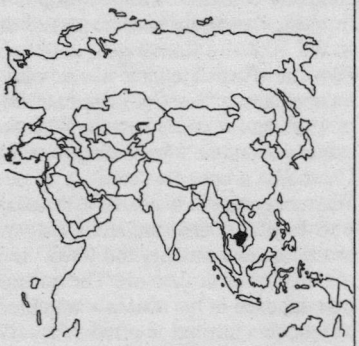

rich. The country produces tropical hardwood trees, as well as rubber, coconut, mango, orange, banana, and kapok trees.

People. About 90% are Khmers. The Chinese and Vietnamese are minorities and there are Chams, Europeans, Indians, Thai, and primitive tribes. The modern official language is Khmer, spoken by about 60% of the population, and French is used by a sizable minority. Numerous other languages are found among the hill peoples. Theravada Buddhism is practiced, and most Kampuchean males spend at least a short time in Buddhist monasteries, many of which are also educational establishments. There are several technical schools, and the Buddhist University and the former Royal Khmer University are located in Phnom Penh. The literacy rate is about 40%.

Located at the confluence of the Mekong and Tônlé Sap rivers, Phnom Penh is the principal city of the country. Other towns are generally much less than 50,000 in population. The majority of Khmers live in villages in the Mekong and Tônlé Sap basins. Their houses, often of bamboo and thatch, are built on stilts in preparation for the rainy season. Most Kampucheans are skilled in art, music, and dancing, and their many temples are elaborately carved.

Economy. Small and often primitive rice farms on the plains around the Tônlé Sap are the basis of Kampuchea's economy. Rice is the most important export product. Rubber is the second most important. In addition, corn, livestock, sugar, pepper, tobacco, cotton, coffee, and soybeans are raised. Deep-sea fishing in the Gulf of Siam is an important commercial activity, while the Tônlé Sap and the Mekong rivers provide one of the greatest concentration of freshwater fish in southeast Asia. The extensive forests are largely untouched and, because of transport problems, high-grade iron ore deposits in the north are also unexploited.

History. Mythology claims that the country was founded by a Hindu king, Kambu, who gave the country the name Kambuja. In the 1st century A.D., Hindu people established the flourishing kingdom of Funan, which ruled large areas. Toward the end of the 6th century, the territory was split up among rival groups. The most powerful of these, the Khmer, founded the great Angkor Dynasty between 800 and 850. This Khmer kingdom reached its greatest power about 1100 and attained a high level of civilization. Much of Thailand, Laos, and Vietnam were part of the Khmer empire, which began its decline in the late 14th century. By the middle of the 19th century the

country was approximately its present size and in 1863, to prevent its complete conquest, King Norodom asked for the protection of the French. In 1887, Cambodia became part of the French Union of Indochina.
In the 1930s, a Cambodian nationalist movement gained strength and by 1940 anti-French feeling was running high. In 1953 Cambodia achieved full independence. Norodom Sihanouk became prime minister after the elections of 1955 and remained so for 5 years. In 1960 Sihanouk was made head of state, without the title of king. A member of the United Nations since 1955, Cambodia proclaimed a policy of neutrality. Aid from both communist and Western countries was used to develop the economy: to build roads, air-transport facilities, and irrigation systems. In 1963, Sihanouk refused further economic and military aid from the United States, and in 1965 diplomatic relations were broken off. The military coup d'etat of 1970, when Sihanouk was deposed in his absence, together with incursions of North Vietnamese troops, precipitated internal crises. General Lon Nol established a military government (the Khmer Republic) in Phnom Penh, but the new and inexperienced Cambodian army proved a poor match for the Vietcong. U.S. and South Vietnamese forces crossed the border to clear out enemy "sanctuaries" in April 1970, but American troops soon withdrew.
The Cambodian communists (Khmer Rouge) emerged in 1970 as a powerful political group. In alliance with the Khmer Rouge, Sihanouk formed an exile government in Peking. Civil war raged between Lon Nol's government forces and the Khmer Rouge, who were gaining control of the country despite intensive U.S. bombing. In Apr. 1975 Phnom Penh was besieged and surrendered to the Khmer Rouge. "The Royal Government of the National Union of Cambodia (Kampuchea)" returned from exile under Sihanouk. Following the resignation of Sihanouk in 1976, Pol Pot became prime minister of the newly named Democratic Kampuchea. The regime enacted harsh measures, evacuating all cities and suppressing opposition. Hundreds of thousands of people died or were killed. In 1978 Vietnam launched attacks against Kampuchea, and in 1979 Vietnamese troops captured Phnom Penh and proclaimed the People's Republic of Kampuchea. Pol Pot, as commander-in-chief of the Khmer Rouge forces, continued to fight the Vietnamese from unoccupied parts of the country. In 1983, Vietnam launched major offensives against the rebel forces and by Feb. 1985 had overrun all Khmer Rouge bases. In 1989 the Vietnamese forces withdrew. The U.N. established a preliminary government in 1991, which prepared free elections to be held in 1993, combined with the restauration of the monarchy. Sihanouk became King, and his son Ranarridh prime minister. In 1997 however, Ranarridh was deposed by Hun Sen.

Kanawha River, chief river of West Virginia, formed by the confluence of the New and Gauley rivers. It flows about 97 mi (156 km) northwest to join the Ohio River at Point Pleasant.

Kandinsky, Wassily (1866-1944), Russian painter and theorist, widely regarded as one of the originators of abstract art. Influenced by fauvism in postimpressionist Paris, his early work aimed at pure aesthetic expression by using bursts of color in nonrepresentational paintings. He was a founder, along with Paul Klee, of the Blaue Reiter art movement in Munich (1911; named for his own painting, *Le cavalier bleu*, "The Blue Rider"). He studied the psychology of color and its effects in *Concerning the Spiritual in Art*

(1912) and expressed his viewpoint on art and color in *The Art of Spiritual Harmony* (1914). Geometric compositions came into play in his paintings of the 1920s, at which time he also joined the faculty of the Bauhaus design school in Weimar (1922-33).

Kanem, African empire that lasted from 700 A.D. through the 1800s. It included parts of modern Cameroon, Chad, Libya, Niger, Nigeria, and the Sudan. Kanem declined in the late 1800s when trade routes shifted away from it.

Kangaroo, herbivorous, marsupial mammal of the family Macropodidae, with large hind feet, strong hind legs, and a tail used for balancing, native to Australia and nearby islands. Like other marsupial females, female kangaroos have a pouch in which they carry and suckle their young. The red kangaroo (*Megaleia rufa*) of the Australian plains may reach 7 ft (2.1 m) in height and over 200 lb (90 kg) in weight. Its top speed is about 40 miles (64 km) an hour, with each hop extending as much as 18 ft (5.5 m). Other members of the kangaroo family, classified as genus *Macropus*, include wallabies and tree kangaroos.

Kangaroo apple *See:* Solanum.

Kangaroo court, unofficial and illegal gathering of unauthorized persons for the purpose of passing sentence upon a wrongdoer. Such sentences have been imposed in many countries by citizens' groups, such as vigilante societies in the United States and the illegal Irish Republican Army. The name was first used c.1853 to refer to the "instant justice" meted out by frontier judges in the United States who "hopped" like kangaroos from place to place on their legal circuits.

Kangaroo rat, pouched, burrowing, nocturnal rodent (genus *Dipodomys*) similar to the gerbil. It has long hind legs, a long tail, and moves by jumping. Kangaroo rats live in arid regions of the southwestern United States.

Kanishka (d.A.D. 160?), greatest king of the Kushan Empire, which included what is now Pakistan, Afghanistan, and northern India. A patron of Buddhism, Kanishka built a monument in his capital, Peshawar, to house relics of Buddha. He established the Gandharan school of art, which blended eastern and western influences in sculpture.
See also: Kushan Empire.

Kanpur (pop. 1,879,400), city in the state of Uttar Pradesh, north central India, on the Ganges River. An industrial center manufacturing silk, cotton, wool, and leather goods, Kanpur first became an economic power in 1801, when it was ceded to the British East India Company. During the Sepoy Rebellion of 1857 the entire British garrison of the city was wiped out.

Kansa, also known as Kaw or Kansas, Native American tribe of eastern Kansas. This agricultural and hunting plains tribe, for whom the state of Kansas was named, lived along the Kansas River until their lands were taken by the U.S. government (1873) and they were moved to a reservation in Oklahoma. Decimated by disease, very few Kansa survive today.

Kansas

Capital:	Topeka
Statehood:	Jan. 29, 1961 (34th state)
Familiar name:	Sunflower State
Area:	82,277 sq mi (213,098 sq km); ranks 14th
Population:	2,595,000 (1997); ranks 32nd
Elevation:	Highest—4,039 ft (1,231 m), Mt. Sunflower; Lowest—680 ft (207 m), Verdigris River in Montgomery County
Motto:	*Ad Astra per Aspera* (To the Stars Through Difficulties)
Flower:	Sunflower
Bird:	Western meadowlark
Tree:	Cottonwood
Song:	"Home on the Range"

Kansas, state in the central United States; bordered by Nebraska to the north, Missouri to the east, Oklahoma to the south, and Colorado to the west. Nicknamed "Midway, U.S.A." and "Heart of the Nation," Kansas is halfway between the Atlantic and Pacific Oceans.

Land and climate. Kansas lies in the transition area between the prairies and the high plains. It consists of 3 principal land regions: the Great Plains, covering the western two-thirds of the state; the Dissected Till Plains in the northeast corner; and the Southeastern Plains. The Great Plains are slightly rolling, rather dry land, sloping downward from the Colorado border to the east. The Dissected Till Plains region was the only one covered by glaciers during the Ice Ages; as a result, it has deposits of rich soil cut through by rivers to leave high bluffs. The Southeastern Plains are often divided into the Flint Hills in the west and the Osage Plains in the east. Kansas does not have extensive water resources, but more than 100 artificial lakes add to its irrigation and recreation resources. Its major river systems are the Kansas, the Arkansas, and their tributaries. Kansas soils are generally dark, fertile loam suitable for raising a variety of crops. Like most of the U.S. interior, Kansas has cold winters and warm-to-hot summers. Principal cities are Wichita, Kansas City, and Topeka.

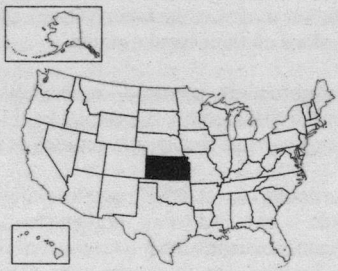

Economy. Often called the "Breadbasket of America," Kansas is one of the top agricultural states. It leads the nation in wheat production, and is the leading producer of beef cattle. Other major crops include grain sorghum, hay, corn, and hogs.

Kansas's leading industrial products are transportation equipment, processed foods, and printed materials. Wichita is the nation's largest aviation-produc-

tion center. Automobiles, trucks, and railroad cars are produced in Atchison, Kansas City, Lawrence, Topeka, and Wichita. One of the world's largest meat-packing plants is in Garden City; large producers of pharmaceuticals and other chemicals operate in the Kansas City area. Service industries account for the largest share of the state's income. Kansas's mineral resources include petroleum, natural gas, helium, limestone, coal, and salt.
Government. The Kansas constitution was adopted in 1859. The governor serves a 4-year term. The state's legislature consists of 40 senators serving 4-year terms and 125 representatives serving 2-year terms. In the U.S. Congress, Kansas is represented by 2 senators and 5 representatives.
History. Native Americans inhabited the region long before the first white settlers arrived. Gold-seeking Spaniards were the first Europeans to enter the area (1541); in the late 1600s, French explorers claimed the land. The U.S. acquired most of Kansas as part of the Louisiana Purchase (1803). In the mid-1800s, the nationwide debate over slavery led to a series of disorders and killings that earned the territory the nickname of "Bleeding Kansas." In 1861 Kansas became the 34th state, supporting the Union cause during the Civil War. After the war, settlement and economic expansion progressed rapidly until the 1930s, when Kansas was hit hard by drought and depression. World War II brought recovery to agriculture, and new cultivation methods restored prosperity. In the decades since, Kansas's small towns have declined in population as its urban centers and industries have grown.

Kansas City (pop. 1,758,500), name of 2 adjacent cities at the junction of the Missouri and Kansas rivers, one in northeast Kansas (inc. 1859) and one in northwest Missouri (inc. 1850). This area, as eastern terminus of the Santa Fe trail (1850), served as the starting point for many Western expeditions and gave rise to several settlements in the early 19th century. The building of the railroads increased the importance of Kansas City. Today the cities serve as an industrial, cultural, transportation, and commercial center, with extensive stockyards, grain elevators, mills, and refineries. Leading products include automobiles, farm machinery, and printed materials. Sights include the Nelson Gallery-Atkins Museum (Missouri), a Shawnee mission (1839), and an agricultural museum (Kansas).
See also: Kansas; Missouri.

Kansas-Nebraska Act, bill passed by the U.S. Congress (1854) to establish the territories of Nebraska and Kansas. Territorial organization of this region had been stalled due to conflict over slavery and the routes of the transcontinental railroad. The proposed Missouri Compromise, which would have organized the area as one territory but would not have allowed slavery in the region, was not supported by the South, and was defeated at every presentation. As a compromise, Sen. Stephen Douglas proposed the creation of 2 territories, each to decide the slavery question for itself. As both North and South flooded the territories with settlers in an attempt to establish control, the conflict escalated, culminating in the Civil War.
See also: Slavery; Civil War, U.S.

Kant, Immanuel (1724-1804), German philosopher, founder of critical philosophy. Though originally influenced by the rationalism of Leibniz, Kant was awakened from his "dogmatic slumber" by the work of skeptic David Hume and thus led to greatness as a metaphysician. In *Critique of Pure*

Reason (1781), Kant proposed that objective reality (the phenomenal world) can be known only because the mind imposes its own structure (time and space) on it. Things beyond experience (noumena) cannot be known, though we may presume to know them. The questions of the existence of God, immortality, freedom—all metaphysical questions—cannot be answered by scientific means, and thus cannot be proved or disproved. But, according to Kant in *Critique of Practical Reason* (1788), their existence must be presumed for the sake of morality. Kant's absolute moral law states, "Act as if the maxim from which you act were to become through your will a universal law." In *Critique of Judgment* (1790), beauty and purpose form the bridge between the sensible and the intelligible worlds that he sharply divided in his first 2 *Critiques*. Kant's influence is extensive, particularly in Germany. G.W.F. Hegel, F.W.J. von Schelling, and J.G. Fichte, influenced by Kant, developed German idealism; Ernst Cassirer of the physical sciences and Heinrich Rickert of the historical and cultural sciences applied neo-Kantian insights to their studies. Kant influenced the theology of F.D.E. Schleiermacher, the pragmatism of U.S. philosophers William James and John Dewey, and Gestalt psychology.
See also: Metaphysics; Philosophy.

Kantor, MacKinlay (1904-77), U.S. screenwriter and author. A newspaper writer (1921-31), Kantor also wrote screenplays and several books, including *Long Remember* (1936), *The Voice of Bugle Ann* (1935), *Arouse and Beware* (1936), *Happy Land* (1943), and *Andersonville* (1955).

Kaolin, or china clay, soft, white clay composed chiefly of the mineral kaolinite, mined in England, France, former Czechoslovakia, China, and the southern United States. It is used for filling and coating paper, filling rubber and paints, making pottery and porcelain, and in medicine, to treat diarrhea.

Kapitsa, Pyotr (1894-1984), Russian physicist best known for his work in low-temperature physics (cryogenics). During the 1920s and early 1930s he worked at Cavendish Laboratory in Cambridge, England. After returning to the USSR (1934) he directed the Institute for Physical Problems. He was an outspoken advocate of freedom of thought and scientific exchange and was awarded the 1978 Nobel Prize for physics.
See also: Physics.

Kapok (*Ceiba pentandra*), tropical tree; also, the water-repellent fiber of its seeds. Kapok is used as a stuffing for life jackets, mattresses, pillows, and cold-weather clothing, and as insulation against heat and sound. Oil from its seeds is used in the manufacture of soap. Kapok trees are found in India, Indonesia, Africa, and other tropical regions.

Karachi (pop. 5,208,000), former capital (1947-59) of Pakistan, and the country's largest city, major port, and industrial center. It stands on the Arabian Sea near the Indus River delta in Sind province, of which it is the capital. Among its manufactures are automobiles, steel, petroleum products, and textiles. Karachi began to develop as a trading center in the early 18th century. In 1843 the British took over and made it a military outpost, a major seaport, and the seat of the Sind government. Upon independence, Karachi became the capital of the new nation, until the new city of Islamabad was

made capital in 1960. The tomb of Pakistan's founder, Muhammad Ali Jinnah, rests there.
See also: Pakistan.

Karajan, Herbert von (1908-89), Austrian conductor. He directed the Berlin State Opera (1938-45), the Vienna State Opera (1956-64), and the Berlin Philharmonic Orchestra (1955-89).

Karakorum, ancient capital of Genghis Khan's empire. Its ruins, discovered in 1889, stand in what is now the Mongolian People's Republic, on the Orhon River. Established c.1220, it fell into decay by the 16th century. Marco Polo visited Karakorum c.1275.
See also: Genghis Khan.

Karakul, any of several species of sheep of Central Asia, bred primarily for their fur-bearing skin. The pelts of the Karakul are called Persian lamb, broadtail, and caracul. The wool of the lamb is lustrous, smooth, and often black. A mature Karakul's fleece is thick and rough in texture and may have a range of colors including white, brown, gray, and yellow.

Kara Kum, desert region in Turkmenistan, in central Asia, covering about 135,000 sq mi (330,000 sq km) in area. The Kara Kum canal, extending from the Amu Darya River through two oases to the city of Ashkhabad, enables parts of the desert to be irrigated and used for grazing sheep, goats, and camels.

Karamanlis, Constantine *See:* Caramanlis, Constantine.

Kara Sea, branch of the Arctic Ocean about 300 miles (480 km) long and 200 miles (320 km) wide off the north central coast of Siberia. The sea is bounded on the east by the Yamal Peninsula and on the west by the Novaya Zemlya Islands.
See also: Arctic Ocean.

Karate (Japanese: "empty hand"), unarmed combat and sport, originating in the Orient. Hands, knees, elbows, and feet are all used to deliver blows against vulnerable pressure points on the body of the attacker.

Karelia, self-governing republic in northwestern Russia. Its capital city is Petrozavodsk. Bordering Finland, it has an area of about 70,000 sq mi (181,000 sq km), with vast pine forests and more than 2,000 lakes. Lumbering, forest industries, iron working, and fishing are the major sources of employment.
See also: Union of Soviet Socialist Republics.

Karl-Marx-Stadt, nowadays Chemnitz (pop. 291,400), industrial city in eastern Germany and chief center of the Karl-Marx-Stadt district, situated on the Chemnitz River. Famous since medieval times for its textiles, Karl-Marx-Stadt now also produces machinery, machine tools, chemicals, and optical instruments. The city was chartered in 1143, destroyed during the Thirty Years War, and severely damaged in World War II. It was renamed

Karl-Marx-Stadt in 1953. In 1990 the name reverted back to Chemnitz.
See also: Germany.

Karloff, Boris (William Henry Pratt; 1887-1969), English-born U.S. actor renowned for his parts in horror films. His most famous roles were as the monster in *Frankenstein* (1931) and *The Bride of Frankenstein* (1935).

Karlovy Vary (pop. 58,600), resort and spa in western Bohemia, Czech Republic, famed for its mineral springs. The most celebrated of its 17 functioning springs is the Vridlo. Glassware, china, and pottery are the main industrial products.
See also: Czech Republic.

Karma, Sanskrit term denoting the inevitable effects of a person's physical and mental actions on his or her destiny in successive lives, central to Buddhist and Hindu thought.
See also: Sikhism.

Karnak, village east of Luxor, on the Nile in central Egypt, part of ancient Thebes. It is the site of the Great Temple of Amon, perhaps the finest example of ancient Egyptian religious architecture.
See also: Egypt.

Karnak, Temple of *See:* Thutmose III.

Karpov, Anatoly (1951-), a Russian chess prodigy who became the Soviet champion in his early twenties. He was awarded the world chess championship in 1975, after reigning champion Bobby Fischer of the United States had repeatedly refused to defend his title. In 1981 Karpov defeated his principal challenger, Viktor Korchnoi, for the second time. In 1985 he lost his title to Gary Kasparov in a second match for the world title. Karpov's most recent attempt to regain his championship ended unsuccessfully when he was beaten again by Gary Kasparov in a 24-game match in Dec. 1990. In 1993 and 1996 Karpov became world champion in the FIDE version.
See also: Chess.

Karsh, Yousuf (1908-), Canadian portrait photographer of Turkish-Armenian birth. In 1935 he was appointed the Canadian government's official photographer.
See also: Photography.

Kart racing, sport that features single-seated, rear-engine racing cars. Referred to as go-karts, these automobiles can reach speeds of 140 mph (225 kmph) In most national competitions, drivers must be 16 years or older, but competitions for children ages 8 and 9 are quite popular. Very popular in Europe, kart racing was invented in 1956 in the United States.

Kasavubu, Joseph (1917?-69), African politician, first president (1960-65) of the Republic of the Congo (now Zaïre). He ousted Premier Patrice Lumumba but was himself supplanted (1965) by Gen. Joseph Mobutu.
See also: Zaïre.

Kashmir, disputed territory in southern Asia, administered since 1972 as the Indian state of Jammu and Kashmir (capital: Srinagar; 54,000 sq mi/139,000 sq km) and the Pakistani Azad Kasmir (capital: Muzafarabad; 32,000 sq mi/82,900 sq km), bordering China. This beautiful region, which includes sections of the Himalayan and Karakorum mountain ranges, centers around the Vale of Kashmir, the agricultural area where rice and wheat are grown, fed by the Jhelum River. After years of rule by Hindus and Buddhists, Islam took hold in the late 14th century, and Kashmir became part of the Mogul empire (1586). In the mid-19th century the British restored Hindu rule. Since India's partition (1947) the territory has been the source of a dispute between India and Pakistan, with some interference from China (1959-63). Current boundaries were established in 1972. In 1996 the Indian government sent troops to fight armed movements such as the Hizbul-Mujahedeen and the Harkat-al-Ansar. In the same year, elections for a representative for the federal parliament took place. The elections caused turmoil when the Islamic parties called for a boycot of the elections whereas the government sometimes tried to force people to vote.
See also: India; Pakistan.

Kasparov, Gary (1963-), Russian chess prodigy who at 22 became the sport's youngest world champion by beating Anatoly Karpov (1985). He has successfully defended his title, most recently by beating Anatoly Karpov in a 24-game match that ended on Dec. 31, 1990. In 1993, he was one of the founders of the Professional Chess Association (PCA), which organized its own world championship. In 1995 Kasparov prolonged his world title in the PCA version. In 1996 he defeated Deep Blue, the IBM chess computer. The next year, however, Deep Blue won.

Kassebaum, Nancy Landon (1932), U.S. Republican senator from Kansas since 1978. Having never held political office before, Kassebaum became the first woman ever elected to the U.S. Senate without having first been appointed to a congressional seat to complete a spouse's term. Her father, Alfred M. Landon, was one-time governor of Kansas and lost the 1936 presidential election to Franklin D. Roosevelt by a wide margin.

Katayev, Valentin Petrovich (1897-1987), Russian novelist, poet, and playwright. Among his best-known works are the novels *The Embezzlers* (1926) and *Lonely White Sail* (1936), and the farce *Squaring the Circle* (1928).

Kathmandu (pop. 393,500), capital of Nepal, 4,500 ft (1,370 m) above sea level in a Himalayan valley in central Nepal. The city lies on an ancient route from India to Tibet and China and is a vital commercial and administrative center. Important sites include temples, the royal palace, and Sanskrit libraries.
See also: Nepal.

Katmai National Park, large wilderness region covering 4,430,125 acres (1,792,810 hectares) in southwestern Alaska. The violent eruption of the Novarupta volcano in 1912 eradicated Mount Katmai and created a broad dish of ash known as The Valley of Ten Thousand Smokes. There are fifteen volcanoes in the area, although none are very active. The Katmai National Park has a rich range of wildlife, including Alaskan brown bears, sea otters, and bald eagles.

Katydid, name for several large, green, winged insects of the long-horned grasshopper family (Tettigoniidae), native to the Western Hemisphere. Katydids, which range in length from 1.25 to 5 in. (3 to 12.5 cm), are tree-dwelling and nocturnal. Males produce a song, which sounds like "Katy did, Katy didn't," by rubbing together specialized parts of their wings.

Katyn forest, site in the former USSR of a massacre of some 4,250 Polish officers in World War II. The mass grave was reported in 1943 by the Germans, who accused the Soviets, who in turn accused the Germans. Stalin refused a Red Cross inquiry, and the Polish government-in-exile in London took this as an admission of Soviet guilt. A U.S. congressional investigation in 1952 charged the Soviets with responsibility. In 1990 the Soviet government admitted responsibility for the massacre.
See also: World War II.

Kauffmann, Angelica (1741-1807), Swiss painter. Her works often depict mythological and historical events from ancient Greece and Rome. Initially a portrait painter in Italy, she traveled to England and in 1768 became a founding member of London's Royal Academy of Arts. Kauffmann returned to Italy in 1781. She is known for her wall paintings decorating English residences designed by Robert Adam. Other works include Religion and La Pensierosa.

Kaufman, George S. (1889-1961), U.S. playwright and stage director. His collaborations (over 40 plays and musicals), often noted for their satire, included *Beggar on Horseback* (1924, with Marc Connelly), *Of Thee I Sing* (1932, with Morrie Ryskind and George Gershwin; Pulitzer Prize), *Dinner at Eight* (1932, with Edna Ferber), and some of his most successful, written with Moss Hart, *You Can't Take It with You* (1936, Pulitzer Prize) and *The Man Who Came to Dinner* (1939).

Kaunas (pop. 429,000), former capital city of Lithuania. Founded in 1030, it is Lithuania's second largest city and produces one-quarter of its manufactured goods, which include machine tools, paper, radio, and textiles. A cultural center as well, Kaunas has several museums and many buildings dating from the 15th century.
See also: Lithuania.

Kaunda, Kenneth David (1924-), African political leader, president of Zambia (1964-91). From 1953 he worked for African rule in Northern Rhodesia, which was then a British dependency, suffering exile and imprisonment. Released in 1960, he headed the new United National Independence Party, and became Zambia's first president upon independence (1964). In December 1997, Kaunda was arrested on suspicion of involvement in the attempted coup in October. In 1998 he was acquitted
and left active politics.
See also: Zambia.

Kazakhstan

Capital:	Astana
Area:	1,049,150 sq mi (2,717,300 sq km)
Population:	16,847,000
Language:	Kazakh
Government:	Presidential republic
Independent:	1991
Head of gov.:	Prime minister
Per capita:	U.S. $1,330
Mon. unit:	1 Tenge = 100 tiyn

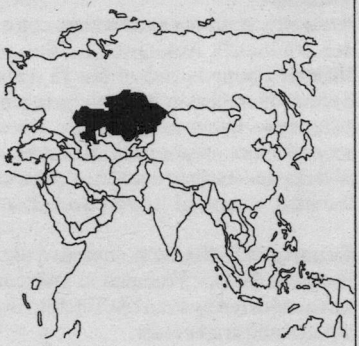

Kava, shrub (genus *Piper*) native to the Pacific Islands and Australia, closely related to the pepper plant. Kava may reach a height of 5 ft (1.5 m), and has round leaves and yellowish-cream flowers. Juice taken from the root of the shrub is used to produce a nonalcoholic intoxicant called kava or kavakava.

Kaw *See:* Kansa.

Kawabata, Yasunari (1899-1972), Japanese novelist. He is noted for his impressionistic, lyrical style and a preoccupation with loneliness and death. One of his best-known works is *Snow Country* (1947). He was awarded the 1968 Nobel Prize for literature, the first Japanese to win the prize.

Kawasaki disease, disease believed by many doctors to be caused by a virus, affecting children, primarily boys of Asian ancestry from middle- and upper-class backgrounds. Its symptoms include high fever, sore throat, redness of the eyes, and sore, bleeding lips. It can result in inflammation and scarring of the artery walls. Palliative treatment with aspirin and gamma globulin reduces the risk of heart damage.

Kaye, Danny (1913-87), American comedian and entertainer whose films, television shows, and personal appearances made him an international personality. He first gained attention in 1940 in the Broadway musical *Lady in the Dark*. Among his more important films were *The Secret Life of Walter Mitty* (1947), and *The Inspector General* (1949). He was an ambassador-at-large for Unicef.

Kazakhstan (Republic of), independent country in central Asia, bordered on the west and the north by Russia, on the east by China, on the south by Kirghizstan, Uzbekistan, and Turkmenistan, and on the west by the Caspian Sea. The capital is Astana (since 1997, Astana was formerly called Akmola). ***Land and people.*** Two thirds of the country is (semi) arid. The Caspian Sea is a great salt lake (92 ft/28 meters below sea level). Kazakhstan has a continental climate, with considerable differences between different areas. The population is 40% Russian and Ukrainian, 40% Kazakh. One half of the

population are Christians, the other half are Muslims. The official language is Kazakh.
Economy. A producer of wheat, cotton, sheep, and cattle, Kazakhstan is also rich in minerals. Amongst other things, it possesses huge oil and gas supplies.
History. Formerly one of the 15 constituent republics of the USSR (Soviet Union), Kazakhstan became independent in 1991. After independence the differences between the north, where most Russians live, and the south became more pronounced. Kazakhstan is a member of the Commonwealth of Independent States and has close ties with Russia.
See also: Union of Soviet Socialist Republics.

Kazan (pop. 1,103,000), capital of the Tatar Autonomous Republic in eastern European Russia. Founded in 1401, it is the cultural center for the Tatars. It was conquered by Ivan the Terrible in 1552. A major port on the Volga River, it is an industrial center.
See also: Union of Soviet Socialist Republics.

Kazan, Elia (1909-), Turkish-born U.S. film and stage director. He is best known for realistic films on social issues, such as *On the Waterfront* (1954). Other films include *A Streetcar Named Desire* (1951) and *Viva Zapata!* (1952). He also wrote and directed *The Arrangement* (1967) and *The Assassins* (1972). At the 1996 Berlin Film Festival he was awarded a Golden Bear for his complete works.

Kazantzakis, Nikos (1883-1957), Greek writer and statesman. He served as minister of public welfare (1919-27) and minister of state (1945-46). Among his best-known works are the novels *The Greek Passion* (1938) and *Zorba the Greek* (1946) and his epic poem *The Odyssey: A Modern Sequel* (1938).
See also: Greece.

Kea (*Nestor notabilis*), New Zealand parrot with an immensely powerful bill. Keas live in flocks and feed mainly on insects, leaves, buds, nectar, and berries; in winter they occasionally attack living sheep.

Kean, Edmund (1787-1833), English actor. Popular both in England and the United States, he was known for his roles in Shakespearean tragedy, notably Othello, to which he introduced a dynamic naturalistic style, and Shylock in *The Merchant of Venice*.

Kearny, Stephen Watts (1794-1848), U.S. general. During the Mexican War (1846-48) he conquered New Mexico by diplomacy, persuading the more powerful Mexican force to withdraw peacefully. He subdued California also, despite conflict with fellow officers Robert Stockton and John Frémont. Governor of Veracruz and Mexico City in 1848, he died there of yellow fever.
See also: Mexican War.

Keaton, Buster (Joseph Francis Keaton; 1895-1966), U.S. silent-film comedian and director. In such films as *The Navigator* (1924) and *The General* (1927), masterpieces of comic inventiveness, he created the character of a deadpan innocent in conflict with malevolent machinery. Keaton designed and performed his own elaborate and often dangerous film stunts.

Keats, John (1795-1821), English Romantic poet. He gave up medicine in 1816 to devote himself to poetry. The epic "Hyperion," the ballad "La Belle Dame sans Merci," and "The Eve of St. Agnes" were written about 1817. In May 1819 he wrote 4 great odes—"To a Nightingale," "On a Grecian Urn," "On Melancholy," and "On Indolence." "Lamia" and "To Autumn," effectively his last works, followed that summer. In 1820 he developed tuberculosis and died in Rome at age 25.

Keelboat *See:* Flatboat.

Keeshond, or Dutch barge dog, national dog of the Netherlands, related to the Samoyed and chow chow. The keeshond has a foxlike face with a long, thick, black-tipped gray coat. Fully grown, it stands 17-18 in (43-46 cm) and weighs 35-40 lb (16-18 kg). Keeshonden make excellent guards and companions.

Kefauver, Estes (1903-63), U.S. Democratic senator from Tennessee, known for his investigations into organized crime. He studied law at Yale, supported Franklin D. Roosevelt's New Deal, and entered Congress in 1939, becoming a senator 10 years later. In 1952 Adlai Stevenson defeated Kefauver for the Democratic presidential nomination, but lost the election to Dwight Eisenhower. In 1956 he was Stevenson's running mate for the presidency, but the Democrats again lost to Eisenhower.

Keillor, Garrison Edward (1942-), U.S. writer, creator of the fictional town of Lake Wobegon, Minnesota. Keillor has told stories about the town on his radio program *A Prairie Home Companion* (1974-87, 1989-) and in *New Yorker* magazine articles. His books include *Happy to Be Here* (1982), *Lake Wobegon Days* (1985), *Leaving Home* (1987), *We Are Still Married* (1989), *WLT: A Radio Romance* (1991), and *The Book of Guys* (1993).

Keitel, Wilhelm (1882-1946), German field marshal, head of the armed forces high command during World War II. On May 8, 1945, he ratified Germany's unconditional surrender in Berlin. He was convicted at Nuremberg of violations of international law and executed.
See also: World War II.

Kekkonen, Urho Kaleva (1900-86), president of Finland, 1956-81. Head of the Agrarian Party, he held cabinet posts and was prime minister 1950-56. He resigned the presidency in 1981 because of poor health and was succeeded in 1982 by Mauno Koivisto.
See also: Finland.

Kekulé von Stradonitz, Friedrich August (1829-96), German chemist regarded as the father of modern organic chemistry. At the same time as Archibald Scott Couper (1831-82) he recognized the quadrivalency of carbon and its ability to form long chains. With his later inference of the molecular structure of benzene as a ring, structural organic chemistry was born.
See also: Chemistry; Organic chemistry.

Keller, Helen Adams (1880-1968), U.S. author and lecturer. Blind and deaf from age 1 1/2, she was taught by Anne Sullivan from 1887, learned to read, write, and speak, and graduated from Radcliffe College with honors in 1904. Her books include *The Story of My Life* (1902) and *Helen Keller's Journal* (1938).

Kelley, Florence (1859-1932), U.S. social reformer and lawyer. A campaigner for labor legislation to protect women and children and for minimum wage laws, she was director of the National Consumers League from 1899.

Kellogg, Frank Billings (1896-1937), U.S. diplomat, senator (1917-23), ambassador to Great Britain (1924-25), and U.S. secretary of state (1925-29). His most important achievement was the Kellogg-Briand Peace Pact (1928). He was awarded the Nobel Prize for peace and became a judge of the Permanent Court of International Justice (1930-35).
See also: Kellogg-Briand Peace Pact.

Kellogg, Will Keith (1860-1951), U.S. industrialist and philanthropist. He made his fortune through the breakfast cereal industry he established in 1906 at Battle Creek, Mich., originally to manufacture the cornflakes developed as a health food by his physician-brother.

Kellogg-Briand Peace Pact, or Pact of Paris, agreement signed on Aug. 27, 1928, by 15 nations (eventually ratified by 64) renouncing "war as an instrument of national policy." Conceived by Aristide Briand of France and U.S. Secretary of State F.B. Kellogg, it lacked enforcement powers and proved ineffectual.

Kelly, Gene (1912-96), U.S. actor, dancer, and director, known for his spontaneous, athletic dancing routines. Kelly made his Broadway debut in *Leave It to Me* (1938), gained recognition for his role in *Pal Joey* (1940), and made his first film appearance in *For Me and My Gal* (1942). He helped choreograph many of his musicals, including *Cover Girl* (1944), *Anchors Aweigh* (1945), *On the Town* (1949), and *Singin' in the Rain* (1952).

Kelly, George Edward (1887-1974), U.S. playwright. Kelly achieved success with his satiric renderings in *The Torch Bearers* (1922), *The Show-Off* (1924), and *Craig's Wife* (1925), for which he received the Pulitzer Prize (1926).

Kelly, Grace (1929-82), U.S. motion picture actress and, later, Princess of Monaco. Kelly first appeared in the film *Fourteen Hours* (1951) and her first starring role was opposite Gary Cooper in *High Noon* (1952). She won an Academy Award for her role in *The Country Girl* (1954) and appeared in several other films, including *Dial M for Murder* (1954), *To Catch a Thief* (1955), and *High Society* (1956). Kelly married Prince Rainier III of Monaco in 1956. She died in an automobile crash near Monaco.

Keloid, scar tissue raised above the skin surface at the site of a wound. Keloids result from an overproduction of fibrous tissue in the skin. They can be surgically removed but frequently reappear. Keloids are found most frequently in people of African descent.

Kelp, name for various large brown seaweeds of orders Laminariales and Fucales. Edible kelps are rich in iodine, calcium, potassium, and the trace minerals. Dehydrated kelp tablets, powder, and granules are used as a mineral supplement and as a salt substitute.

Kelvin, William Thomson, Lord (1824-1907), British physicist. He formulated the second law of thermodynamics and introduced the Kelvin, or absolute temperature, scale. His work on electromagnetism gave rise to the theory of the electromagnetic field, and his papers influenced J. Clerk Maxwell's work on the electromagnetic theory of light. His work on telegraphic signaling played an essential part in the successful laying of the first Atlantic cable.
See also: Galvanometer; Thermodynamics.

Kelvin scale *See:* Absolute zero; Kelvin, William Thomson, Lord; Metric system; Temperature.

Kemal Atatürk *See:* Atatürk, Kemal.

Kempis, Thomas à *See:* Thomas à Kempis.

Keneally, Thomas (1935-), Australian writer, known for his powerful and turbulent novels, which often take place in a particular historical period. His works include *The Chant of Jimmie Blacksmith* (1972), *Schindler's List* (1982), *Jacko: the Great Intruder* (1993), *River Town* (1995), and *Homebush Boy* (1995).

Kennan, George Frost (1904-), U.S. diplomat, one of the main authors of the U.S. postwar policy of "containment" of Russian expansionism. He served as ambassador to the USSR (1952) and Yugoslavia (1961-63). His books include *Russia Leaves the War* (1956) and *Memoirs, 1925-1950* (1967), both Pulitzer Prize winners.

Kennebec River, river in southern Maine, flowing about 150 mi (240 km) southward from Moosehead Lake to empty into the Atlantic at Popham, Maine's first English settlement (1607). The state capital, Augusta, lies on the Kennebec. The river is an important source of power for Maine's industries.

Kennedy, U.S. family prominent in government, politics, and business. **Joseph Patrick Kennedy** (1888-1969) chaired the Securities and Exchange Commission (1934-35) and the U.S. Maritime Commission (1936-37) and served as U.S. ambassador to Great Britain (1937-40). The oldest son of Joseph Patrick and Rose Kennedy, **Joseph P. Kennedy, Jr.** (1915-44), a U.S. Navy pilot, was killed in World War II. **John Fitzgerald Kennedy** (1917-63) was elected 35th president of the United States in 1960. **Robert Francis Kennedy** (1925-68) was appointed U.S. attorney general in 1961 and elected U.S. senator from New York in 1965. A fourth son, **Edward Moore Kennedy** (1932-), has been a U.S. senator from Massachusetts since 1962. The 5 Kennedy daughters are Rosemary, Kathleen, Eunice, Patricia, and Jean.
See also: Kennedy, Edward Moore; Kennedy, John Fitzgerald; Kennedy, Robert Francis; Smithsonian Institution.

Kennedy, Anthony McLeod (1936-), associate justice of the United States Supreme Court (1988-), appointed after Justice Lewis Powell retired. A Stanford University graduate (1958), Kennedy earned a law degree from Harvard University (1961). He practiced law until 1975, when he was appointed to the United States Court of Appeals (Ninth Circuit) by President Gerald Ford. Kennedy taught constitutional law at the McGeorge School of Law (1965-88).

Kennedy, Edward Moore (1932-), U.S. political leader, U.S. senator from Massachusetts since 1962. Like his brothers John and Robert, "Ted" Kennedy became a national leader of the Democratic party and an articulate advocate of liberal causes. His career suffered (1969) when a woman companion drowned after he drove his car off a bridge on Chappaquiddick Island, near Martha's Vineyard, Mass. He unsuccessfully challenged Carter for the 1980 presidential nomination.

Kennedy, John Fitzgerald (1917-63), 35th president of the United States. Kennedy was the youngest person and the first Roman Catholic ever elected to the post. Kennedy was shot in Dallas, Tex., after 1,037 days in office. After his death, a legend grew up around his youth, good looks, intelligence, idealism, and vigor that has become inseparable from his more concrete accomplishments.

Early life. Kennedy graduated *cum laude* from Harvard University in 1940. While serving in the Navy (1941-45), he was honored for his heroism.

Entering politics. At age 29, Kennedy was elected to the U.S. House of Representatives (1947-53). In 1953, he married socialite Jacqueline Lee Bouvier. In 1952, Kennedy was elected to the U.S. Senate; he was reelected in 1958. While convalescing from 2 spinal operations, he wrote *Profiles in Courage*, which won a Pulitzer Prize.

In 1956, Kennedy narrowly lost the Democratic vice-presidential nomination. In 1960, he won the presidential nomination. He and running mate Lyndon B. Johnson narrowly defeated Republicans Richard M. Nixon and Henry Cabot Lodge.

President. Kennedy changed the style of the presidency. His White House was known for its elegant receptions for artists and intellectuals and for the restoration of the White House supervised by Mrs. Kennedy. For its gracious social atmosphere and Kennedy's outstanding Cabinet appointments and new "brain trust" of political advisers, his administration was dubbed "Camelot."

John Fitzgerald Kennedy

35th U.S. President

Born:	Brookline, Mass.; May 19, 1917
Term:	Jan. 1961-Nov. 1963
Vice president:	Lyndon B. Johnson
Political party:	Democratic
Spouse:	Jacqueline Lee Bouvier Kennedy
Children:	2
Died:	Dallas, Tex.; Nov. 22, 1963

Kennedy's program was largely unsuccessful in Congress. He failed to win approval of expanded medical care for the elderly, tax reform, the creation of an urban-affairs department, comprehensive federal aid to education, and a new farm program. The major civil-rights bill he drafted passed only after his death. However, he did obtain the first major minimum-wage increase in a generation and passage of an urban-renewal and housing program. He also called for a bold new space program, and, in 1961, pledged that the United States would land a man on the moon within the decade. Kennedy was able to accomplish more through executive action, particularly in civil rights.
Kennedy promoted foreign aid and freer trade, launched a new program of cooperation for economic and social development in Latin America, and created the Peace Corps to aid underdeveloped areas of the world.
In 1961 Kennedy sent military advisers and equipment to Vietnam; allowed a U.S.-backed invasion of Cuba at the Bay of Pigs, which failed; and called up U.S. army reserves after East Germany erected the Berlin Wall. In Oct. 1962 the Cuban Missile Crisis took the United States to the brink of nuclear war with the Soviet Union. Kennedy demanded that the USSR remove its missile bases from Cuba. After a tense stalemate, the missiles were removed. Afterward U.S. and Soviet leaders signed a treaty banning atomic tests in the atmosphere.
Death in Dallas. Kennedy was fatally shot as he rode in an open car through Dallas, Tex., on Nov. 22, 1963. The presumed assassin, Lee Harvey Oswald, was shot to death 2 days later. Despite an investigation by a special commission headed by Chief Justice Earl Warren, the circumstances of the assassination remain a source of controversy.

Kennedy, Robert Francis (1925-68), U.S. attorney general (1961-64) and U.S. senator from New York (1965-68). He was chief counsel to the Senate subcommittee investigating labor union racketeering in the late 1950s, and elder brother John's senatorial campaign manager in 1962. As attorney general in President John F. Kennedy's cabinet, Robert Kennedy supervised enforcement of civil rights legislation in the South. After his brother's death he led the liberal wing of the Democratic party. In a controversial move after Eugene McCarthy's strong showing in the New Hampshire primary of 1968, Kennedy entered the race for his party's presidential nomination. On the evening of his victory in the California primary, June 5, 1968, he was shot and killed in Los Angeles by Sirhan Sirhan.

Kennedy, Ted *See:* Kennedy, Edward Moore.

Kennedy Center for the Performing Arts, part of the Smithsonian Institution, Washington, D.C., designed by U.S. architect Edward Durell Stone as a national memorial to the late president. The center, which opened 1971, houses 3 main theaters: the Eisenhower Theater, which seats 1,000 persons and offers dramatic productions; the Opera House, which seats 2,200 and presents opera, ballet, and musical comedies; and the Concert Hall, which seats 2,750 and features concert music.

Kenny, Elizabeth (1886-1952), Australian nurse. She is best known for developing the treatment of infantile paralysis combining hot, moist applications with exercise. She coauthored *the Kenny Concept of Infantile Paralysis and Its Treatment* (1942) and *And They Shall Walk* (1943).

Kensington rune stone, inscribed stone found in 1898 on a farm near Kensington, Minn. The inscription in runes (alphabet used by Germanic and Scandinavian peoples in the Middle Ages) is purportedly an account of Norse exploration of the Great Lakes in 1362. Most scholars now agree that the stone is of much more recent origin, probably a hoax.

Kent, James (1763-1847), U.S. jurist. He was the first professor of law at Columbia College (1793-98; 1823-26) and judge and chief judge (1798-1823) of the New York Supreme Court. As chancellor of the New York Court of Chancery (1814-23) he revived equity law in the United States. He wrote the monumental *Commentaries on American Law* (1826-30).

Kent, Rockwell (1882-1971), U.S. writer and artist. He is best known for his illustrations of popular classics and for his original works, which include the paintings *Toilers of the Sea* and *Winter* and the books *Wilderness* (1921) and *This Is My Own* (1940).

Kenton, Stan (1912-79), U.S. bandleader, pianist, and composer. Kenton experimented with the size and concept of his bands and sometimes combined Afro-Cuban music, modern jazz, and classical music. He introduced a brass instrument called the mellophonium, with a range between the trumpet and the trombone. His compositions include "Artistry in Rhythm" and "Eager Beaver." He helped establish the careers of jazz greats Lee Konitz and Art Pepper on alto saxophone, trumpeter Maynard Ferguson, drummer Shelly Manne, and trombonist Kai Winding.

Kentucky, state in the south central United States; bordered by Illinois, Indiana, and Ohio to the north; West Virginia and Virginia to the east; Tennessee to the south; and Missouri to the west.
Land and climate. Kentucky can be divided into 3 distinct topographical regions: the Gulf Coastal Plain, the Interior Low Plateau, and the Appalachian Plateau. The Gulf Coastal Plain in the extreme west has wide flood plains that are the site of cypress swamps and oxbow lakes. The Interior Low Plateau in central and northern Kentucky consists of the Western Coal Field, with its rich coal reserves and good farmland; the Bluegrass Region (named for the blue blossoms of its grasses), with its gently rolling pastureland and farm areas; and the Pennyroyal Region (named for an herb common in the area), with its flat and rolling farmland in the south, treeless "Barrens" in the center, and rocky ridges and bluffs in the north. The Appalachian Plateau in the east is a mountainous area of narrow valleys and sharp ridges. Kentucky lies in the drainage basin of the Mississippi River and the Ohio, which forms the state's northern boundary. Important rivers include the Tennessee, Cumberland, Green, Kentucky, and Licking rivers. Kentucky's largest lakes were created by dams built by the Tennessee Valley Authority. Kentucky is generally warm and rainy. Principal cities are Louisville and Lexington.
Economy. Service industries account for more than half of Kentucky's gross state product (GSP)—the total value of all the goods and services a state produces in a year. Manufacturing, however, is Kentucky's major economic activity. Leading manufactured products are transportation equipment, chemicals, electrical equipment, and machinery; others include processed foods and beverages, tobacco products, printed materials, and bourbon whiskeys. Kentucky's agricultural income is led by livestock and livestock products,

Kentucky

Capital:	Frankfort
Statehood:	June 1, 1792 (15th state)
Familiar name:	Bluegrass State
Area:	40,409 sq mi (104,660 sq km); ranks 37th
Population:	3,908,000 (1997); ranks 23rd
Elevation:	Highest—4,145 ft (1,263 m), Black Mountain; Lowest—257 ft (78 m), Mississippi River in Fulton County
Motto:	United We Stand, Divided We Fall
Flower:	Goldenrod
Bird:	Kentucky cardinal
Tree:	Kentucky coffee tree
Song:	"My Old Kentucky Home"

including beef cattle, milk, hogs, eggs, and broilers (chickens). The state is famous for its thoroughbred horses—and the annual Kentucky Derby horse race. Important crop products include tobacco, soybeans, corn, and wheat. Kentucky leads the U.S. in coal production. Other important mining products include natural gas, petroleum, and limestone.

Government. Kentucky's present constitution was adopted in 1891. The governor serves a 4-year term. The state's legislature, called the General Assembly, consists of 38 senators serving 4-year terms and 100 representatives serving 2-year terms. In the U.S. Congress, Kentucky is represented by 2 senators and 7 representatives.

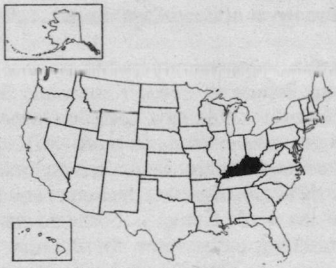

History. Native Americans lived in the area well before the first white settlers arrived in the mid-1700s. In the late 1760s, Daniel Boone opened settlement by blazing the Wilderness Trail through the Appalachians' Cumberland Gap. After the American Revolution, thousands of new settlers poured into the area. Originally part of Virginia, Kentucky gained statehood in 1792, becoming the first state west of the Appalachians. In the Civil War, Kentucky was a border state, drawn to both North and South. It eventually declared allegiance to the Union. World War I prosperity was followed by economic distress in the 1920s and 1930s; World War II brought recovery. Industrial expansion has continued in recent decades, but pockets of poverty still exist, particularly in eastern coal-mining areas, where unemployment is high (due to mechanization of the industry) and adequate health and education services are lacking.

Kentucky and Virginia Resolutions, resolutions in support of states' rights and civil liberties, passed by the legislatures of Kentucky and Virginia in 1798 and 1799, in response to the Alien and Sedition Acts. The Kentucky

Resolutions, drafted by Thomas Jefferson, claimed that the states could declare unconstitutional any congressional acts based on powers not specifically delegated to the federal government. The Virginia Resolutions, drafted by James Madison, declared the same theory in milder form.
See also: Alien and Sedition Acts.

Kentucky coffeetree (*Gymnocladus dioica*), state tree of Kentucky. Its natural range is from New York to Oklahoma. In colonial times its seeds were used as a coffee substitute. It grows to 30 m (100 ft) and has a dark gray scaly bark. The Kentucky coffee tree is one of the first trees to lose its leaves in autumn and one of the last to open its buds in spring. Its fruit are dark brown seed pods 6-10 in (15-25 cm) long.

Kentucky Derby, annual thoroughbred horse race for 3-year-olds run over a course of 1 1/4 mi (2 km) at Churchill Downs, Louisville, Ky. The Derby was founded in 1875 by Col. M. Lewis Clark, and is currently attended by more than 120,000 fans each year, and is the most popular horse race in the United States. The Preakness and the Belmont Stakes are the other 2 races which comprise the Triple Crown of horse racing.

Kentucky Lake, one of the world's largest human-made lakes. It covers 247 sq mi (640 sq km) in Kentucky and Tennessee, and was created as a reservoir by the vast Tennessee Valley Authority (TVA) Kentucky Dam, built across the Tennessee River in the 1940s.

Kentucky River, 250 mi (402 km) long, rises in the Cumberland Mountains, flows northwest through Kentucky's bluegrass region, and empties into the Ohio River at Carrollton. Small craft navigate as far upstream as Frankfort.

Kenya, independent republic of East Africa. Since achieving independence from Britain in 1963, Kenya has been one of the most prosperous and politically stable new African states for a long time. Economic and social progress has been made more difficult by the rapid growth of population.
Land and climate. Kenya has an area of 224,960 sq mi (582,646 sq km). Its northern neighbors are the Sudan and Ethiopia, with Somalia in the northeast. On the west, Kenya is bordered by Uganda; on the south, by Tanzania. Straddling the equator, the country has a varied landscape, with 4 main regions: the coastal strip bordering the Indian Ocean; the vast, dry plains of the Nyika; the highlands; and the western plateau.
The coastal strip is narrow and fertile, with scattered rain forest, mangrove swamps, and coconut palms. The plains extend from northern Kenya over more than half of the country, and are about 150 mi (240 km) wide in the south, where they are crossed by Kenya's 2 chief rivers, the Tana and the Athi. They are mostly scrubland pasture, but the Tana Valley and the Taita Hills are cultivated.
The highlands, where most Kenyans live, are mainly in the southwest, and are cut from north to south by the Great Rift Valley, of which Lake Rudolf (in the north) is part. They are mostly 5,000-8,000 ft (1,525-2,440 m) above sea level, but volcanic action has raised such lofty cones as Mount Kenya (17,058 ft/5,200 m), Kenya's highest mountain, and Mount Elgon (14,178 ft/4,321 m). With rich volcanic soils, moderate temperatures, and ample rainfall, the highlands provide most of Kenya's farm crops.

Kenya

Capital:	Nairobi
Area:	224,022 sq mi (580,367 sq km)
Population:	28,337,000
Language:	Swahili
Government:	Presidential republic
Independent:	1963
Head of gov.:	President
Per capita:	U.S. $280
Mon. unit:	1 Kenya shilling = 100 cents

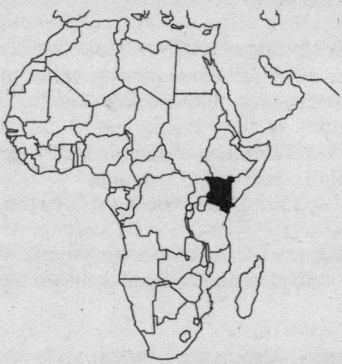

Beyond the Great Rift Valley and the highlands, the western plateau (sometimes called the Nyanza Plateau) stretches to Lake Victoria. At an average altitude of 4,000 ft (1,220 m), this well-watered plateau has good farmlands, forests, and grasslands. Kenya is famous for its big game, including elephants, hippos, giraffes, and antelopes. There are many national parks and game reserves, the largest and best known being the Tsavo National Park (8,034 sq mi/20,809 sq km) in southeast Kenya. Every year many visitors come from abroad to go on safari.

People. Nearly 98% of the population is African, comprising more than 40 ethnic groups, chief among which are the Kikuyu. There are also Indian, Arab, and European (primarily British) communities. Most Kenyans live in the southwest, mainly in the highlands where Nairobi, the capital and largest city, is situated.

Economy. Agriculture is the major occupation, with coffee, tea, timber, fruit, and vegetables the main exports. Chief industries center around food processing, textiles, footwear, and clothing. There is also a large livestock industry. Kenya has few natural resources, and its reliance upon imported oil places a strain on the economy. Hydroelectric and geothermal power sources are being developed. Tourism is also important.

History. Until 1887 the coast was under Arab control. The British then opened the interior with imported Indian labor and encouraged European settlement. In 1944 the first African nationalist party was set up, and Jomo Kenyatta became its leader in 1947. Discontent led to the formation of the Mau Mau terrorist organization. Pacified by reforms, Kenya gained independence in 1963, becoming a republic in 1964 under Kenyatta's presidency. In 1978 Kenyatta died. His vice president, Daniel arap Moi, was elected unopposed and rules since then. In 1998 the American embassy was the target of an attack by Muslim fundamentalists.

Kenyatta, Jomo (1893?-1978), Kenya's first president (1964-78). His early political career was concerned with rights of his Kikuyu people. In 1953 he was imprisoned by the British on charges of leading the Mau Mau, a terrorist Kikuyu group. His release came in 1961 following pressure from African nationalists; he negotiated Kenya's independence in 1963.

See also: Kenya.

Keogh plan *See:* Pension.

Kepler, Johannes (1571-1630), German mathematician and astronomer. Kepler advanced Copernicus's heliocentric model of the solar system in showing that the planets followed elliptical paths. His 3 laws describing the revolution of the planets around the sun, presented in *Astronomia nova* (1609) and *Harmonice mundi* (1619), guided Isaac Newton to the formulation of his theory of gravitation.
See also: Copernicus, Nicolaus; Newton, Sir Isaac.

Keratin, any of various fibrous proteins concentrated in the outermost layer of the skin of vertebrates and acting as a constituent of hair, nails, claws, and horns.

Kerensky, Alexander Feodorovich (1881-1970), Russian revolutionary, head of the provisional government that followed the Russian Revolution from July to Oct. 1917. Overthrown in the Bolshevik Revolution (Nov. 1917), he fled to Western Europe and in 1940 escaped to the United States. His books include *The Prelude to Bolshevism* (1919), *The Catastrophe* (1927), and *The Kerensky Memoirs* (1966).
See also: Russian Revolution.

Kerguelen Islands *See:* French Southern and Antarctic Territories.

Kern, Jerome (1885-1945), U.S. composer. His most famous musical is *Show Boat* (1927), which includes the song "Ol' Man River." Among his classic songs are "Smoke Gets in Your Eyes" and "The Song Is You."

Kerner Commission, appointed by President Lyndon B. Johnson in 1967 to investigate the causes of the race riots of the mid 1960s. The commission, headed by Gov. Otto Kerner of Ill., put most of the blame on "white racism." It concluded that the United States was moving toward 2 societies, one black and one white—"separate but unequal." It suggested improvements in schools and housing and better police protection for residents of black neighborhoods.

Kerosene, colorless, thin oil, a mixture of hydrocarbons, used mainly as a fuel for jet engines, and also for heating and lighting and as a solvent and paint thinner. Although it can be derived from oil, coal, and tar, most kerosene is produced from distilled petroleum.

Kerouac, Jack (Jean-Louis Lebris de Kerouac; 1922-69), U.S. novelist and poet. His best-known book is *On the Road* (1957), describing his life of freedom from conventional middle-class values. He was a leading figure of the beat generation.

Kerry blue terrier, breed of dog produced by the union of the Irish terrier and the Dandie Dinmont. Named for County Kerry in Ireland, where it was originally bred in the 1700s to herd sheep and cows, the Kerry blue has a thin, elongated body, stands about 18-19 inches tall (46-49 cm), and weighs 33-38 pounds (15-17 kg).

Kesselring, Albert (1885-1960), German field marshal of World War II. He became commander in chief in Italy (1943) and in the West (1945). He was convicted of war crimes (1947) and sentenced to life imprisonment, but he was released in 1952.

Kestrel, name given in the Old World to various small falcons. The European kestrel (*Falco tinnunculus*) is closely related to the American sparrow hawk.

Ketchikan, town in southeastern Alaska, on the southwestern edge of Revillagigedo Island, a port of entry for ships and vessels navigating the Inside Passage. Fishing, logging, and tourism are the major sources of income.

Kettering, Charles Franklin (1876-1958), U.S. inventor of the first electric cash register and the electric self-starter. He made significant contributions to automobile technology.

Kettledrum *See:* Drum.

Kettle hole, depression or cavity in solid rock formed by a block of glacial ice. The size may vary from 15 ft (5 m) to 8 mi (13 km) in diameter with depths of up to 140 ft (45 m).

Key, musical term denoting the arrangement of notes in a certain kind of scale. On the piano keyboard there are 12 notes, black and white, between each octave, each of which can be the starting point for 2 scales, one in the major mode and one in the minor mode. Thus if a piece of music is written for a major scale starting on the note C, then the key of the piece will be C major. If the piece is written for the minor scale starting on the note G, then the key will be G minor. Major scales all have one particular sequence of pitch intervals between the notes, while all the minor scales have a different sequence of pitch intervals. To maintain the same sequence of pitch intervals for all the major and minor scales, adjustments to the pitch of individual notes need to be made from scale to scale. Notes will either need to be raised by half a tone (sharpened) or lowered by half a tone (flattened). The number of sharpened or flattened notes required for any key is called the *key signature* and is always written at the start of a piece. Each major key has a corresponding minor key in terms of a shared key signature. For example, a sharpened F is the key signature for both the key of G major and E minor; a flattened B indicates either the key of F major or D minor; and so on through the 24 major and minor keys.

Key, Francis Scott (1779-1843), U.S. poet and lawyer who wrote the words to the "Star-Spangled Banner" after witnessing the night bombardment of Fort McHenry by the British in Sept. 1814. It became the U.S. national anthem by act of Congress (1931). Key's works include *The Power of Literature and Its Connection with Religion* (1834) and *Poems* (1857).
See also: Star-spangled Banner.

Keyboard instrument *See:* Celesta; Clavichord; Harpsichord; Organ; Piano.

Keynes, John Maynard (1883-1946), British economist at Cambridge University, a pioneer in the development of modern economics. He resigned in protest as treasury representative at the Versailles Peace Conference after World War I, stating his objections to the possible outcome of the treaty in *The Economic Consequences of the Peace* (1919). His chief work, *The General Theory of Employment, Interest, and Money* (1936), formed the basis of Keynesian economics, showing how government intervention could be used to maintain high levels of economic activity.
See also: Economics.

Key West (pop. 24,382), city on an island at the southwestern tip of the Florida Keys, about 150 mi (240 km) from Miami and 90 mi (145 km) from Cuba. Key West, the southernmost point of the continental United States, is a fishing and vacation center and has long been considered a dwelling for artists.

KGB, Committee for State Security, government organization in the former USSR functioning as a secret police force. The KGB is one of the state bodies exercising control over Soviet oppositionists. Its intelligence network keeps track of political and military activities abroad as well. Given its present name in 1953, the KGB is the successor to the earlier state security groups, the Cheka and the NKVD.

Khachaturian, Aram Ilich (1903-78), Soviet-Armenian composer. His music was influenced by the folk music of Armenia and the Orient. He is famous for the *Violin Concerto* (1940), the "Saber Dance" in his ballet *Gayané* (1942), and the orchestral suite *Masquerade* (1944).

Khalid ibn Abd al-Aziz Al Saud (1913-82), king of Saudi Arabia (1975-82). Appointed crown prince in 1965, Khalid acceded to the throne in 1975 on the death of his brother Faisal. His regime showed some restraint on oil prices and otherwise took cautious positions on Middle East issues.

Khamenei, Hojatolislam Ali (1939-), Iranian religious and political leader (1989-). He served in the legislature (1980-81) and as Iran's president (1981-89). A Shi'te Muslim and follower of the Ayatollah Ruhollah Khomeini, he took part in the 1979 revolution which overthrew the shah.

Kharkov (pop. 1,536,000), city in Ukraine, at the confluence of the Kharkov, Lopan, and Udy rivers. Founded in the 18th century, Kharkov is now the fifth largest city in the Soviet Union and was the capital of the Ukraine until 1934, when it was superseded by Kiev. An industrialized city, Kharkov produces metals, chemicals, and heavy machinery.
See also: Ukraine.

Khartoum (pop. 557,000), capital of Sudan. It is a cotton trading center linked by rail and river to Egypt and Port Sudan, and headquarters for the Bank for African Development, linking North and South Africa economically. The city was founded in 1821 as an Egyptian army camp. British General Gordon was killed here in 1885 defending the city against the Muslim religious leader known as the Mahdi.

Khayyam, Omar *See:* Omar Khayyam.

Khazars, Turkic people whose empire in southern Russia and the Caucasus controlled trade between the Slavs, Byzantium, and the Far East from 550 until the Byzantines and Russians overwhelmed it (969-1030). The king and nobility adopted Judaism in about 740.

Khmer *See:* Kampuchea.

Khmer empire, ancient Southeast Asian empire dating from the 6th century, occupying much of modern Laos, Thailand, and Vietnam. Its Angkor period (889-1434) produced beautiful architecture and sculpture. After the empire fell to the Thais in 1434, the court moved to Phnom Penh.

Khmer Rouge *See:* Kampuchea.

Khoikhoi, or Hottentot, member of a southern African group similar to the San. Members of the group call themselves "Khoikhoi"; "Hottentot" is now considered an insulting name. Small in stature, they have brown skin, prominent cheekbones, broad noses, and coarse hair. They were nomadic herders and farmers, but this way of life largely disappeared as a result of conflicts with other tribes and the Dutch settlers. Remaining members of the group live in Namibia.

Khomeini, Ruhollah (Ruhollah Moussavi; 1900?-89), spiritual and political leader of Iran, 1979-89. Khomeini received the title Ayatollah (Persian, "reflection" or "sign") for achieving the highest status that can be bestowed upon a Shi'te Muslim. He was forced into exile in 1963 because of his opposition to the rule of the shah (king), Muhammad Reza Pahlevi. In exile in Turkey, Iraq, and France, he emerged as the leader of the anti-shah forces, which overthrew the Pahlevi regime. He returned to Iran in Jan. 1979 to become absolute leader of his new Islamic republic. He held U.S. hostages (1979-81) and waged war with Iraq (1980-88).
See also: Iran.

Khrushchev, Nikita Sergeyevich (1894-1971), Soviet premier, 1958-64. As a loyal Stalinist during the great purges of the 1930s he managed the Communist Party in the Ukraine. During World War II he was a political adviser in the army, defending Stalingrad. When Josef Stalin died in Mar. 1953, Khrushchev became a member of the Soviet Union's "collective leadership," taking over as first secretary of the Central Committee. His famous "secret speech" of 1956, attacking Stalin, inaugurated the policy of "de-Stalinization," and by 1958 Khrushchev had made himself both premier and party head. During his rule Khrushchev traveled extensively, addressing the UN General Assembly in New York in 1959 on disarmament, and meeting with President Kennedy in Vienna in 1961. His main setback in foreign policy came in 1962, when the United States forced him to withdraw Soviet missiles secretly installed in Cuba. This crisis, his rift with the People's Republic of China, and repeated crop failures led to his removal from power.
See also: Union of Soviet Socialist Republics.

Khufu, or Cheops (fl. c.2680 B.C.), Egyptian pharaoh of the 4th dynasty. He built the greatest pyramid at Gizeh, near Cairo; it is known as one of the Seven Wonders of the Ancient World.
See also: Egypt, Ancient.

Khyber Pass, mountain pass on the Pakistan-Afghanistan border, about 3,500 ft (1,070 m) high and 28 mi (45 km) long. For centuries it was the main western land entry to India. Now a modern highway and a 34-tunnel railroad are on this site.

Kibbutz, type of collective farm in Israel established in the early 20th century. Land held by the Jewish National Fund is rented to the kibbutz inexpensively. Nearly all property on the kibbutz is collectively owned. All work, economic, and municipal activities are done communally. Kibbutzim provide food, accommodations, nurseries, and elementary education.

Kickapoo, Algonquian-speaking Native American tribe living in the Great Lakes region at the time of the arrival of European settlers. The Kickapoo lived by hunting, fishing, and farming. Opposed to the Europeans' incursion in their lands, they became formidable warriors, fighting against the United States in the American Revolution and the War of 1812. Forced to cede their land to the United States in 1819, most went to Kansas or Missouri, but later some went to Mexico. Today only 800 Kickapoo remain in Oklahoma, Kansas, and along the Texas-Mexico border.

Kidd, William (1645?-1701), British pirate. Employed in 1695 by the British to privateer against French ships in King William's War, he later plundered the British in the Indian Ocean and was hanged in London for murder and piracy.
See also: Pirate.

Kidnapping, the forcible abduction of a human being, whether or not for ransom. A famous early example was the kidnapping of Richard I of England for a huge ransom, on his way home from the crusades in 1192. In the 17th century the term referred to the practice of abducting children for labor on U.S. plantations. The first major U.S. kidnapping case occurred in 1874, but after 1920, with the growth of gangsters kidnappings increased at an alarming rate. The abduction and murder of the infant son of Charles A. Lindbergh in 1932 so aroused the public that legislation making kidnapping a federal crime, in some cases punishable by death, was passed in 1932 and 1934. Thereafter, kidnappings for ransom in the United States declined sharply. In modern times revolutionary groups have kidnapped ambassadors, consuls, businesspersons, and politicians, sometimes for ransom, sometimes to force the release of political detainees.

Kidney, one of a pair of organs of the urinary system, located in the back part of the abdomen, on each side of the vertebral column; the left lies slightly higher than the right. A high concentration of blood vessels gives the kidney a dark, reddish-brown color, and each is bean-shaped and slightly tilted. In adults, the kidney is about 4 in (10 cm) long and 2.5 in (6.5 cm) wide. At least one kidney must function for life to be maintained.

Through the activity of millions of nephrons, filtering units that are the organ's basic functional components, the kidneys perform a number of tasks: the removal from the blood of nitrogenous waste, mostly in the form of urea (a main constituent of the urine that the kidneys form); the maintenance of the body's electrolyte balance; the maintenance of the body's water balance; the regulation of the body's acid-base balance. In addition, the kidneys release a number of chemical substances (acting as hormones) into the blood. Urine is formed in the kidneys as an aqueous solution (95% water) containing metabolic waste products, foreign substances, and water-soluble constituents of the body. The quantity of urine produced by the kidneys depends on the balance of water and other essential substances in the body.
Among the most common kidney diseases are pyelonephritis, or kidney infection, and a type of inflammation called glomerulonephritis (formerly Bright's disease). If a person loses or suffers damage to both kidneys, he or she may be kept alive by a dialysis machine. The machine is attached to an artery in the patient's arm; blood flows through one tube into the machine, which removes wastes, and then flows back into the patient through a second tube. The patient must undergo this procedure for several hours, three days a week.

Kidney stone, hard mineral deposit that forms in the kidney as a result of excessive concentrations of mineral salts in the urine. If the stone is not passed through the urine or dissolved by natural or medical means, it can seriously disrupt regular kidney function.

Kidney transplant *See:* Tissue transplant.

Kiel (pop. 246,600), city in northwest Germany, on the Baltic Sea at the eastern end of the Kiel Canal. An important shipping and industrial center, it was Germany's chief naval base, 1871-1945. Kiel was founded in 1242 and joined the Hanseatic League in 1284.
See also: Germany.

Kiel Canal, German canal extending 61 mi (98 km) from the mouth of the Elbe River to Holtenau near Kiel. It opened in 1895 to facilitate movement of the German fleet between the North and Baltic seas. Because of its military and commercial value, it was internationalized after World War I until Hitler denied its status in 1936.

Kierkegaard, Søren Aabye (1813-55), Danish religious philosopher, precursor of existentialism. Opposing G.W.F. Hegel, he emphasized that one has a free will and can pass from the aesthetic (or material) to the ethical point of view and finally, through "a leap of faith," to the religious. Ignored in the 19th century, he has influenced 20th-century Protestant theology and modern literature and psychology. His main works are *Either/Or* (1843), *Fear and Trembling* (1843), and *Philosophical Fragments* (1844).
See also: Existentialism.

Kiev (pop. 2,600,000), capital and largest city of Ukraine, on the Dnieper River. Founded before the 9th century, it was the seat of the Russian Orthodox Church from 988. More than 40% of Kiev was destroyed in World

War II, but after extensive reconstruction it is now an industrial, communications, and cultural center.
See also: Ukraine.

Kigali (pop. 182,000), capital and largest city of Rwanda. Established by German colonists in 1907, Kigali is now an administrative and commercial center. In 1994 life in the capital was brutally disturbed by the genocide that followed the death of president Habyarimana.
See also: Rwanda.

Kikuyu, agricultural Bantu-speaking tribe, one of the largest groups (about 2 million) in Kenya, living north of Nairobi. Racial and tribal tensions led to the formation of the Mau Mau, a secret terrorist Kikuyu group involved in a nationalist uprising against European colonists in the late 1940s and 1950s.

Kilauea, world's largest active volcano, located on the southeastern part of Hawaii island. It is about 8 mi (13 km) in circumference and 3,646 ft (1,111 m) deep, with a lake of molten lava 740 ft (230 m) below its rim.

Kilimanjaro, extinct volcano and Africa's highest mountain, in northeastern Tanzania, near the Kenyan border. Its highest, snow-capped peaks are Kibo (19,340 ft/5,895 m) and Mawenzi (17,564 ft/5,354 m).

Killarney (pop. 7,800), town district in southwestern Ireland, County Kerry. Though it has some light industry, Killarney is primarily a tourist center, the main attraction being the surrounding countryside, especially the Lakes of Killarney.
See also: Ireland.

Killdeer (*Charadrius* or *Oxyechus vociferus*), shorebird, named for its noisy call. Marked with bold black and white rings on head and breast, killdeer breed from Canada to Chile, spending the winter in large flocks. They feed on insects and other small animals and kill harmful ticks and boll weevils.

Killer whale (*Orcinus orca*), small, toothed, carnivorous whale of the dolphin family, but lacking a beak. Voracious predators, killer whales eat dolphins, porpoises, seals, and fish. They may hunt in small groups or form packs of 40 or more, driving their prey into shallow water where escape is impossible. Their average length is about 20 ft (6 m), and they are found worldwide.

Kilmer, Joyce (1886-1918), U.S. poet remembered for his sentimental poem "Trees" (1913). He was killed in World War I.

Kiln, oven or furnace usually designed for "firing" earthy materials to make bricks, pottery, or quicklime. Limestone for quicklime is often roasted in a *shaft kiln*, being heated by hot gases flowing upward as it falls through the shaft. Clay and limestone, used to make cement, are usually burned in a *rotary kiln*, a long tube (up to 610 ft/186 m) that rotates slowly. The materials are heated as they shift gradually along it. Bricks and pottery, stacked on small cars, may be fired continuously in a *tunnelkiln*. The clay is prewarmed and hardened as it approaches the center firing zone and gradually cools as

it leaves. Clayware is also fired in batches in *periodic kilns*. Ware is stacked, heated, and allowed to cool before repeating the process.
See also: Pottery and porcelain.

Kimberley (pop. 150,000), city in Cape Province, South Africa, about 540 mi (870 km) northeast of Capetown, famed for having some of the world's largest diamond mines. The city was named for the Earl of Kimberly, colonial secretary at the time the area was settled by Britons.

Kim Il Sung (1912-94), North Korean political leader, premier 1948-72, president (1972-94). Trained in Moscow, he returned to Korea as head of a provisional Soviet-supported government in 1946. His invasion of South Korea precipitated the Korean War, and only Communist Chinese intervention saved his regime. He then launched a vast industrial and military buildup.

Kindergarten, school for children aged 4-6, conceived by German educator F.W.A. Froebel in 1837. The school aims to develop a child's self-expression and sociability through games, play, and creative activities. One of the first American kindergartens was opened in 1860 by E. Peabody.
See also: Froebel, Friedrich Wilhelm August.

Kinesics, systematic study of nonverbal communication through body motions. Developed by Ray L. Birdwhistell, an American anthropologist, kinesics examines gestures such as winking, or eyebrow raising, as well as involuntary reactions like blushing, in an effort to interpret the feelings and messages being relayed through such gestures.

King, Billie Jean (Billie Jean Moffitt; 1943-), U.S. tennis player. She was a prominent figure in the international game, whose efforts have done much to improve the status of women in tennis. Kings achievements include winning the U.S. Open 4 times (1967, 71, 72, 74), Wimbledon 6 times (1966, 67, 68, 72, 73, 75), and the Australian Open and French Open once (1968, 1972).

King, Coretta Scott (1927-), U.S. civil rights leader, widow of Martin Luther King, Jr. As president of the Martin Luther King, Jr. Center for Social Change, she continues the legacy of her late husband's work. She is the author of *My Life with Martin Luther King, Jr.* (1989).
See also: Civil Rights; King, Martin Luther, Jr.

King, Ernest Joseph (1878-1956), U.S. admiral, commander of the U.S. fleet and naval operations chief in World War II. His recognition of the importance of the air war and the superiority of aircraft carriers to battleships led to Japan's naval defeat.
See also: World War II.

King, Karl (1891-1971), U.S. composer and conductor of musical bands, creator of more than 300 musical works, 200 of which were marches. King composed most of his pieces with the circus in mind. His "Barnum and Bailey's Favorite" (1913) became the theme song of the circus of that name.

King, Martin Luther, Jr. (1929-68), black U.S. clergyman and civil rights leader, recipient of the 1964 Nobel Peace Prize for his work for racial equality in the United States. King organized the boycott of the Montgomery, Ala., transit company in 1955 to force desegregation of the buses. Under his leadership in the late 1950s and 1960s, civil disobedience and nonviolent tactics, like the Washington March of 250,000 people in 1963, brought about the Civil Rights Act of 1965. Black militants challenged his methods in 1965, but in 1966 he extended his campaign to slum conditions in the northern cities of the United States, and in 1968 he set up the Poor People's Campaign. He was less successful in this effort because the Vietnam War distracted national attention from civil rights and urban issues. He was assassinated in Memphis, Tenn. In 1983 Congress designated the third Monday in January a national holiday to commemorate his birthday.

King Arthur *See:* Arthur, King.

King, Stephen (1947-), U.S. novelist and short-story writer. His best-selling occult thrillers about families threatened by malevolent supernatural forces include *Carrie* (1974), *The Shining* (1976), *Cujo* (1981), and *Misery* (1987). Other works include *Gerald's Game* (1992), *Insomnia* (1994), and *Wizard and Glass* (1997).

King, William Lyon Mackenzie (1874-1950), Canadian statesman, Liberal prime minister (1921-30, 1935-48). He established Canada's right to act independently of Great Britain in international affairs, introduced old age pensions (Canada's first national social security scheme), and directed the Canadian war effort in World War II.
See also: Canada.

King, William Rufus Devane (1786-1853), U.S. politician. King served as U.S. senator from North Carolina and was elected vice president under President Franklin Pierce. He died before being inaugurated.

Kingbird, aggressive North American flycatcher (genus *Tyrannus*), usually with gray head and a black stripe through the eye. It feeds on insects and defends its nest vigorously, even attacking humans.

King crab *See:* Horseshoe crab.

Kingdom, in biology, large group of organisms that share basic characteristics. Biologists recognize 5 kingdoms of organisms: Monera, Protista, Fungi, Plantae, and Animalia.
See also: Classification.

Kingfish, any of several large food and game fishes, including the mackerel and drum, especially of the genus *Menticirrhus*. Kingfish live in the warm waters of the Atlantic and Pacific coasts.

Kingfisher, family (Alcedinidae) of brightly colored, strong-beaked birds of rivers, lakes, and streams worldwide. The bird perches until prey is sighted, then dives arrowlike into the water to take the fish. The belted kingfisher (*Megaceryle alcyon*) is the only species widely found in the United States.

King George VI Falls, collection of waterfalls and rapids descending some 1,600 feet (488 meters), situated in northwestern Cape Province, South Africa. The falls, on the Utishi river, are the major attraction of the Aughrabies National Park.

Kinghead *See:* Ragweed.

King James Version *See:* Bible.

Kinglet, tiny, olive-green songbird (genus *Regulus*) living in the temperate woodlands of the Northern Hemisphere. It feeds on small insects with its thin, pointed bill.

Kingmaker *See:* Warwick, Earl of.

King Peak, one of the highest mountains in North America, rising 17,130 ft (5,221 m) in the St. Elias Mountains of northwestern Canada.

King Philip's War (1675-76), last Native American resistance to the whites in New England. In 1675 the Plymouth Colony executed 3 Native Americans for an alleged murder. Metacom, a Wampanoag chief also called King Philip, led an alliance of tribes in fierce guerrilla raids. The whites replied in kind, and Metacom was killed when his secret refuge was betrayed. The colonists then drove most of the Native Americans from New England.

Kings, Books of, in the Old Testament, called First and Second Kings in the Authorized Version, and Third and Fourth Kings in the Greek versions and the Western canon. They cover Israelite history from the reign of Solomon through the period of the 2 kingdoms of Israel and Judah to the destruction of Judah by the Babylonians.
See also: Old Testament.

Kings Canyon National Park, area of about 460,100 acres (186,200 hectares) in the Sierra Nevada, south central California, established as a national park in 1940. Two immense canyons are formed by the Kings River. The park features snow-covered peaks, rich wildlife, and sequoia trees.

Kingsley, Charles (1819-75), English writer and clergyman and an advocate of social reform. His early novel Alton Locke (1850) is a sympathetic study of working-class life. He also wrote historical novels, notably Westward Ho! (1855) and the children's fantasy *The Water Babies* (1863).

Kingsley, Sidney (1906-), U.S. playwright noted for his treatment of social problems. His first play, *Men in White* (1933), won a Pulitzer Prize.

Kingsnake, nonpoisonous snake (genus *Lampropeltis*) of the central and southern United States. Kingsnakes grow up to 6 ft (2 m) long and are often brightly colored. They feed on rodents, birds, and snakes, even rattlesnakes, since kingsnakes are immune to venom.

Kingston (pop. 24,481), industrial city of New York, on the west bank of the Hudson River about 92 mi (148 km) north of New York City. Founded by

the Dutch (1652), the city was burned by the British a few months after being made the state capital in 1777.
See also: New York.

Kingston (pop. 643,800), capital and largest city of Jamaica, in the Caribbean Sea. Famed for its botanical gardens, Kingston is the economic hub of the island nation. Industries include oil refining, food processing, and tourism. The city was founded in 1693 and superseded Port Royal as capital in 1872.
See also: Jamaica.

Kingstown (pop. 19,000), capital of St. Vincent and the Grenadines, in the Caribbean Sea. Situated on the southwest seashore of St. Vincent's island, Kingstown is the country's chief port. The economy is based largely on import/export activities. Kingstown was ruled by England for nearly 200 years (1783-1979), until its integration with the self-governing body of St. Vincent and the Grenadines.
See also: Grenadines.

King William's War *See:* French and Indian Wars.

Kinkajou (*Potos flavus*), relative of the raccoon that can hang by its tail. It grows up to 3 ft (1 m) long and has short legs and a very long tail covered in soft fur. The kinkajou lives in tropical forests from southern Mexico to Brazil. It moves cautiously through the branches using its tail as an anchor. Although kinkajous are members of the Carnivora (flesh eaters), they eat mainly fruit and a few insects.

Kinnock, Neil Gordon (1942-), British politician, elected youngest Labour Party leader in 1983 at the age of 41. Known for his left-wing views and fervent public speaking skills, Kinnock has strived to promote unity between the party's left-wing and moderate factions in the area of policy. In 1993 he was succeeded by John Smith. Kinnock became a member of the European Commission in 1994.

Kino, Eusebio Francisco (1644?-1711), Italian Jesuit missionary who explored lower California and parts of Arizona. His map (1705) remained the basis of maps of the southwest and northwest Mexico for a century.
See also: Jesuits.

Kinsey, Alfred Charles (1894-1956), U.S. biologist best known for his statistical studies of human sexual behavior, published as *Sexual Behavior in the Human Male* (1948) and *Sexual Behavior in the Human Female* (1953).
See also: Biology; Sex.

Kinshasa (pop. 2,800,000), capital and largest city of Zaïre. It was founded in 1881 by the British explorer Henry M. Stanley, who named it Leopoldville after King Leopold II of Belgium. Its name was changed to Kinshasa in 1966, after Zaïre became independent.
See also: Zaïre.

Kiowa, Native American tribe of the North American plains. A nomadic people, they were followers of sun dance and ghost dance cults. A Kiowan

Kirghizstan

Capital:	Bishkek
Area:	76,600 sq mi (198,500 sq km)
Population:	4,522,000
Language:	Russian, Kirghiz
Government:	Presidential republic
Independent:	1991
Head of gov.:	Prime minister
Per capita:	U.S. $700
Mon. unit:	1 Som = 100 tyin

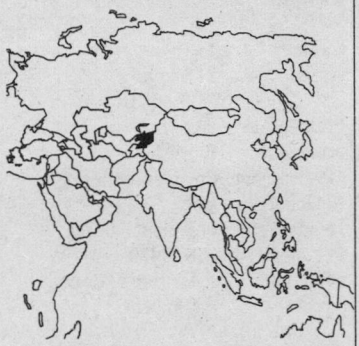

uprising was put down by the U.S. army in 1874. They were settled in Oklahoma, and presently number about 2,000.

Kipling, Rudyard (1865-1936), Indian-born English writer. Among his works are short stories about Anglo-Indian life, such as *Plain Tales from the Hills* (1888); poems, including "Mandalay" and "Gunga Din"; and children's books, including *The Jungle Book* (1894), *Kim* (1901). He won the Nobel Prize for literature in 1907.

Kirchhoff, Gustav Robert (1824-87), German physicist best known for his work on electrical conduction, showing that current passes through a conductor at the speed of light, and deriving Kirchhoff's Laws. With Robert Bunsen he discovered the elements cesium and rubidium and pioneered spectrum analysis, which he applied to the solar spectrum, identifying several elements and explaining the Fraunhofer lines.
See also: Physics.

Kirchhoff's Laws, two laws governing electric circuits involving Ohm's law conductors and sources of electromotive force, stated by Kirchhoff. They assert that the sums of outgoing and incoming currents at any junction in the circuit must be equal and that the sum of the current-resistance products around any closed path must equal the total electromotive force in it.
See also: Kirchhoff, Gustav Robert.

Kirchner, Ernst Ludwig (1880-1938), German expressionist graphic artist and painter, cofounder of the Brücke (bridge) movement (1905-13). He is noted for his powerful, savagely expressive woodcuts and, in his painting, for his vigorous, distorted use of color and form. When his work was condemned by the Nazis as degenerate, Kirchner committed suicide.

Kirghizstan, or Kyrgyzstan, republic in central Asia, bordered by on the north by Kazakhstan, on the east by China, on the south by Tajikistan, and on the west by Uzbekistan. Its capital is Bishkek.
Land and climate. The country is almost entirely mountainous, it is part of the Tien Shan mountains (highest peak 24,406 feet/7440 meters). The rivers

Kiribati

Capital:	Tarawa
Area:	277 sq mi (717 sq km)
Population:	84,600
Language:	English
Government:	Presidential republi
Independent:	1979
Head of gov.:	President
Per capita:	U.S. $920
Mon. unit:	1 Australian dollar = 100 cents

are important for irrigation and for generating electricity. The climate varies from subtropical to alpine in the high mountains.
People. About 60% of the population are Kirghiz, a Muslim people speaking a Turkic language; other inhabitants include Russians and Uzbeks. Official languages are Khirgiz and Russian. Besides Islam, one can find Christianity and Buddhism in Khirgizstan.
Economy. The wool from its sheep is an important product, and the region also has deposits of coal and natural gas. When after 1991 the economic ties with Russia disappeared, this had a disastrous effect on the Kirghiz economy
History. Formerly one of the 15 constituent republics of the USSR (Soviet Union), the country became independent in 1991. After independence the political and economic policies of the government have been aimed at reforming the old communist structures. The country is a member of the Commonwealth of Independent States en made radical reforms during the last years.
See also: Union of Soviet Socialist Republics.

Kiribati, independent island republic in the central Pacific, consists of 3 groups of coral atolls and 33 islands astride the equator. The land area is 324 sq mi (811 sq km), spread across 2,400 mi (3,860 km) of ocean. The population of 75,000 is mostly Micronesian. The capital, Bairiki, is on Tarawa, where over 30% of the total population lives. Fishing constitutes the mainstay of the subsistence economy, supplemented by the cultivation of taro and fruits. Formerly part of the British protectorate called British Gilbert and Ellice Islands (since 1892), Kiribati was granted independence in 1971.

Kiritimati Atoll, or Christmas Island, one of the largest coral islands in the Pacific, covering 140 sq mi (360 sq km) and with a coastline of 80 mi (130 km). It is 1,300 mi (2,100 km) south of Honolulu. On Christmas Day, 1777, British explorer James Cook became the first European to reach the island. It was used for nuclear testing by both Britain and the United States. In 1979 it became part of the nation of Kiribati.

Kirkland, Lane (1922-), U.S. labor leader, president of the American Federation of Labor and Congress of Industrial Organizations (AFL-CIO) since 1979. He was executive assistant to AFL-CIO president George Meany

(1961-69) and secretary-treasurer from 1969. Succeeding Meany as president, he became known as a strong supporter of civil rights and national defense.

Kirkpatrick, Jeane Jordan (1926-), U.S. ambassador to the United Nations (1981-85). A professor of political science at Georgetown University, she was a charter member of the conservative Coalition for a Democratic Majority, advocating a tougher U.S. foreign policy. After leaving her UN post she joined the Republican Party and was appointed by President Ronald Reagan to serve on the National Commission on Space and the Foreign Intelligence Advisory Board.

Kirlian photography, or electromagnetic discharge imaging (EDI), technique of recording an image on photographic film by applying a high-frequency electric field to it and recording the resulting pattern of luminescence. The electromagnetic field causes electrons and positive ions in the gas surrounding an object to accelerate and frees them from the object's surface. When the electrons and ions recombine, the objects photographed appear surrounded by light. The process is named after Soviet scientists Semyon and Valentina Kirlian, who systematized it c.1940.
See also: Photography.

Kirstein, Lincoln (1907-96), U.S. ballet promoter who persuaded George Balanchine to come to the United States and helped him organize the School of American Ballet in New York (1934) and the New York City Ballet (1948). Kirstein also wrote several books on ballet.
See also: Ballet.

Kirtland Air Force Base, nuclear research facility in Albuquerque, N.M., established 1941. It is named after Air Force Col. Roy S. Kirtland. The U.S. Air Force Weapons Laboratory and Special Weapons center are located here.
See also: Nuclear energy.

Kissinger, Henry Alfred (1923-), German-born U.S. adviser on foreign affairs. Professor at Harvard when his book Nuclear Weapons and Foreign Policy (1957) brought him international recognition, Kissinger served as special assistant for national security affairs (1969-75) and secretary of state (1973-77) under presidents Nixon and Ford. He was instrumental in initiating the Strategic Arms Limitation (SALT) Talks on disarmament (1969), in ending U.S. involvement in Vietnam, and in opening U.S. policies toward China.

Kitasato, Shibasaburo (1852-1931), Japanese bacteriologist. He discovered with Emil von Behring that graded injections of toxins could be used for diphtheria immunization (1890). He also discovered (1894) the infectious agent of bubonic plague (which he described simultaneously with A.E.J. Yersin).
See also: Bacteriology.

Kitchen Cabinet, popular name for an unofficial body of advisers to President Andrew Jackson (1829-31). It included editors F.P. Blair and Amos Kendall, politicians, and government officials.

Kitchener (pop. 356,400), Canadian cultural and industrial city 65 mi (105 km) west of Toronto. Named Berlin in 1830 and populated by German immigrants, it is noted for an Oktoberfest celebration based on the beer festival of Munich, Germany. During World War I the city's residents renamed it after the British war hero Horatio H. Kitchener to demonstrate support for Canada and Great Britain.
See also: Canada.

Kitchener, Horatio Herbert (1850-1916), British field marshal, secretary of state for war in World War I. In the Sudan in 1898, he defeated the Mahdis at Omdurman and retook Khartoum. He was commander in chief in the Boer War, 1900-2, and in India, to 1909. His appeals during World War I raised thousands of army volunteers. He drowned when a ship taking him to Russia hit a mine and sank.
See also: Boer War; World War I.

Kite, any of various predatory birds of the hawk family (Accipitridae) with long, pointed wings and a forked tail. Kites live near water in tropical zones, preying on reptiles, frogs, and insects.

Kite, aircraft consisting of a light frame covered with thin fabric (e.g., paper) and flown in the wind by aerodynamic lift at the end of a long string. Originating in the ancient Far East, kite flying has long been a popular sport, and has been used for meteorological observations.

Kittiwake, small gull (genus *Rissa*) that nests on narrow cliff ledges around the coasts of the North Atlantic, the North Pacific, and on the islands of the Arctic Ocean. Named for its noisy call, the kittiwake feeds on fish, mollusks, and plankton and flies far out to sea.

Kitty Hawk *See:* Wright brothers.

Kiwanis International, community service association for business and professional men, having some 4,500 clubs and 285,000 members in the United States and Canada. Its objectives are to promote higher standards in business, to promulgate the Golden Rule, and to take part in community affairs. Founded in Detroit in 1915, its headquarters are in Chicago.

Kiwi, 3 species of flightless New Zealand birds (genus *Apteryx*), about 18 in (46 cm) high, lacking a tail, with gray-brown, hairlike feathers concealing their wings. The long slender bill probes into soil at night for worms, insects, and berries.

Kiwi fruit, or Chinese gooseberry (*Actinidia chinensis*), fruit originating in China and named for the kiwi bird of New Zealand (where it was first established as a commercial crop). Green-fleshed, with a thin, fuzzy, brown skin, it is similar in size and shape to an egg. It has a pungent flavor and is rich in vitamin C. The fruit is also found in France, the United States, Italy, Spain, and Japan.

Klaipeda, or Memel (pop. 191,000), city in western Lithuania, on the Baltic Sea. Named Memelburg by Teutonic Knights who conquered a fort here in

1252, it was renamed after the Memel Territory became part of Lithuania in 1923. It is an ice-free seaport and trade center specializing in fishing, food processing, shipping, shipbuilding, and textile production.
See also: Lithuania.

Klamath, Native American tribe of southeastern Oregon and northern California, neighbors of the Modoc tribe, with whom they share a reservation around Upper Klamath Lake, established in 1864.

Klee, Paul (1879-1940), Swiss painter, graphic artist, and art theorist. From 1906, he exhibited with the German expressionist Blaue Reiter (Blue Rider) group. He taught at the Bauhaus 1920-31, publishing a textbook on painting (*Pedagogical Sketchbooks*, trans. 1944). Sensitive line, color, and texture are combined in Klee's paintings with wit and fantasy: *Landscape with Blue Birds* (1919), *Jorg* (1924), and *Diana* (1931).

Klein, Lawrence Robert (1920-), U.S. economist. A professor at the Wharton School of the University of Pennsylvania from 1958, he was an adviser to President Jimmy Carter (1976-81) and winner of the 1980 Nobel Prize in economic science.
See also: Economics.

Kleist, Heinrich von (1777-1811), German dramatist and writer of novellas, known for his power and psychological insight. His works include the plays *Penthesilea* (1808) and *Prince Friedrich von Homburg* (1821) and the novels *Michael Kohlhaas* (1808) and *The Marquise of O* (1810-11).

Klemperer, Otto (1885-1973), German conductor. As director of the Kroll Opera House, Berlin (1927-33) he introduced many modern works and new interpretations of classics. After a period of crippling illness he revived his career in 1947, notably as an interpreter of Beethoven and Mahler.

Klimt, Gustav (1862-1918), Austrian painter and designer, a leader of the Vienna Secession (1897), noted for his lavishly ornamented, mosaic-patterned style. His interior designs, as for the Palais Stoclet, Brussels, and in Vienna, influenced Jugendstil (German "art nouveau").

Kline, Franz (1910-62), U.S. abstract expressionist painter. His huge, stark, black-and-white compositions influenced the "calligraphic" style of the 1950s New York school. Later, Kline reintroduced color into his works.

Klondike, subarctic region in the west central Yukon Territory, northwest Canada, site of the gold rush of 1896. By 1900 $22 million was being panned annually from a tributary of the Klondike River, but the creeks were mined out in about 10 years.
See also: Yukon Territory.

Knee, front of the leg where the femur (thighbone) and tibia (shinbone) meet, and the joint itself, covered by the patella, or kneecap. Because the bony surfaces do not match exactly, the knee joint is one of the body's weakest joints. Its strength lies in the number, size, and arrangement of

the ligaments, and the powerful muscles and fibrous membranes that pass over the joint and enable it to withstand the leverage of the 2 longest bones in the body.
See also: Joint.

Knife, hand-held cutting instrument used as a tool and a weapon since early history. Made from stone, bone, metal, wood, and plastic, knives are broadly categorized as fixed-blade or folding, also known as pocket knives.

Knight, Eric (1897-1943), English-American author best known for his children's novel *Lassie Come Home* (1940). Other works include the novels *The Flying Yorkshireman* (1937), *This Above All* (1941), and the short-story collection *Sam Small Flies Again* (1942). He was killed in an airplane crash while on a World War II mission.

Knighthood, Orders of, religious, honorary, or other fraternal society. Knights of the Middle Ages, vowing loyalty to their king, formed orders to defend his lands. During the crusades religious orders of knights fought the Muslims for the Holy Lands. The most famous of the religious orders were the Knights of St. John, the Knights Templars, and the Teutonic Knights. In Great Britain honorary orders of knights include the Order of the Garter (1349), the Order of the Thistle (1687), the Order of the Bath (1725), the Order of St. Michael and St. George (1818), the Royal Victorian Order (1896), and the Order of the British Empire (1917). Other European orders are the Seraphim of Sweden (1748), the Golden Fleece of Spain and Austria (1429), the Danish Order of the Elephant (1462), St. Andrew of Russia (1698), the Black Eagle of Prussia (1701), the Legion of Honor of France (1802), the Order of St. Olaf in Norway (1847). In the United States, the Knights of Columbus are a fraternal order of Roman Catholic men.

Knights and knighthood, part of the feudal system of the Middle Ages in Europe. Knights were mounted and armed sworn defenders of a feudal superior, generally having previously served as page and squire. Chivalry was the code of honor practiced by knights. They were known by their clothing, armor, and participation in tournaments in which they fought each other. The legend of King Arthur is the most famous literary account of knighthood.
See also: Feudalism.

Knights Grand Cross of the Bath *See:* Bath, Order of the.

Knights Hospitallers *See:* Knights of Saint John.

Knights of Columbus, U.S. fraternal organization for Roman Catholic men, founded at New Haven, Conn., in 1882 and now claiming more than a million members. The society sponsors charitable and educational causes and protects the interests of the Roman Catholic Church.
See also: Roman Catholic Church.

Knights of Labor, U.S. labor organization founded in 1869 in Philadelphia. Some of its goals were an 8-hour work day, abolition of child labor, and equal pay for equal work. It led successful strikes in 1884-86, but declined after the Haymarket Square riot in Chicago in 1886.
See also: Labor movement.

Knights of Pythias, U.S. fraternal organization, incorporated by an act of Congress in 1864. Its aims are charity, friendship, and benevolence. It contributes to disaster funds, blood banks, children's camps, and other humanitarian causes.

Knights of Saint John (officially, Order of the Hospital of St. John of Jerusalem; also known as Hospitallers, Knights of Rhodes, or of Malta), religious order founded by papal charter (1113) to tend sick pilgrims in the Holy Land. It became a military order as well in 1140, and after the fall of Jerusalem was based successively on Cyprus (1291), Rhodes (1309), and Malta (1530) to provide a defense against Muslim seapower. Expelled from Malta by Napoleon in 1798, the Knights have been established at Rome since 1834.
See also: Knighthood, Orders of.

Knights of the Bath *See:* Bath, Order of the.

Knights of the Round Table *See:* Arthur, King; Round Table.

Knights Templars, Christian military order founded in 1118, with its headquarters on the site of Solomon's Temple in Jerusalem, to protect pilgrims. It provided elite troops for the kingdom of Jerusalem. Its immense riches from endowments and banking excited the greed of Philip IV of France, who (1307-14) confiscated its property and forced the pope to suppress the order.

Knitting, production of fabric by using needles to interlock yarn or thread in a series of connected loops, using basic knit and purl stitches. It was practiced in North Africa in the 3rd century B.C. and was taken to Europe by Arab traders.

Knitting machine, manufacturing device for knitting fabrics ranging from delicate lace to rugs, invented by the Englishman William Lee in 1589. The 2 main types of machines are weft, which produces fabric that stretches elastically, and warp, with lengthwise stitches that produce a flat, less elastic fabric.
See also: Knitting.

Knopf, Alfred A. (1892-1984), U.S. publisher. He founded Alfred A. Knopf, Inc. (1915), a prestigious publishing house with many Nobel Prize-winning authors. Random House acquired the company in 1960, but the imprint remains.

Knossos, ancient city on the north coast of Crete, the center of Minoan civilization. Excavations by Sir Arthur Evans revealed settlements dating from before 3000 B.C.. The great palace of Knossos comprises more than 5 acres (2 hectares) of halls, ceremonial rooms, and staircases, with magnificent fresco decorations, advanced sanitation, and every luxury. Fire destroyed it c.1400 B.C.
See also: Crete.

Knotgrass, knotweed, or doorweed (*Polygonum aviculare*), plant of the buckwheat family, found in Canada and the northern United States. It is short and thick with bluish green leaves and pinkish green flowers.

Knots, hitches, and splices, methods to tie or fasten ropes. A knot is a fastening of cord or ropes. A hitch is used to tie a rope to a ring, spar, post, or other object. A splice joins 2 rope ends permanently. Sailors, explorers, mountain climbers, and builders make wide use of knots. The Gordian knot of Greek mythology, which reputedly could not be untied except by a person predestined to do so, is used as a metaphor for any unsolvable problem.

Know-Nothing Party, U.S. political party formed in the 1840s to exclude recently immigrated Roman Catholics from politics. The party sought to elect only native-born citizens to office and to require 25 years of residence for citizenship. It won success in the 1854 election as the American Party, but split irremediably in 1856 over the slavery issue. Its name came from its members' habit of saying they "knew nothing" of the movement.

Knox, John (1514?-72), Scottish Protestant Reformation leader. A Catholic priest, Knox converted to Protestantism and fled in 1554 from the Roman Catholic regime of English queen Mary I to Geneva, where he became a follower of John Calvin. He returned to Scotland in 1559 ardently preaching Protestantism. When it became the state religion (1560) Knox gained great political influence, opposing Mary Queen of Scots. His writings include his unfinished *History of the Reformation in Scotland* (pub. 1644), *First Blast of the Trumpet Against the Monstrous Regiment of Women* (1556-58), and the *Book of Common Order*.
See also: Reformation.

Knoxville (pop. 604,816), city in eastern Tennessee, at the edge of the Great Smoky Mountains on the Tennessee River. Founded in 1785, Knoxville was occupied by Union troops during the Civil War. In the 1930s the dam complex of the Tennessee Valley Authority was built nearby.
See also: Tennessee.

Koala, or koala bear (*Phascolarctos cinereus*), pouched tree-dwelling mammal of eastern Australia. Koalas have thick, gray fur, a black nose, and no tail, and are 2-2$^1/_2$ ft (60-75 cm) long. They eat only eucalyptus leaves. Koalas are marsupials, bearing and nursing their young in a pouch, although unlike must marsupials, they do have a true placenta. The koala has been considered an endangered species.

Kobe (pop. 1,468,000), city located on the southern coast of the island of Honshu, Japan. This major seaport is a hub for export and import as well as industry and shipbuilding. It is also considered to be a cultural center, with many places of worship and centers of learning. Modern Kobe is largely the result of rebuilding after the heavy bombings of World War II. In 1995 the city was struck by an earthquake that destroyed thousands of houses and buildings and caused the death of more than 5,000 people.
See also: Japan.

Koblenz, or Coblenz (pop. 110,800), city in west-central Germany, located on the Rhine River in the state of Rhineland-Palatinate. It serves as an administrative, industrial, trade, and cultural center for Germany. One of the oldest German settlements, it was founded in 9 B.C. as a Roman fortress. A popular landmark is the Ehrenbreitstein Castle, a fortress built

around the 11th century, destroyed by the French in 1801, and restored by 1832.
See also: Germany.

Koch, Edward Irving (1924-), U.S. Democratic representative from New York (1969-77), and mayor of New York City (1977-89). He steered the city through a severe fiscal crisis by cutting city expenditures, while trying to maintain essential services. As a popular, hard-working mayor, Koch won both the Democratic and Republican party nominations for reelection in 1981. Koch's third term in office was marked by political scandal within his administration and racial unrest in the city of New York. These events contributed to Koch's failure to gain his party's candidacy to run for a fourth term of office.

Koch, Robert (1843-1910), German bacteriologist. He was awarded the 1905 Nobel Prize for physiology or medicine for developing a test for tuberculosis. His innovative methods of obtaining pure cultures are still used. He discovered the bacilli responsible for anthrax (1876), tuberculosis (1882), and cholera (1883).
See also: Bacteriology.

Kocher, Emil Theodor (1841-1917), Swiss surgeon. He won the 1909 Nobel Prize for medicine for his research of the physiology, pathology, and surgery of the thyroid gland. In 1878 he performed the first operation for the removal of an enlarged thyroid gland.

Kodály, Zoltán (1882-1967), Hungarian composer and, with Béla Bartók, an ardent researcher of Hungarian folk music. Folk influences are evident in such works as the cantata *Psalmus Hungaricus* (1923), the opera *Háry János* (1926), and the orchestral *"Peacock" Variations* (1938-9).

Koestler, Arthur (1905-83), Hungarian-born British writer. His novel *Darkness at Noon* (1941), based on his own experiences in a Spanish death cell, analyzed the psychology of victims of Stalin's 1930s purges. Many later works on philosophical and scientific subjects include *The Sleepwalkers* (1964), *The Case of the Midwife Toad* (1971), and *The Thirteenth Tribe* (1978).

Koffka, Kurt (1886-1941), German-born U.S. psychologist who, with Wolfgang Köhler and Max Wertheimer, was responsible for the development of Gestalt psychology.
See also: Gestalt psychology; Köhler, Wolfgang; Wertheimer, Max.

Kohl, Helmut (1930-), German politician and chancellor (1982-98). Leader of the conservative Christian Democratic party, he succeeded Social Democrat Helmut Schmidt as chancellor of West Germany in 1982 and sanctioned U.S. nuclear missile installations there (1983). Under his leadership West Germany was reunited with East Germany in 1990.

Köhler, Wolfgang (1887-1967), German-born U.S. psychologist, a founder of Gestalt psychology. He studied problem-solving among chimpanzees.
See also: Gestalt psychology; Koffka, Kurt; Wertheimer, Max; Gestalt psychology.

Kokoschka, Oskar (1886-1980), Austrian expressionist painter and writer. He is known for psychologically acute portraits such as *The Tempest* (1914) and forlyric land- and townscapes including *Jerusalem* and *View of the Thames* (1925-26).

Kola, tropical tree (genus *Cola*, especially *C. nitida*) that yields fruit containing caffeine-producing seeds. In its native West Africa, the seeds are chewed to combat feelings of tiredness and are also exported for use in beverages (colas) and medicine.

Kollwitz, Käthe (1867-1945), German artist known for her lithographs, woodcuts, and sculpture. Opposed to social injustice, she often depicted human misery and tragedy using the theme of mother and child. Among her well-known works are *War* (1923), a series of 7 wood-block prints, and the sculptures *The Mother* and *The Father* (1931-32), a war memorial.

Köln *See:* Cologne.

Komodo dragon (*Varanus komodoensis*), largest of living lizards, reaching a length of 10 ft (3 m). It lives on Komodo and a few other Indonesian islands.

Komondor, all-white Hungarian sheep dog. These dogs weigh approximately 90 lb (40 kg), and are about 31 in (76 cm) tall. Komondors were brought to Hungary in the late 9th century by Magyar invaders.

Kongo, kingdom of central Africa from the 15th to the 18th century, covering an area now in Angola and Zaïre, south of the Congo River. The king or *Mani-Kongo* ruled from the capital of Mbanza over a hierarchy of provincial and village governments, exercising political and religious authority without military force. The Kongolese traded in ivory, copper, and slaves. The Portuguese, who first explored the area in 1482, began converting the Kongolese to Christianity, but soon also became active in enslaving them. Portuguese slave trade seriously weakened the hierarchy of the kingdom, and Portugal took control by invading the Kongo in 1665, killing the king. By the early 18th century the kingdom was destroyed.

Konoye, Prince (Fumimaro Konoye; 1891-1945), Japanese premier (1937-39, 1940-41). A moderate, he appeased the military extremists and so furthered expansionism. His suicide prevented his trial as a war criminal after World War II.
See also: Japan; World War II.

Kon-Tiki *See:* Heyerdahl, Thor.

Kookaburra, or laughing jackass (*Dacelo novaguineae*), crow-sized bird, an Australian kingfisher, named for its gurgling, laughing call.

Koop, Charles Everett (1916-), U.S. surgeon general (1982-89). Known for his vigorous opposition to cigarette smoking and abortion, in 1987 Koop proposed extensive sex education and the use of condoms to halt the spread of AIDS.
See also: Surgeon general of the United States.

Kootenay *See:* Kutenai.

Koppel, Ted (Edward James Koppel; 1940-), U.S. news reporter, host of the popular T.V. news program *Nightline*. A Vietnam war correspondent, Koppel was made chief diplomatic correspondent for ABC News in 1971. He became famous for his coverage of the Iran hostage crisis in 1979 and has won many journalistic awards.

Koran, sacred scripture of the religion of Islam and the supreme authority of the Islamic tradition. To Muslims the book is not only divinely inspired but enshrines the actual words of God, as made known by the angel Gabriel to Muhammad in the 7th century A.D. After his death in 632 these sayings were collected in the Koran, and a standard text was formulated about 652. Basically the Koran is a collection of laws, moral teachings, and stories written in highly charged, poetic Arabic, much of it rhymed. About 80,000 words long, it is made up of 114 *suras*, or chapters, arranged according to length from the longest to the shortest—except for the first, "The Opening," which is a brief prayer, the equivalent of the Lord's Prayer in Christianity. Just as the word *Islam* means "surrender" to the will of God, so the Koran passionately demands this same spiritual surrender. The Koran, it teaches, is the revelation of God, known in Arabic as *Allah*, who is compassionate and merciful. It was given to Muhammad, last and greatest of the prophets, but Adam, Noah, Abraham, Moses, and Jesus are also counted among the prophets. However, the requirement in the Koran that the faithful should make at least one pilgrimage to Mecca probably reflects earlier Arab religions, and the complete subordination of women in the Koran is also in the Arabic tradition.

The Koran sets forth many rules governing moral behavior and social life. Alcoholic drinks and gambling are forbidden. The Koran is far more than a religious scripture. Because, as the first book written in Arabic, it formed a point of unity for all Arabs and for the diverse peoples they conquered, it is in a sense the foundation of Islamic civilization, as well as the molder and preserver of the Arabic language. As it is forbidden to recite the Koran in any language other than Arabic, the language was perpetuated in its purest form, with no corruption from the languages of the many peoples who were converted to Islam. The Koran today is the inspiration and guide for millions of Muslims.

See also: Islam.

Korea, peninsula (600 mi/966 km long) of eastern Asia that separates the Yellow Sea and the Sea of Japan. Korea has been divided since the end of the Korean War in 1953 into 2 countries: the communist Democratic People's Republic (North Korea) and the Republic of Korea (South Korea). This artificial division, and incidents and tensions along the border between the 2 (near the 38th parallel of latitude), give little credibility to the Korean name for the peninsula: *Choson*, Land of the Morning Calm. The Koreans are a remarkable people, the heirs of an ancient civilization. Korean astronomers were studying the heavens one hundred years before the birth of Christ. Koreans were printing from movable metal type in the late 1300s, about 50 years before Johann Gutenberg used this method in Europe. In the late 1500s a Korean engineer built what was probably the world's first suspension bridge.

Land and climate. Korea (85,677 sq mi/221,903 sq km) is mostly mountainous, with the main ranges along the east and in the north. In the extreme northeast, Mt. Kwanmo rises to 8,337 ft (2,541 m). There are large coastal plains in the west, and lesser plains and river valleys among the mountains. The northern boundary with China and the Soviet Union is marked mainly by the Yalu and Tumen rivers. Most Korean rivers flow west and south from the mountains to the Yellow Sea. The southward-flowing Naktong River empties into the Korean Strait, which separates the peninsula from Japan.

Korea has a moderate climate. Winters are mild in the south but cold elsewhere, and summers everywhere are hot. Rainfall, higher in the south than in the north, occurs mainly during summer.

Korea is at present divided into South Korea, with an area of 38,316 sq mi (99,237 sq km) and North Korea, 46,540 sq mi (120,538 sq km). Running along the border between the 2 is a demilitarized zone (487 sq mi/1,261 sq km), in which stands Panmunjom, the scene of North-South negotiations.

People. Although South Korea is smaller, it is much more densely populated than North Korea. Korea's 2 largest cities are the 2 capitals: Seoul (South Korea) and Pyongyang (North Korea). Other important centers in the South are Pusan, the chief port; Inchon, a port on the Yellow Sea; and Taegu and Taeyan. Northern towns include the ports of Chongjin and Hungnam; and Sinuiju, a commercial center. More than 60 of every 100 Koreans live in the towns. Most Koreans are farmers, and many still live in traditional small houses, which have clay walls, thatched roofs, and doors, windows and interior partitions of oiled paper. Buddhism, Confucianism, and Christianity all have followers, and animism also survives. In the North, as in other Communist countries, all religious beliefs are discouraged.

Economy. In both North and South Korea less than half the working population is engaged in agriculture. Rice is the leading crop, followed by barley, wheat, and millet. Other crops include oats, beans, cotton, corn, and potatoes. Most of North Korea's land is farmed by cooperatives and agriculture is highly mechanized. Most of Korea's mineral wealth is in the North, where large amounts of coal, iron ore, lead, zinc, copper, tungsten, nickel, manganese, oil and graphite are mined. The South has some of the world's largest deposits of tungsten (the Sangdong mine) but only small deposits of coal, iron ore, and other minerals.

South Korea's chief industry is cotton textiles, but silk is also important. Other products include cement, paper, chemicals, electrical goods, and steel. The North has many industries, including iron and steel, chemicals, textiles (cotton, wool, silk, and manufactured fibers), cement, and fertilizers. Hydroelectric power production is being expanded.

History. The half-legendary founder of the kingdom of Choson was Kija, who led a group of exiles from China to Korea in 1122 B.C. But there were other kingdoms on the peninsula, and Korea was not united until the 7th century A.D. Most of its early civilization was destroyed by the Mongol invasions (1231-92), but with the establishment of the Yi dynasty (1392) Korea entered a golden age that lasted until 1592, when Japan invaded the peninsula.

Although the invaders were finally driven out, the Koreans never fully recovered from the years of bloody fighting. For 300 years Korea, known as the Hermit Kingdom, cut itself off from the world. In the late 1800s, Japan and the United States began trading with Korea. In 1910 Japan annexed Korea. After 35 years of Japanese exploitation, Korea was liberated in 1945

Korea, North

Capital:	Pyongyang
Area:	46,540 sq mi (120,538 sq km)
Population:	21,234,000
Language:	Korean
Government:	People's republic
Independent:	1948
Head of gov.:	Prime minister
Per capita:	U.S. $3,035
Mon. unit:	1 North Korean won = 100 chon

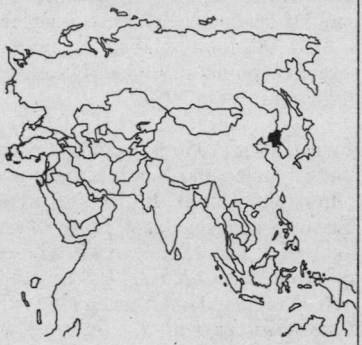

by Russia in the North and by the United States in the South. Despite United Nations intervention, no agreement was reached on a united Korea. The North became a rigidly controlled Communist state under the former guerrilla leader Kim Il Sung. Free elections held in the South, under UN supervision, produced a republic under Syngman Rhee.

On June 25, 1950, the Communists of the North invaded South Korea, thus beginning the Korean War. The heavy fighting was eventually stopped by an armistice between the UN forces and the Communists, and by the establishment of the demilitarized zone (1953). Since then the uneasy peace has often been disturbed.

In South Korea, Syngman Rhee became increasingly autocratic and unpopular, and in 1960, after his opponents charged election-rigging, he left Korea. After a confused period of military rule, democratic government was restored (1963) by General Park Chung Hee, who was elected president and returned to power repeatedly. In July 1979 General Park Chung Hee was assassinated and replaced by General Chun Doo Hwan, who established his own autocratic rule. In 1987 Roh Tae Woo was elected president of South Korea. He was succeeded by the first elected civilian president Kim Young

Korea, South

Capital:	Seoul
Area:	38,316 sq mi (99,237 sq km)
Population:	46,417,000
Language:	Korean
Government:	Republic
Independent:	1948
Head of gov.:	Prime minister
Per capita:	U.S. $9,700
Mon. unit:	1 Won = 100 chon

Sam in 1992, who continued the liberalization proces started in 1987. In North Korea Kim Il Sung continued his policy of regimented development until his death in 1994. He was succeeded by his son Kim Young Il. While in the 1990s the north had to deal with starvation, the south experienced a severe economic recession. In South Korea Kim Dae Young became head of government in 1997.

Korean War (1950-53), conflict between forces of the UN (primarily the United States and South Korea) and forces of North Korea and (later) communist China. In 1945 Korea was divided along latitude 38°N, Russia occupying lands north of this line, and the United States those south of it. The war began when North Korea launched a surprise invasion against South Korea and UN forces were sent to assist South Korea under Gen. Douglas MacArthur. By Nov. 1950 Chinese troops had joined North Korean forces and the fighting was situated over the 38th parallel. MacArthur was replaced in April 1951 by Gen. Matthew B. Ridgway. Two years of negotiations achieved an armistice signed at Panmunjom on July 27, 1953.
See also: Korea; United Nations.

Kornberg, Arthur (1918-), U.S. biochemist awarded with Severo Ochoa the 1959 Nobel Prize for physiology or medicine for discovering an enzyme (DNA polymerase) that could produce from a mixture of nucleotides exact replicas of DNA molecules. He thus extended Ochoa's related work.
See also: Biochemistry; Deoxyribonucleic Acid.

Korsakoff's syndrome, amnesic state in which, because of an inability to record new memory traces, a person can carry out complex tasks learned before his or her illness but cannot learn the simplest new skills. The syndrome is often transient and has a good prognosis in head injury. In alcoholism (where the syndrome, sometimes called alcoholic dementia, is caused by a lack of thiamine, a B vitamin that is destroyed by alcohol) and in other conditions where destruction is irreversible, the prognosis is poor and prolonged institutional care may be required.

Korzeniowski, Józef *See:* Conrad, Joseph.

Kosciusko, Thaddeus (1746-1817), Polish soldier and patriot who fought in the American Revolution. In 1794 he led an unsuccessful fight for Poland's unification and independence from Russia and Prussia.
See also: Poland.

Košice (German: *Kaschau*; Hungarian: *Kassa*; pop. 196,200), city in Slovakia, on the Hornad River. Since the end of World War II it has been the chief industrial city of the region of Slovakia, with large steelworks as well as chemical, food-processing, and textile plants. The old center city was established by Hungary in 1241; its St. Elizabeth cathedral was built in the 14th century. The region became part of the newly established Czechoslovakia in 1918. It was controlled by Hungary and Germany during World War II, but returned to Czechoslovak control in 1945. Since 1993 it is controlled by the Slovak Republic.
See also: Czechoslovakia.

Kosinski, Jerzy (1933-91), Polish-born U.S. writer best known for his semi-autobiographical novel *The Painted Bird* (1965). Its vivid, often shockingly brutal imagery deals with "daily life among the violations of the spirit and body of human beings." Among his other works are *Steps* (1968), for which he won a National Book Award, and *Being There* (1971).

Kossuth, Lajos (1802-94), Hungarian patriot and statesman who campaigned against Austrian rule and led the Hungarian revolution of 1848-49. A minister in the government set up in 1848, he engineered Hungary's declaration of independence as a republic the following year and became president. Austria, with the aid of Russian troops, forced a surrender, and Kossuth fled. He was received as a hero in the United States and England, where he lived for many years, and he died in Italy.
See also: Hungary.

Kosygin, Aleksei Nikolaevich (1904-80), Soviet premier, 1964-80. In 1939 he was appointed to the central committee of the Communist party; in 1960 he became first deputy to Nikita Khrushchev, whom he succeeded. Sharing leadership with Leonid Brezhnev, Kosygin concentrated on modernizing industry and agriculture.
See also: Union of Soviet Socialist Republics.

Koufax, Sandy (1935-), U.S. baseball player. Koufax is considered one of the best left-handed pitchers of all time. His achievements include winning 3 Cy Young awards (1963, 65, 66), the Most Valuable Player (MVP) award (1963), striking-out 382 batters in one season (1965), and pitching 4 no-hit games. Koufax pitched with the Brooklyn and (later) Los Angeles Dodgers (1955-66). In 1972 he was inducted into the National Hall of Fame.

Koumiss *See:* Kumiss.

Kouprey, also known as the Indonesian forest ox, rare wild cattle found in southeastern Asia. Six ft (1.8 m) tall at the shoulder, kouprey have small ears and a long tail, with the males (bulls) having large horns and blackish-brown hides. Females (cows) and calves are gray.

Koussevitzky, Serge (1874-1951), Russian-born U.S. conductor. He left the USSR for England in 1920 and settled in the United States, where he became conductor of the Boston Symphony Orchestra (1924-49). In 1940 he established the Berkshire Music Center at Stockbridge, Mass. He is remembered as a champion of contemporary composers.

Kowloon, Juilong, or Chiulung (pop. 799,100), peninsula across Kowloon Bay from the island of Hong Kong, near Guangzhou (Canton), southern China, but part of the British Crown Colony of Hong Kong since 1860. Only 4 sq mi (10 sq km), it is one of the most densely populated areas in the world. It is an important transportation and commercial link between the People's Republic of China and the West. As part of British Hong Kong it was reverted to Chinese control in 1997.
See also: Hong Kong.

Krakatoa, volcanic island in the Sunda Strait, Indonesia. The eruption of Aug. 1883, one of the most violent ever known, caused a tidal wave killing 36,000 people in neighboring Java and Sumatra, and threw debris as far as Madagascar.

Kraków, or Cracow (pop. 214,400), city in south-central Poland, on the Vistula River. By the 8th century the city was a major trading center on routes between Europe and Asia. It was the capital of Poland from the late Middle Ages until Warsaw was made capital in 1596. Dating from that period are the Jagiellonian University (founded 1364), the 14th-century cathedral and market square, and the 16th-century royal castle. From the 18th century it was at times under Austrian, Prussian, and Russian rule, but it has once again been part of Poland since 1920. It is now a manufacturing center for iron and steel, chemicals, textiles, and other products.
See also: Poland.

Kramer, Jack (John Albert Kramer; 1921-), U.S. tennis player, Wimbledon singles (1947) and doubles (1946-47) champion. He won the U.S. singles (1946-47), doubles (1940-41, 43, 47) and mixed doubles (1941) titles. In 1942, Kramer won 10 straight singles tournaments and in 1946 and 1947 was a member of the United States Davis Cup team that defeated Australia in the finals. An active promoter and organizer of professional tennis tours, Kramer was elected to the National Lawn Tennis Hall of Fame in 1968.

Krebs, Sir Hans Adolf (1900-81), German-born British biochemist awarded (with F.A. Lipmann) the 1953 Nobel Prize for physiology or medicine for his discovery of the citric acid cycle, or Krebs cycle, the principle means by which living organisms produce energy.
See also: Biochemistry.

Kreisler, Fritz (1875-1962), Austrian-U.S. violinist. He was an extremely popular performer, known for his elegance of style. A collector of manuscripts of violin music, he published violin pieces of his own composition which he at first attributed to various baroque and classical composers. He composed the operettas *Apple Blossom* and *Sissy* as well as numerous violin pieces, including *Liebesfreud*, *Liebesleid*, and *Caprice*. His arrangements of compositions by earlier composers became part of the standard repertoire.

Kremlin, fortified portion of medieval Russian cities, originally a place of refuge to nearby inhabitants; especially, the Kremlin in Moscow, now the political and administrative center of the Russian Federation. The greater part of the Moscow Kremlin dates from the 15th and 16th centuries. Peter the Great transferred the capital to St. Petersburg (1712), but in 1918 the Russian regime returned the government to Moscow and the Kremlin. A leading tourist attraction, the Kremlin contains 3 cathedrals, a bell tower, and the throne and banqueting hall of the czars.
See also: Moscow.

Kreps, Juanita Morris (1921-), U.S. economist, author, public official. Kreps was U.S. secretary of commerce (1977-79), the first woman to hold that office. She has been a teacher of economics at colleges since 1945, and vice president of Duke University since 1979. In 1972 Kreps became one of the 10 public directors on the newly reorganized board of directors of the New York Stock Exchange, the first woman to serve on the NYSE's policy-making board. Her writings include books dealing with the rights of women and the aged: Lifetime Allocation of Work and Income: Essays in the Economics of Aging (1971); Women and the American Economy (1976).

Krill, small marine animal (genus *Euphausia*) resembling shrimp. There are over 90 species, ranging from 3/8 in (1 cm) to nearly 6 in (15 cm). Krill live in the open sea at depths of more than 6,600 ft (2,000 m). Most species have special organs (photophores) that make them visible in the dark. At night they swim in swarms of thousands to the surface to feed on microorganisms. Krill are an important food source for birds, seals, and whales, especially blue and finback whales. Rich in vitamin A, krill have been considered as a possible human food source.

Krishna *See:* Bhagavad-Gita; Vishnu.

Kris Kringle *See:* Santa Claus.

Kroeber, Alfred Louis (1876-1960), U.S. anthropologist who made contributions to many areas of cultural anthropology and archeology, particularly with reference to Native Americans. His books include *The Nature of Culture* (1952) and *Style and Civilization* (1957).
See also: Anthropology.

Kruger, Paulus (1825-1904), South African Boer leader. He opposed the annexation (1877) of the Transvaal by the British and the Boer rebellion of 1880. He was elected president of the new self governing Transvaal Republic (1883). During the second Boer War (1899-1902) he went to Europe and sought vainly for support for the Boers.
See also: Boer War.

Krupa, Gene (1909-73), U.S. jazz musician, member of the Benny Goodman Orchestra (1935-38). The first famous drum soloist, Krupa was known for his frenzied performing style and exceptional drum technique. From 1938 to 1951 he played with his own successful band and continued to perform and tour with a quartet throughout the 1950s and 60s.

Krupp, family of German armaments makers. The firm was founded in Essen (1811) by **Friedrich Krupp** (1787-1826) with a small steel casting factory, and under his son, **Alfred Krupp** (1812-87), became the largest cast steel enterprise in the world, playing a key role in the Franco-Prussian War, World War I, and World War II. After World War II, **Alfred Krupp von Bohlen und Halbach** (1907-67), head of the firm from 1943, was imprisoned (1948-51) for war crimes. The company, now a public corporation, concentrates on heavy industrial equipment. In 1992, Krupp merged with Hoesch and in 1997 with Thyssen.

Krupskaya, Nadezhda Konstantinovna (1869-1939), Russian revolutionary and educational theorist. She married Vladimir Ilyich Lenin

(1898) while both were exiled in Siberia, thereafter sharing his life in Europe and after his return (1917) to Russia. An opponent of Stalin, she lost her considerable influence in the Communist party after Lenin's death.
See also: Russian Revolution; Lenin, V.I.

Krypton, gaseous element, symbol Kr; for physical constants see Periodic Table. Krypton was discovered by William Ramsay and M.W. Travers in 1898. It is a colorless, odorless, and chemically inert gas. Krypton is used in certain flash lamps for high-speed photography and some types of electric bulbs.

Kuala Lumpur (pop. 1,103,200), capital and largest city of Malaysia, on the South Malay Peninsula. It was founded in 1857 as a mining camp. The city owed much of its rapid growth to the local abundance of tin and rubber.
See also: Malaysia.

Kublai Khan (1216-94), Mongol emperor from 1259, founder of the Yüan dynasty of China and grandson of Genghis Khan. He defeated the Chinese Sung dynasty in 1279. Under his rule China flourished both economically and culturally; his new capital Cambuluc, described by Marco Polo, became the nucleus of modern Peking.
See also: Mongol Empire.

Kubrick, Stanley (1928-), U.S. film director and writer noted for the strong social commentary of his work. His most famous films include the controversial *Dr. Strangelove* (1964), which treated the accidental triggering of nuclear war as a bitter joke; *2001: A Space Odyssey* (1968), his own story of humanity's distant past and future, which won an Academy Award for special effects; and *A Clockwork Orange* (1971), a terrifying look at criminal rehabilitation. *Paths of Glory* (1958) was Kubrick's first feature-length film, and *Lolita* (1962) his treatment of Vladimir Nabokov's novel of obsession. More recent movies include *The Shining* (1980) and *Full Metal Jacket* (1987).

Kuching (pop. 150,000), capital of Sarawak, a Malaysian state on the island of Borneo. Archeologists confirm it to have been an ancient trading center. The modern city was founded by the British in 1841. Located on the Sarawak River 18 mi (29 km) inland from the South China Sea, it is a major livestock trading and fishing center. It exports rubber, pepper, and timber. Kuching is home to a modern airport and the Sarawak Museum, which is set in scenic gardens and exhibits collections representing the history and archeology of Borneo.
See also: Sarawak.

Kudu, large antelope (*Tragelaphus strepsiceros*) with long spiral horns. It feeds mainly on leaves. The coat is fawn or gray with white spots and stripes. The greater kudu lives in Africa, south of the Sahara, in scrub or dry bush country. The lesser kudu lives in the northeastern corner of Africa.

Kudzu, long semi-woody vine (*Pueraria thunbergiana*) belonging to the pea family. Kudzu is common to the southeastern United States, where it was introduced in the 1800s from Asia. It can grow to 60 ft (18 m) and has broad leaves. The pealike purple flowers have a yellow patch on the upper petal and smell like grapes. Kudzu has been used as a decorative porch vine, as food for livestock, and as ground cover to prevent soil erosion, but it grows so quickly out of control that it is most often treated as a weed. A fine white flour can be made from the peeled and washed roots.

Kuhn, Richard (1900-67), Austrian chemist. He was awarded the 1938 Nobel Prize for chemistry, but the Nazi government prevented him from accepting the award until after World War II. Noted for his research into vitamins and carotenoids (yellow to red coloring found in plants and animals), he isolated vitamins B_2 (riboflavin) and B_6.
See also: Chemistry.

Kuibyshev *See:* Kuybyshev.

Kuiper, Gerard Peter (1905-73), Dutch-born U.S. astronomer who discovered carbon dioxide in the atmosphere of Mars (1948) and satellites of Uranus and Neptune (1948-49). He directed the Ranger space program (early 1960s), which provided close-up photographs of the moon essential in the landing site selection for the moon landings (1969).
See also: Astronomy.

Kukenaan Falls *See:* Cuquenán Falls.

Ku Klux Klan, secret organization originally begun (1866) by ex-Confederates in the U.S. South to conduct a campaign of terror against newly enfranchised blacks. Its members disguised themselves in hoods and white sheets and used whippings and lynchings to terrorize their victims. Although the first Klan was officially disbanded in 1869, many members remained active throughout reconstruction and beyond. The second Klan, organized in 1915, extended its hostilities to Jews, Catholics, pacifists, and the foreign born. In the 1920s it had 5 million members and its political power extended to the North. Officially disbanded in 1944, the Klan revived in response to civil rights activism of the 1960s and was involved in violent racial confrontations in the early 1980s.
See also: Racism.

Kukui (*Aleurites moluccana*), tree of the spurge family, Hawaii's state tree. Commonly found on mountain slopes, it has light green leaves and may grow as tall as 60 ft (18 m). Its branches spread out and grow long, making it a popular shade tree. The oil produced from these trees is used for fuel and in the manufacture of varnish.

Kumiss, koumis, kumys, or koumyss, alcoholic milk beverage of Asian origin. Primarily a product of the former USSR, it is traditionally made from mare's or camel's milk. This thick, sour, effervescent drink was at one time used for treating tuberculosis in sanitoriums.

Kumquat, dwarf evergreen (genus *Fortunella*) belonging to the rue family, grown for its citrus fruits, which resemble small oranges. The kumquat tree measures from 10 to 15 ft (3 to 5 m); it is grown in China, Japan, and in warm regions of the United States such as Florida and California. The fruits are eaten whole or in preserves.

Kuomintang *See:* Chiang Kai-shek.

Kurchatovium *See:* Element 104.

Kurds, people of Kurdistan in western Asia. Traditionally nomadic, most Kurds today are settled farmers and are Muslims. Kurds have struggled vigorously against various rulers for an independent Kurdistan; in the 1970s Kurds fought Iraqi troops unsuccessfully for self-government. With the defeat of Iraq in the Persian Gulf War (1991), the Kurds once again took up arms against Iraqi authority. The Kurds, lacking adequate military equipment, were supressed, but then were subject to massacres staged by the Iraqi military. Fearing annihilation, the Kurds fled their homes for the borders of Turkey and Iran. This mass migration caused incredible suffering and thousands of deaths and forced the U.S. government to establish refugee camps in the north of Iraq.

Kuril Islands, chain of 56 volcanic islands, stretching from the Kamchatka Peninsula of Siberia to Hokkaido Island, Japan. Sparsely inhabited, the islands are the subject of a territorial dispute, held by Russia since the Soviet occupation during World War II but claimed by Japan.

Kurosawa, Akira (1910-), Japanese film director. Renowned for cinematography, his films include *Rashomon* (1950), *Seven Samurai* (1954), and *Ran* (1985), an interpretation of *King Lear*. He often adapts foreign classics, blending Eastern and Western styles.

Kuroshio *See:* Japan Current.

Kush, ancient kingdom located along the Nile River in what is now Sudan. Lasting from about 2000 B.C. to A.D. 350, Kush was an important center of trade and learning. Exports included cattle and gold. It was also an important slave trading center. The people of Kush developed their own spoken language, writing system, architectural styles, and religion. Exact details of the kingdom's decline and end remain unknown.

Kushan Empire, dynasty of northern India, Afghanistan, and central Asia, from A.D. 50 to the 3rd century. Emperors of the dynasty opened important trades routes between China and India and between India and Rome. Along these trade routes both goods and ideas were exchanged. The dynasty's greatest ruler and an important proponent of Buddhism, its chief religion, was Kanishka, who lived in the 1st century A.D. During his reign Buddhism probably first reached China, and influential artistic concepts from Greece and Rome were incorporated into Indian religious art.
See also: Kanishka.

Kuskokwim River, second longest river in Alaska. Originating south of the Yukon, it flows southwest for about 600 mi (970 km) and empties into Kuskokwim Bay, an inlet of the Bering Sea.

Kutenai, Native American tribe of the U.S.-Canadian border. Once mountain dwellers, their activities included hunting and fishing. They now live in reservations in Idaho, Montana, and British Columbia.

Kuvasz, breed of powerful, sturdily built dog. Bred in Hungary, it was popular in the Middle Ages as a guard dog of the nobility. Used now as a shepherd and guard dog, the typical kuvasz has a pure white, mostly short-haired coat, stands 26 in (66 cm), and weighs about 70 lbs (32 kg).

Kuwait, small independent Arab state on the northwest coast of the Persian Gulf, bordered by Iraq (northwest) and Saudi Arabia (south). Though mostly desert, it has been a major oil-producing country and possesses more than 10% of the world's estimated oil reserves. Its independence was jeopardized in Aug. 1990, when Iraq, on the pretext of settling a border dispute but also interested in obtaining control of Kuwaiti oil, invaded the country and announced its annexation. The ensuing Persian Gulf War (begun in Jan. 1991) pitted the United States and its allies, with the sanction of UN resolutions calling for the restoration of Kuwait's independent status, in a military action against Iraq to roll back the invasion.
Economy. Kuwait's traditional economy was based on the export of wool and hides and pearl fishing. With the discovery (1946) and exploitation of its huge oil reserves, the enormous wealth generated by the petroleum industry allowed the government to establish a widespread social welfare system that made Kuwait one of the world's wealthier nations on the basis of per capita income. In the 1960s the government also embarked on an ambitious modernization and diversification program. Until the Iraqi invasion, the capital, also called Kuwait, was a thoroughly modern city. The ruler, called *emir*, appointed the prime minister. More than half the population was madeup of non-Kuwaiti citizens, who held a majority of the jobs, as many native Kuwaitis lacked adequate education and training. The government had put special effort into training Kuwaitis to help them take more control of their economy.
History. In the early 19th century Arabs settled on the southern shore of Kuwait Bay and elected the head of the Al-Sabah family to be their ruler, establishing a dynasty unbroken to the present. Even as part of the Ottoman Empire, Kuwait retained its independent government under the Al-Sabahs. It was a British protectorate from 1897 until 1961, when it became independent. In 1967 Kuwait sided with Egypt in its war against Israel, as it did again in 1973. Also in that year, Kuwait, a member of the Organization of Petroleum Exporting Countries (OPEC), joined with other Arab oil-exporting countries in halting oil shipments to countries that supported Israel. In 1976 the emir dissolved the National Assembly. A new assembly was elected in 1981 but dissolved by the emir in 1986.During the Iran-Iraq War (1980-88) Iran began attacking Kuwaiti oil tankers because Kuwait had sided with Iraq and was aiding that country with financial and other support. In 1987 Kuwait requested help from the Soviet Union and the United States to protect its shipping. The Soviet Union leased some ships to Kuwait that carried the Soviet flag, which prevented Iran from attacking them. The U.S. Navy provided armed escorts for Kuwaiti-flagged ships in the Persian Gulf.

Kuwait

Capital:	Kuwait
Area:	6,880 sq mi (17,818 sq km)
Population:	1,913,000
Language:	Arabic
Government:	Monarchy (Emirate)
Independent:	1961
Head of gov.:	Prime minister
Per capita:	U.S. $17,390
Mon. unit:	1 Kuwaiti dinar = 1,000 fils

Soon after a cease-fire in 1979 ended Iran-Iraq hostilities, Iraq turned on its former ally and demanded settlement of a dispute involving an oil field along their mutual border and some small islands in the Persian Gulf. In Aug. 1990 Iraq sent troops into the lightly defended country and proclaimed it part of Iraq. Saudi Arabia and other Gulf states, fearful that a powerful Iraq might continue its agression against them, asked the United States and the United Nations to condemn the action and restore Kuwait to its independence. A large multinational force, overwhelmingly composed of the U.S. military, rushed to Saudi Arabia to protect it against aggression. In Jan. 1991 this force commenced hostilities against Iraq and its troops in Kuwait with the aim of restoring the pre-invasion status of Kuwait. However, as many Kuwaitis fled the country and as Kuwait itself suffered so much damage from the occupation and the allied efforts to dislodge it, expectations are that restoring Kuwait to its former condition will be a long process.

Kuwait (pop. 44,300), capital and the most important city in the country of Kuwait and founded in the 18th century by a tribal confederation of Arabic people. It is the chief economic center with an excellent harbor on the Persian Gulf. The port was established in the 18th century and was a shipbuilding center. The city is highly modernized because of the wealth generated by the petroleum industry which has developed since the end of World War II. In Aug. of 1990, the military forces of Iraq invaded the nation of Kuwait and occupied the city. This event precipitated the Persian Gulf War.
See also: Persian Gulf War.

Kuybyshev, now known as Samara (pop. 1,300,000), city in east-central European Russia, located on the Volga River. It is an important port and industrial center, where automobiles, locomotives, and aircraft are manufactured. It is also the site of a hydroelectric power plant. Founded as Samara in 1586, renamed in 1935. In 1991 the name reverted back to Samara.
See also: Union of Soviet Socialist Republics.

Kwajalein, world's largest atoll, situated in the Marshall Islands in the west central Pacific. Now in the U.S. Trust Territory of the Pacific Islands, Kwajalein is the site of a U.S. military missile range.

Kwakiutl, Native American tribe of Wakashan linguistic stock, native to Vancouver Island and coastal British Columbia, Canada. Skilled in fishing and crafts, they had a strictly hierarchical society in which the potlatch ceremony played a significant part.

Kwashiorkor, severe condition of protein deficiency common in children of some areas of the Third World. It causes excess body fluid, distended abdomen, skin and hair changes, loss of appetite, apathy, diarrhea, liver disturbance, stunted growth, and sometimes, death. Its name derives from the Ghanaian for "deposed one," from its occurrence in children who are removed from breastfeeding too soon.

Kyanite, or cyanite, blue or white aluminum silicate mineral found in metamorphic rocks, occurring as long crystal blades. Because it is heat resistant, kyanite is used in spark plugs and as lining for ovens used in the manufacture of glass. Some kyanite is used for jewelry. It is found in the United States, India, Italy and the former USSR.

Kyd, Thomas (1558-94), English dramatist whose *The Spanish Tragedy* (c.1586) was a prototype of the Elizabethan and Jacobean revenge tragedy. The work is partly modeled on Seneca but is more lurid and more psychologically acute. Kyd may have written a version of the Hamlet story.

Kyoto (pop. 1,394,900), capital of Kyoto prefecture, Honshu Island, Japan, about 25 mi (40 km) northeast of Osaka. The national capital from its foundation A.D. 794 until supplanted by Tokyo in 1868, Kyoto is rich in architectural relics and art treasures. Still a cultural and religious center, it also has leading educational establishments and large-scale mixed industry with manufactures that include electrical equipment, cameras, chemicals, silk, and porcelain.
See also: Japan.

Kyzyl Kum, or Kizil Kum, sandy desert of Central Asia, lying southeast of the Aral Sea and covering about 88,000 sq mi (228,000 sq km) of southern Kazakhstan and northern Uzbekistan between the Syr Darya and Amu Darya rivers. Some parts have been irrigated for crop growing (cotton, rice, and wheat), and the area has significant deposits of gold.

L

L, the 12th letter of the English alphabet. It is derived from the Semitic *lamedh* (perhaps itself based on an Egyptian hieroglyphic), representing an oxgoad, and from the Greek *lambda*. In Roman numerals, L is 50. The British symbol for the pound sterling (£) is another form of the letter, derived from the Latin *libra*, originally a pound in weight.

Labor *See:* Birth.

Labor *See:* Labor movement.

Labor, Department of, federal department, independent since 1913, responsible for U.S. workers' welfare. Headed by the secretary of labor, a cabinet member, it is concerned with the enforcement of federal laws regulating hours, wages, and safety measures, collects and issues industrial statistics, administers job-training programs, and provides information in labor disputes. Its specialized divisions include the Occupational Safety and Health Administration, the Bureau of Labor Statistics, the Employment and Training Administration, the Bureau of International Labor Affairs, and the Labor-Management Services Administration.

Labor Day, official holiday in the United States and Canada since 1894, held on the first Monday in Sept. to honor the workers. In socialist countries, labor is honored on May Day (May 1).

Labor force, that part of a nation's population that is either employed or capable of employment. In the United States, the labor force includes all citizens above the age of 16 who are working, actively looking for work, or in the armed forces. Those who are retired, full-time homemakers, students, or handicapped are excluded.

Labor movement, movement to organize industrial workers and improve their working conditions. The need for organized labor did not occur until the late 19th century when the poorly treated and underpaid unskilled labor force—including children under 16 years old—in urban areas reached 40%. A secret society made up of Philadelphia garment workers, the Knights of Labor (1869), organized both skilled and unskilled laborers. This group declined by the 1880s after an unsuccessful strike against the railroad tycoon Jay Gould (1886).

In 1881 the predecessor of the American Federation of Labor (AFL) had its beginning. It was organized by specific craft unions, not workers as a whole; therefore unskilled workers were not represented. This loose federation consisted of the iron workers, molders, printers, carpenters, glass workers, and cigar makers. Samuel Gompers, its leader from the cigar makers group, proposed a 3-point program: practical benefits of higher wages and better working conditions, federalism allowing each union considerable internal freedom to organize and operate according to its own needs and style, and non-federally involved collective bargaining that also rewarded politicians who held pro-Union opinions and defeated those that did not.

Despite the successful beginning of the AFL, labor organizers faced employers reluctant to recognize and work with unions; *blacklisting* (agreement between companies not to hire pro-union workers or to hire those who signed anti-union documents called *yellow dog contracts*), and court injunctions, which usually resulted in pro-management decisions. It was not until the failure of business in the Great Depression and the New Deal policy of President Franklin Roosevelt that union organization and workers' rights found widespread support.

The Congress of Industrial Organizations (CIO) helped with a favorable attitude in Congress, launched a campaign to organize great industries such as steel, automobiles, oil, and rubber—over the bitter opposition of the managements of these corporations. Federal legislation favored both sides: the *Wagner Act* (1935), which protected the right for unions to organize and participate in *collective bargaining*—negotiations between management and elected union officials—and the *Taft-Hartley Act* (1947), which protected non-union workers and allowed the Attorney General to suspend strikes after 90 days.

In 1955, headed by George Meany (president of the AFL), the AFL and CIO merged to represent an organized labor voice before Congress and a strong united stand against industry. Not all unions became or remained members of this federation—such as the automobile workers headed by former CIO head Walter Reuther—due to political differences. Using AFL-CIO guidelines, unions and collective bargaining have become an essential part of U.S. industry. The groups elected to represent workers follow procedures for negotiations with management on wages, hours, pensions and health insurance, seniority rights of workers, and grievance procedures. When agreement is reached, a contract is signed by both sides—often to cover a 2 to 3 year period. If agreement cannot be reached by both parties, a neutral third party called a *mediator* suggests solutions. If a mediator cannot bring both parties to agreement, a specialist called an *arbitrator* hears both sides and renders a binding decision to which both sides must adhere.

Since the 1880s unions have helped to increase hourly wages, to reduce the length of the work week, to increase worker safety, provide insurance and pensions, and to support paid vacation and holiday time for workers. New and important unions have been established since the AFL-CIO merger, such as the United Farm Workers Union (UFW) in the 1960s, led by the Mexican-American labor leader Cesar E. Chavez of California.

Labor union *See:* Unions, labor.

Labour Party, English political party founded in 1900 by trade unions and socialist groups—the Independent Labour Party (1893) and the Fabian Society—with James Keir Hardie as its first leader. It gained nationwide support after World War I, first coming to power under Ramsay MacDonald in 1924. His second administration (1929-31) ended in coalition with the Conservatives, division within the party, and electoral defeat. The first effective socialist program was implemented by the Labour government of Clement Attlee (1945-51), instituting the National Health Service and nationalizing the Bank of England and major industries. Attlee was followed as leader by Hugh Gaitskell, who was succeeded at his death (1963) by Harold Wilson. Prime minister in 4 Labour governments (1964-70, 1974-76), he was succeeded by James Callaghan. Callaghan yielded leadership in 1979 to Michael Foot, a member of the party's left wing. As Labour became deeply embroiled in factionalism, several leaders resigned to form the new Social Democratic Party in 1981. After the party's decisive loss in the June 1983 general election, Neil Kinnock replaced Foot as leader. At the 1997 general elections, Labour achieved the highest gain in seats ever. Tony Blair became the new prime minister.

Labrador, large peninsula in northeast Canada. It is a land of long, severe winters with temperatures falling to –40°F (–40°C), and short, hot summers, during which temperatures rise to 80°F (27°C). Its population is about 97% white and 3% Inuit (Eskimos), Naskapi, and Montagnais. Labrador is rich in iron ore, timber, and cod fish. Its hydroelectric plant, which began operation in 1971 on the Churchill River at Churchill Falls, is one of the

largest in the Western Hemisphere, with a capacity of $5^1/_4$ million kilowatts of electricity.
See also: Canada.

Labrador retriever, breed of sporting dog originating in Newfoundland, Canada and further developed in England. A strongly built dog standing 21-24 in (93-100 cm) and weighing 60-75 lb (27-34 km), the Labrador has a stable temperament, a keen sense of smell, and an innate love of water. Distinctive features are its short, thick, water-resistant coat (usually black, but sometimes yellow or dark red-brown) and its thick-based "otter tail." The Labrador is used in hunting to retrieve waterfowl and other small game.

Labrador tea, 6 species of small evergreen shrubs (genus *Ledum*; especially, *L. groenlandicium*) containing in their aromatic leaves tannin and a mild narcotic that is the active ingredient in the tea and beer brewed from the leaves. These plants are found in swampy areas of subarctic North America, Greenland, and northern Europe.

La Brea tar pits, asphalt bog in Hancock Park, Los Angeles, containing skeletons of prehistoric (Pleistocene) animals, including mammoths, saber-toothed cats, and giant sloths, preserved by tar.
See also: Prehistoric animal.

Laburnum, genus of small trees belonging to the pea family (Fabaceae or Leguminosae), characterized by glossy green leaves, yellow blossoms, and fine-grained, hard wood. A poison called cytisine is present in their roots, seeds, and other parts. The common laburnum (*L. anagyroides*) is native to Asia and is also called golden chain, bean tree, and bean trefoil.

Labyrinth, complex of buildings or hedges with many passages and dead ends, designed to baffle strangers trying to find the way in or out; a maze. The most famous labyrinth of antiquity, according to Greek legend, was built in Crete by Daedalus to house the Minotaur. Other famous labyrinths were in Lemnia and in Italy. The maze at Hampton Court Palace, England, is an example of a garden labyrinth.

Lac, sticky residue secreted by a species of scale insect (*Laccifer lacca*) and used to produce shellac and lac dye. The secretion, called stick lac in its natural state, is harvested by gathering the twigs in which the insect resides.

Lace, fine openwork decorative fabric made by braiding, looping, knotting, or twisting thread, usually linen or cotton, sometimes silver and gold. Before 19th-century mechanization, it was handmade by needlepoint or with bobbins. Lace was developed in 16th-century Italy and Flanders.

La Ceiba (pop. 61,900), city in northern Honduras, located in the Gulf of Honduras at the base of Mt. Bonito. It is an industrial center and a major Caribbean port for the distribution of goods produced locally.
See also: Honduras.

Lacewing, insect of the order Neuroptera, named for its double pair of delicate, lacy wings. The two most common families are the green or golden-eyed lacewings (Hemerobiidae) and the smaller brown lacewings (Chrysopidae). These insects are also called stinkflies because of the strong odor they emit to repel predators. Larvae, often called aphid lions, use their large jaws to suck fluids from aphids and other insects.

Lacquer, solution used as a coating for wood, metal, paper, clothing, or porcelain to provide a lustrous, protective finish. Lacquers can be made from either natural (tree sap, resins, lac, cellulose) or synthetic compounds.

Lacrimal gland *See:* Tears.

Lacroix, Christian (1950-), French designer of *haute-couture* fashion. In 1987 the Council of Fashion Designers of America voted him best foreign designer. He is best known for his "bubble" dress.

La Crosse (pop. 97,904), city in western Wisconsin, seat of La Cross County, located at the junction of the Black, La Crosse, and Mississippi rivers. Founded in 1842, the city was named after the Native American game of lacrosse. Today it is active in manufacturing auto parts, aircraft instruments, and consumer goods.
See also: Wisconsin.

Lacrosse, team game derived by French settlers from the Native American game of baggataway, now the national game of Canada. It is played with a stick called a crosse having a net at one end. The crosse is used to catch, throw, and carry a hard rubber ball, with the aim of sending it into the opposing goal. In men's lacrosse, played in Canada, the United States, and the United Kingdom, each team has 10 members. Women's lacrosse is usually played with 12 to a side.

Lactic acid ($C_3H_6O_3$), organic acid that is the end product of the metabolism of sugar, the formation of which causes milk to sour. Lactic acid is produced in muscles after their cells have broken down glycogen for energy; it is this accumulation of lactic acid that causes muscle fatigue. Blood levels of lactic acid are also elevated in persons with lactic acidosis, diabetes, anemia, leukemia, and other abnormal conditions.
See also: Scheele, Carl Wilhelm.

Ladybug, lady beetle, or ladybird, small, almost round beetle of the family Coccinellidae. Ladybugs are named for their association with the Virgin Mary. Their shiny wing-cases are brightly colored (red, yellow, or black) and usually have patterns of spots (black with a red or yellow case, or red or yellow with a black case). They hibernate in groups under bark or in caves and rock crevices. They emerge in the spring to lay their eggs, and both adults and larvae feed on aphids and scale insects, thus playing an important role in controlling these insect pests. A few species eat plants, and the Mexican bean beetle is a pest of beans, alfalfa, clover, and other crops.

Lady's-slipper, moccasin flower, or squirrel's shoes, any of various species of the orchid family that bear a single flower on each stem. The lower petal is shaped like a slipper, and the sepals look like a bow securing it. Lady's-slippers are found in damp woodlands and bogs in North America, Europe, and Asia. They are fertilized by queen bumblebees, which are heavy enough to force their way in through a slit in the "slipper."

Lady's-thumb *See:* Smartweed.

Laënnec, René Théophile Hyacinthe (1781-1826), French surgeon, physician, and inventor of the stethoscope. Laënnec specialized in heart and lung pathology and is considered the founder of chest medicine. He described his research in *A Treatise on Mediate Auscultation* (1819).
See also: Stethoscope.

Laetrile, alleged anticancer drug (chemical name, amygdalin) created from an extract of apricot pits in 1926 by Ernst Krebs, Sr., and refined by his son, Ernst Krebs, Jr., who patented it in 1949. Though considered worthless by the medical establishment and banned by the U.S. Food and Drug Administration, it was legalized in 14 states by 1978, when a U.S. appeals court ruled that the drug could not be withheld from terminally ill people, since the government's criteria of "safety" and "effectiveness" had no meaning in their case.
See also: Cancer.

La Farge, John (1835-1910), U.S. artist and writer. He was noted for his fine mural painting and stained glass, chiefly executed for churches, such as the mural *Ascension* in the Church of the Ascension, New York City. He also produced fine watercolors and drawings and was a lecturer and writer of art criticism.

La Fayette, Marie Madeleine Pioche de la Vergne (1634-93), French writer. She is epsecially noted for *The Princess of Clèves* (1678), whose sensitivity and psychological realism make it the first great French novel. She also wrote *The Princess of Montponsier* (1622) and *Zayde* (1670).

Lafayette, Marquis de (1757-1834), French soldier and statesman who fought in the American Revolution and worked for French-American alliance. He came to America in 1777, joined George Washington's staff as major general, and fought in the campaigns of 1777-78 and at Yorktown (1781). On a visit to France (1779) he persuaded Louis XVI to send troops and a fleet to aid the colonists. In the French Revolution he supported the bourgeoisie, helped set up the National Assembly, drafted the Declaration of the Rights of Man, and commanded the National Guard, but he fell from power after ordering his troops (July 1791) to fire on the populace. In 1824 he revisited the United States, hailed as a hero. He was a leader of the July Revolution (1830) in France.
See also: French Revolution; Revolutionary War in America.

Laffite, Jean (c.1780-1825?), French pirate and smuggler who attacked Spanish ships south of New Orleans. He and his men received a pardon from President James Madison in return for aiding General Andrew Jackson against the British in 1815, but they later went back to piracy. When Laffite attacked U.S. ships (1820), the navy sailed against him, and he set out in his favorite ship, the *Pride*, never to be seen again.

La Follette, family name of 2 generations of influential U.S. politicians from Wisconsin. **Robert Marion La Follette, Sr**. (1855-1925) was a U.S. statesman and reform legislator. He served in the House of Representatives, 1885-91. As Wisconsin governor (1901-6), he was supported by progressive Republicans, and initiated the "Wisconsin idea" reform program, proposing direct primaries and a state civil service. He served as U.S. senator, 1906-25, during which time he founded the Progressive Party, opposed U.S. entry to World War I and the League of Nations, and ran unsuccessfully for president in 1924. One son, **Robert Marion La Follette, Jr.** (1895-1965), was U.S. senator from Wisconsin (1925-47) and another, **Philip Fox La Follette** (1897-1965), was governor of Wisconsin (1931-33, 1935-39).

La Fontaine, Jean de (1621-95), French writer. He is remembered especially for his *Fables* (1668-94), moral tales drawn from Aesop and Asian sources that he used to comment satirically on contemporary society, and for his humorous, bawdy *Tales and Novels in Verse* (1664-66).
See also: Canada.

LaFontaine, Sir Louis Hippolyte (1807-64), Canadian politician and judge. Leader of the French Canadians from 1837 and twice joint prime minister with Robert Baldwin (in 1842-43 and 1848-51, when the "great ministry's" legislation included the Rebellion Losses Bill). He was chief justice of Lower Canada from 1853-64.

Lagerkvist, Pär Fabian (1891-1974), Swedish poet, novelist, and dramatist, winner of the 1951 Nobel Prize for literature. He was much disturbed by World War I and later also protested against fascism. His works, which include the novels *The Hangman* (1933) and *Barabbas* (1950), and the play *Man Without a Soul* (1936), explore the problem of good and evil in humanity.

Lagerlöf, Selma (1858-1940), Swedish novelist, the first woman to win a Nobel Prize for literature (1909). Her works, rooted in legend and the folklore of her native Värmland, include *The Story of Gösta Berling*, *The Wonderful Adventure of Nils* (1906, a children's classic), and a trilogy, *The Ring of the Lowenskolds* (1931).

Lagos (pop. 1,125,000), former capital and chief port of Nigeria, on the Gulf of Guinea (West Africa). The city occupies Lagos, Victoria, and Iddo islands, between the Bight of Benin and Lagos Lagoon, and also part of the mainland, where its main deepwater harbor and the terminal of the Lagos-Kano-Nguru railroad are located at Apapa. Lagos has been a trade center since the 15th century. It now handles most of Nigeria's seaborne exports, mainly palm products, peanuts, cocoa, tin, hides, and skins. Manufactures include textiles, furniture, and metal products. Its university (1962) specializes in law, medicine, and business administration.
See also: Nigeria.

Lagrange, Joseph Louis (1736-1813), French mathematician and astronomer who made important contributions to calculus and differential equations and was influential in adopting the decimal system in metrics. He worked also on celestial mechanics, in particular explaining the moon's libration

(swinging movement). His most important work is the *Mécanique analytique*.
See also: Number theory.

La Guardia, Fiorello Henry (1882-1947), U.S. statesman and mayor of New York City. As a Republican member of Congress (1917-19, 1923-33) he supported liberalizing and prolabor measures, including the Norris-La Guardia Act forbidding the use of injunctions in labor disputes. As mayor (1933-45) he instituted major reforms in New York and fought corruption.

Lahore (pop. 3,150,000), city in eastern Pakistan, capital of the province of Punjab, lying on the Ravi River. Lahore is Pakistan's second largest city and is a center for education, steel production, film-making, and textile manufacturing. The city served as a capital for the Mogul and Sikh empires before being taken over by the British in 1849.
See also: Pakistan.

Laissez faire (French, "leave alone"), doctrine that opposes state intervention in economic affairs. First enunciated by the French physiocrats in the 18th century as a reaction against mercantilism, the idea was taken up by Scottish economist Adam Smith and became a cornerstone of classical economics.
See also: Smith, Adam.

Lake Agassiz, ancient North American lake that covered much of what is now the Canadian province of Manitoba and parts of other provinces and the United States. It was formed by melting glaciers during the last ice age. Lake Agassiz was the largest of the glacial lakes, reaching its maximum size (approximately 135,000 sq mi/350,000 sq km) between 7900 and 7500 B.C. The continued runoff from the glaciers caused the lake to drain into the Hudson Bay, except for the deeper areas that became smaller lakes such as Manitoba, Winnipeg, and Winnipegosis.

Lake Albano, crater lake inside an extinct volcano in west-central Italy, southeast of Rome in the Albani hills. Lake Albano served as a vacation spot for ancient Romans and is still a site for resorts, including Castel Gandolfo, the papal summer residence.

Lake Albert, or Lake Mobutu Sese Sekolake, lake in east central Africa between Zaire and Uganda, linked to Lake Edward to the south by the Semliki River. It was named (1864) for England's Prince Albert, husband of Queen Victoria. The lake is approximately 100 mi (160 km) in length and 20 mi (32 km) in width, covering about 2,059 sq mi (5,333 sq km). It is a water source for the Nile River.

Lake Baikal, world's deepest lake (maximum depth 5,315 ft/1,620 m), located in southeastern Siberia, USSR. It is about 395 mi (636 km) long and 49 mi (79 km) wide, covering an area of about 12,200 sq mi (31,500 sq km). It contains about 20% of the world's unfrozen fresh water (more than any other lake).

Lake Chad, largest lake in west central Africa, fourth largest on the African continent. Lake Chad lies within the boundaries of 4 African nations: Chad (containing the major portion of the lake), Cameroon, Nigeria, and Niger. Its shallow basin, approximately 22 ft (7 m) at the deepest, allows easy overflow into surrounding areas. The size of the lake fluctuates depending on the season, the volume of water received from inflowing rivers, and the rate of evaporation.

Lake Champlain, long, narrow lake forming much of the border between New York State and Vermont, with its northern tip extending into the Canadian province of Quebec. Named after the first European to see it, French explorer Samuel de Champlain, it is 107 mi (172 km) long, 1-14 mi (1.6-22 km) wide, and up to 400 ft (122 m) deep. Lake Champlain was the site of many naval battles during the Revolutionary War and the War of 1812.

Lake Charles (pop. 168,134), inland port city of southwest Louisiana, on the Calcasieu River, linked by a 33-mi (53-km) channel with the Gulf of Mexico. It lies at the center of a rich rice- and cattle-producing region. A commercial and industrial city, it ships chemicals, synthetic rubber, petroleum products, timber, rice, and cotton.

Lake Como (Italian: *Lago di Como*), lake in the northern Italian province of Lombardy, at the foot of the Alps, 25 miles (40 km) north of Milan. Lake Como is a popular tourist attraction, famed for the beauty of its setting and the elegant villas lining its shores.

Lake District, scenic region in northwestern England, about 30 mi (50 km) wide. It contains the highest mountain in England (Scafell Pike, 3,210 ft/978 m) and 15 lakes, including Windermere, Ullswater, and Derwentwater. William Wordsworth, Samuel Coleridge, and Robert Southey are among the writers and artists who lived here in the early 19th century.

Lake dwelling, shelter built on stilts or piles in the waters of a lake. Stone Age and Bronze Age lake dwellings can be found in parts of Europe, and in some parts of the world they are still built. Crannogs, strongholds built on artificial islands, were built in Ireland, Scotland, and England from the Late Stone Age until the Middle Ages.

Lake Edward, lake in the Rift valley of East Africa, on the border between Uganda and Zaire. Explorer Henry M. Stanley named it in 1889 for Albert Edward, Prince of Wales (later King Edward VII). Lake Edward, approximately 40 mi (64 km) long, 32 mi (51 km) wide, and 830 sq mi (2,150 sq km) in area, is a water source for the Nile. The Semliki River connects it to Lake Albert to the north.

Lake Erie, one of the 5 Great Lakes, fourth on the border between the United States and Canada. Lake Erie is 240 mi (386 km) long, 38-57 mi (61-92 km) wide, and has an area of about 10,000 sq mi (26,000 sq km). It is the southernmost of the Great Lakes and is a link in the St. Lawrence Seaway.
See also: Great Lakes.

Lake Garda, largest lake in Italy, about 143 sq mi (370 sq km). Its southern end is about 65 mi (105 km) east of Milan. Its scenery has made it a popular resort area.

Lake Geneva, crescent-shaped lake, one of Europe's largest, between southwestern Switzerland and France. With an area of about 224 sq mi (581 sq km), Lake Geneva is known for the clear, blue water of its western end and its lakeshore resorts.

Lake George, long, narrow, deep lake in the Adirondack Mountains of New York state. Now a summer resort, the lake was the scene of several important clashes during the American Revolutionary War.

Lake Huron, one of the 5 Great Lakes, 206 mi (332 km) long and 183 mi (295 km) wide, with an area of about 23,000 sq mi (60,000 sq km). Lake Huron is bordered by the Canadian province of Ontario on the north, east, and southeast, and by Michigan on the west and southwest. It is part of the St. Lawrence Seaway and is heavily used by maritime commercial traffic.
See also: Great Lakes.

Lake Itasca, lake of glacial origin in Minnesota. The chief source of the Mississippi River, Lake Itasca is about 1.8 sq mi (4.7 sq km) in area.

Lake Ladoga, lake in northwest Russia, about 40 mi (64 km) northeast of Leningrad. At 6,835 sq mi (17,703 sq km), Lake Ladoga is the largest in Europe. It forms part of a canal system connecting the Baltic and White Seas.

Lakeland terrier, dog originally bred in northern England's Lake District to hunt foxes and protect sheep. The average lakeland has a narrow body, stands 14.5 in (37 cm) at the shoulder and weighs 17 lbs (7.7 kg). It has a wiry coat, a bearded chin, and an upright, docked tail.

Lake Lugano, lake on the border between Switzerland and Italy. It is located east of Lake Maggiore at the southern foot of the Alps. It is connected to Lake Maggiore by the Tresa River. It is 20 m (32km) in length and 2 m (3 km) wide.

Lake Maggiore, lake lying mostly in Italy, but extending into the Swiss Alps. Its area is 82 sq mi (212 sq km), making it Italy's largest lake. The western and eastern shores are home to lakeside resorts and small villages.

Lake Manitoba, narrow, shallow lake in south-central Manitoba, Canada. There is an important waterfowl-research station on the lake's southern shore.

Lake Maracaibo, lake in northwestern Venezuela, in the oil-producing region. Connected to the Carrribean Sea by a dredged channel, Lake Maracaibo has an area of 5,217 sq mi (13,512 sq km), making it South America's largest lake. The southern shore produces agricultural products, notably sugarcane, coconuts, cacao, and coffee.

Lake Mead, largest reservoir in the United States, located in northwestern Arizona and southeastern Nevada, built by confining the Colorado River at the Hoover (Boulder) Dam. Lake Mead is located approximately 15 mi (24 km) east of Las Vegas, Nev. It is about 250 sq mi (650 sq km) in area, 115

mi (185 km) long, and 1-10 mi (2-16 km) wide. It was named after Elwood Mead, reclamation commissioner (1924-36).
See also: Hoover Dam.

Lake Michigan, largest freshwater lake lying entirely within the United States, and the third largest of the 5 Great Lakes. It is 307 mi (494 km) long, 118 mi (190 km) at its widest point, and up to 923 ft (281 m) deep. Its borders are Wisconsin and Illinois on the west, Michigan on the east and north, and Indiana on the southeast. It is connected to the Great Lakes St. Lawrence Seaway that goes east to the Atlantic Ocean and south to the Gulf of Mexico via the Mississippi River, serving international commerce.
See also: Great Lakes.

Lake Neagh *See:* Lough Neagh.

Lake of Lucerne (German: *Vierwaldstätter See*), major lake in Switzerland, between the Rigi and Pilatus mountains. It is around 24 mi (39 km) long and up to 2 mi (3 km) wide and has the appearance of an imperfect cross. Adventures of the legendary William Tell took place along Lake Uri's shores.
See also: Tell, William.

Lake of the Woods, lake located mostly in Ontario, Canada along the Minnesota border, with 2 bays reaching into Manitoba. It is 100 mi (160 km) long and 10-50 mi (16-80 km) wide, with an area of 1,485 sq mi (3,846 sq km). Waters from the Rainy River run into the lake from the southeast. The lake is drained in the north by the Winnipeg River, which flows into Lake Winnipeg in Manitoba. At the end of the Revolutionary War it was declared an official boundary. The island-filled lake is now a tourist attraction.

Lake Okeechobee (Seminole, "big water"), largest freshwater lake in the southern part of the United States, located in central Florida just north of the Everglades. The lake is 35 mi (56 km) long, about 680 sq mi (1,760 sq km) in area, and up to 15 ft (4.6 m) deep. In 1937 a 155-mi (249-km) cross-state waterway was completed to control seasonal flooding. Canals were constructed as outlets to the Atlantic Ocean and Gulf of Mexico, and to supply needed water to communities along Florida's eastern coastline.

Lake Onega, second largest lake in Europe (3,753 sq mi/9,720 sq km), located in the northwestern part of the former USSR. It is an important transportation connection between the Baltic and White seas. The lake has productive fisheries along its coast.

Lake Ontario, one of the 5 Great Lakes, located in New York State and Ontario, Canada. It is fed mainly by the Niagara River, and flows into the Atlantic Ocean through the St. Lawrence River, making it an important part in transportation of goods through the St. Lawrence Seaway system. It is about 193 mi (311 km) long and 53 mi (85 km) wide, with depths ranging from 500 to 802 ft (152 to 244 m). Its low elevation above sea level (245 ft/75 m) and great offshore depths keep it from freezing during the winter. It tempers the surrounding climate, producing cool summer days along the

eastern shore and allowing fruit crops to produce successfully on the southern shore.
See also: Great Lakes.

Lake Peipus, or Chudskoe, lake in the former USSR between Estonia and Russia. It has depths up to 50 ft (15 m) and an area of 1,400 sq mi (3,626 sq km), and is frozen about 6 months out of the year. During World War II, when the Germans surrounded Leningrad and cut off all supply routes, Russian volunteers used small trucks to transport food across the thick ice to feed more than 3 million starving people.

Lake Placid, small lake in the northeastern Adirondack Mountains, New York, about 3 mi (5.6 km) long and 1 mi (2.4 km) wide. Its beauty attracts visitors for boating, swimming, hiking, ice skating, and skiing. It was the site of the 1980 Winter Olympics. Just south of Lake Placid lies the grave of abolitionist John Brown.

Lake Poets, name given to the English poets William Wordsworth, Samuel Taylor Coleridge, and Robert Southey, who lived in the Lake District for a time. The critic Francis Lord Jeffrey was first to characterize them as constituting the "Lake school of poetry," although the 3 friends do not form a group stylistically.
See also: Coleridge, Samuel Taylor; Wordsworth, William.

Lake Pontchartrain, lagoon-like lake in southern Louisiana, connected to the Mississippi River through the Inner Harbor Navigation Canal. Its briny water provides abundant game fish for the numerous small resorts along its shores. It is 40 mi (64 km) long and 25 mi (40 km) wide. It is crossed by the Lake Pontchartrain Causeway, the world's longest bridge (29.2 mi/47 km).

Lake Powell, lake on the Utah-Arizona border, formed by the Glen Canyon Dam and fed by the Colorado River. It is 186 mi (299 km) long and 500 ft (150 m) deep. The dam was built to produce hydroelectric power. Lake Powell is a popular recreation site.

Lakes of Killarney, 3 scenic lakes lying southwest of the town of Killarney in County Kerry, Ireland. The lakes—Lough Leane ("Lower Lake"), Muckross Lake, and Middle Lake—have a combined area of nearly 10 sq mi (17 km). They form part of Killarney National Park, a popular tourist attraction.

Lake Superior, largest freshwater lake in the world, largest of the 5 Great Lakes, located along the United States-Canadian border, with Michigan and Wisconsin on the south, Minnesota on the west, and Ontario on the north. It is 350 mi (563 km) long, 160 mi (257 km) wide, and up to 1,333 ft (406 m) deep. An important waterway for shipping, it connects to the Atlantic Ocean through the St. Lawrence Seaway, and to the Gulf of Mexico through the Great Lakes and the Mississippi River.
See also: Great Lakes.

Lake Tahoe, deep glacial lake on the California-Nevada border. It is 22 mi (35 km) long, 12 mi (19 km) wide, and up to 1,640 ft (500 m) deep. Its waters flow into the Truckee River and on to Pyramid Lake. It is a popular tourist resort offering fishing, boating, waterskiing, and hunting.

Lake Tana, major water source for the Blue Nile River, located in northwestern Ethiopia. Its blue color comes from the lake's silt-free water. It is 47 mi (76 km) long and 44 mi (71 km) wide, and lies 6,000 ft (1,800 m) above sea level.

Lake Tanganyika, longest freshwater lake in the world (420 mi/680 km), located in the Great Rift valley between Tanzania and Zaire in east central Africa. The lake has depths to 4,708 ft (1,435 m).

Lake Texoma, one of the largest artificially created lakes in the United States, formed by the Denison Dam and located along the Texas-Oklahoma border. The dam was built in 1944 to produce hydroelectric power and control flooding. Lake Texoma provides recreational boating, waterskiing, hunting, and fishing.

Lake Tiberias *See:* Galilee, Sea of.

Lake Titicaca, highest lake in South America, located in the Andes Mountains between Peru and Bolivia. Its altitude of 12,507 (3,812 m) makes it the highest lake in the world to provide large boat transportation. It is 110 mi (180 km) long and 45 mi (72 km) wide, with depths up to 900 ft (270 m). There are 41 islands of varying size throughout the lake. Over 25 rivers empty into the lake, but only the Desaguadero River acts as drainage. The shores have been home to Native American settlements for centuries.

Lake trout *See:* Trout.

Lake Victoria, largest freshwater lake in Africa, located in Tanzania, Uganda, and Kenya; major water source for the Nile River. The lake is 210 mi (337 km) long and 150 mi (241 km) at its widest point. The Owen Falls Dam, constructed on the Nile River to generate hydroelectric power (1954), raised the level of the lake about 3 ft (1 m) to a depth of 270 ft (82 m). Numerous islands rise from the lake, Ukerewe being the largest and most populated. There are several million people living within a 50-mi (80-km) radius of Lake Victoria, making it the most heavily populated area in Africa.

Lake Volta, one of the largest human-made reservoirs in the world, in Ghana, West Africa. Created by the construction of the Akosombo Dam across the Volta River (1965), it is 250 mi (400 km) long and covers 3,275 sq mi (8,482 sq km). Water from the lake is used to produce electric power.

Lake Winnebago, lake in east-central Wisconsin. It is connected to the Fox River, which flows into the lake on the west and leaves at the northwest end. It is the largest lake in the state, measuring about 30 m (48 km) in length and 5 to 10 m (8 to 16 km) in width.

Lake Winnipeg, located in Manitoba, Canada, it is one of the largest lakes in Canada. The lake is 258 miles (416 km) long and ranges from 20 to 60 miles (32 to 97 km) in width. The fisheries on the lake are the most important in Manitoba.

Lake Winnipesaukee, lake in east-central New Hampshire. It lies in a depression caused by glacial activity. It measures almost 70 sq m (180 sq km) and contains 365 islands. During the summer, it serves as a popular recreational spot.

Lake Xochimilco, 5 shallow "floating garden" lakes in Mexico City, Mexico, made by building mud dikes in the original lake and seeding them with flowers and vegetables. The gardens thus created are a tourist attraction.

Lalo, Édouard (1823-92), French composer. Many of his works were influenced by Spanish music, including *Symphonie Espagnole* (1875) for violin and orchestra, first performed by Spanish virtuoso violinist Pablo Sarasate. Other famous works are the ballet *Namouna* (1882) and the opera *Le Roi d'Ys* (1888).

Lamaism, popular term for Tibetan Mahayana Buddhism, which evolved from Indian Buddhism starting in the 7th century A.D. This religion combined intellectual discipline with the ritual of tantric yoga and shamanism. The spiritual and political head of the hierarchy of monks or *lamas* is the Dalai Lama (Tibetan, "oceanic teacher"). He is chosen as a young boy and considered to be the reincarnation of previous lamas and of Avalokitesvara, a *bodhisattva* (spiritually enlightened being who remains on earth to help others achieve enlightenment). The intensely religious society remained unchanged until the Communist Chinese invasion of Tibet (1959), which forced the Dalai Lama into exile.
See also: Buddhism.

Lamarck, Jean Baptiste de Monet, chevalier de (1744-1829), French biologist whose pioneering work in taxonomy (especially that of the invertebrates) led him to formulate an early theory of evolution. Where Darwin was to propose natural selection as a mechanism for evolutionary change, Lamarck theorized that organisms could develop new organs in response to their need for them and that these acquired characteristics could be inherited. His theory is known as Lamarckism.
See also: Biology; Evolution.

Lamartine, Alphonse Marie Louis de (1790-1869), French poet and politician, briefly head of government after the 1848 revolution. His collection *Poetic Meditations* (1820) was a landmark of French Romantic literature and contains the famous poem "The Lake"; lyric evocations of love and nature are underlaid by gentle melancholy and religious feeling. *Harmonies* (1830) and *Jocelyn* (1836) were other poetic works.

Lamb, Charles (1775-1834), English essayist and critic who often wrote under the name "Elia." With his sister Mary Ann Lamb he wrote *Tales from Shakespeare* (1807) for children. His *Essays of Elia* (1823, 1833) contain insightful and humorous personal comments on many subjects. He helped revive interest in Elizabethan drama with *Specimens of English Dramatic Poets* (1808).

Lamb's-quarters, pigweed, or goosefoot (*Chenopodium album*), annual herbaceous plant related to spinach, sugar beets, and chard. The plants, native to Europe, Asia, and North America, grow from 1 to 10 ft (30 cm to 3 m) and have diamond-shaped leaves and groups of small greenish flowers.

Lamentations, book of the Old Testament, traditionally ascribed to the prophet Jeremiah, though this is disputed by modern scholars. It consists of a series of 5 poems (the first 4 are acrostics) lamenting the fall of Jerusalem at the hands of the Babylonians (586 B.C.).
See also: Bible.

Lammergeier, bird belonging to the Old World vulture family and native to the mountain regions of Europe, Asia, and Africa. One of the largest of the vultures, it has a wingspread of 9 to 10 ft (2.7 to 3 m). It is recognized by its dark wings with white streaks, its orange neck and breast, and by the black feathers underneath its bill. It subsists on the flesh of dead animals but is also known to kill live ones.

L'Amour, Louis (1908-1988), popular U.S. novelist who wrote stories about the American frontier, many of which have been adapted for film and television. He is noted for his compassionate treatment of Native Americans and Mexicans and for the authenticity of his historical and geographic detail. Much of his material was drawn from his own travels in the West as well as from the stories told to him by his grandfather. His most popular novels include *Hondo* (1953), *The Daybreakers* (1960), and *The Lonesome Gods* (1983).

Lamp, implement that produces light and usually heat using one of 3 methods: combustion of fats or oils, combustion of gases, or electricity. Fat lamps burn fat, oil, paraffin, or grease utilizing a simple wick that pulls the fuel up to the flame. These were the first lamps, dating from prehistoric times, when they were made of hollowed rocks with grass wicks. Gas lamps, dating from 1792, produce light when air mixes with such gases as natural gas, butane, or acetylene. Electric lamps, developed about 1879, utilize electrical energy by directing it through a glass bulb containing inert gas that charges a tungsten filament.

Lamprey, primitive fish of the Petromyzontidae family, one of the 2 remaining groups of jawless fish (Agnatha), found both in freshwater and in the sea. Its body is eellike, and its round, sucking mouth has horny teeth with which it rasps away at its prey. Many species are parasitic when adult, feeding on the flesh of living fishes. The blind, wormlike, filter-feeding larva is totally unlike the adult.

Lanai *See:* Hawaii.

Lancaster, English royal family. **Edmund Crouchback** (1245-96), second son of Henry III, was first earl of Lancaster (1267); his son **Thomas** (d. 1322) led baronial opposition to Edward II. **John of Gaunt** (1340-99) became duke of Lancaster by marriage in 1362, and his son and grandson became Henry IV (1399) and Henry V (1413). The Lancastrians were deposed by the house of York during the Wars of the Roses (1455-85), which began during the

reign of Henry VI, but the heir to Lancaster claims, Henry Tudor, reestablished the line (as the house of Tudor) in 1485, becoming Henry VII.
See also: England.

Lancaster (pop. 422,822), city in southeast Pennsylvania, county seat of Lancaster County. It is located 60 mi (96 km) west of Philadelphia, on the Conestoga River. Lancaster, settled in 1709 by the Amish, Moravian, and German Mennonites, is an agricultural, manufacturing, and marketing center. Points of interest include President James Buchanan's home, Wheatland; Mill Bridge Village; and nearby Amish and Mennonite farms.
See also: Pennsylvania.

Lancelet *See:* Amphioxus.

Lancelot, Sir, legendary medieval knight. The son of the king of Brittany, he was taken as an infant to the undersea castle of the Lady of the Lake, who brought him to the court of King Arthur after he had attained manhood. As a Knight of the Round Table, he achieved great fame and fortune, however his passionate involvement with King Arthur's wife, Queen Guenevere, led to scandal and Lancelot's ultimate ruin. During his life he involved himself in the search for the Holy Grail, but his moral flaw prevented him from finding it. The Holy Grail was, however, found by Galahad, Lancelot's illegitimate son—the product of Lancelot's youthful affair with a British Princess. Lancelot was the hero of various medieval romances. He was also a central figure in a series of poems by Alfred Lord Tennyson called *Idylls of the King.*
See also: Arthur, King; Round Table.

Lan-chou *See:* Lanzhou.

Land, Edwin Herbert (1909-91), U.S. physicist, inventor, and manufacturer. He invented a material called Polaroid, which provided a cheap and adaptable means of polarizing light (1932), and the Polaroid Land Camera (1947). In 1937 he set up the Polaroid Corporation to manufacture scientific instruments and antiglare sunglasses incorporating Polaroid.

Land Bank, Federal *See:* Farm Credit System.

Landes, Bertha Knight (1868-1943), first female mayor (1926-28) of a major U.S. city. Landes, a Republican, was elected mayor of Seattle, Wash., after serving on the city council (1922-26).

Land-grant colleges, U.S. colleges set up by the Morrill Act of 1862. Congress granted the states federal lands to be sold to establish agricultural, engineering, and home economics colleges. There are some 70 land-grant colleges today, including many state universities.

Landon, Alfred Mossman (1887-1984), U.S. politician. He was governor of Kansas (1933-37) and Republican presidential candidate in 1936. His daughter, Nancy Landon Kassebaum, was elected to the Senate in 1978.

Landowska, Wanda (1877-1959), Polish harpsichord virtuoso, largely responsible for the revival of the harpsichord. Living in Paris (1900-40), she founded the Ecole de Musique Ancienne. In the United States after 1940, she was famous as a performer, teacher, and authority on early music.

Land reform, governmental redistribution of land ownership, the purpose of which is to lessen the personal wealth, power, and political influence accorded those with large land holdings. Land reform is usually utilized at times of social or political unrest to more fairly distribute land, particularly farmlands, to those with little or no land of their own. The recipients of land are often given technical training, favorable financing, and low tax rates.

Land's End, England's westernmost point of land, located in Cornwall. Land's End, a turf-covered headland of granite cliffs 60-100 ft (18-30 m) high, juts into the English Channel, near the Atlantic Ocean, and is surrounded by rocky shores and hazardous reefs.

Landsteiner, Karl (1868-1943), Austrian-born U.S. pathologist. He was awarded the 1930 Nobel Prize for physiology or medicine for discovering the major blood groups and developing the ABO system of blood typing. He also contributed to the identification of the Rh factor.
See also: Blood type; Rh factor.

Lanfranc (d. 1089), archbishop of Canterbury (1070-89). He appointed reforming Norman bishops, enforced clerical celibacy, and strengthened the monasteries. As a scholar he helped shape the doctrine of Transubstantiation, writing *Concerning the Body and Blood of the Lord* (c. 1059).
See also: Church of England.

Lang, Andrew (1844-1912), Scottish writer and scholar. He explored folklore in *Custom and Myth* (1884) and *Myth, Literature, and Religion* (1887), and published translations of Homer, fairy tale collections, poetry, and historical works.

Lang, Fritz (1890-1976), Austrian-U.S. film director. He first established himself as a leading director of expressionist silent films, including *Metropolis* (1926), a bleak futuristic drama. In *M* (1931), a sound film about a child murderer, Lang explored the psychology of evil. After emigrating to the United States in 1933, he created such Hollywood films as *Fury* (1936), *Clash by Night* (1952), and *Beyond a Reasonable Doubt* (1956).

Lange, David Russell (1942-), New Zealand's prime minister from 1984-89. He received a law degree at the University of Auckland and has been active in politics since 1976.

Lange, Dorothea (1895-1965), U.S. documentary photographer. Her powerful, stark pictures of Depression victims, migrant workers, and the rural poor greatly influenced photo-journalistic technique. In 1939 she published *An American Exodus*.

Langland, William (1332-1400), presumed poet of *The Vision of Piers Plowman*, a religious allegory representing a dream-vision of the Christian life and a satire, one of the finest examples of Middle English alliterative verse.

Langley, Samuel Pierpont (1834-1906), U.S. astronomer, physicist, and meteorologist. He invented the bolometer, which measures radiant energy (1878), and an early heavier-than-air flying machine. His most important work was in the investigation of the sun's role in bringing about meteorological phenomena.
See also: Bolometer.

Langmuir, Irving (1881-1957), U.S. physical chemist awarded the 1932 Nobel Prize for chemistry for his work on thin films on solid and liquid surfaces (particularly oil on water), giving rise to the new science of surface chemistry.

Langton, Stephen (c. 1155-1228), English cardinal and theologian whose appointment as archbishop of Canterbury (1207) led to a quarrel between Pope Innocent III and King John. Langton led opposition to the king, and his is the first signature on the Magna Carta.
See also: Magna Carta.

Langtry, Lillie (Emily Charlotte Le Breton; 1853-1929), English actress. Known, because of her birthplace (Jersey, Channel Islands), as the Jersey Lily. In 1881 she made a sensation by being the first society woman to go on the stage, making her debut at the Haymarket Theatre, London, in *She Stoops to Conquer*.

Language (from Latin *lingua*, "tongue"), means by which humans express themselves vocally and communicate with others. A language subset is part of a language that can be used independently of the rest of the language. Language translation is the process of changing information from one language to another.

Langur, any of various brightly colored, long-tailed monkeys (family Colobidae) of India and Southeast Asia. Langurs have patches of colored skin, crests of hair on the head, bushy eyebrows, and a chin tuft, and some have long, upturned noses, as in the proboscis monkey. Langurs live in troops in forests, where they eat leaves. The entellus, or Hanuman langur, is sacred in India.

Lanier, Sidney (1842-81), U.S. poet and musician. A Southerner who fought in the Civil War (recalled in his novel *Tiger-Lilies*, 1867), he practiced law, and became a professional flutist, writing a study of the interrelation of music and poetry, *The Science of English Verse* (1880). He also published *Poems* (1877).

Lansing (pop. 432,674), capital of Michigan, in the southern part of the state at the junction of the Grand and Cedar rivers. It is an important automobile-manufacturing and transportation center and the trading center of a rich farming area. Lansing was settled c.1837, succeeding Detroit as state capital in 1847. It was chartered as a city in 1859. Michigan State University is in East Lansing.
See also: Michigan.

Lansing, Robert (1864-1928), U.S. international lawyer and statesman. He founded the *American Journal of International Law* (1907), and as secretary of state (1915-20) he concluded the Lansing-Ishii agreement with Japan (1917), reaffirming the Open Door policy toward China.

Lanternfish, deep-sea fish (family Myctophidae) that has numerous light organs along the sides of its body and on its head. Lanternfish are found in both the Atlantic and Pacific oceans. The particular pattern of light identifies sex and species. Lanternfish come to the surface at night to feed on small animals.

Lanthanide *See:* Rare earth.

Lanthanum, chemical element, symbol La; for physical constants see Periodic Table. Lanthanum was discovered by Carl Mosander in 1839. It occurs in the minerals *cerite*, *bastnasite*, and *monazite* which is the principal source of the element. The metal is prepared by reducing the anhydrous fluoride with calcium. Lanthanum is silvery-white, malleable, ductile, and soft enough to be cut with a knife. Ion-exchange and solvent extraction techniques have led to much easier isolation of the so-called "rare-earth" elements. Lanthanum and its compounds are used in carbon lighting applications, special glasses, hydrogen sponge alloys, and misch metal.

Lanzhou, or Lanchow (pop. 1,510,000), capital city of Gansu Province in northwestern China, on the Huang He River. An industrial and transportation hub, the city produces chemicals and petroleum products and is the center of China's nuclear energy industry.
See also: China.